ESSENTIALS OF
EQUITY AND TRUSTS LAW

John Duddington

Worcester College of Technology

Harlow, England • London • New York • Boston • San Francisco • Toronto
Sydney • Tokyo • Singapore • Hong Kong • Seoul • Taipei • New Delhi
Cape Town • Madrid • Mexico City • Amsterdam • Munich • Paris • Milan

Pearson Education Limited
Edinburgh Gate
Harlow
Essex CM20 2JE
England

and Associated Companies throughout the world

Visit us on the World Wide Web at:
www.pearsoned.co.uk

ISBN-10 0-582-89406-9
ISBN-13 978-0-582-89406-8

British Library Cataloguing-in-Publication Data
A catalogue record for this book is available from the British Library

Library of Congress Cataloging-in-Publication Data
A catalog record for this book is available from the Library of Congress

10 9 8 7 6 5 4 3 2 1
10 09 08 07 06

Typeset in 9.5/12.5 pt Stone Serif by 35
Printed and bound by Henry Ling Ltd., at the Dorset Press, Dorchester, Dorset

The publisher's policy is to use paper manufactured from sustainable forests.

ESSENTIALS OF
EQUITY AND TRUSTS LAW

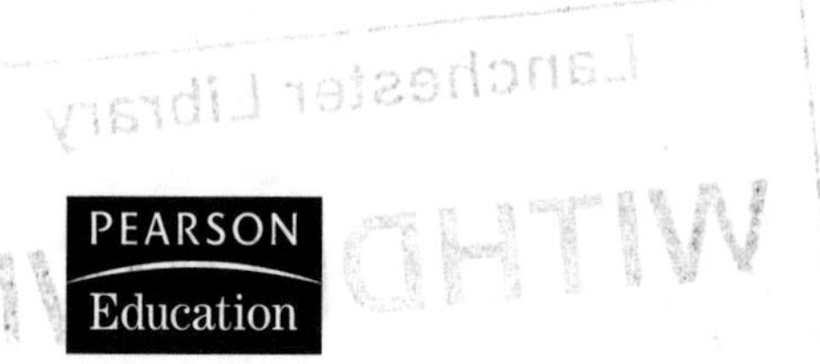

We work with leading authors to develop the strongest educational materials in law, bringing cutting-edge thinking and best learning practice to a global market.

Under a range of well-known imprints, including Longman, we craft high quality print and electronic publications which help readers to understand and apply their content, whether studying or at work.

To find out more about the complete range of our publishing, please visit us on the World Wide Web at: www.pearsoned.co.uk

Visit the *Equity and Trusts* Companion Website at **www.pearsoned.co.uk/duddington** to find valuable **student** learning material including:

- Sample examination questions to aid examination preparation
- Seminar activity questions to check your understanding
- An online glossary to explain key terms
- Annotated links to relevant sites on the web
- Regular updates in the field of equity and trusts

Brief contents

Full contents

Part Three
RESULTING AND CONSTRUCTIVE TRUSTS: TRUSTS OF THE HOME

Supporting resources

Visit **www.pearsoned.co.uk/duddington** to find valuable online resources

Companion Website for students

- Sample examination questions to aid examination preparation
- Seminar activity questions to check your understanding
- An online glossary to explain key terms
- Annotated links to relevant sites on the web
- Regular updates in the field of equity and trusts

For more information please contact your local Pearson Education sales representative or visit **www.pearsoned.co.uk/duddington**

Guided tour

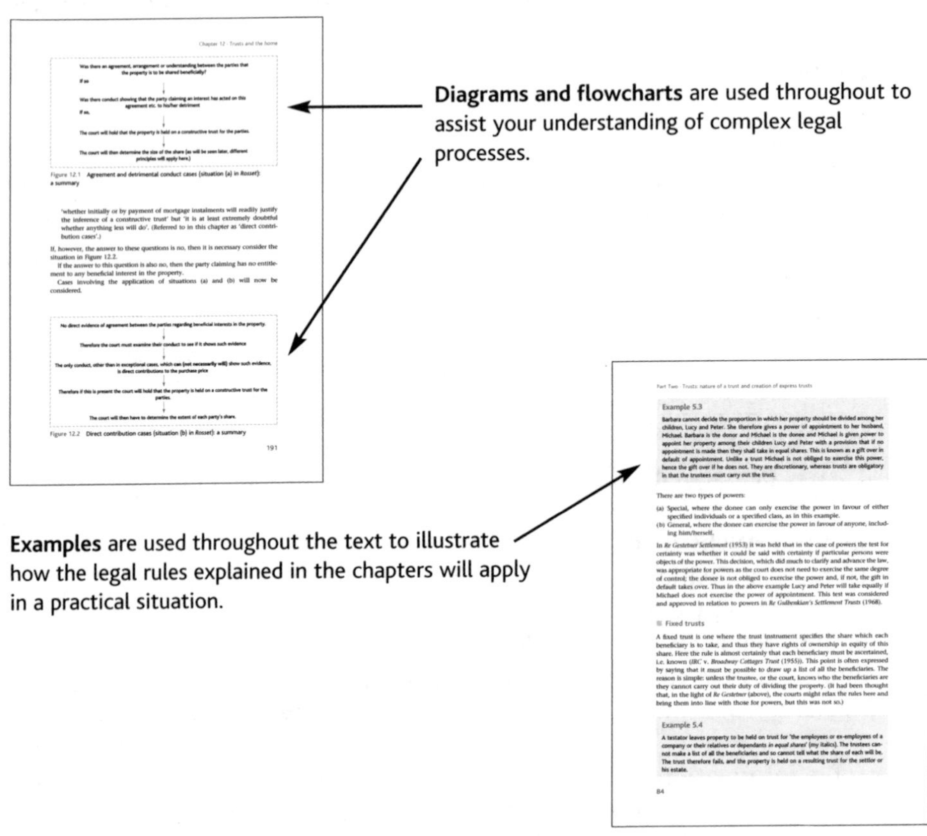

Diagrams and flowcharts are used throughout to assist your understanding of complex legal processes.

Examples are used throughout the text to illustrate how the legal rules explained in the chapters will apply in a practical situation.

Part Two Trusts: nature of a trust and creation of express trusts

FURTHER READING

Jones (1997) 'Uses, trusts and a path to privity', 56 CLJ 175. Good on an aspect of the early development of the trust.

Hayton, 'Developing the law of trusts for the 21st century', 106 LQR 87. Essential reading on the possible way forward for the law of trusts.

Kerridge (1994) 'Taxation of trust income', 110 LQR 84. Essential further reading on taxation of trusts, a topic which this book has only been able to glance at.

Simpson (1986) *A History of the Land Law*, Oxford: Oxford University Press. Especially Chapter 8 on the development of the trust.

CHAPTER SUMMARY

- What is a trust?
- History of the development of trusts.
- Split between legal and equitable interest.
- Functions of trusts today.
- Equitable proprietary interest.
- Types of trust.

QUESTION

'The great value of the trust today is in its versatility.' Do you agree?

Note 4.4: You will find suggested points for inclusion in this answer in Appendix 2. (You may prefer to complete this question when you have read further about the details of trusts.)

74

Further reading – each chapter is supported by a list of further reading directing you to relevant academic commentary to encourage independent exploration of the subject. You can also find a list of useful websites on the book's companion website at **www.pearsoned.co.uk/duddington,** allowing you to link directly to relevant resources.

Summaries at the end of each chapter enable you to identify and focus on the key points to be taken from each chapter.

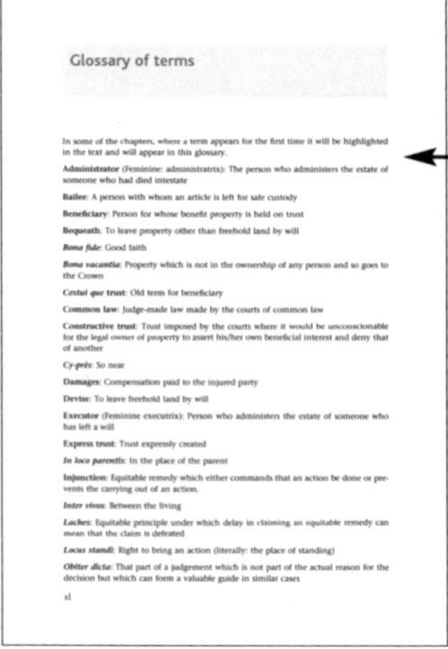
Glossary of terms

In some of the chapters, where a term appears for the first time it will be highlighted in the text and will appear in this glossary.

Administrator (Feminine: administratrix): The person who administers the estate of someone who had died intestate

Bailee: A person with whom an article is left for safe custody

Beneficiary: Person for whose benefit property is held on trust

Bequeath: To leave property other than freehold land by will

Bona fide: Good faith

Bona vacantia: Property which is not in the ownership of any person and so goes to the Crown

Cestui que trust: Old term for beneficiary

Common law: Judge-made law made by the courts of common law

Constructive trust: Trust imposed by the courts where it would be unconscionable for the legal owner of property to assert his/her own beneficial interest and deny that of another

Cy-près: So near

Damages: Compensation paid to the injured party

Devise: To leave freehold land by will

Executor (Feminine executrix): Person who administers the estate of someone who has left a will

Express trust: Trust expressly created

In loco parentis: In the place of the parent

Injunction: Equitable remedy which either commands that an action be done or prevents the carrying out of an action

Inter vivos: Between the living

Laches: Equitable principle under which delay in claiming an equitable remedy can mean that the claim is defeated

Locus standi: Right to bring an action (literally: the place of standing)

Obiter dicta: That part of a judgement which is not part of the actual reason for the decision but which can form a valuable guide in similar cases

xl

Glossary of legal terms – this can be referred to throughout your reading of the text to clarify unfamiliar terms. The glossary is also available on the book's companion website at **www.pearsoned.co.uk/duddington.**

Exam-style questions end each chapter to encourage you to practice applying your knowledge and assist in exam preparation. Further exam questions and guidelines on how to answer them can be found on the book's companion website at **www.pearsoned.co.uk/duddington.**

Exam study skills – an Appendix at the end of the book gives guidelines on good exam answer technique, and hints on what to include in essay and problem questions in specific topic areas, to help you prepare for assessments.

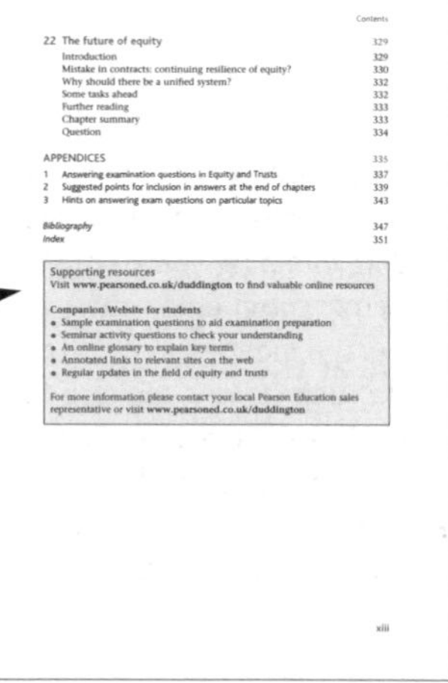
Contents

Supporting resources
Visit www.pearsoned.co.uk/duddington to find valuable online resources

Companion Website for students
- Sample examination questions to aid examination preparation
- Seminar activity questions to check your understanding
- An online glossary to explain key terms
- Annotated links to relevant sites on the web
- Regular updates in the field of equity and trusts

For more information please contact your local Pearson Education sales representative or visit www.pearsoned.co.uk/duddington

xiii

Companion website www.pearsoned.co.uk/duddington – the book is accompanied by a companion website with regular updates on major legal changes affecting the book, further exam questions and guidelines on answering them, weblinks to useful resources, and an online glossary to explain key legal terms.

Preface

Two old chestnuts are told about equity and trusts. One is that it is a difficult and dull subject, the other that it is concerned largely with the problems of a bygone era. The study of equity and trusts is not difficult; it is challenging, which is something very different. How could the study of a subject which combines the great themes of justice and fairness with the detailed working out of those themes ever be difficult and dull? A quick glance through the book will dispel the second chestnut: note, for instance, the importance of equity in dealing with breach of the obligation of confidence (Chapter 3), disputes over the family home (Chapter 12), and charities (Chapters 13 and 14). Make no mistake, a person who is fascinated by a study of this subject becomes fascinated for ever.

This book is intended to be a useful guide to students of equity and trusts who should find that there is enough material here, especially on areas of which examiners are especially fond, to enable them to have a sound basis on which to approach those examinations with some confidence. Clearly a book of this size cannot deal with all aspects of topics on which there are different views, and so I have included references to further reading at the end of each chapter. In addition, I have tried, by the use of flow charts, diagrams, specimen questions (with points for inclusion in the answers at the end) and chapter summaries to make this book as readable as possible. I have had in mind students, perhaps trying to make sense of some abstruse area, who are simply stuck on a particular point, and to provide a clear path for them through what may seem a maze. I also hope that this book will be of use to those who have to actually deal with trust law in practice, for instance, trustees and administrators of charitable trusts.

I have tried to cover all the areas likely to be dealt with in an equity and trusts course although some areas, such as perpetuities and trusts of land, are only covered to the extent that they are relevant to trust law. Readers may also find an explanation of the order of topics useful. There is a tendency, regrettable I think, to regard this subject as really trusts with a passing nod in the direction of other areas of equitable jurisdiction, usually thrown in at the end. This is, I think, a mistake. There is a great deal of vitality in equity apart from trusts and I have tried to show this by looking in Chapter 3 at two areas which are particularly active at the moment, undue influence and the equitable duty of confidentiality. Nevertheless, anyone who wishes to begin with trusts and only later return to equity can easily do so as the parts dealing with trusts and other areas of equity are quite distinct.

There is no ideal time for a book on any area of law, which, as ever, rushes on like 'an ever rolling stream' and in this case, the Charities Bill 2005 will, if enacted, change some of the material in Chapters 13 and 14. Not only this, but this book will have a free updating service and, when and if the Charities Bill becomes law, revised Chapters 13 and 14 will be available.

I must express my heartfelt thanks to the staff of Pearson Publishing, especially Rebekah Taylor, Cheryl Cheasley, Michelle Gallagher and Lissa Matthews, whose professionalism and helpfulness make them such a pleasure to work with, and to many generations of students at Worcester whose persistent questioning and capacity for original thought have helped to clarify my ideas and suggest new lines of argument. My colleagues in the Law School at Worcester provide the kind of cheerful and stimulating company which makes working with them a joy, and the Law Library has been an excellent resource when writing this book. Thank you also to two reviewers of this book: Richard Clements and Christine Ocran, LLB, LLM, Barrister-in-law (non-practising), Associate Lecturer, University of East London.

I cannot speak for other authors, but I know in my case that I could not write my books alone. My wife Anne has, as with all my writing over many years, been the absolute bedrock on which these efforts have rested, not only with her expertise in so many areas but with her constant support. My daughter Mary has been absolutely indispensable with her ability as a proofreader, her custodianship of my grammar and spelling and her knack of spotting an infelicitous phrase, while my son Christopher has, as always, simply been an inspiration.

In short, this book is the product of teamwork, and if, at the end of what has been a long task, I can say with Virgil '*haec olim meminisse iuvabit*' ('one day this too will be pleasant to remember') the credit goes to my family and to them alone, and it is of course to them that this book is dedicated.

A final thought. On the day on which this preface is written, news come to hand of a cabinet minister who has divested himself of his interest in some shares and has instead placed those shares in trust for his children. At the same time, not far from here, 'A Man for All Seasons', Robert Bolt's play on one of the greatest of all the Chancellors, Thomas More, is playing to sold out notices. To those who feel that equity's role as a separate area of jurisdiction is about played out, here is their answer!

John G. Duddington
Worcester College of
Technology
2006

NOTE

This book is primarily concerned with the law of trusts as it applies in England and Wales. Scottish law does not recognise a separate branch of law known as equity and so rights which in England depend for their validity on equity are either enforced by the common law or not at all. Scottish law does, however, recognise the trust. In Northern Ireland and Eire the basic principles of equity and trusts are the same as in England, although the statutory provisions are sometimes different.

Table of cases

Table of statutes

Abbreviations used when referring to judges

As we shall see, the judgments of individual judges are of great importance both in the interpretation of statutes and other statutory materials, such as regulations, and also in directly making law through the system of precedent. When referring to the judgments of individual judges, standard abbreviations are used to indicate particular members of the judiciary. These are as follows and the imaginary name in this context of 'Smith' is used to make the examples clearer.

Smith J	Mr or Mrs Justice Smith, a judge of the High Court
Smith LJ	Lord Justice or Lady Justice Smith, a judge of the Court of Appeal
Lord or Lady Smith	A Law Lord, i.e. a member of the House of Lords, who sits as a judge to hear appeals
Smith MR	The Master of Rolls, the presiding judge of the Court of Appeal, Civil Division
Smith LCJ	The Lord Chief Justice, who is the presiding judge of the Court of Appeal, Criminal Division
Smith LC	The Lord Chancellor, who, amongst other functions, sits as a judge in the House of Lords
Smith V-C	Vice Chancellor

Glossary of terms

In some of the chapters, where a term appears for the first time it will be highlighted in the text and will appear in this glossary.

Administrator (Feminine: administratrix): The person who administers the estate of someone who had died intestate

Bailee: A person with whom an article is left for safe custody

Beneficiary: Person for whose benefit property is held on trust

Bequeath: To leave property other than freehold land by will

Bona fide: Good faith

Bona vacantia: Property which is not in the ownership of any person and so goes to the Crown

***Cestui que* trust**: Old term for beneficiary

Common law: Judge-made law made by the courts of common law

Constructive trust: Trust imposed by the courts where it would be unconscionable for the legal owner of property to assert his/her own beneficial interest and deny that of another

Cy-près: So near

Damages: Compensation paid to the injured party

Devise: To leave freehold land by will

Executor (Feminine executrix): Person who administers the estate of someone who has left a will

Express trust: Trust expressly created

In loco parentis: In the place of the parent

Injunction: Equitable remedy which either commands that an action be done or prevents the carrying out of an action.

Inter vivos: Between the living

Laches: Equitable principle under which delay in claiming an equitable remedy can mean that the claim is defeated

Locus standi: Right to bring an action (literally: the place of standing)

Obiter dicta: That part of a judgement which is not part of the actual reason for the decision but which can form a valuable guide in similar cases

Pari passu: On an equal footing or proportionally

Personalty: Personal property i.e. property other than freehold land

Private trust: Trust for the benefit of individuals as distinct from a public trust which is for purposes

Realty: Real property i.e freehold land

Rescission: Equitable remedy restoring the parties to their pre contract position

Rectification: Equitable remedy rectifying a contract to make it accord with the intentions of the parties

Residuary estate: Property left by will which is anything not disposed of specifically

Resulting trust: A trust which is implied by the court which has the effect of returning property to the settlor

Settlor: Creator of an *inter vivos* trust

Specific performance: Equitable remedy which commands the carrying out of contractual obligations

Sui juris: Of full age and capacity

Testator (Feminine Testratrix): Person who executes a will which may contain a trust

Tracing: The process of identifying assets against which an equitable remedy may be sought

Trustee: A person who holds property in a fiduciary capacity for the benefit of another

Trustee in bankruptcy: A person who acts on behalf of creditors

Unjust enrichment: Means by which a defendant who has been unjustly enriched at the expense of the claimant is compelled to restore property

Ultra vires: Beyond the powers

Volunteer: Person who is promised property without having provided consideration

Part One

EQUITY: GENERAL PRINCIPLES

The focus of this part is on equity in general, rather than on the trust, which is the major creation of equity. As such it looks at the general nature of equity and its remedies and doctrines. Some teachers leave this area until the end of the course. If this is so in your case then, as this part is self-contained, you can return to it later. It is, however, recommended that you do read Chapter 1, which sets the scene for the study of equity as a whole.

1 Nature of equity

INTRODUCTION

Welcome to the study of equity! This chapter introduces you to the study of equity by looking at a case study based on *Patel* v. *Ali* and then aims to give you a framework for studying equity. It looks at the meaning of the term 'equity' and then at its history. The history is important as otherwise it is impossible to understand why equity developed not only as a separate system of laws but also why it developed its own courts to administer it. The extent to which equity has a discretionary character is often misunderstood and this chapter aims to clarify this issue and finally it considers the place of equity today, including the extent to which it can be said that equity and the common law are 'fused'. The last chapter, Chapter 22, picks up some of the themes in this chapter and you may find it useful, when you reach Chapter 22, to refer back to Chapter 1.

AN INTRODUCTION TO EQUITY TODAY – A CASE STUDY

In 1979 Suriya Ali and Nazir Ahmed, who were joint owners of a house, contracted to sell it to Mr and Mrs Patel. In May 1979 Mr Ali, Suriya Ali's husband, was adjudged bankrupt and within a week his **trustee in bankruptcy** had obtained an **injunction** preventing a sale. The reason was to preserve the house, as a claimed asset of Mr Ali, for his creditors.

In January 1980 the court allowed the sale of the house to proceed on the basis that the trustee's claim would be met out of the proceeds of sale. In August 1980 the Patels brought a claim for **specific performance** of the contract of 1979 but had difficulty in serving the claim on Mr Ahmed as he had left the country and, indeed, plays no further part in the story. At about that time Mrs Ali became seriously ill with bone cancer. In July 1980 she became pregnant and then had a leg amputated. As a result she needed help with household duties and shopping. A month later she give birth to their second child. In 1981–82 Mr Ali was in prison and in August 1983 Mrs Ali gave birth to their third child. By this time she was very much dependent on her family and close friends nearby for help. An additional factor was that she spoke virtually no English.

The facts above are those of *Patel* v. *Ali* (1984). Did the court grant the remedy of specific performance which was sought? The answer depends on an examination of some fundamental principles of equity.

There was undoubtedly a breach of the contract made in 1979. Mrs Ali and Mr Ahmed had not given the Patels possession of the house as agreed. Therefore at **common law** the Patels had a right to damages for breach of contract. However, damages were not the appropriate remedy. The Patels, having contracted for the purchase of a particular house, wanted that house and not money instead. This is where we reach equity, as the remedy sought, specific performance, is an equitable one that compels a party to perform their contractual obligations. In this case, that meant giving up possession of their house.

However, as we shall see in more detail later, equity has a discretion whether to grant its remedies. Indeed the very word 'equity' implies a desire to be fair and just. In this case the court had to balance the position of Mrs Ali, who needed to remain where she was, against that of the Patels, who not unreasonably wanted what they had contracted for, the house.

The court held that, if the defendants were forced to complete the sale and Mrs Ali had to move out, there would be 'hardship amounting to injustice', in the words of Goulding J. The fact that a person would suffer hardship in having to complete a sale was not in itself enough to justify the court in refusing an order for specific performance. Hardship would, said the court, only justify the refusal of an order in an exceptional case. This was one.

That was not the end of the matter, though. The court also had to be satisfied that the remedy at common law, in this case, **damages**, would be effective. Otherwise the Patels would have no remedy at all. Here it was felt that it would be and there was evidence that the Muslim community would pay the damages awarded against Mrs Ali and Mr Ahmed.

The following points emerge from this case:

(a) The discretion of the court is guided by principles. Thus here the court did not have a complete discretion whether or not to grant specific performance. Instead it considered whether hardship would be caused if it did grant the remedy and not only hardship but also 'hardship amounting to injustice'. In addition it had to be satisfied that the common law remedy would be effective. The extent to which equity exercises discretion is considered below.

(b) Common law remedies (damages here) are considered first. Only if they are not adequate will equitable remedies be considered.

(c) The equitable remedy of specific performance is directed against particular persons rather than their money, like the common law remedy of damages.

(d) In some cases equity is not discretionary at all and the common law at times exercises what amounts to a discretion, a point to which we shall return at the end of this chapter.

Note also that this case illustrates two other areas of equity, which have been highlighted above:

(a) The equitable remedy of an **injunction**, which in this case forbade the doing of an act, here the sale of the house. Injunctions normally are negative although they can be positive.
(b) The idea of a **trust**. The property of Mr Ali, when he was made bankrupt, was then held by his trustee in bankruptcy for the benefit of his creditors. The trustee in bankruptcy was the legal owner of the property although he did not hold it for his own benefit but for the benefit of the creditors.

Injunctions and specific performance will be dealt with in Chapter 2 and trusts in Chapter 4.

EQUITY AND DISCRETION

Although a court, when awarding equitable remedies has some discretion, it is not a complete discretion. The court, when applying equity, does not start with a blank sheet of a paper. It cannot simply do what it feels to be just in the circumstances and it must be emphasised that the fact that equity is a discretionary system should not lead to the idea the equity is all about vagueness. It has been said that 'there is a real danger in simply assuming that equity stands for flexibility and vagueness. Equity needs to be principled and equity needs to be clear' (Virgo 2003). Indeed in many areas, as we shall see, there is no more discretion in equity then there is in the common law. A good example is the rules on constitution of a trust in Chapter 7. Furthermore, there are many areas of the common law where the courts exercise discretion, such as judicial review and the imposition of a duty of care in negligence.

Having looked at a modern application of equity we can now turn to the questions of how equity developed and what equity means.

A DEFINITION OF EQUITY?

A simple definition might be that equity consists of the body of rules, which was developed to mitigate the harshness of the common law. This takes us some way, but not far enough.

The first stage is to define the term 'common law'. This term has different meanings depending on the context in which it is used. It can mean all law made by the courts in opposition to law made by parliament, but in this context it means that part of judge-made law made by the courts of common law as distinct from judge-made by the courts of equity.

Before moving on, it is well worth thinking briefly about what this definition does, and what it does not, tell us:

(a) **That equity is a body of rules**. This is, in fact, true of much of equity, especially of the law of trusts.
(b) **That the rules were developed to mitigate harshness**. This tells us that equity must be concerned with what the word 'equity' might indicate to the

layperson, that is, certain broad notions of fairness with which the harshness of the common law could be mitigated. As such, we begin to see that the first part of the definition is partly misleading. Although there are areas of equity, for example, the rules on the formation of trusts, which are just as rule bound as the common law, if not more so, other areas have much more of the flavour of broad principles about them. Contrast, for example, Chapter 5, on the formation of trusts, and Chapter 11 on constructive trusts.

✓(c) **That equity was developed as a reaction to the harshness of the common law**. The word 'harshness' although appropriately vivid, is not entirely accurate. The common law was not always harsh. Sometimes it was, but at other times it would be truer to say that equity was found more suitable to certain needs of society than the common law.

✓(d) **That equity was a reaction to developments, or the lack of developments, in the common law**. Here we arrive at a very significant point. Unlike all other branches of English law, equity is not a complete system of law in itself. Take the law of contract. This deals, of course, with the law of agreements. The law of tort deals with civil wrongs. It is not possible to state so simply precisely what area of human behaviour is covered by equity. This is because equity deals with a great variety of different aspects of life where, for one reason or another, its intervention was found necessary. Therefore in many cases equity simply adds to what the common law had already done. A good example is in the area of remedies. If one removed all equitable remedies there would still be a workable system of common law remedies. These would be much less satisfactory without the equitable remedies but would still manage to function. However, the oft-quoted statement of Maitland (1936) that 'equity is a gloss on the common law' is misleading. There are areas of law which owe everything to equity and nothing to the common law. The best example is the law of trusts, but there are others, such as the law on breach of confidence and much of the law on mortgages.

✓(e) **The concluding point to make here is that an attempt to arrive at a definition of equity is bound to fail**. Equity cannot be confined within some tightly drawn formula. The most that can be done is to indicate the main areas in which equity intervenes in the legal system, to estimate the value of those interventions, and to try to estimate where equity may travel to in the future. This is what this book tries to do.

However, before looking at these topics, it is necessary to glance at two connected topics: what does the term 'equity' mean and how and why did equity develop? A knowledge of these issues is perhaps more important, for example, than a knowledge of the history of the law of contract, as the very term 'equity' and the rationale for its development still influence current thinking about the place of equity is our society.

✓ 'Equity' contrasted with 'justice'

One difficulty is that the term 'equity' does not have a certain meaning. To the layperson it means fairness and, perhaps, reasonableness. The word 'equity' is sometimes used in this sense in our legal system. For example, s. 98(4) of the Employment Rights Act 1996 provides that a decision on whether a dismissal was fair or unfair shall be determined in accordance with various factors including, crucially for our purposes, 'equity and the substantial merits of the case'. In this context equity means that the decision on the fairness or unfairness of a dismissal shall not be arrived at on the basis of technical rules, but shall be influenced by whether the decision to dismiss was actually fair. This is distinct from the position where the claim is for wrongful dismissal when the issue is whether the dismissal was in breach of contract. (In reality there is not so much difference between them but that is another story!)

Equity as a branch of our legal system can also be said to be governed by fairness but if that was all there was to say about equity there would be no need for this, or any, book on the subject. The challenge is to try to discover some distinguishing features of the term 'equity' as it is used in the context of a branch of our law.

The problem is that equity can be described by other words, which themselves do not have precise meanings and may indeed be different from each other. The words justice, mercy, fairness and conscience, to take four obvious examples, are often used as synonyms for equity. The task is to try to disentangle the term 'equity' from these if possible or, if not, at least to seek to mark areas where equity takes on the characteristics of these terms.

A starting point is found in the *Nicomachean Ethics* of Aristotle (Book 5) where the distinction between justice and equity is discussed. It is pointed out that it is not easy to distinguish between them. However, a distinction is found by regarding justice as dealing with what is lawful, so that the just man observes the law whilst the unjust man is grasping and unfair. A discussion of justice follows in which it is clear, in very broad terms, that justice is essentially a virtue associated with law. However, Aristotle also observes that there is a need at times to have a kind of corrective to legal justice. This is because a law is obviously universal in that it applies to all in particular situations without being able to take account of individual circumstances. This is where equity comes in, as it can take account of these circumstances and, as Aristotle puts it: 'say what the legislator would have said had he been present'. This notion of equity is undoubtedly still present in equity today, as illustrated by *Patel* v. *Ali* (above) later in this chapter and *Rochefoucauld* v. *Boustead* (see later in this chapter and also Chapter 11). Worthington (2003) refers to this principle of Aristotle's as distinguishing between bright line rules and fact sensitive rules in that the latter lend themselves to discretionary justice. Indeed, something like this principle needs to exist in every legal system. The question is whether, given that Aristotle's principle is one feature of modern equity, anything else can be said of the distinguishing features of equity.

We shall see shortly that equity was largely developed by churchmen and so the next question is clearly whether equity was influenced by Christian and, in particular, by biblical views of justice. As McIlroy points out (McIlroy 2003) the biblical view of justice was, on one level, that one should 'Give to each what is due to him', a statement found also in the Digest of the Emperor Justinian.

Whilst this is true, the statement does not have any distinctive Christian flavour, but can be found both in the notion of the inherent dignity of each member of the human race and in the fact that a misuse of power is unjust as it takes away what God has given to each individual. The question is whether these principles are also characteristic of equity and here we must turn to the medieval canon lawyers.

It is with the medieval canon lawyers that we see the distinction between justice and equity more fully thought through (see Brundage 1995). If a generalisation (always dangerous) may be attempted here, one could say that the notion of Aristotle (above) that equity was a kind of principle of mitigation, 'which adjusted the rigours of strict law to the varied needs of individual situations' (Brundage) was also accepted by the canonists. Justice, on the other hand, was sometimes regarded as a principle of retribution where offenders were given what they deserved (rather in line with the statement in Justinian (above) but at other times it was given a much deeper meaning. For example, fourteenth-century canonists thought of justice as an ideal to which humans on earth could only aspire to and not attain, and law was thus only the best attempt which humans could make towards the ultimately impossible pursuit of absolute pursuit of justice.

The foregoing discussion has, if nothing else, shown that the terms 'justice' and 'equity' have not necessarily been regarded as the same, which is itself significant in that judges even today use the term 'justice' as synonymous with equity. However, we are not yet at the end of our quest. Instead we have reached the fourteenth century, and the system of equity in English law is just beginning its journey. It is to this that we must now turn.

✓ EARLY DEVELOPMENT OF EQUITY

There is a potted version of the development of equity, which is often related to students, and which runs like this:

The early common law, although beneficial, became too hidebound and unable to respond to the needs of society. Accordingly, those with grievances started to take them direct to the King who, in time, passed them on to his Chancellor. The Chancellor, being an ecclesiastic, decided them according to general principles of justice and so equity was born. Later on, after equity had become a regular system of law, and a rival to the common law, it became just, if not more, hidebound by technicalities than the common law had been and so the disease ended up worse than the cure. This was ended by the Judicature Act of 1873, which completed the process of reform of equity, and now both equity and the common law are administered side by side in the same courts.

There is a good deal of truth in this account but it contains some ancient myths which need debunking, not only for the sake of accuracy but also to clear the ground for a better appreciation of equity today.

The early common law courts were certainly a success in bringing a common system of justice across England. Nor were they rule-bound in the way that a court today is bound to apply the words of statute law, even if it regrets having to do so. It is a myth that the Chancellor was the first to apply broad notions of justice. The early courts of common law, when applying the law, were willing to disapply it when otherwise injustice would be done. Allen (1964) mentions a case of 1309 when a man had promised to hand over a document by a certain day and to pay a penalty if he did not do so. He was, however, unable to do so as he was overseas at the time and pointed out that the creditor had suffered no damage by the delay. The court took the point and told the creditor that he would have to wait seven years for the money. (The judge, Bereford CJ, was in some ways a medieval Lord Denning and it is a pity that more is not known about him.) Here at a very early date we see the courts applying very much the idea of equity suggested by Aristotle. Not only this, but there is evidence that the common law courts were prepared to grant remedies which look very similar to the equitable remedies granted later by the Chancellor and which have been seen as one of the distinctive contributions of equity to English law. Thus there are examples from the early cases of the remedies of specific performance and injunction (see below). In addition the Kings themselves were prepared on occasion to intervene. The coronation oath of King Edward II, for example, required him to do justice 'in mercy and truth' (Baker 2002). Edward III granted what amounted to an injunction in 1350 and in 1381, during the Peasants' Revolt, Richard II was persuaded by a man near him to intervene in a land dispute (see Musson 2001.) Accordingly, the picture of the common law as administering a rigid system of rules not tempered by any higher principles is wrong.

Nevertheless, it is true to say that there were increasing complaints about the ability of the common law courts to deal with a variety of matters and there is evidence of increasing rigidity by the mid-fourteenth century. Some examples were:

(a) Juries were bribed or intimidated so that a litigant could not obtain justice. As Plucknett (1948) observes, 'Distrust of juries is an important factor in the early popularity of equity courts'. This appears to have been a particularly significant factor in the general unrest and dislocation in the time of the Wars of the Roses (for our purposes 1455–71) when equity was just beginning to burgeon out.

(b) The use of juries in civil cases also hampered the development of the law as the judges needed to concentrate on explaining the law to them at the expense of developing it.

(c) The procedures of the common law courts were often ill-suited to deal with cases which required the personal attendance of the parties and witnesses and commanding a party to actually do, or not do, something. The common law courts were far better suited to disputes concerning land where, rather than deal with an individual direct, his land could be taken from him.

(d) The writ system had become an obstacle to the proper development of the law. A writ is in essence simply a command to a person to appear and answer a complaint against him and the modern successor of writs is the claim form, writs having been abolished in 1999. Today a few types of forms suffice for all claims but in 1258 the Provisions of Oxford laid down that any new writ had to fit the formula of a previous one and so, if one could not be found in the register of writs, the plaintiff was unable to bring his case. Whatever the reason for this, its effect was far reaching as it stultified the development of the common law and the gap had to be filled by another system of law.

For these, and other reasons, litigants took to petitioning the King's Council to do justice. These petitions were presented by a bill, which had no prescribed form, and, although in many cases these were simply passed to the courts with a command to deal with the matter, in others the King in Council dealt with it directly. By the mid-fourteenth century this practice was becoming increasingly common and it was by this means that what we now know as equity eventually developed.

The Chancery was the royal secretariat and its clerks issued the writs referred to above. As such it constituted a permanent body of trained personnel headed by the Chancellor, who was generally a lawyer and also an ecclesiastic as well as being one of the chief ministers of the Crown. It was therefore a natural process to pass these petitions to the Chancery, especially where the complaint was the failure to issue a writ. Originally the Chancery saw its function as assisting the common law courts in dispensing justice but from around 1350 onwards the Chancery began to deal with cases itself and by 1390 petitions were directed to the Chancellor directly rather than to the King in Council.

The advantages of the Chancellor over the common law courts were that:

(a) The Chancery was able to deal with the case without a jury.
(b) The Bill procedure did not require any particular form and so the bar on new types of actions being brought disappeared if the action was begun in Chancery.
(c) The Bill procedure was also quicker than that by writ as the Chancellor, on receipt of a bill, then issued a writ in a general form without being bound, as were the common law courts, to follow the form of a previous writ (see (d) above).
(d) The relative informality of procedure at this early date meant that the services of a lawyer were not always needed.
(e) The Chancellor acted *in personam*. This famous phrase, one of the great characteristics of equity, meant that the Chancellor acted against a person rather than against his land, and so he could be ordered to carry out an obligation by a decree of specific performance or do, or refrain from doing, an act by an injunction. However, it should be pointed out that the early common law courts also acted *in personam* but their jurisdiction withered away.
(f) The fact that the Chancellor recognised and enforced trusts. This topic is dealt with in more detail in Chapter 2 but, briefly, the essential feature of a trust is that the ownership of the property in law and the rights over it in equity are split. The **trustee** is the owner in law but others may have rights over it in equity.

Thus we can see that equity was of great use to private litigants but in its early days in the period from around 1380 to 1420 it was also used by the Crown as a means of enforcing law and order.

Example 1.1

John has a daughter, Angela, aged three, to whom he wishes to give £25,000 so that it will be securely in Angela's name should John die. Clearly a child of three is too young to be able to deal with a sum as large as this and so John creates a trust under which a friend, Michael, agrees to act as trustee. The money is legally in Michael's name but equity recognises Angela as having rights over the money so that, for instance, if Michael withdrew the money and spent it on himself, equity would grant Angela a remedy. The common law, by contrast, would not, and the development of the law of trusts is one of the greatest contributions which equity has made to the English law.

LATER DEVELOPMENT OF EQUITY

Once fairly launched the development of equity was rapid. Its function of being used as a kind of law enforcement agency largely disappeared and the Chancellor's jurisdiction increased threefold between 1420 and 1450 (Avery 1970). This now mainly concerned trusts (90 per cent) and contracts (6 per cent). Avery successfully challenges the myth that there was rivalry between the common law courts and the Chancellor at this time: common law judges frequently sat with the Chancellor to hear cases and it was not until 1473 that the Chancellor issued a decree in his own name. It is at this time that we should now refer to an actual Court of Chancery. It is in fact a sobering thought that even at this time the Court of Chancery was subject to the problems which plagued it later, such as delay, and its orders, granted *in personam*, were not always obeyed. Chancery was never a knight in completely shining armour.

This rapid development continued under a succession of vigorous Chancellors and reached a peak under Wolsey who held office from 1515–29. He was followed by Thomas More (1529–32) and the growth of Chancery jurisdiction can be judged by the fact that he heard 2,356 cases in the 31 months when he held office. The type of cases dealt with by the Chancellor have been analysed by Guy (1980) as follows: 47 per cent concerned real property, 15 per cent mercantile and the rest were a mixed bag consisting of e.g. fraud, forgery, defamation and false imprisonment. It is this last part of the Chancellor's jurisdiction which has very largely died away.

In the early Tudor period the history of the Court of Chancery becomes entangled to some degree with that of the Court of Star Chamber. This was not strictly a court at all but was part of the judicial business of the King's Council. The medieval and Tudor kings were constantly on the move and so part of their court went with them. Part, however, stayed at Westminster, dealt with judicial work and met in the Star Chamber. Unlike the Chancellor this court did not administer a law of its own but was concerned to see that existing law was properly administered. It dealt with cases involving civil disorder and also with property disputes. Guy points out that the basis on which lawyers recommended either Chancery or Star Chamber is obscure, but records show that where the claim was complex or some form of personal violence was involved then Star Chamber was the chosen forum. At all events, Star Chamber went on its own way, but as it was closely associated with Royal power, it fell victim to the upheavals of the seventeenth century and was finally abolished at the Restoration in 1660.

The growing popularity of the Court of Chancery (and also Star Chamber) led to a decline of the business dealt with by the common law courts so that in 1515/1516 the level of business in the Courts of Common Pleas and King's Bench combined was only 62 per cent of what it was in 1439/1440 (Guy 1980). Although the extent of the division between the Court of Chancery and the common law courts at this date can be exaggerated (judges in the common law courts could still, when the need arose, be found also sitting in Chancery), there was a growing dislike of the practice of the Chancellor issuing injunctions preventing either the issuing of proceedings, or the enforcement of a judgment obtained, at common law. On a celebrated occasion, Thomas More invited the common law judges to dine with him and offered to issue no more injunctions if the common law judges would reform the law themselves. The attempt failed but one interesting point is that More thought that the judges had enough discretion vested in themselves to achieve this and were 'in conscience bound' (Roper 1979).

'Conscience' in equity

The use of the term 'conscience' as a means of identifying the fountain-head of equitable jurisdiction was not new. Many times in the middle ages the judges often used it to describe the way in which the Chancellor operated, and indeed it was a more familiar term than the very word 'equity', but the term conscience seems to acquire a particular resonance at the time of More, partly due no doubt to the emphasis which he himself put on the word in his struggle with Henry VIII. In addition Nicholas St Germain, in his influential work *Doctor and Student* published around 1530, emphasised the importance of the principle of conscience both from a moral standpoint and also as a corrector of strict legal rules which should be applied according to their intention and not necessarily their strict meaning.

The location of conscience as perhaps the mainspring of equitable jurisdiction has been enormously significant in the development of equity, especially in more recent years and there is now an increasing tendency for the courts to rest their decision in an equity case on whether an act was 'unconscionable'. However, before looking at this, we need to briefly survey the rest of the story of the development of equity.

EQUITY INTO THE MODERN ERA

After the era of Wolsey and More there was a gradual hardening of equitable jurisdiction and a move towards definite principles and rules. In one way this was surprising, given that, as we have just seen, the idea of conscience was now seen as a vital feature of equity. In effect equity began to turn in on itself and this phase lasted until the middle of the last century. This was probably inevitable as far as trusts were concerned, as the actual administration of a trust needs to be governed by clear rules. But in addition there was a reluctance to extend equity into new fields as, when in 1676, in *Bennett* v. *Honeywood* the Court of Chancery declined to give relief against unfair terms in contracts. The well-known jibe of Selden in 1689 that 'equity varies with the length of the Chancellor's foot' was not only half serious but also becoming out of date. Indeed thirteen years earlier, in 1676, Lord Nottingham had stated that the conscience of the Chancellor was not simply his own ideas of what was right. Even so, equity at this date was by no means stagnant. When the Statute of Frauds was passed in 1677 it quickly developed the doctrine of secret trusts (see Chapter 8) and redeveloped the rules of *donatio mortis causa* (see Chapter 7) to deal with cases where property had been left outside a will. Also, this was the era when the maxims were developed as a guide to equitable jurisdiction. (References to these will be found throughout this book and they are gathered together at the end in Chapter 21.) Nevertheless, it is difficult to avoid the impression that equity had lost its early vigour. Throughout the eighteenth century the notion of equity as a general corrector of injustice was increasingly repudiated and Chancellors as notable as Lords Hardwicke and Eldon, by their developments of equitable doctrines, made equity an increasingly rigid system. This development was aided by the availability for the first time of proper reports of Chancery decisions. Not only this, but it was clear that the Chancellors did not see their role in any wider sense. In 1818 Lord Eldon said, in *Gee* v. *Pritchard* that nothing would give him greater pain 'quitting this place' than recollecting that he had done anything 'to justify the reproach that the equity of this court varies like the chancellor's foot'. Not only were the rules hardening, but also the procedures of the Court of Chancery were becoming a by-word for delay, incompetence and hopelessness amongst litigants. One particular example (quoted in Baker 2002) was the case of *Morgan* v. *Lord Clarendon* which was commenced in 1808 and which, by 1824, was still in its preliminary stages and no counsel had as yet been briefed. This situation was made worse by the fact that it was not until 1885 that the Chancellor was aided by the creation of a separate department which dealt with administrative matters. Until then the Chancellor dealt with far too many routine matters. Moreover, until 1813, when a Vice Chancellor was appointed, there were only two judges, the Chancellor and the Master of the Rolls.

In Dickens' *Bleak House*, in which the practices of the old Court of Chancery are mercilessly exposed, Miss Flite, the perpetual suitor, observes, with considerable understatement, that 'Chancery justice is so ve-ry difficult to follow'. As it happened, by the time *Bleak House* was published in 1852, one of the first steps had been taken to reform the procedures of the court with the passage of the Chancery Procedure Act. This was part of a series of measures culminating in the Judicature Acts of 1873 and 1875. The old Court of Chancery was abolished along with the old common law courts of Queen's Bench, Common Pleas and Exchequer. In their place a new High Court was established which also incorporated the old courts of Probate, Divorce and Admiralty. Much of the work of the

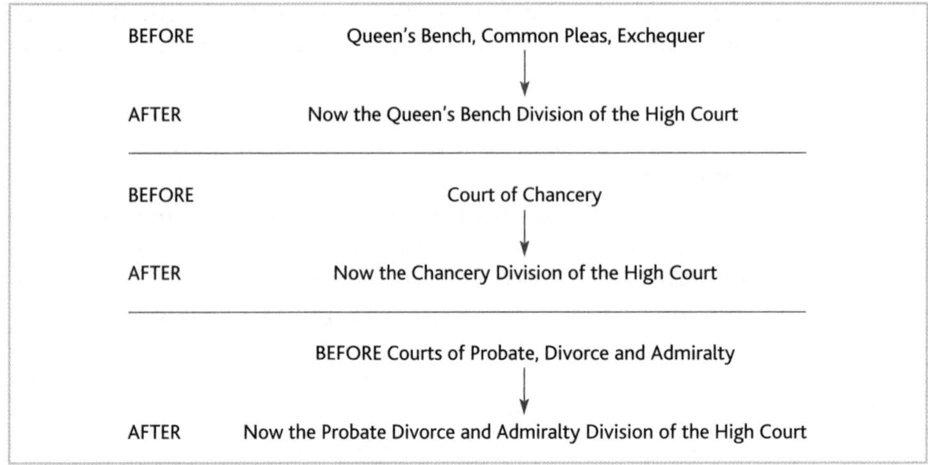

Figure 1.1 The court system before and after the Judicature Acts

Court of Chancery was assigned to the new Chancery Division of the High Court, but the vital point was that equity jurisdiction could be exercised by any of the divisions of the High Court and this is the case today. In addition County Courts have a limited equity jurisdiction, the relevant statute being the County Courts Act 1984. The effect was that equity was no longer administered separately from the common law; instead they are both now administered side by side in all courts.

The effect was that the seven courts which existed prior to the Judicature Acts were merged into three divisions of the High Court. Although the Chancery Division deals with many areas which were previously dealt with by the former Court of Chancery, each division of the High Court has, by virtue of s. 24 of the Judicature Act, jurisdiction in both law and equity.

The High Court, with a new Court of Appeal, formed the Supreme Court (it was originally intended to abolish the House of Lords as the final court of appeal but this did not happen and so the title of Supreme Court is misleading. It is now proposed to change this with the establishment of a new Supreme Court which will replace the House of Lords but that is another story). What is important here is that as the new Court of Appeal heard appeals from all three divisions of the High Court the old separation between common law and equity was inevitably broken down. A final twist in the story of the development of equity is that the Constitutional Reform Bill of 2003 (now the Constitutional Reform Act 2005) proposed to abolish the historic office of Lord Chancellor but, following misgivings expressed in many quarters, the Bill was amended so that the office will remain. However, the Lord Chancellor has, under the Act, been shorn of many of his judicial functions.

EQUITY TODAY

It will be easier to appreciate the importance of the issues raised here when the subject of equity has itself been mastered, but at this point it is a good idea to remember that, when studying equity, the following main themes should be kept in mind. We shall look at them again, in Chapter 22, in the light of some of the material which will be covered.

The fusion debate

The administration of equity and the common law are fused by the Judicature Acts, but are equity and the common law themselves fused so that it is no longer correct to speak of equity and the common law as distinct systems? This question has been much debated. Did fusion occur with the Judicature Acts, has it occurred since and, if not, should it occur now? The general view is that it has not. This was expressed in a well known metaphor by Ashburner (1933): 'the two streams of jurisdiction, though they run in the same channel, run side by side and do not mix their waters'. This view has been contradicted, most notably by Lord Diplock in *United Scientific Holdings* v. *Burnley Borough Council* (1977) who said that this 'fluvial metaphor' is 'mischievous and deceptive' and that the two systems of law, common law and equity, were indeed fused by the Judicature Acts. The truth is, however, that they have not, as any glance at the areas covered in this book will show. Equitable and common law remedies operate together but are not governed by the same principles, as shown by *Patel* v. *Ali* (see beginning of this chapter). Another example is *Walsh* v. *Lonsdale* (1882) (below).

The fusion debate has been revived from another angle by Worthington (2003), who suggests that it is time that equity and the common law were fully integrated. This approach goes beyond the somewhat sterile discussion as to the effect of the Judicature Acts and argues that, in any event, there is now no reason why integration should not be pursued. She points out that it is untrue to say that it is only equity which permits the exercise of discretion; so does the common law. She instances, for example, the discretionary element in deciding if a duty of care exists in tort or if a consumer contract contains unfair terms. At times, on the other hand, equity has no discretion at all, for example, in deciding if equitable proprietary remedies should be awarded or not. She makes the telling point that, if there were discretion here, the law of insolvency would turn into a farce. Moreover, she rightly draws attention to the increased willingness of the common law to adjudicate according to the standard of reasonableness. This is true, as in the above examples, but one could say that there is an undoubted flavour of equity which could be lost if it was simply taken under the umbrella of the common law. Furthermore, the common law standard of reasonableness is not the same as some equitable principles which have a specifically ethical dimension to them which is not necessarily present in the standard of reasonableness. This issue is discussed again in Chapter 22 in the light of the material covered in this book.

Section 25(11) of the Judicature Act 1873 (the rule is now in s. 49 of the Supreme Court Act 1981) provided that where the rules of equity and common law conflict then equity shall prevail. The effect of this can be exaggerated as in many cases there is no conflict. In the administration of the law of trusts equity holds undisputed sway and in the case of remedies equity and the common law work alongside each other so the court may award the appropriate remedy, whether it be equitable or common law. An instance is *Patel* v. *Ali* (above) where it was felt that the equitable remedy of specific performance was inappropriate and so common law damages were awarded. However, in some cases there is the possibility of conflict and so s. 25(11) comes into play.

The outcome of the decision in *Walsh* v. *Lonsdale* can be illustrated by Figure 1.2.

Case study 1.1
Equity versus the Common Law

In *Walsh* v. *Lonsdale* (1882) the parties had agreed on the lease of a mill for seven years. Rent was payable quarterly in arrears but the landlord was entitled to demand a year's rent in advance. However, the agreement was not contained in a deed as required to make it binding in law (this requirement is now in s. 52(1) of the Law of Property Act 1925). The result was that the lease was void in law.

Nevertheless the tenant entered into possession and paid rent in accordance with the lease for eighteen months. The landlord then demanded a year's rent in arrears and when the tenant refused to pay the issue was whether the terms of the agreement for a lease could be relied on. At common law the landlord could not have demanded a year's rent in advance as the lease was void and the yearly periodic tenancy which arose when the tenant went into possession excluded a right to claim payment of rent in advance. However, equity could be applied and here the maxim 'equity looks on that as done which ought to be done' meant that, as the parties had *agreed* on a lease equity would then act on the principle that the agreement had now been given effect to by a deed as this was what the parties *ought* to have done. When the agreement was applied it was seen that it allowed the landlord to claim payment of rent in advance and so the landlord's claim succeeded.

Note 1.1: The principle in this case is not only important from the point of s. 25(11) but as an example of where equity has looked behind formal requirements and given effect to what the parties actually intended, a point which will arise on many occasions later.

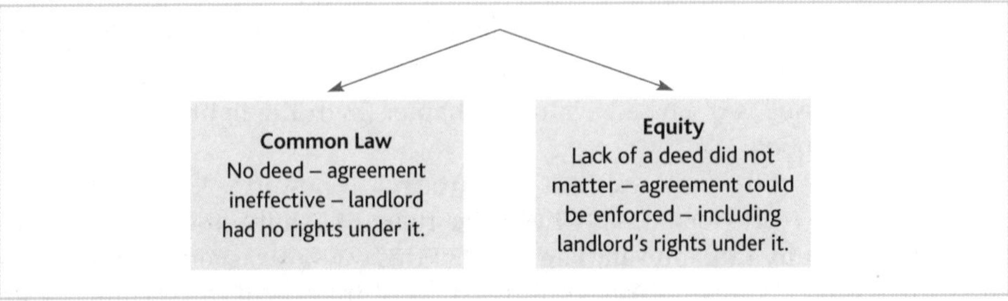

Common Law
No deed – agreement ineffective – landlord had no rights under it.
Equity
Lack of a deed did not matter – agreement could be enforced – including landlord's rights under it.

Figure 1.2 The outcome of the decision in *Walsh* v. *Lonsdale*

Is equity 'past the age of child bearing?'

Is equity still able to react to new challenges, especially in the light of changing social circumstances, or has it now reached the limit of its creative activity? This debate raged with particular vigour when Lord Denning was Master of the Rolls (1962–82) as it was the contention of Lord Denning MR that, as he put it: 'Equity is not past the age of childbearing' (*Eves* v. *Eves* (1975)). This statement was made in connection with the 'new model constructive trust' which, as we shall see, is in decline, but it is undoubtedly true that equity remains capable of developing new principles to meet new situations, as in *Barclays Bank* v. *O'Brien* (1994) (undue influence – Chapter 3), equitable estoppel (Chapter 11) and equitable remedies (Chapter 2). This is, in fact, uncontroversial, and would be approved by Bagnall J, who, in *Cowcher* v. *Cowcher* (1972) insisted that, although equity is not past the age of childbearing, 'its progeny must be legitimate – by precedent out of principle'. The debate is really one of degree and relates back to the point made earlier about the extent of equitable discretion. Should equity strike out into previously uncharted waters, as Lord Denning MR would have had it, in order to meet a need, or should it develop from clear existing principles which can then be developed? Examples of opposing views on this will be found throughout this book and especially in Chapters 10 and 11.

Although, as stated earlier, it is impossible to define equity, one ought to ask if it is possible to at least indicate the basis on which equity operates. The way forward, it is suggested, is to separate that area dealing with the creation and administration of express private trusts and charitable trusts from the rest of equity. This specific area is governed by rules which are as rigid (and not as rigid) as the common law. A straightforward example is *Re Compton* (1945) where the court felt unable to alter the anomalous rule that there is no requirement of public benefit in charitable trusts for the relief of poverty, a situation which is only now being addressed by statute in the Charities Bill 2005 (see Chapter 13). This instance shows how rigidly bound by precedent equity can be. These apart it is possible to see certain principles emerging. One, which runs right through equity, is that equity will displace a particular rule where its workings would cause injustice, although even here, this will only apply in areas where equity has traditionally intervened and not, for instance, in the criminal law. However, if this is all that we can say about equity, then it will amount to saying that the role of equity is essentially reactive: it only comes into play when a legal rule is perceived to be working injustice. In fact, equity has developed doctrines on its own, for example, those of undue influence, equitable estoppel and the equitable duty of confidence. On what basis has this been done?

Equity and unconscionability

In this chapter, we have looked at a number of concepts: justice, mercy, fairness and conscience. It is this last term which best describes the basis of equity and, in recent years, the term 'unconscionability' has been increasingly used, especially in Commonwealth jurisdictions, where much of the current thought on equity comes and it has, of course, played a major part in the development of equity, as we have seen. As Morris (1996) has said: 'The point has now been reached in Australia that equity now recognises a general principle pursuant to which transactions may be set aside on the ground of a party's unconscionable conduct'. We have not reached this stage in England but the passage does emphasise the part played by the notion of unconscionability in modern equity. It is also seen in the Australian decision of *Baumgartner* v. *Baumgartner* (1987) on family property and in many English decisions on, for example, constructive trusts (see Chapter 12). As Lord Browne–Wiulkinson observed (in the context of trusts) in *Westdeustsche Landesbank Girozentrale* v. *Islington LBC* (1996): 'Equity operates on the conscience of the owner of the legal interest'. Moreover, in the recent decision of the Court of Appeal in *Pennington* v. *Waine* (2002), which may have liberalised the law on incompletely constituted trusts, Arden LJ expressly based her decision on unconscionability (see Chapter 7). Not only this, but the notion of unconscionability is making its way into equitable remedies and what may be considered fairly routine decisions at first, such as *Gafford* v. *Graham* (1998) (see Chapter 2).

If it is true that conscience is now a mainspring of equity then the question is: what do we mean by unconscionability? This is more difficult to pin down but two points may be made: it indicates a particular ethical flavour to equity and, more particularly, it indicates a willingness on the part of equity to intervene on the side of the weaker party where there is what has been called 'transactional imbalance' coupled with unconscionable conduct on the part of the stronger party. Beyond this it is not really possible to go. For example, attempting to produce a list of what constitutes unconscionable conduct will only put equity into the very straightjacket which it is necessary to avoid. Thus unconscionability is valuable as a general pointer to the direction which equity should take, but it is of no use as a practical tool in the application of equitable principles, for, in the end, principle is what equity is about.

CONCLUSION

This chapter has attempted to provide a sketch of what equity is about, how it has developed and its role today. Having read through it, do remember to refer to it as you go deeper into your studies to see how the issues outlined here have been developed in practice.

FURTHER READING

Allen (1964) *Law in the Making*, 7th edn, Oxford: Oxford University Press.

Avery (1970) 'The Court of Chancery under the Lancastrian Kings', 86 LQR 84.

Baker (2002) *Introduction to English Legal History*, 4th edn, Oxford: Oxford University Press. This standard work provides extra detail on the development of equity.

Brundage (1995) *Medieval Canon Law*, London: Longmans.

Dickens C. *Bleak House*. The early chapters, especially Chapter 1, give a flavour of equity before the reforms culminating in the Judicature Acts.

Mason (1994) 'The Place of Equity and Equitable Remedies in the Common Law World', 110 LQR 238. This looks in detail at the possible future development of equity and the Australian perspective is especially useful. You will find it helpful to return to this article later.

McIlroy (2003) *Christian Perspectives on Law: A Biblical View of Law and Justice*, Carlisle: Paternoster Press.

Polden (2002) 'Mingling the Waters: Personalities and Politics in the Making of the Supreme Court of Judicature', 61 CLJ 575. Puts flesh on the bones of an aspect of legal history. Most enjoyable.

Roper (1979) *A Life of Thomas More*, Folio Society Edition.

Virgo (2003) 'Restitution Through the Looking Glass: Restitution within Equity and Equity within Restitution', in Getzler (ed.) *Rationalising Property, Equity and Trusts: Essays in Honour of Edward Burn*, London: Butterworths.

Worthington (2003) *Equity*, Oxford: Oxford University Press. A stimulating, readable and provocative study of equity today. One of the most valuable monographs to appear on this topic for some time.

CHAPTER SUMMARY

- Nature of equitable and common law remedies contrasted.
- Equitable remedies are discretionary – what does this mean?
- Equity developed as a response to perceived failures in the common law.
- Later history of equity – became stagnant.
- Vigour of equity today.
- Search for a definition of equity really pointless but on what principle is equitable jurisdiction based?
- Justice? Mercy? Fairness? Unconscionability?

QUESTION

'It is the function of equity to restrict the exercise of legal rights where it would be unconscionable for them to be asserted.'

Consider and illustrate this statement by reference to modern equity.

> *Note 1.2: You will find suggested points for inclusion in this answer in Appendix 2.*

2 Equitable remedies

INTRODUCTION

Chapter 1 dealt with the grant of equitable remedies in *Patel* v. *Ali* and this chapter first looks at the general principles governing their exercise. It then looks at specific remedies but it does not include remedies for breach of trust as these are dealt with in Chapter 20, after trusts have been studied.

General characteristics of equitable remedies

(a) They are discretionary, whereas the common law remedy of damages is available as of right. This does not, however, mean that everything is left to the discretion of the court in each case: as we shall see, there are clear principles governing the grant of equitable remedies. The word 'discretionary' simply means that there are situations where, for various reasons, the court is unlikely to grant an equitable remedy.

(b) They are granted where the common law remedies, e.g. damages, would be inadequate or where the common law remedies are not available because the right is exclusively equitable, e.g. a right of a beneficiary under a trust.

(c) They act *in personam*, i.e. against the defendant personally. Thus failure to comply with an order giving effect to an equitable remedy is contempt of court punishable either by imprisonment or, where the order can be enforced without a personal restraint on the defendant, then an order against his property can be made, such as an order of sequestration. Under this order the court can appoint sequestrators to take possession of the defendant's property until he has complied with the original order.

INJUNCTIONS

An injunction is a court order requiring a party either to do or not to do a particular act. It can be sought by anyone who alleges that a legal or equitable right of theirs has been infringed. If so, they have ***locus standi***. An example of where such a right was held not to exist is *Paton* v. *Trustees of the British Pregnancy Advisory Service* (1979) where the claimant was refused an injunction to prevent his wife from having an abortion. The Abortion Act 1967 gave the father no right to be consulted about the termination of a pregnancy. The issue of *locus standi* in public law actions for an injunction is dealt with below.

The High Court has jurisdiction to grant injunctions by virtue of s. 37(1) of the Supreme Court Act 1981. The County Court has the same powers as the High Court has here (the statutory basis being s. 38 of the Courts and Legal Services Act 1990) except that only the High Court has jurisdiction to grant a Freezing (Mareva) or Search (Anton Piller) Order other than in family proceedings or in aid of the execution of a county court judgment.

Here are some examples of the use of injunctions:

(a) To restrain a breach of contract. There is an overlap here with specific performance and this topic is therefore considered below.
(b) To restrain the commission of a tort e.g. a nuisance or a trespass.
(c) To restrain a breach of confidence.
(d) To restrain a breach of trust. Thus in *Fox* v. *Fox* (1870) trustees were restrained from distributing the estate in a way which was inconsistent with the trust instrument, and in *Buttle* v. *Saunders* (1950) from selling trust property at a price below that offered by a prospective purchaser.
(e) In matrimonial and family matters. The Family Law Act 1996 gives the courts extensive powers to grant injunctions in divorce proceedings, other than matrimonial proceedings and where the parties are cohabitees. Injunctions can require the respondent, for instance, to refrain from assaulting, molesting or otherwise interfering with the other party to the marriage, or a cohabitee, and their children.
(f) In disputes between members of unincorporated associations. An injunction can be granted to restrain a member from being expelled from the association in breach of the rules (*Lee* v. *Showmen's Guild of Great Britain* (1952)).
(g) In public law matters. See below.
(h) Freezing orders (formerly known as Mareva injunctions). See below.
(i) Search orders (formerly known as Anton Piller Orders). See below.

We will now consider the various types of injunctions.

1. Perpetual injunctions

These are known as perpetual injunctions in contrast to interlocutory and *quia timet* injunctions which by their nature will only last for a certain time. Perpetual injunctions will not necessarily last forever but they are final in that they will finally resolve the issue between the parties. There are two types of perpetual injunction:

(i) Prohibitory

This restrains a person from doing some particular act e.g. breaking a contract.

(ii) Mandatory

This commands a person to perform some positive act. It is less frequently granted than a prohibitory injunction and, because it is similar to an order of specific performance, it is subject to similar restrictions as to when it may be granted, e.g. where supervision would be difficult. A mandatory injunction which is positive does, by its nature, have a more drastic effect than a prohibitory injunction and this was recognised in *Wrotham Park Estate Ltd* v. *Parkside Homes Ltd* (1974). Here the court refused to grant a mandatory injunction requiring the demolition of houses built in breach of a restrictive covenant which the builder had thought was unenforceable, as this would have meant the waste of much needed houses. However, in *Wakeham* v. *Wood* (1981) an injunction was granted requiring the demolition of houses built in deliberate breach of a restrictive covenant. A mandatory injunction is rarely granted in industrial disputes although it was granted in *Parker* v. *Camden LBC* (1986) to require the turning on of a boiler when a strike of boilermen meant that tenants of council houses had no heating or hot water.

Interlocutory injunctions

The object of an interlocutory injunction is to preserve the *status quo* until the trial of an action. They have been granted, for example, to prevent a dismissal alleged to be in breach of agreed procedures (*Irani* v. *Southampton and South-West Hampshire Health Authority* (1985), to restrain an association from holding a meeting without allowing certain members to attend (*Woodford* v. *Smith* (1970)), and to restrain the removal of a child from the jurisdiction of the courts. (*Re N (No. 2)* (1967)). Important instances are Freezing and Search Orders – see below.

Interlocutory injunctions may be prohibitory, mandatory or *quia timet* (see below) and normally remain in force until the trial, although a shorter period may be specified. Mandatory interlocutory injunctions are less often granted but see *Sky Petroleum* v. *VIP Petroleum* (1974) below. Where speed or secrecy is of the essence they may be granted without notice (the former term, still used in practice, was *ex parte* (as with Freezing and Search orders) and *Re N (No. 2)* (above) was an *ex parte* application. In most cases, however, the defendant is given the right to be heard.

When will an interlocutory injunction be granted?

In *American Cyanamid Co* v. *Ethicon Ltd* (1975) Lord Diplock laid down the following rules:

(a) Is there a serious question to be tried? The claimant must show that his claim is not frivolous and he must adduce sufficient evidence to satisfy the court that his claim has a real prospect of success at the trial. If the defendant has no arguable defence at all then an injunction will be granted and points (b) and (c) below do not arise (*Official Custodian for Charities* v. *Mackey* (1985)). Otherwise the court will consider the following points:

(b) If there is a serious issue, will damages be an adequate remedy so that an injunction will not be needed? This must be looked at from the point of view of:
   - (i) The claimant i.e. would damages be adequate compensation for loss caused to him by acts of the defendant before the trial?
   - (ii) The defendant i.e. if the claimant loses at the trial then could any loss to him be compensated by the claimant giving an undertaking in damages? (see below)

In *Hubbard* v. *Pitt* (1976) picketing by the defendants of the claimant's estate agents premises was held to be likely to result in serious damage to the business and there was also doubt about whether the defendants could pay damages. Thus an injunction was granted.

(c) If damages would be inadequate, then should an injunction be granted taking into account the balance of convenience to each party? In *Hubbard* v. *Pitt* it was held that the disadvantage of lost trade suffered by the claimants was greater than the disadvantage suffered by the defendants, who were complaining of certain local housing developments, in having to argue their case elsewhere.

(d) There may be other special factors to be considered as in the *American Cyanamid* case (1975) itself, where an interlocutory injunction was granted to prevent infringement of a patent for a pharmaceutical product and partly because of the argument that if the defendant's product had been used prior to the trial, and the claimants then obtained a permanent injunction against its further marketing, the claimants would themselves lose goodwill. Accordingly the interlocutory injunction prevented the defendants from marketing the product at all.

In *Cream Holdings* v. *Banerjee* (2004) it was held that where an injunction is sought to restrain publication before cases involving libel, breach of confidentiality and privacy, *American Cyanimid* should not be applied and the court must look at the actual strength of the case.

Undertakings on the grant of an interlocutory injunction

(a) Damages.
A claimant who is granted an interlocutory injunction is almost always required to undertake that if he does not succeed at the trial he will compensate the defendant for any damage suffered because the injunction was granted. The undertaking is given to the court and so a failure to comply with it is contempt of court.

(b) Other undertakings.
One example is an undertaking to notify the defendant of the terms of an injunction forthwith in a case where the application was made without notice.

(c) No undertaking is required in matrimonial cases which do not involve property rights (Practice Direction 1974).

(d) Applications by the Crown to enforce the law. The court has a discretion whether to require an undertaking in damages from the Crown. There is no automatic rule that an undertaking should be required, especially where the Crown is bringing an action to enforce a statutory provision in a case where there is no other method of enforcement because here the Crown is fulfilling a duty owed to the public at large. (See Lord Diplock in *Hoffmann-La Roche & Co* v. *Secretary of State for Trade and Industry* (1975). Therefore in this case the Secretary of State was held not to be obliged to give such an undertaking when bringing proceedings for an injunction against a company to prevent it from charging higher prices for drugs other than those prescribed by an Order. This principle was applied to local authorities in *Kirklees MBC* v.

Wickes Building Supplies Ltd (1992) where a local authority, acting under its powers in s. 222 of the Local Government Act 1972, was seeking an injunction to prevent Sunday trading contrary to s. 47 of the Shops Act 1950. It was not required to give an undertaking in damages. However, the Crown can be required to give an undertaking if it is simply asserting a proprietary or contractual right on behalf of another as in *A-G* v. *Wright* (1988) where the Crown was asserting rights on behalf of a charity.

Freezing Order

This is an interlocutory injunction designed to prevent the defendant from disposing of assets which would otherwise be available to meet the claimant's claim or removing them from the courts' jurisdiction. Since its introduction in 1975 (in *Mareva Compania Naviera SA* v. *International Bulk Carriers SA*) it has become widely used, especially because of the ease with which assets can now be moved from one country to another with modern systems of banking and finance. The injunction is normally granted without notice to the other side because of the need for speed and is now granted under s. 37 of the Supreme Court Act 1981. It is sometimes granted together with a Search order – see below.

The general principles laid down in the *American Cyanimid* case apply together with the following points:

(a) The claimant must have a good arguable case. The court will therefore need to form a provisional view on the final outcome of the case on the evidence before it and where there are substantial disputes of fact the requirement of a 'good arguable case' will be difficult to meet. (See Kerr LJ in *The Niederesachen* (1984).)
(b) The claimant should make full and frank disclosure of all material matters (*Brink's-Mat Ltd* v. *Elcombe* (1989)) together with full particulars of his claim and its amount and should state fairly the points made against it by the defendant.
(c) The claimant should normally give grounds for believing that the defendants have assets in the jurisdiction. All assets are within the scope of a Freezing Order which has thus been ordered in relation to, for example, bank accounts (the most frequent situation), motor vehicles, jewellery and goodwill. A limit is normally specified on the amount to which the injunction applies. In *Derby & Co Ltd* v. *Weldon (No. 2)* (1989) Donaldson MR suggested that it could include a disposition of a freehold interest in a house. In *Ghoth* v. *Ghoth* (1992) it was held that there was no reason why, in matrimonial proceedings, a Freezing Order should extend to all the respondent's assets because it was unlikely that the petitioners would get all those assets.
(d) Territorial extent of Freezing Orders. In *Republic of Haiti* v. *Duvalier* (1989) an injunction was granted in respect of worldwide assets alleged to have been embezzled by Jean-Claude Duvalier, the former president of the Republic. The court, though, observed that this was a most unusual measure. A similar injunction was granted in *Derby & Co Ltd* v. *Weldon* (1989) where the court held that in such a case the claimant must show that the defendant has insufficient assets within the jurisdiction to meet the claim. In *Rosseel NV* v.

Oriental Commercial Shipping (UK) Ltd (1990) the court refused to grant a worldwide Mareva injunction to enforce an arbitration award in New York. It held that only exceptional circumstances, which did not exist here, would justify the court enforcing an award which was itself granted by a court in another jurisdiction against assets which were themselves beyond the courts' jurisdiction. However, in *Alltrans Inc* v. *Intercom Holdings Ltd* (1991) the court held that it did have jurisdiction to grant a Mareva injunction, or any other form of interim relief, in aid of proceedings commenced in a state which has signed the Convention on Jurisdiction and the Enforcement of Judgments in Civil and Commercial Matters 1968. Furthermore, this jurisdiction applies even when the proceedings were begun before the Convention came into force in that state.

(e) The claimant should normally give grounds for believing either that the assets will be removed from the jurisdiction before the claim is satisfied or that in some way they might be dissipated. In either case there will be a real risk that a judgment in the claimant's favour will not be satisfied (see *Babanaft International Co* v. *Bassatne* (1989)).

(f) Freezing Orders and Third Parties. In *TSB Private International* v. *Chabra* (1992) an order was granted against a company owned and controlled by the defendant as well as being granted against the defendant himself, even though there was no cause of action against the company. There was an arguable case that some assets held in the company's name were the beneficial assets of the defendant. In *Atlas Maritime Co SA* v. *Avalon Maritime Ltd (No. 3)* (1991) the court refused to vary an order so that some of the money frozen by it could be used to pay legal fees. It was permissible to lift the corporate veil and see if funds were available from the defendant's parent company which, on the facts, was the case.

(g) The scope of Freezing Orders. This was clarified in *Polly Peck International plc* v. *Nadir* (1992) where it was held that:
   (i) They are only appropriate where the claim is not a proprietary one to the very funds in question, such as a tracing remedy, where the proper remedy is an interlocutory injunction to preserve the assets in question.
   (ii) A Freezing Order should not be granted against a bank except where the bank was likely to attempt to evade a judgment.
   (iii) The court should take into account the harm which a Freezing Order might do to the defendant's commercial reputation.
   (iv) The object of a Freezing Order is not to give the claimant security in advance of judgment but to prevent the defendant from dissipating his assets in order to prevent the claimant recover under judgment.

Search Orders

These orders owe their origin to the decision in *Anton Piller KG* v. *Manufacturing Processes Ltd* (1975). In contrast to Freezing Orders, where the claimant has the evidence for commencing proceedings but is concerned about enforcement, here the claimant may lack even the evidence to begin. It is especially useful in cases of e.g. alleged video pirating or cases of passing off where, once proceedings have been served, the defendant may destroy evidence. The order allows the search of the defendant's premises and seizure of articles, making lists, taking photographs etc. It does not allow forcible entry.

In *Anton Piller* Omrod LJ laid down the following conditions which must be satisfied by the claimant for the grant of the order:

(a) An extremely strong *prima facie* case.
(b) Actual, or potential damage of a very serious nature.
(c) Clear evidence that the defendant has incriminating documents or items and a real possibility of their destruction before an application without notice can be made.

Despite these apparently formidable hurdles to the grant of a Search Order there was evidence that they were bring granted too routinely (see Dockray and Laddie (1990) and so in *Universal Thermosensors Ltd* v. *Hibben* (1992) conditions were imposed on their use which are have now been incorporated into the standard form (see also Practice Direction CPR 25 para. 7).

(a) Supervision by an independent solicitor.
(b) Service between 9.30 am and 5.30 pm on weekdays.
(c) Search must be in the presence of the defendant.
(d) A female must be present at a private house when a woman may be alone.
(e) A list of items must be prepared before they are removed so that the defendant can check them.
(f) The defendant may apply on short notice to vary or discharge the order.

Quia timet injunctions

These are granted to restrain a threatened apprehended injury to the claimant's rights even though no injury has yet occurred. The claimant must show 'a strong case of probability that the intended mischief will in fact arise' (Chitty J in *A-G* v. *Manchester Corporation* (1893). Thus just to say '*timeo*' (I am afraid) is not enough. In *Torquay Hotel Co Ltd* v. *Cousins* (1969) the defendants, members of a trade union, intended to picket the claimant's hotel to prevent the delivery of fuel oil which would interfere with the execution of contracts which the claimants had made for the supply of fuel oil. A *quia timet* injunction was granted.

Defences to a claim for a perpetual or interlocutory injunction

(a) Delay (*laches*)
Delay by itself may not be fatal to the grant of a perpetual injunction as in *HP Bullmer Ltd* v. *J Bollinger SA* (1977) where an injunction was granted to restrain the use by the respondents of the description 'champagne cider' which had been used by the appellants for many years, even though the appellants had known for over 40 years of its use by the respondents. The wrong was held to be a continuing one. However, the court held that an injunction would not be granted if delay was 'inordinate'. Delay can be fatal to an

application for a without notice interlocutory injunction if the delay shows that the matter is not urgent (*Bates* v. *Lord Hailsham of St Marylebone* (1972)).

(b) Acquiescence
A claimant will not obtain an injunction if he has acted in such a way that the wrongdoer believes that the claimant does not 'intend to enforce his legal rights'. In *Sayers* v. *Collyer* (1884) the claimant was refused an injunction to restrain a house being used as a beershop in breach of covenant because the claimant had known of this for three years and had bought beer there. There can be, of course, a link between delay and acquiescence, as illustrated by this case. In *Gafford* v. *Graham* (1999) injunctions were sought to demolish a building erected in breach of covenant and to restrain an unlawful use of the land. Relief in respect of the breach of covenant by building was refused as the defendants had acquiesced in this. They had known of it for more than three years before taking action. In the case of unlawful use, although here there was no acquiescence, there was sufficient inactivity to make the award of an injunction unconscionable, but the claimants were still awarded equitable damages (see later in this chapter).

(c) The claimant's conduct
A claimant who has failed to 'come to equity with clean hands' may not be granted an injunction. Thus in *Goddard* v. *Midland Railway Co* (1891) it was held that a claimant who has not complied with a restrictive covenant may not be able to enforce it against another.

(d) Hardship to the defendant
This is especially relevant in considering whether to grant an interlocutory injunction and a perpetual mandatory injunction. Hardship can sometimes be mitigated by suspending the operation of an injunction. (See above.)

Suspension of injunctions

Where it would be difficult for the defendant to comply with an injunction immediately or where it would cause him/her undue hardship the court may grant the injunction but suspend its operation for a specified time. In *Pride of Derby Angling Association* v. *British Celanese Ltd* (1953) an injunction restraining a local authority from polluting a river by discharging sewage into it was suspended to give the local authority time to make other arrangements.

Public interest

The court, in deciding whether or not to grant an injunction, may sometimes take the wider public interest into account. In *Miller* v. *Jackson* (1977) the court refused to grant an injunction restraining a ground from being used for the playing of cricket because of cricket balls landing on the claimant's garden. The public interest in being able to enjoy the playing of cricket outweighed the claimant's need for protection although they were awarded damages. However, in *Kennaway* v. *Thompson* (1981) an injunction was granted to restrain excessive noise from a motor boat racing club which was annoying the claimant and the court held that the claimant's legal rights should not be subordinated to the interests of the public. In the *Pride of Derby* case (see above) it was no defence that the local authority was performing a public service in disposing of sewage.

Effect of the Human Rights Act 1998

This may be relevant where an injunction is sought which could, for example, affect freedom of expression and this is dealt with in Chapter 3. See, in particular, *Venables* v. *News Group Newspapers* (2001) and *Douglas* v. *Hello! Ltd* (2001).

The use of injunctions in public law

An injunction is one of the remedies that can be used against a public body which is alleged to be in breach of the law, the others being a declaration and quashing, prohibitory or mandatory orders. These remedies are normally sought in an 'application for judicial review' (s. 31 Supreme Court Act 1981). An old example is *A-G* v. *Fulham Corporation* (1921) where an injunction was obtained to prevent a local authority from acting *ultra vires* by running a municipal laundry. Two particular problems arise with the use of injunctions in this area:

(a) The question of *locus standi*
In *Gouriet* v. *Union of Post Office Workers* (1978) it was held that an individual who seeks an injunction to protect a public right must ask the Attorney-General, as the guardian of public rights, to 'lend his name' in a relator action. Once the Attorney-General has agreed to do so, he virtually drops out of the proceedings but his decision on whether to lend his name cannot be questioned in the courts. Thus here he refused to lend his name to an action for an injunction to prevent a threatened boycott of mail to South Africa in breach of the Post Office Act 1953. If the claimant had suffered special damage because of the boycott (e.g. if his own mail had been delayed) then he could have sought an injunction in his own name because his private rights would have been infringed. Local authorities have a general power to seek injunctions under s. 222 of the Local Government Act 1972.

(b) Injunctions and legislation
An injunction cannot be granted to restrain the making of delegated legislation. In *Harper* v. *Secretary of State for the Home Dept* (1955) it was held that an injunction could not be granted to restrain the Home Secretary from submitting draft Orders in Council implementing the recommendations of the Boundary Commission to the Queen in Council for approval. There is no doubt that an injunction is not normally available to challenge the validity of a statute (*British Railways Board* v. *Pickin* (1974)) but what if it is alleged that the statute conflicts with the UK's obligation under the European Communities Act 1972? In *Factortame Ltd* v. *Secretary of State for Transport (No. 2)* (1991) the House of Lords refused to grant an interim injunction restraining the enforcement of Part II of the Merchant Shipping Act 1988 pending a decision on whether it was invalid as being in breach of European

Community Law. This Act was passed to prevent Spanish owned fishing vessels from being registered under the British flag and so sharing in UK fishing quotas. The court held that 'the presumption that a statute is compatible with Community Law unless and until declared to be incompatible' (Lord Bridge) applied and so it would be wrong to grant an injunction which disapplied the provisions of an Act until the issue of incompatibility had been decided. However, the European Court of Justice, in *Factortame Ltd* v. *Secretary of State for Transport (No. 2)* (1991), held that Community Law required the UK courts, in an appropriate case, to grant an interim injunction where the validity of a UK statute was being challenged as being incompatible with Community Law, and so in this case the House of Lords then granted such an injunction. It held that, although a court should not restrain an apparently authentic law unless satisfied that there was a firmly based challenge to its validity, there was such a challenge here. In addition, there would be obvious and immediate damage to the applicants if an interim injunction was not granted because their ships would not be able to operate as British fishing vessels. In effect the court did not apply the 'serious question' test in *American Cyanamid* v. *Ethicon Ltd* and instead held that in cases where the validity of a statute was in question there was a presumption in favour of its validity. (Subsequently in *R* v. *Secretary of State for Transport, ex parte Factortame* (1991) the European Court of Justice held that the nationality and residence requirements of the Merchant Shipping Act 1988 were indeed incompatible with Community law.)

Specific performance

A decree of specific performance orders the defendant to perform his contractual obligations, i.e. to do what he promised to do. The grant of a prohibitory injunction can have the same effect as in *Sky Petroleum* v. *VIP Petroleum* (1974) (see below).

Grounds on which specific performance may be refused

The best way to consider the remedy of specific performance is to look first at the grounds on which it may be refused:

(a) *Where damages would be an adequate remedy*, e.g. specific performance will not normally be ordered against a borrower in a contract of loan because damages would be adequate. This principle is also a factor in the courts' reluctance to enforce contracts of personal service (see *Warren* v. *Mendy* (1989) below). In some cases damages are not always considered to be adequate and so specific performance may be ordered:
   (i) Contracts for the sale of land, each piece of land being regarded as unique. In *Verrall* v. *Great Yarmouth BC* (1981) a contractual licence granted by the local authority to the National Front allowing it to hold a conference on council property was specifically enforced.

(ii) Contracts for the sale of stocks or shares which cannot be bought in an open market, e.g. shares in a private company (see the discussion in *Oughtred* v. *IRC* (1960) in Chapter 6).

(iii) Contracts for the sale of chattels which are especially rare, beautiful or of particular value to the claimant. Although s. 52 of the Sale of Goods Act 1979 empowers the court to grant specific performance of a contract for the sale of specific or ascertained goods, this does not seem to have extended the grounds on which equity will grant specific performance. Thus in *Cohen* v. *Roche* (1927) specific performance was refused of a contract to sell Hepplewhite chairs. A less restrictive attitude was taken in *Sky-Petroleum* v. *VIP Petroleum* (1974) where an injunction was granted restraining the defendants from withholding supplies of petrol which they had contracted to supply to the claimant. There was a petrol shortage at the time and so if only damages had been awarded to the claimants they would have been unlikely to obtain supplies elsewhere. The effect of the injunction was to compel defendants to continue to supply the petrol and so it was in effect an order of specific performance. Although this contract concerned unascertained goods, which are not covered by s. 52 of the Sale of Goods Act, the court was still able to make the order. There is also an independent equitable jurisdiction to order the delivery of chattels wrongly detained by the defendant as in *Pusey* v. *Pusey* (1684) which involved the Pusey horn reputedly associated with King Canute.

(b) *Where an order of specific performance would require constant supervision.* In *Ryan* v. *Mutual Tontine Westminster Chambers Association* (1893), specific performance of a contractual obligation to provide a porter constantly in attendance at a service flat was refused but in *Posner* v. *Scott-Lewis* (1987) specific performance of a covenant to employ a resident porter for certain duties, although not to be constantly in attendance, was granted. The court felt that enforcing compliance would not involve it in an unacceptable degree of supervision and this case was felt to be an example of the approach noted in *Sky Petroleum* v. *VIP Petroleum* (1974) of an increasing willingness of the courts to grant specific performance. However, in *Co-operative Insurance Society* v. *Argyll Stores Ltd* (1998) specific performance was refused of an undertaking to keep a supermarket open during the usual hours of business in a lease which had 19 years still to run. The supermarket was an 'anchor store' in a shopping centre and its closure would badly affect the viability of the rest of the centre. However, the House of Lords considered that if the store was ordered to be kept open the loss to the tenant would exceed that which would be suffered by the landlord if the supermarket closed. In addition, the principle that the court would need to supervise any order of specific performance remained important. It is fair to say that this decision was regarded as a setback by those who favour an extension of this remedy.

(c) *Contracts for personal service.* Various reasons have been suggested for equity's refusal to grant specific performance here: the difficulty of supervision, the undesirability of one person being compelled to submit to the orders of another and the difficulty of deciding whether an employee was actually performing his contract. Thus as Megarry J observed in *Giles (C.H.) & Co* v. *Morris* (1972) 'if a singer sang flat, or sharp, or too fast, or too slowly . . . who could say whether the imperfections of performance were natural or self-induced?' The adequacy of damages is also a factor. In *Hill* v. *Parsons* (1972) (below) their inadequacy was a reason for granting equitable relief and in *Warren* v. *Mendy* (1989) (below) their adequacy was a reason for not granting such relief.

(d) *Statutory position with regard to enforcement of contracts of personal service.* Section 236 of the Trade Union and Labour Relations Act (Consolidation) 1992 prohibits the courts from enforcing performance of contracts of employment either by specific performance or injunction but equitable principles are still important in three areas:

(i) Where the contract is not covered by the Act, e.g. a contract for services made with an independent contractor. Such a contract was specifically enforced in *Posner* v. *Scott-Lewis* (1987) (above);

(ii) Where the remedy is sought by an employee against an employer to compel him to continue to employ him. Recently the courts have been willing to grant interlocutory injunctions restraining dismissal of an employee where such an injunction has had the effect of an order of specific performance. In *Hill* v. *Parsons* (1972) such an injunction was granted restraining an employer from implementing a notice of termination of the contract which was in breach of that contract. In *Irani* v. *Southampton and South West Hampshire Health Authority* (1985) the injunction restrained implementation of a dismissal notice until a disputes procedure had been complied with. However, in both cases there was the special factor that the grant of an injunction would enable the claimant to seek some other remedy: in *Hill* v. *Parsons* (1972) he would, as a result, still be an employee when the unfair dismissal provisions of the Industrial Relations Act 1971 came into force and in *Irani* he would be able, as an employee, to use the disputes procedures. In addition, in both cases the effect of the injunction was only that the employee still received his wages and remained an employee. The employer did not actually have to give him work.

Equity's traditional reluctance to order specific performance against an employer was shown in *Page One Records Ltd* v. *Britton* (1967) where the claimant who had been dismissed as manager of 'the Troggs' pop group sought an injunction to restrain the group engaging anyone else as manager. This was refused as its effect would be to compel the defendant to continue to employ the claimant because it would need a manager. Under the Employment Rights Act 1996 an employment tribunal may order the re-instatement or re-engagement of an unfairly dismissed employee but the employer cannot be compelled to take the employee back; if he fails to comply with the order he is simply ordered to pay extra compensation to the employee.

(iii) Where the grant of an injunction would amount to indirect specific performance. This point is illustrated by Example 2.1.

Example 2.1

An actress has a contract under which she agrees to work only for Y who are film-makers, for a period of five years. X leaves the employment of Y. Y cannot obtain an injunction preventing X from working for someone else because the practical effect of this would be to compel X to work for Y in order to earn a living.

The position where the employee's contract stated only that she would not act for any other *employer* during that time.

This was the situation in *Warner Bros Pictures Inc* v. *Nelson* (1937), where the court granted the injunction (the actress being Bette Davis) on the grounds that Miss Davis could earn a living doing other work. However, in *Warren* v. *Mendy* (1989) a boxer had given the claimant exclusive rights to act as his manager but then engaged the defendant as manager instead. The court refused to grant the claimant an injunction restraining the defendant from acting as manager as this would compel the boxer to be managed by the claimant. The court also held that damages could be an adequate remedy as the defendant could be asked to keep an account of his receipts and pay a sum into court to preserve funds to meet any order that might be made.

(e) *Where the party seeking the remedy is a volunteer.* See the discussion in Chapter 7 on enforcement of incompletely constituted trusts.

(f) *Contracts to build or repair.* In *Wolverhampton Corporation* v. *Emmons* (1901) it was held that specific performance can be ordered if all these three conditions are satisfied:
   (i) the building work is clearly specified in the contract so that the court can see what has to be performed;
   (ii) the claimant has a substantial interest in the performance of the contract and so damages would be an inadequate remedy;
   (iii) the defendant is in possession of the land so that the claimant cannot employ another to build without a trespass being committed.

In *Rainbow Estates Ltd* v. *Tokenhold Ltd* (1999) it was held that in rare cases specific performance may be granted of a tenant's obligation to repair where there was no other remedy. Here there was a listed building which was in serious disrepair and the lease contained no right for the landlord to forfeit it for breach of covenant.

(g) *Other contracts where specific performance may not be granted:*
   (i) Contracts to transfer the goodwill of the business (*Baxter* v. *Connolly* (1820)). If the contract is to sell both the premises and the goodwill then specific performance can be ordered (*Darbey* v. *Whittaker* (1857)).
   (ii) Contracts to leave property by will.

(iii) Contracts to refer a dispute to arbitration, although the arbitrator's award can be specifically enforced.
(iv) Where only part of a contract can be specifically enforced, e.g. if a contract contains two terms, one of which is to perform a personal service, then specific performance of the other will not be decreed (*Ogden* v. *Fossick* (1862)). In *Giles (C.H.) and Co* v. *Morris* (1972) Megarry J doubted if this was a rigid rule and it does not apply anyway to divisible contracts.

Requirement of mutuality

Equity will not generally grant specific performance to one party if it could not grant specific performance against him. Thus in *Flight* v. *Bolland* (1828) a minor was not granted an order of specific performance because specific performance could not be granted against him. In *Price* v. *Strange* (1978) it was held that the time for looking at mutuality was not the date of the contract but the date of the judgement. If, at this date, those obligations which could not be enforced by an order of specific performance had nevertheless been performed by a party then an order of specific performance could be granted to that party. Here specific performance was granted of a promise by the defendant to grant an underlease of a flat to the claimant. Although at the time of the contract there was no mutuality because the claimant's obligation to repair the flat was not specifically enforceable, at the date of the hearing the claimant had completed half of the repairs and would have done the rest had the defendant allowed him to do so. Instead the defendant had made her own arrangements to have the repairs done. Specific performance was granted to the claimant on condition that he compensated the defendant for the repairs she had done.

Defences to an action to specific performance

(a) *Where the contract was obtained by unfair means*, e.g. undue influence or taking advantage of another's mistake. In *Webster* v. *Cecil* (1861) the defendant offered to sell land to the claimant for £1,250. The claimant accepted although, as his own offer to buy at £2,000 had been rejected by the defendant, he must have known that the defendant had meant £2,250. Therefore specific performance was refused to the claimant. If the party seeking specific performance has not contributed to the mistake then specific performance will only be refused in an appropriate case if hardship would be caused to the mistaken party and it would be unreasonable to hold him to the contract. In *Tamplin* v. *James* (1880) the defendant bid at an auction for an inn mistakenly believing that it included a garden. However, the property had been correctly described and so specific performance was ordered.
(b) *Where to grant the remedy would cause undue hardship*. In *Patel* v. *Ali* (1984) (which was considered in detail in Chapter 1) it will be recalled that the vendor, a Pakistani woman, who could hardly speak English, contracted to sell her home to the claimants. After the contract was made her husband became bankrupt, she bore two more children and had a leg amputated. Friends and

relatives helped her but if she had been forced to move she would probably lose this help. Specific performance was refused to the purchasers and they were left to their remedy of damages.

(c) Where the claimant has been guilty of undue delay (doctrine of *laches*). This will depend on the circumstances. In *Lazard Bros & Co Ltd* v. *Fairfield Properties* (1977) specific performance was granted where there had been over two years' delay and Megarry V-C disapproved of the idea that specific performance was a prize to be awarded to the zealous and denied to the indolent.

(d) The claimant's conduct. The claimant must show that he has either performed his part of the contract or has tendered performance and is willing to perform any further obligations under the contract (*Chappell* v. *Times Newspapers Ltd* (1975)).

(e) Misdescriptions in contracts for the sale of land. Where a vendor of property has failed to describe it correctly the claimant may be able to resist an action for specific performance but not where the misdescription was only trivial. Here the purchaser will be compensated for the misdescription but the contract of sale may still be enforced against him (note *Cedar Holdings* v. *Green* (1981)).

(f) Where it would compel the defendant to embark upon uncertain litigation. In *Wroth* v. *Tyler* (1974) specific performance of a contract to sell a house was refused as it would require the defendant to embark on uncertain litigation to compel his wife to leave it when her rights of occupation had been registered under the Matrimonial Homes Act 1967.

EQUITABLE DAMAGES

Note 2.1: The topic of equitable damages in also considered in Chapter 20 as a remedy against defaulting trustees.

(a) *Lord Cairns' Act (Chancery Amendment Act) 1858*. Section 2 of this Act gave the Court of Chancery power to award damages either in addition to, or in substitution for, an injunction or specific performance. These provisions are now found in s. 50 of the Supreme Court Act 1981. The object of this provision was to give the court power to award damages where they would not be available at common law, as in *Wrotham Park Estate* v. *Parkside Homes Ltd* (1974) where damages were awarded for breach of a restrictive covenant. However, no jurisdiction exists to award damages here unless there is jurisdiction to grant one of the equitable remedies. In *Surrey CC* v. *Bredero Homes Ltd* (1993) a developer exceeded the number of houses which he was allowed to build by a restrictive covenant, but, by the time the action was brought on the covenant, he had sold all the houses. Thus no injunction could have been granted under Lord Cairns' Act and so damages in equity were not available either (contrast with *Wakeham* v. *Wood* (1981)).

(b) *Basis of damages in equity*. In *Johnson* v. *Agnew* (1980) Lord Wilberforce held that the principles under which damages would be assessed were the same in equity as at common law. There was, however, some authority that damages in equity can be on a different basis. In *Wroth* v. *Tyler* (1974) damages for breach of contract for the sale of land were assessed by Megarry J on the basis that they must be a substitute for specific performance. The normal rule is that damages for breach of a contract for the sale of land are measured by the difference between the contract price and the market price at the time of completion (i.e. the date of the breach) but he held that damages here could be assessed as at the market price at the date of judgment. The result was that while damages applying the common law rule would have been £1,500, in fact £5,500 was awarded. In *Johnson* v. *Agnew* (1980) Lord Wilberforce said that this decision could in any case be reconciled with common law principles because damages could be measured as at the date of judgment in cases where the innocent party has reasonably tried to press for completion. However, in *Surrey CC* v. *Bredero Homes Ltd* (1993) Ferris J held that only nominal damages could be awarded at common law where the value of other land retained by the claimants had not diminished. The effect of this decision was that it seemed possible for a defendant to escape from paying anything other than nominal damages even though he was in clear breach of contract. However, in *A-G* v. *Blake* (2000) the House of Lords held that damages in contract as well as in tort are not always confined to recovering financial loss. In some cases damages can be measured as the loss gained by the wrongdoer from the breach.

(c) *Relationship between common law damages and the equitable remedy of specific performance*. The following points emerge from *Johnson* v. *Agnew* (1980):

(i) If the defendant repudiates the contract and the claimant accepts that repudiation as discharging the contract then although the claimant can seek damages he cannot seek specific performance because by accepting the defendant's repudiation the dependant has now been relieved from further liability to perform.

(ii) If, however, the claimant, following a breach of contract by the defendant, obtains an order of specific performance then this time the contract remains in force precisely because the claimant is asking for it to be performed. Accordingly the claimant can then come back to court and ask the court to dissolve the decree of specific performance and request damages instead.

Section 49 of the Supreme Court Act 1981 allows the court to award common law damages together with specific performance. A possible case would be where even though the order for specific performance was complied with, performance was late and so damages could be awarded for the late performance.

(d) *Damages in equity and injunctions*. In *Shelfer* v. *City of London Electric Lighting Co* (1895) A.L. Smith LJ said that a 'good working rule' should be that damages under Lord Cairns' Act in substitution for an injunction should be granted if:

(i) the injury to the claimant's legal right is small;
(ii) the injury is capable of being estimated in money;
(iii) it is an injury which can be adequately compensated for by a money payment;
(iv) the case is one where it would be oppressive to grant an injunction.

However, these are not definitive rules (*Fishenden* v. *Higgs and Hill Ltd* (1935)). In *Kennaway* v. *Thompson* (1981) the High Court had initially awarded damages of £16,000 because of the nuisance caused by excessive noise from motor boat racing. The Court of Appeal held that points (i), (ii) and (iii) above were not satisfied and an injunction was granted instead.

(e) Damages for breach of confidence (see Chapter 3).

RESCISSION

Rescission sets the contract aside and restores the parties to their pre-contract positions. It often occurs without the intervention of the courts, e.g. Y buys a car from X as a result of a misrepresentation made by X. Y, on learning that he has been deceived, returns the car to X who gives him his money back.

Rescission applies in situations such as this where the contract is voidable because of some vitiating factor, e.g. mistake, misrepresentation or undue influence. The word rescission is sometimes also applied to the situation where there is a serious breach of contract and the innocent party is said to have a right to rescind the contract and so is relieved from performing his part although he can sue the party in breach for damages. In *Photo Production* v. *Securicor Transport Ltd* (1980) Lord Wilberforce disapproved of the word rescission in this context and in any event it is not an area in which equity plays a part. This discussion will therefore deal only with rescission where the contract is voidable.

Grounds for rescission

(a) *Mistake*. Where a mistake is not operative at common law, because it is not sufficiently fundamental then equity may rescind the contract and impose terms designed to ensure that justice is done. In *Grist* v. *Bailey* (1967) both the buyer and seller of a house believed that the tenant in it was protected by the Rent Acts. The purchase price was £850. The tenant was not protected and had the parties known this the price would have been about £2,250. The contract was rescinded on terms that the seller would make a new offer to the buy at a proper price.

The precise scope of equity's jurisdiction here is uncertain. How, for instance, does it relate to the common law rules in e.g. *Bell* v. *Lever Bros Ltd* (1932)? This issue was recently considered in *Associated Japanese Bank (International) Ltd* v. *Credit du Nord SA* (1988) and in *Great Peace Shipping Ltd* v. *Tsavliris (International) Ltd* (2002) and is considered further in Chapter 22.

(b) *Misrepresentation*. Rescission can be awarded for all types of mis-representation and in addition damages in lieu of rescission can be awarded under s. 2(2) of the Misrepresentation Act 1967.
(c) *Undue influence*. See Chapter 3.

Loss of the right to rescind

(a) *Affirmation*. Where the party seeking rescission affirms the contract with full knowledge of his right to rescind, e.g. if he knows that the prospectus on which he took shares contained a false statement but he still accepts a dividend on them.
(b) *Where precise restitution is impossible*. However, rescission can still be granted if substantial restitution can be made, e.g. if the subject matter can be returned even though it is altered and an allowance made for any deterioration caused by its use (*Erlanger* v. *New Sombrero Phosphate Co* (1878)). See also *Cheese* v. *Thomas* (1994)).
(c) *Rights of third parties*. The contract is valid until rescinded. Thus if an innocent third party acquires for value rights under the contract then the right to rescind is lost (see *Phillips* v. *Brooks Ltd* (1919)).
(d) *Lapse of time* will constitute a bar to rescission where a misrepresentation is innocent. In other cases it is just evidence of affirmation.

RECTIFICATION

This remedy is used where a written instrument does not accord with the intentions of the parties and so it is rectified to make it do so. It is available for contracts, deeds, and by s. 20 of the Administration of Justice Act 1982 it is also available for wills. In *Craddock Bros Ltd* v. *Hunt* (1923) a written agreement for the sale of a house included its adjoining yard which had not been intended. The court rectified the written agreement to exclude the yard and ordered specific performance of the rectified agreement.

Rectification is possible in two situations:

(a) *For common mistake*. It must be shown that there was a prior agreement under which the parties expressed a common intention regarding the point in question although it does not have to be shown that there was an enforceable contract. In *Joscelyne* v. *Nissen* (1970) an agreement was negotiated for the transfer of business premises between a father and a daughter, it being understood that the father would continue to live in the premises and the daughter would pay his gas and electricity bills and some other household expenses. However, the formal contract as executed did not mention these payments. Rectification was ordered even though the agreement had no contractual force until the formal contract was executed.
(b) *For unilateral mistake*. In *Bates & Son Ltd* v. *Wyndham's (Lingerie) Ltd* (1981) it was held that rectification can only be ordered here if one party (X) was

aware of the other's (Y's) mistake and X had failed to draw Y's attention to it and the mistake would benefit X. In *Roberts* v. *Leicestershire CC* (1961) an agreement for the building of a school provided that it should be completed in 18 months but the officers of the local authority altered this to 30 months in the draft contract, but failed to draw the claimant's attention to the change. Rectification was ordered.

Bars to rectification

(a) Third party rights as in rescission.
(b) Lapse of time. This time probably runs from when the mistake should have been discovered by reasonable diligence (*Leaf* v. *International Galleries* (1950)).
(c) Judgment given in proceedings when the issue of rectification could have been raised.

FURTHER READING

Devonshire (2002) 'Freezing Orders and the problem of enjoining non-parties', 118 LQR 124. A more up-to-date account than Zuckerman (below) and should be read in conjunction with it.

Dockray and Laddie (1990) 'Piller problems', 106 LQR 601. An excellent in-depth study of the problems caused by the Anton Piller (Search) Order and which led to changes in the way in which it is granted.

Phang A. (1998) '*Specific Performance*: "Explaining the roots of settled practice"', 61 MLR 421. An excellent survey of the developing case law on this remedy.

Zuckerman (1993) 'Mareva injunctions and security for judgment in a framework of interlocutory remedies', LQR 432. Very good on the development of Mareva (Freezing) Orders.

CHAPTER SUMMARY

- Equitable remedies are discretionary but this does not mean that the court has an unfettered discretion on whether to grant them.
- Types of injunctions – perpetual, interlocutory, *quia timet.*
- Injunctions in public law.
- Freezing Orders.
- Search Orders.
- Specific performance compels the performance of contractual obligations.
- Injunctions either restrain an unlawful act or compel a lawful act.
- Rescission restores the parties to their pre-contract position.
- Rectification brings a written contract into accord with what was orally agreed.

QUESTION

'Equitable remedies are discretionary.' Consider the extent to which this is an accurate statement of the law.

Note 2.2: You will find suggested points for inclusion in this answer in Appendix 2.

3 Equitable doctrines

INTRODUCTION

Equity developed various doctrines and it would be impossible to deal with them all in a book of this nature especially as particular doctrines are sometimes best studied in other contexts. One example is the equitable doctrine of redemption of mortgages, which is really part of Land Law and another is assignment of choses in action in equity which, if it is studied at all today, is part of contract. This chapter therefore makes a selection and begins by looking at two equitable doctrines which have great vitality at the moment, undue influence and confidentiality and then looks at four traditional equitable doctrines: conversion, reconversion, election and satisfaction.

UNDUE INFLUENCE

Nature of the doctrine

Undue influence is a doctrine that, by its nature, is difficult to define precisely, but in essence it aims to prevent the vulnerable from exploitation. It is really directed at the manner in which a transaction is entered into: as Lord Eldon observed in *Huguenin* v. *Baseley* (1807) in relation to a person who, it was claimed, was the victim of undue influence: 'The question is, not whether she knew what she was doing, had done or proposed to do, but how the intention was produced'. Millet LJ (as he then was) therefore argued (Millett 1998) that, by analogy with public law, undue influence is concerned 'with procedural rather then with substantive unfairness'. In practice it is difficult to pin the doctrine down to an exact formula and in this way it is classic equity. As Lord Scarman observed in *National Westminster Bank plc* v. *Morgan* (1985): 'This is the world of doctrine, not neat and tidy rules'. A straightforward case of undue influence which gives a clear account of what it is about is *Re Craig* (1971).

Duress at common law is often with linked with undue influence but it can be argued that here the situation is different: it is that the unlawful conduct, such as actual violence or the threat of it, or economic duress, results in a person entering into a transaction which they do not intend to enter into. Where there is undue influence the person may act freely but, as explained above, it is the way in which their intention is procured which may lead the court to set the transaction aside (Millett 1998). Worthington (2003) looks at the matter slightly differently: she argues that in cases of both duress and undue influence, consent has apparently been given, but in reality there has been no genuine consent. What has happened is that a person has entered into a transaction as a result of being pressurised into doing so and the law has to determine which types of pressure are legitimate and which are not.

In reality cases of possible undue influence have to be looked at from the point of view of both sides: not just to examine what pressure was brought by one side, but to see the extent to which the other was vulnerable to that pressure because, for example, of their dependency on the one bringing the pressure to bear. There are a few cases where there is no dependency (identified by Birks and Chin (1997) as 'transactional reliance cases') but the majority are of the other type, identified as relational undue influence cases.

Case study 3.1
Undue influence

A wealthy elderly lady, Florence, has become a recluse and relies for advice on her accountant, Tom, who is the only person she sees regularly apart from her carers. She tells the accountant that she intends to make a will but has no one to leave her property to. Tom says that he will give the matter some thought and, in the course of many conversations, gradually persuades her to leave a substantial part of her property to him.

Here there is no actual duress and indeed there may have been no wrongdoing at all. However, it looks as though Tom was placed in a position where he was able to use his existing influence over Florence to persuade her to make the gift in her will to him. This could be a case of undue influence. By its nature it is more subtle and more difficult to pin down than duress, partly because usually, but not always, it consists of conduct over a period of time.

In *Royal Bank of Scotland* v. *Etridge* (1997) the Court of Appeal held that undue influence 'is brought into play whenever one party has acted unconscionably in exploiting the power to direct the conduct of another which is derived from the relationship between them'. This is a deliberately broad statement of the law because the doctrine of undue influence applies in a variety of situations and it is vital that it is not too tightly drawn.

The following general points can be made:

(a) The above remarks of the Court of Appeal do not apply where undue influence is alleged in the making of a will where a different test applies: whether the testator was coerced (see *Wingrove* v. *Wingrove* (1885)). A distinction is drawn between legitimate persuasion and legitimate pressure (see *Hall* v. *Hall* (1868)). There are other differences between the situation where a will is alleged to have been made through undue influence and where other transactions are involved (see below).

(b) There is no closed list of relationships which can give rise to undue influence. Indeed, the Court of Appeal in *Ettridge* went on to observe that the relationship of trust and confidence may be one of 'ascendancy and dependency'. See Burns (2002) who looks at this area from the standpoint of undue influence and the elderly.

(c) Undue influence usually arises as a result of conduct over a period of time although one case where this was not so is *Tufton* v. *Sperni* (1952) where the claimant was influenced into buying a house from the defendant at a grossly inflated price and then leasing it to the defendant on terms which were very favourable to him.

The statement of the Court of Appeal in *Etridge* that conduct must be unconscionable, whilst doubtless true, is of little use as a practical guide as to what may be sufficient to constitute undue influence, and the words of Lindley LJ in *Allcard* v. *Skinner* (1887) are still useful. He observed that undue influence may be said to involve 'some unfair and improper conduct, some coercion from outside, some overreaching, some form of cheating, and generally, though not always, some personal advantage obtained by a donee placed in some close and confidential relationship to the donor'. As a working guide this is as good as any although it should not be taken as a statement of rigid categories. In *Tufton* v. *Sperani* (1952) Evershed MR vividly expressed the situation as one where the domination of the one by the other is so complete that the 'mind of the latter became a mere channel through which the wishes of the other flowed'. In *Yorkshire Bank plc* v. *Tinsley* (2004) it was held that where a wife executed one mortgage of the matrimonial home through the undue influence of her husband and then executed a second mortgage over a new home the court could assume that, as the two transactions were linked, the undue influence applied to the second mortgage also.

Types of undue influence

In *Bank of Credit and Commerce International SA* v. *Aboody* (1992) the Court of Appeal classified the different types into Class 1 and Class 2, which was itself divided into 2A and 2B. This classification will be adopted here, as can be seen in Figure 3.1.

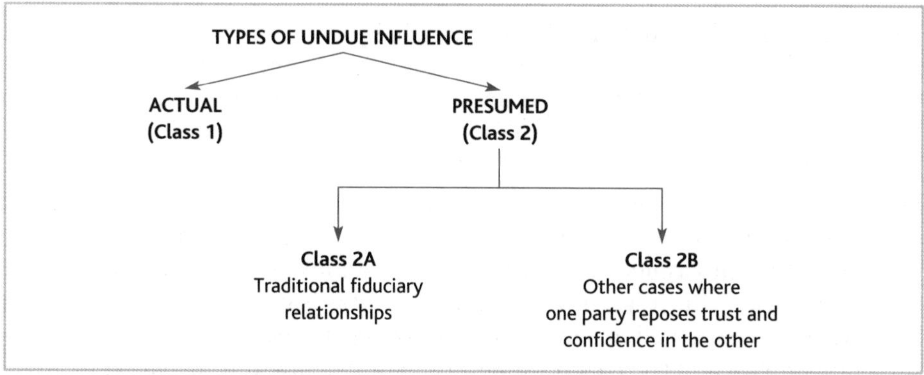

Figure 3.1 The classification of the types of undue influence

Class 1 Actual (or express) undue influence

This is where undue influence must be proved. Here it is necessary for the claimant to prove that she entered into the transaction not of her own free will but through the exercise of undue influence on her of another. The question here is a factual one: has there actually been undue influence? A good, if old, example, is *Williams* v. *Bayley* (1866) where a father was induced to enter into a mortgage in order to prevent his son from being prosecuted by a lender for forgery of some bills held by the lender.

Class 2 Presumed undue influence

Here the claimant must establish a relationship of trust and confidence between him and the wrongdoer together with the existence of a transaction that appeared to result in some unfair advantage to the alleged wrongdoer. This then brings the presumption into play so that it is up to the alleged wrongdoer to prove that there was no undue influence.

There are therefore three differences between actual and presumed undue influence:

(a) In presumed, but not actual, undue influence there must be a relationship of trust and confidence.
(b) In actual undue influence the undue influence must be proved whereas in presumed undue influence, once the initial facts have been established the burden shifts to the alleged wrongdoer to prove that there was none.
(c) In presumed undue influence there must be some unfair advantage which results to the claimant from the transaction whereas in cases of actual undue influence this seems not to be required. (See *Royal Bank of Scotland* v. *Etridge*.) This distinction may be more apparent than real as there would seem little point in challenging a transaction which was to one's advantage.

Having established that there is a relationship of trust and confidence, Class 2 is then subdivided into:

Class 2A

These are traditional situations where equity has presumed a relationship of trust and confidence and so where a transaction is entered into by the 'weaker' party in favour of the 'stronger' one then undue influence is presumed. The main situations are: parent and child, doctor and patient, clergy and parishioner, trustee and beneficiary.

Class 2B

These are other situations where the claimant establishes that she reposed trust and confidence in the alleged wrongdoer. Once this is done and the transaction is shown to have resulted in some unfair advantage to the claimant then the presumption applies and the burden shifts. The leading case is *National Westminster Bank plc* v. *Morgan* (1985) where a husband and wife mortgaged the matrimonial home to the bank as security for a loan to the husband, whose business was in financial difficulties. The wife claimed that her signature to the loan was obtained by undue influence on the part of the bank manager when he visited her at home. Her claim failed as there was no evidence that the relationship went beyond the normal one of banker and customer and, in addition, there was no evidence that the transaction was to the wife's disadvantage.

Requirement of 'manifest disadvantage'

Lord Scarman, in the House of Lords, held that in cases of presumed undue influence there was a requirement that a transaction must be to the 'manifest disadvantage' of the claimant before the presumption arose. The reason for this requirement was that otherwise every transaction between parties where the presumption applies would be open to attack on the basis that it had been procured by undue influence. This would be ridiculous where a child gave a Christmas present to its parent. However, the phrase 'manifest disadvantage' has been criticised on the basis, for example, that it is inapplicable in cases examined below where a wife agrees to guarantee her husband's business debts. In the narrow sense this is to her manifest disadvantage as she gains nothing: the debts are those of her husband. But in a wider sense it is not to her manifest disadvantage because, as Lord Nicholls pointed out in *Etridge*, there are many reasons why such a transaction might be for her benefit. For example, the finances of the husband and wife may in reality be linked and then there are ties of mutual affection. He therefore preferred the test of Lindley LJ in *Allcard* v. *Skinner* (1887): 'if the gift is so large as not to be reasonably accounted for on the ground of friendship, relationship, charity, or other motives on which ordinary men act, the burden is on the donee to support the gift'.

Independent advice

The fact that a party has received independent advice before entering into the transaction is a factor in deciding whether there has been undue influence but it is not decisive. As Lord Nicholls pointed out in *Etridge*, 'a person may understand fully the implications of a proposed transaction . . . and yet still be acting under the undue influence of another'.

Undue influence and third parties

This area has become of great importance in recent years especially since the decision of the House of Lords in *Barclays Bank* v. *O'Brien* (1994). This case has really led to a new area of equitable intervention and can be seen as one example of the modern renaissance of equity.

This situation is illustrated in diagrammatic form in Figure 3.2.

It should be noted that liability can arise not only where there has been undue influence but also in cases of misrepresentation.

In these circumstances Lord Browne-Wilkinson in the House of Lords in *Barclays Bank* v. *O'Brien* laid down how a third party might be liable and how

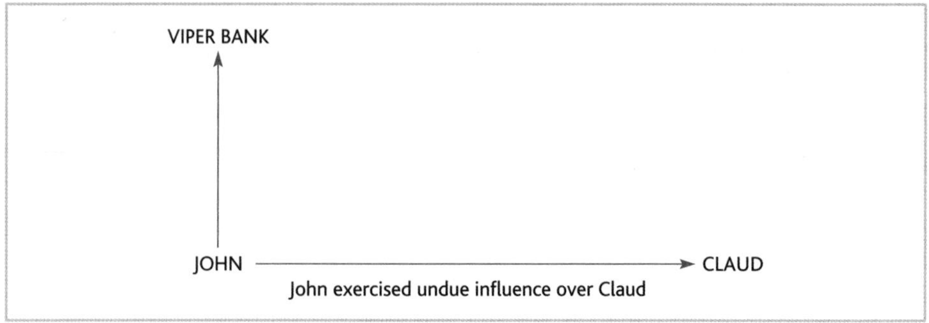

Figure 3.2 Is the Viper Bank bound by John's undue influence?

Example 3.1

John persuades Claud, his partner, to enter into a second mortgage of their jointly owned home to the Viper Bank in order to secure some business debts of John. It is clear that John exercised undue influence over Claud to persuade him to sign. The question is whether the Viper Bank is affected by what John has done. If it is not, then, although John may be liable to Claud the actual mortgage is unaffected.

they might avoid liability. He held that, in cases where a wife is induced to stand surety for her husband's debts, a lender will be put on notice if the transaction is not to the financial advantage of the wife and there is a substantial risk that the husband has committed a legal or equitable wrong in persuading the wife to enter into the transaction. If so the lender has constructive notice of any rights which the wife may have to set aside the transaction. He pointed out that the principle also extended to cohabitants and possibly other relationships and in *Royal Bank of Scotland* v. *Etridge (No. 2)* (2002) it was held that it could apply in all 'non commercial relationships'.

The principle laid down by *Barclays* v. *O'Brien* can be expressed as seen in Figure 3.3.

What steps are sufficient to ensure that the 'weaker' party has entered into the transaction freely?

In *Royal Bank of Scotland* v. *Etridge (No. 2)* (2001) Lord Hobhouse pointed out that the application of the principle in *O'Brien* boils down to three issues:

(a) Has the wife proved what is necessary for the court to be satisfied that the transaction was affected by the undue influence of the husband?
(b) Was the lender put on enquiry?
(c) If so, did the lender take reasonable steps to ensure that there was no undue influence?

Before discussing the application of this principle it should be pointed out that the use of the term 'notice' is not notice in the traditional sense in which it is

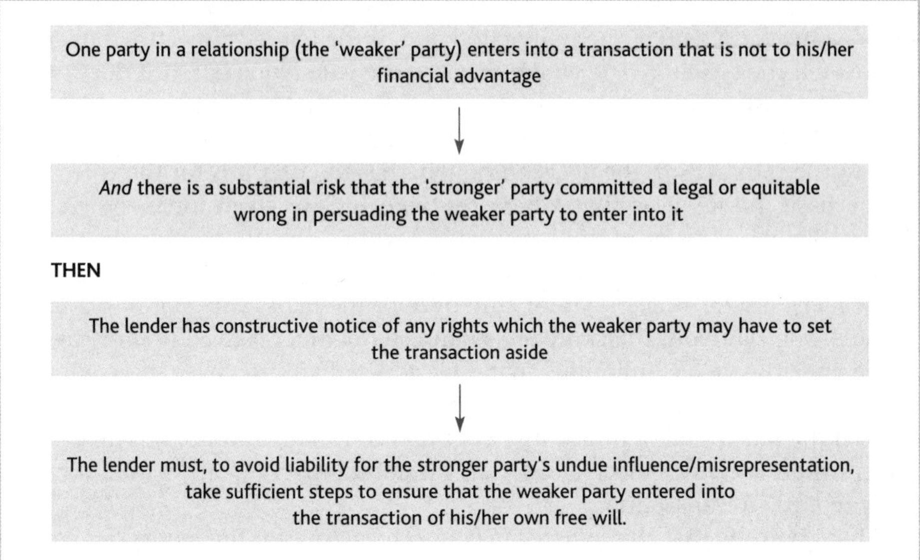

One party in a relationship (the 'weaker' party) enters into a transaction that is not to his/her financial advantage
And there is a substantial risk that the 'stronger' party committed a legal or equitable wrong in persuading the weaker party to enter into it
THEN
The lender has constructive notice of any rights which the weaker party may have to set the transaction aside
The lender must, to avoid liability for the stronger party's undue influence/misrepresentation, take sufficient steps to ensure that the weaker party entered into the transaction of his/her own free will.

Figure 3.3 What steps are sufficient to ensure that the 'weaker' party has entered into the transaction freely?

used by equity. Equity, as we have seen, uses this term to denote situations where the transferee of property may, because of lack of notice, acquire a better title to it than the transferor. Here the question is not one of title but whether a party is bound by a transaction at all.

The issue of notice was emphasised in *CIBC Mortgages plc* v. *Pitt* (1994) where it was held that if it appears to the lender that the transaction was not to the wife's financial disadvantage then the lender is not put on notice and no steps need be taken. Thus the lender was told that the loan was to be used to buy a holiday home for both the husband and wife when it was used to pay off an existing mortgage and the surplus was used by the husband to speculate on the Stock Exchange. The wife failed in her application to set the mortgage aside.

Following the decision in *Barclays Bank* v. *O'Brien* there was a stream of cases which attempted to clarify precisely what steps a lender needed to take to avoid liability for the undue influence or misrepresentation of another. In *Royal Bank of Scotland* v. *Ettridge (No. 2)* (2001) the House of Lords reviewed the authorities since *O'Brien* and laid down the flowing guidance. (In this explanation it is assumed that the relationship is between husband and wife, although the principle is not, of course, confined to this situation). The furthest the lender can be expected to go is to take reasonable steps to satisfy itself that the wife appreciated the practical implications of the proposed transaction. It should take reasonable steps to satisfy itself that the implications of the transaction have been fully explained to the wife and ask the wife who she wishes to act for her. The lender must explain that it will require confirmation from the solicitor who has advised the wife and the lender must see a certificate from the person who gave the independent advice (e.g. a solicitor) confirming that advice has been given, but it does not have to satisfy itself that the advice was correct. However, the solicitor must explain the nature, effect and risks of the transaction and, if the lender suspects wrongdoing, it must tell the solicitor. The lender may see the wife alone but, if it does not do so, then it must provide all the relevant information to the solicitor who must then see her alone. A fundamental principle is, however, that it is not for the solicitor to veto the transaction; the decision on whether to enter it is for the wife.

The basic principle is that where the wife had received independent legal advice then it will be most unlikely that she will be able to set aside the transaction against the lender. A 'most unlikely case' was *Credit Lyonnais Bank Nederland NV* v. *Burch* (1997) where a junior employee of the bank, who was also a family friend of the claimant, the company's main shareholder, agreed to mortgage her home and to give an unlimited guarantee to the bank to cover the company's overdraft. It was held that as the bank knew of the relationship it should have realised the likelihood of undue influence and so it had notice of it. This is really a case where a lender must know that no competent solicitor would advise a party to enter a transaction.

A final point is that the solicitor may also be acting for the lender or the husband as the lender is entitled to assume that the solicitor, who must of course see the wife separately, will be acting professionally in her best interests.

Position where there is a right to set the transaction aside

Assuming that there is a right to set the transaction aside, precisely what will this mean?

Example 3.2

The appropriate remedy here is rescission and whether the party seeking to rescind can claim to set the whole transaction aside seems to depend on whether they have received a benefit. In *Dunbar Bank plc.* v. *Nadeem* (1997) 2 All ER 253 it was held, obiter, that if the wife did have the charge which was procured by undue influence set aside then she would have to account to the mortgagee for any benefit she had received under the loan. However, in *TSB* v. *Camfield* (1995) the wife had received no benefit. The husband had misrepresented to his wife that the security was limited to £15,000 but in fact it was unlimited and it was held that she had no liability at all.

The principle is that where there is a right to set aside a transaction that right is absolute and so here the husband was worse off than if he had told the truth.

CONFIDENCE

The doctrine which protects confidences, although perhaps originally a child of equity, is now to be found in other areas of the law. In particular, an obligation of confidence may be either an express or an implied term of the contract but in *Stephens* v. *Avery* (1988) Browne-Wilkinson V-C said that 'the basis of equitable intervention to protect confidentiality is that it is unconscionable for a person who has received (confidential) information . . . subsequently to reveal that information'. Thus the duty of confidentiality does not depend on the existence of any contract or other legal relationship.

Thus breach of confidence may also be a tort and, in addition, the right of personal privacy, which can be considered an offshoot of the obligation of confidence, is now enshrined in the European Convention on Human Rights, which is incorporated into UK law by the Human Rights Act 1998. Article 8 protects the right to respect for private and family life and Article 10 protects the right to freedom of expression. It is, however, unfortunate that the basis of the jurisdiction is not clear but this is still so. In one of the most recent cases, *Venables* v. *News Group Newspapers Ltd* (2001), Butler-Sloss P referred at different times to both the tort of breach of confidence and the duty of confidence which may arise in equity, although Sedley LJ in *Douglas* v. *Hello! Ltd* (2001) considered that it was equitable. Most helpfully, Sedley LJ also felt that English law does now recognise a right to personal privacy which is grounded in this equitable duty of confidence (see also below). This is not a quibble as the basis of equitable jurisdiction differs from the common law. The Law Commission suggested a statutory tort of breach of confidence but this has not been acted on. The whole topic is an excellent example of the way in which equitable jurisdiction operates today and should be more widely studied. The best modern account is the essay by Gurry in Finn (1985).

In *Coco* v. *A.N. Clark (Engineers) Ltd* (1969) Megarry J held that if there was no contractual duty of confidence then three elements were required:

(a) The information has 'the necessary quality of confidence about it'.
(b) It was imparted in circumstances importing an obligation of confidence.
(c) There was an unauthorised use of that information to the detriment of the party communicating it, although in *X* v. *Y and others* (1988) Rose J held that detriment was not required.

In *A-G* v. *Guardian Newspapers Ltd (No. 2)* (1988) Lord Goff stated that there were three limiting principles to the operation of the doctrine:

(a) When the information has entered the 'public domain' it cannot, as general rule, be regarded as confidential.
(b) The duty does not apply to useless or trivial information.
(c) The duty of confidence may be outweighed by a greater public interest in its disclosure (but see *Venables* below).

An example of point (a) above is the decision in *A-G* v. *Guardian Newspapers (No. 2)* (1988) (the *Spycatcher* case) itself. It was held that the Crown could not obtain a permanent injunction restraining newspapers from publishing extracts from a book written by Wright, a former member of MI5, because its contents had already become known.

The remedy sought is almost always an injunction to restrain the breach of confidence together with, if appropriate, an account of profits made from its use. Damages can also be awarded (see below).

The duty of confidence, the right to privacy and the impact of the Human Rights Act 1998

A perennial topic in the law has been the extent to which a right to privacy is recognised. In *Kaye* v. *Robertson* (1991) no actionable right to privacy was held to exist when journalists entered the hospital where the claimant, an actor, was and photographed him in his bed. However, in *Douglas* v. *Hello! Ltd* (2001) Brooke LJ considered that an action for breach of confidence could become the way in which rights of privacy were protected and now the impact of the Human Rights Act has given a further push in the direction of the protection of privacy.

This whole topic was examined in *Venables* v. *News Group Ltd* (2001). This case concerned two ten-year-old boys (the claimants) who had been convicted of the murder of James Bulger, a little boy of two, in shocking circumstances. When they were about to be released on parole there was concern that their own lives could be in danger in view of the very strong feelings which their killing of James had aroused. Therefore injunctions worldwide were sought which would prohibit the publication of information leading to the identification of their whereabouts. The court granted them on the basis that there was a real risk of harm to the claimants and was greatly influenced by the effect of the European Convention on Human Rights (ECHR), which is incorporated into UK law by the Human Rights Act 1998. Article 10 of the ECHR guarantees freedom of expression, and, although there are circumstances where Art. 10 recognises that this freedom must be curtailed, the importance of Art. 10 is underlined by s. 12(4) of the Human Rights Act, which provides that the courts must have particular regard to this right. However, the counter-argument for an injunction to maintain confidentiality was bolstered by Art. 2 (the right to life, as without an injunction the lives of the claimants would be in danger), by Art. 3 (the right not to be subjected to torture or inhuman or degrading treatment as this could also occur) and by Article 8 (right to respect for private and family life). Moreover, the court felt that Lord Goff's third principle in the *Spycatcher* case (above – the public interest in the disclosure of information) could no longer be valid in view of Art. 10 and s. 12(4). The effect of this decision was therefore to give increased protection to confidentiality by linking the duty of confidentiality with the Human Rights Act.

In *Douglas* v. *Hello! Ltd* (2001) the issue was not the existence of the duty which was in issue but the remedy for its breach and here also the Human Rights Act was considered. A celebrity couple gave exclusive rights to publish their wedding photographs to one magazine but then a rival publication surreptitiously obtained photographs and intended to publish them. The court refused to grant an injunction restraining this, as the claimants had lessened the degree of privacy by allowing photographs to be taken of their wedding, resulting in the photographs not being confidential, and they were left to a claim in damages. On the Human Rights Act point, Sedley LJ observed that 'no right (i.e. a right under the Act) was a trump card' and the courts would need to take into account the full range of convention rights, as occurred in *Venables*. Even so, one wonders what actual effect the ECHR had in either of these cases. In *Venables* the right of confidentiality was upheld and in *Douglas* the court reached its decision on remedies in a very traditional equitable way, applying the discretion of the court.

The most recent major case where the courts have considered the relationship between the duty of confidentiality and the Human Rights Act is *Campbell* v. *MGN Ltd* (2005). An internationally famous model stated, falsely, that she did not take drugs but was photographed by a newspaper leaving a meeting of a self-help group. It was held that, although it was a matter of legitimate public interest to show that the claimant had deceived the public the publication of the photographs went beyond this and might cause damage to her health if the result was that she did not attend further sessions of the group. Her right to privacy under Art. 8 outweighed the newspaper's right to freedom of expression under Art. 10.

In view of *Venables* and *Campbell* the status of earlier cases, where the defence that disclosure was in the public interest was considered, is unclear. In *A-G* v. *Guardian Newspapers (No. 2)* (1988) the court held that Wright, a secret agent, had a lifelong obligation of confidence owed to the Crown but, on the other hand, was there a public interest in being kept informed of the operation of the security service which overrode this? The House of Lords found it difficult to envisage such a situation ever arising. Although the public interest can require the disclosure of 'iniquity', such as criminal offences, here the alleged iniquity amounted to allegations of subversive activities by MI5 contained in only a few pages of a book. In *X* v. *Y and others* (1988) an injunction was granted restraining the publication of information in a newspaper of the identities of two doctors who were carrying on general practice despite having contracted the AIDS disease. The public interest in preserving the confidentiality of hospital records was held to outweigh the public interest in the freedom of the press to publish such information. The most that can be said is that all of these decisions will now have to be reconsidered in the light of the remarks in *Venables* on the impact of the Human Rights Act.

The duty in operation

In *Argyll* v. *Argyll* (1967) a spouse was prevented from publishing confidential information communicated by the other spouse during marriage and in *A-G* v. *Jonathan Cape* (1976) a Cabinet minister might have been restrained from publishing information about Cabinet meetings but as the events concerned occurred ten years previously an injunction was refused as the need for confidentiality had ceased. In *Stephens* v. *Avery* (1988) the court held that a duty of confidentiality could arise between close friends so that it might be a breach of the duty for the defendant in this case to disclose information obtained from the plaintiff about the plaintiff's lesbian relationship with a woman subsequently killed by her husband.

A third party can be bound by the duty of confidence as in *A-G* v. *Guardian Newspapers* (1987) where interlocutory injunctions were obtained at an earlier stage of the litigation against newspapers restraining them from publishing extracts from *Spycatcher*.

> *Note 3.1:* Boardman v. Phipps (1967) *could have been decided on the basis of the duty of confidence (see Chapter 10).*

Damages for breach of confidence

In *Seager* v. *Copydex Ltd* (1967) the plaintiff, an inventor, gave information in confidence to the defendants about a carpet grip which he had patented. Subsequently the defendants brought out their own carpet grip which was very similar to the plaintiff's. The court held that the defendants had made use of confidential information received from the plaintiff and awarded the plaintiff damages. In *Saltman Engineering Co Ltd* v. *Campbell Engineering Co Ltd* (1963) it was held that damages for breach of confidence were awarded under the principle in Lord Cairns' Act (see Chapter 2). However, in the New Zealand case of *Aquaculture Corporation* v. *New Zealand Green Mussel Co Ltd* (1990) Prichard J, in the High Court, denied the existence of any jurisdiction to award compensatory damages for breach of confidence because he said that these are common law damages and as such are not available for breach of an equitable right because the Judicature Act 1873 has not merged common law and equity (see Chapter 1). This was, however, reversed by the New Zealand Court of Appeal which held that such jurisdiction does exist. The measure of damages would be the same as at common law (see *Wroth* v. *Tyler* – Chapter 2).

> *Note 3.2: Equitable damages are also considered in Chapter 20.*

THE EQUITABLE DOCTRINES OF CONVERSION, RECONVERSION, ELECTION, SATISFACTION AND PERFORMANCE

CONVERSION

The doctrine of conversion states that:

(a) Money directed to be used in the purchase of land shall be considered as land.
(b) Land directed to be sold and turned into money shall be considered money (Sewell MR in *Fletcher* v. *Ashburner* (1779)).

Therefore as soon as there is a duty to convert money into land or land into money, equity acts as though the conversion had taken place even though this may not actually be so. The doctrine is an illustration of the maxim that 'Equity looks on that as done which ought to be done'. The reason for the doctrine is that equity feels that the rights of individuals should not be adversely affected merely because a person has not carried out his duty either to purchase land or to sell land and turn the proceeds into money. The doctrine was partially abolished by the Trusts of Land and Trustees Act 1996, which altered the rule that where land was held on trust then a trust for sale came into operation and therefore the land was regarded as money. This rule has now gone and the land is no longer regarded as money. The change affects all trusts of land, whether created before or after the passing of the Act, with the exception that a trust of land created by will is still a trust for sale if the testator died before 1 January 1997. In addition, Pettit (2005) argues that there is nothing to prevent the parties expressly agreeing that there shall be a trust for sale.

Examples of the operation of the doctrine

(a) Where W enters into a specifically enforceable contract to sell Blackacre but dies before completion, Blackacre is treated as money. Thus if W's will left his realty to X and his personalty to Y, Y would receive the purchase money on the sale of Blackacre because equity would act as though Blackacre had been sold.

(b) Where W enters into a specifically enforceable contract to buy Blackacre but dies before completion. The money which was to be used to buy Blackacre is treated as having already been used to buy Blackacre which will pass to the person entitled to W's realty under his will, subject to an obligation to pay the purchase price.

Duty to convert

(a) The general rule is that the doctrine of conversion only applies where there is a duty to convert, e.g. where there is a specifically enforceable contract for the sale of land or where trustees have a duty (rather than a discretion) to purchase realty (or personalty). The doctrine will not apply where the duty is not legally enforceable, e.g. a direction in a trust for sale which is void for perpetuity was held not to cause a conversion (*Re Daveron* (1893)). Although trusts for sale have gone, the case is still a good example of the perpetuity point.

(b) An exception to this principle is the rule in *Lawes* v. *Bennett* (1785) which provides that where there is only an option (as distinct from a binding contract to purchase land) the exercise of that option, even after the testator's death converts the property retrospectively to personalty.

Example 3.3

W grants Z an option to purchase Blackacre. W's will leaves his realty to X and makes Y his residuary legatee. When Z exercises the option a conversion into personalty is effected and the purchase money goes to Y. However, pending the exercise of the option any rents from Blackacre will go to X (*Townley* v. *Bedwell* (1808)). In *Re Sweeting* (1988) the rule was held also to be applicable to a conditional contract for the sale of land where the condition was fulfilled after the vendor's death.

Failure of conversion

(a) *Total failure.* Where the purposes of the intended conversion have totally failed at or before the time when the will or deed or any other trust instrument came into effect there can be no conversion because there is no one who can enforce the duty to convert, e.g. if there are no beneficiaries under a trust.

(b) *Partial failure*

(i) Where the trust was created by deed and there is a partial failure of beneficiaries then a notional conversion occurs and so the failed share reverts to the settlor in its converted form *Clarke* v. *Franklin* (1858).

(ii) Where the trust was created by will the failed share goes under the will in its unconverted form, no notional conversion having occurred (*Ackroyd* v. *Smithson* (1780)), although because trustees have a duty to convert the recipient will actually receive it in its converted form.

Example 3.4

X and Y are beneficiaries under a trust for sale of Blackacre created by the will of T. X and Y predecease T. There is no conversion and Blackacre goes to T's residuary devisee as realty. If only X had predeceased T then X's share would go to T's residuary devisee, W, but, because of the trust to sale imposing a duty to convert, W will actually receive it as personalty. If, however, the trust had been created by deed X's share would have gone to T's residuary legatee, or, if T was still alive, to T.

ELECTION

The principle

The word election really means choice. In *Birmingham* v. *Kirwan* (1805) Lord Redesdale said that 'a person cannot accept and reject the same instrument, and this is the foundation of the law of election'. Thus a person may not accept a benefit but reject an associated burden, and in practice today the doctrine usually arises in mistakes in wills. This will happen when a testator has made a mistake, for example, by giving a beneficiary property under the will but by the same will the beneficiary's own property is given to another person. The beneficiary must choose which to do: give away his property and receive the gift or forgo the gift. (There is an interesting account of the doctrine by Histed (1998) which argues for its reappraisal in order to place it on a solid foundation for the future.)

Election must be distinguished from the giving of property subject to an express condition. Here, if the condition is not complied with the donee forfeits the gift whereas election is concerned with the paying of compensation. Although election normally arises in connection with gifts made by will it can apply to deeds also.

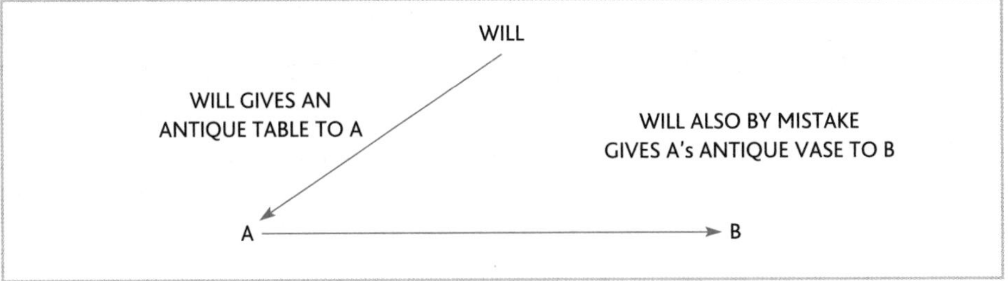

Figure 3.4 The principle of election in action

Example 3.5

Examples of the principle in action

T attempts to devise Blackacre by will to Y although in fact Blackacre belongs not to T but to Z. In the same will he also bequeaths £10,000 to Z. Z cannot be compelled to transfer Blackacre to Y but he can be made to choose either to transfer Blackacre to Y and receive £10,000 under X's will, or to keep Blackacre. In this case, although he will initially receive the £10,000 under the will, he must then compensate Y for his failure to receive Blackacre by paying its value out of the £10,000 which he receives. If Blackacre is worth more than £10,000 then clearly Z must pay Y the whole £10,000 but does not have to pay him more than this sum.

A simpler instance, to which I am indebted to Histed's article (see above), is where an antique table has been bequeathed to beneficiary A but the will also by mistake gives A's antique vase to beneficiary B. A must choose between giving the vase to B and taking the table or keeping the vase and forgoing the table. This can be seen in Figure 3.4.

Conditions for an election

In *Re Edwards* (1958) Jenkins LJ laid down the following conditions:

(a) The testator must intend to dispose of property which does not belong to him. This can be intentional or, probably as in most cases, by mistake. However, where a disposition in a will can be construed as either disposing of another's property or not doing so the courts will construe it as not doing so (Page-Wood V-C in *Howells* v. *Jenkins* (1863)). Thus if a testator uses words which are wide enough to dispose of the absolute interest in property but in fact the testator only has a limited interest then the words will be construed as only disposing of this limited interest.

(b) Where the property which the testator tries to dispose of cannot be alienated by the person whom it is alleged should elect then he/she does not have to do so, because election, being based on choice, is not possible here. In *Re Lord Chesham* (1886) heirlooms were held on trust to be enjoyed with settled land of which X was tenant for life. T bequeathed the heirlooms to Y and his residuary estate to X. X was allowed to take the residuary estate without electing because he had no power to dispose of the heirlooms. However, there can be an election if the person whose property the testator has attempted to dispose of absolutely has only a limited interest in it.

In *Re Dicey* (1957) T devised property to X and attempted to dispose of other property to Y even though the property was owned jointly by X, Y and Z. It was held that X must elect and if he elected to take the property devised to him by T then he must then release to Y his interest in the property jointly owned. In *Woolaston* v. *King* (1869) it was held that election only applies where the property, which the testator attempts to dispose of, belongs to the person who should elect independently of the will. The situation where the principle in this case applies is illustrated in Example 3.6.

Example 3.6

T leaves Blackacre to X but, through failure to comply with the requisite formalities, the gift is void. Y, as the residuary beneficiary, therefore takes Blackacre. Y receives other property also as residuary beneficiary. No question of election arises. See also *Re Macartney* (1918) where the rule in *Woolaston* v. *King* was not applied although *Re Macartney* is generally regarded as an unsatisfactory decision.

(c) The testator must, in the same instrument, have given property to the person required to elect. In *Bristow* v. *Warde* (1794) T had a power to appoint stock among children who were also entitled in default of appointment. He did appoint part of the stock to the children but also made an invalid appointment to persons who were not objects of the power. He gave no property of his own to the children, and thus it was held that the children could claim the part appointed to the strangers and did not have to elect because there was nothing to elect between. On the contrary in *Whistler* v. *Webster* (1794) the facts were similar except that the children were given legacies out of their own property. Accordingly they had to elect.

Making the election

(a) An election can be express or implied (e.g. by receipt of rents from the property) but is only binding if made with full knowledge of all relevant facts, including the relative value of the properties that election has to be made between (*Dillon* v. *Parker* (1833)).
(b) Election relates back to the date of the gift and so the amount of compensation is assessed on the value of the property as at testator's death and not when the election is made (*Re Hancock* (1905)).
(c) A modern application of election in the context of restrictive covenants is *Halsall* v. *Brizell* (1957) where a purchaser of land had been given an easement over some roads and in return agreed to contribute to the cost of maintaining them. The court held that his successor in title could not claim the benefit of the easement whilst refusing to contribute to the cost of maintenance.

SATISFACTION

Where a person is legally obliged to do one thing, but in fact does a different thing, the doing of this may be held to satisfy the obligation on the principle that 'Equity imputes an intent to fulfil an obligation'. However, subjective intention does not play a large part here: instead the courts rely frequently on presumptions. The doctrine can apply in the following situations.

Satisfaction of debts by legacies

Where a testator, who owes a person a debt, gives a legacy to that person which is either equal to or which exceeds the amount of the debt there is a presumption that the legacy extinguishes the debt (*Talbott* v. *Duke of Shrewsbury* (1714)). However, the presumption will not apply where:

(a) The debt was incurred after the making of the will (*Cranmer's Case* (1701)).
(b) The debt is not a specific sum but a running account, such as a trade account (*Rawlins* v. *Powel* (1718)).
(c) The will contains a direction to pay debts, which is normally the case.

These cases all constitute situations where there is evidence of a lack of intention to satisfy the debt, e.g. in (b) the testator will not know the amount of the debt at the date of his death.

Satisfaction of portion debts by legacies or by subsequent portions

The principle here is that equity leans against double portions and feels that, in general, parents wish to give their property in equal shares to their children.

Example 3.7

H in a marriage settlement covenants to provide each child of the marriage with a portion of £5,000 but the money has not yet been paid. There is thus a portion debt. He has two children, X and Y, and he leaves a legacy of £5,000 to X. It is presumed that this is in satisfaction of the portion debt and so if H dies before paying the portion debts it will be presumed that X's legacy was a satisfaction of his portion debt and so X receives only the legacy of £5,000 and Y receives his £5,000 portion.

The presumption applies between father and legitimate child and between a person *in loco parentis* to the child as in *Pym* v. *Lockyer* (1841) where the presumption applied to a grandfather. Unlike satisfaction of debts by legacies, here a smaller legacy may be satisfaction *pro tanto* of a portion debt. This principle also applies where a convenantor, having incurred a portion debt, makes some other provision for the child during his lifetime. The subsequent portion satisfies the portion debt (*Lawes* v. *Lawes* (1881)).

Ademption of legacies by portions

A legacy made by way of portion is adeemed (i.e. cancelled) if, subsequently to the making of the will, the legatee receives a portion or acquires the right to receive one, e.g. under a covenant. This is the converse situation to that in the above section and in general the same rules apply.

However, the presumption of ademption is stronger than the presumption of satisfaction of a debt by subsequent legacy. In *Chichester* v. *Coventry* (1867) it was explained that this is because a will is a revocable instrument and if a subsequent portion is given the presumption is that the benefit provided by the will has been anticipated. If, however, an **irrevocable** settlement is made and the will then follows, the presumption is that the benefit provided by the will has been anticipated. If, however, an irrevocable settlement is made and the will then follows, the presumption may be rebutted by evidence that, as without the consent of the donee, he could not simply substitute the gift in the will for that in the settlement. Therefore, as consent was not obtained, satisfaction was not intended.

PERFORMANCE

Where a person is bound in equity to do an act, and he/she does another act but not the one he was bound to do, then equity may still regard the performance of that act as performance of the original obligation. The doctrine (which must not be confused with part performance (see Chapter 10)) is thus similar to satisfaction and also rests on the maxim that 'Equity imputes an intention to fulfil an obligation'.

The doctrine applies in two types of case:

(a) **Where there is an obligation to purchase land**
Here if the obligation has not been carried out but subsequently land has been bought it is presumed that they were bought in performance or part performance of the covenant (*Lord Lechmere* v. *Lady Lechmere* (1735)).

(b) **Where there is a covenant to leave money**
Where a person (X) has covenanted that he will leave a sum of money by will to Y, or that his executors will pay Y a sum of money and then dies intestate, Y is entitled to a share of X's personal estate and cannot claim the agreed sum as well (*Blandy* v. *Widmore* (1716)).

FURTHER READING

Bigwood (2002) 'Undue influence in the House of Lords: principles and proof', 65 MLR 435. Discusses the decision in *Royal Bank of Scotland* v. *Etridge*.

Birks and Chin (1997) 'On the Nature of Undue Influence' in *Good Faith and Fault in Contract Law*, Beatson and Freidman (eds), Oxford: Oxford University Press.

Burns (2002) 'Undue Influence Inter Vivos and the Elderly', *26 Melbourne University Law Review 499*. This survey is especially useful for its emphasis on practical issues.

Draper (1999) 'Undue influence: a review', 63 Conv. 176. Useful discussion of cases.

Gurry (1985) 'Breach of confidence' in Finn, *Essays in Equity*, Sydney: Law Book Company. Explains the development of the law on breach of confidence.

Phillipson (2003) 'Transforming breach of confidence? Towards a common law right of privacy under the Human Rights Act', 66 MLR 726. Very valuable discussion on the future development of the law on breach of confidence in the context of the Human Rights Act.

Ridge (2004) 'Equitable undue influence and wills', LQR 120. Looks at the extent to which the law of undue influence in connection with wills differs from that in other areas and asks if this is justified.

Wishart (1997) 'The O'Brien principle and substantive unfairness', 56 CLJ 60. Analysis of the decision in *Barclays Bank* v. *O'Brien*.

Millett (1998) 'Equity's place in the Law of Commerce', 114 LQR 214.

CHAPTER SUMMARY

- Types of undue influence: actual and presumed.
- When a third party can be liable for the undue influence of another.
- Duty of confidence: is it equitable?
- Impact of the Human Rights Act on the duty of confidence.
- Conversion: equity may regard land as money and vice versa.
- Election: a person may not accept a benefit under an instrument but reject an associated burden e.g. mistakes in wills.
- Satisfaction: when a person is obliged to do one thing but does another this may satisfy the original obligation.
- Performance: performance of an obligation which a person is not bound to do may satisfy the obligation which they were bound to do.

QUESTION

Explain the equitable remedies which would be appropriate in the following cases:

(a) Abdul wishes to restrain publication of a book which he believes contains confidential information about him.

(b) Shalid, a typist, has been issued with a dismissal notice alleging that the quality of her work is poor. She says that in fact her work is excellent and also that she should not be dismissed until an agreed disputes procedure has been complied with.

Consider also how and to what extent the Human Rights Act would affect the outcome in these situations.

Note 3.3: *You will find suggested points for inclusion in this answer in Appendix 2.*

Part Two

TRUSTS: NATURE OF A TRUST AND CREATION OF EXPRESS TRUSTS

This part looks at the concept of a trust (Chapter 4) and then at the essential requirements in the creation of a trust. Initially there is the need for some degree of certainty in the creation of a trust (Chapter 5), followed by compliance with the formal requirements both for the creation of a trust and for the transfer of interests under a trust (Chapter 6) and then the requirement that the trust property must be transferred to the trustee or the settlor must declare herself a trustee, which is known as constitution of a trust (Chapter 7). This chapter then looks at cases where a trust has been set up to take effect on death but without complying with the formalities required by the Wills Act (Chapter 8). (One ought to point out that one type of trust dealt with in Chapter 8, a secret trust, is almost certainly not an express trust but this topic is most conveniently placed here bearing in mind the types of examination questions which are set.) Finally, Chapter 9 considers the position where the objects of the trust are in conflict with the law and so the trust is void or voidable.

4 The concept of a trust

Note 4.1: in this chapter, as in Chapter 1, where a term which appears in the glossary appears here for the first time it is highlighted in the text unless its meaning is explained alongside it.

INTRODUCTION: DEFINITION OF A TRUST

A precise definition of a trust is difficult because the trust concept has been adapted to so many different ends. Underhill's (2003) definition is one commonly given: 'A trust is an equitable obligation, binding a person (who is called a trustee) to deal with property over which he has control (which is called trust property) for the benefit of persons (who are called **beneficiaries** or ***cestuis que* trust**) of whom he himself may be one and any one of whom may enforce the obligation'. Even so, this definition does not cover charitable trusts, which are not enforceable by the beneficiaries but by the Attorney-General or the Charity Commissioners (see Chapter 14) nor those trusts for non-charitable purposes which are recognised as valid despite the absence of beneficiaries who can enforce them (see Chapter 15). Maitland's (1936) definition is: 'When a person has rights which he is bound to exercise on behalf of another or for the accomplishment of some particular purpose he is said to have those rights in trust for that other or for that purpose and he is called a trustee'.

ESSENTIAL FEATURES OF A TRUST

The essential idea behind a trust is that the right of legal ownership over property and the right to enjoy that property is split between two persons. The trustee is the legal owner and the beneficiaries' right of enjoyment is known as equitable ownership because, as we shall see, it was only equity which recognised the rights of beneficiaries in trusts. It must be pointed out, however, that it is possible for trustees to be beneficiaries as well under the same trust (see e.g. 'Trusts and the Home' Chapter 12). Note that the other party involved, the creator of the trust, is known as the settlor in an ***inter vivos*** (between the living) transaction, or the testator, if it is by will.

From these definitions we can pick out the essential features of a trust:

- The legal ownership of the trust property is held by the trustee(s).
- In equity the beneficiaries are the owners.
- It is the beneficiaries who enforce the trust and so private trusts (i.e. trusts for the benefit of individuals) must have beneficiaries who can enforce it. Charitable trusts are enforced by the Attorney-General and there are also exceptional cases of trusts for non-charitable purposes.
- Trustees may also be beneficiaries. (Subject to this, it is a fundamental principle of trust law that the trustee must not let his own personal interests conflict with those of the beneficiaries.)
- The creator of the trust is the **settlor** if the trust is created by a living person and is the **testator** if it is created by will.
- The trustee is bound to exercise his duties and powers as a trustee for the benefit of the beneficiaries.
- A trust may be set up to benefit either individuals or purposes.
- A trustee is subject to both common law and equitable rules whilst the beneficiaries' rights are governed solely by equity.

All of the above points are dealt with in this book.

Example 4.1 illustrates the main features of a trust.

Example 4.1

Eileen is the legal owner of a house, 'The Gables', which she holds on trust for Aidan and Josephine. Irrespective of the trust, Eileen is the legal owner with the same rights and duties as any other owner of property. For example, she can be liable for the (common law) tort of nuisance if there is unreasonable use of the property. In addition, though, she owes duties in equity to the beneficiaries both under general equitable principles (e.g. no conflict of interest) and under statutes dealing with trustees (e.g. the Trustee Acts 1925 and 2000).

Aidan and Josephine have only rights in equity as their position as beneficiaries was only recognised by equity.

ORIGIN OF THE TRUST

The trust originated in medieval times when it was known as a 'use', i.e. the trustee held property to 'the use' of a beneficiary. (The word 'use' bore no relation to the modern verb 'to use' but was derived from the Latin *ad opus* 'to the use or benefit of'.) Beneficiaries were referred to as *cestui que* use and indeed today they are still some times called '*cestui que* trust'. The term 'trust', which reflects the equitable notion of conscience, came later. (See Jones (1997) on the relationship between the use and the trust.)

Uses were found in very early times in English law. Simpson (1986) points out that instances of them can be found at the time of the Domesday Book (1086). They were always of land and various reasons have been put forward for their use. It is instructive to look at some of these and see how today trusts are still used for the same reasons:

(a) To assist in a fraud. Simpson observes that when someone was proposing to engage in some treasonable enterprise, which could lead to his lands being forfeited to the Crown if he was caught and punished, he might put his lands in the ownership of a 'blameless confederate' who would then hold them to his use. Today it is still the case that persons put their property in the hands of others to hold on trust for them to attempt, for example, to keep it from their creditors if they become insolvent (see Chapter 9).

(b) To enable property to be used for the benefit of causes. The Franciscan friars were not allowed to own property, either individually or as an Order, in imitation of the poverty of Christ. Thus any houses and land of theirs had to be owned by others for their use. In effect it was held for the Order rather than individual friars. Today, a trust is often used to enable property to be used for purposes. For example, suppose that there is an appeal for funds to be donated for the relief of victims of an earthquake in Asia. The money will not be directly transferred from the donees in the United Kingdom to the disaster victims but will instead be channeled through a fund. This will have a bank account which will need to be in the names of individuals or organisations. These will hold the fund on trust for the disaster victims.

(c) To avoid or minimise tax. The main reason for the emergence of 'the use' was the desire to escape from the rigidity of the feudal system. Once caught in it, what we would now call various taxes could be demanded from the landowner and the object of the use was to escape these. The cornerstone of the feudal system was the relationship between the tenant who held land from his lord and from whom the lord was entitled to demand various services and from which there were various incidental consequences for the lord (incidents). For example, a 'relief' had to be paid to the lord when a tenant succeeded to land by descent from the previous tenant. A way to avoid this was for a tenant (X) to grant the land on trust to some friends (Y and Z), who in turn were to grant the land to a named beneficiary (W) after the tenant's death. As the land did not now pass by descent the payment of a relief was avoided. The effect was to allow land to be devised by will although wills of land, as such, were not allowed. Suppose that Y and Z in the above example refused to carry out X's wishes and instead conveyed the land to a stranger? The common law refused to recognise the trust as it was unable to devise procedures which would protect someone who had a beneficial interest in land but not ownership. Thus it would not allow any claim by W, the beneficiary. The Chancellor, however, held that the trustees had obligations imposed on them in conscience and so would enforce the rights of beneficiaries.

DEVELOPMENT OF THE TRUST

The person who suffered most from this was the King himself, who as the greatest of all feudal lords stood to gain the most from payments associated with feudal incidents. It is curious that the Chancellor, one of the King's principal ministers, upheld a system which deprived his master of a great part of his revenue but the fact was that by 1500 most land was held on trust and as a result the feudal system was of little importance. Not only this, but the fact that uses facilitated fraud (above) caused concern. The earliest statute to attempt to control uses was passed in 1377 and a statute of 1489 attempted to prevent uses being the means of avoiding feudal dues. However, uses continued to be extremely popular and so more drastic action seemed to be called for.

Statute of Uses 1535

Henry VIII was, by the early 1530s, in financial difficulties because of his extravagance and so he determined to exact his feudal incidents. He did this by the Statute of Uses 1536 which dealt with the issue in a straightforward fashion: it provided that, where one person X (i.e. a trustee to us) held land to the use of (i.e. on trust for) another Y (i.e. the beneficiary) then the legal title was vested in Y. Legally, the use was 'executed' by the Statute. By this brilliantly simple device Y would die as the legal owner of the land and the feudal incidents would fall due. The Statute was also believed to prevent wills of land. This, together with the sudden reimposition of the feudal system, evoked strong opposition and was one of the reasons for the Pilgrimage of Grace in 1536. It seems that the Government realised that it had gone too far. In 1540 the Statute of Wills gave express power to make wills of most land and ways were found round the Statute of Uses. It did not apply where the trustees had active duties to perform, nor did it apply to property other than freeholds. Even so, it did work. Large quantities of feudal dues flowed into the pockets of the Crown and the sense of grievance which this produced was one of the causes of the Civil War (1642–51). Eventually, a way was found to circumvent the Statute of Uses itself, around 1660, by the courts allowing the device of a 'use upon a use' i.e. if land was granted to X to the use of Y to the use of Z then the Statute executed the first use, so that Y became the legal owner but did not execute the second one, so that Z remained the beneficiary. A shorter formula eventually evolved 'unto and to the use of Y to the use of Z'. In any event, in 1660 feudal dues were abolished by the Tenures Abolition Act.

LATER DEVELOPMENT OF THE TRUST

The trust, in medieval times, was seen as an essentially static institution designed to achieve a particular purpose. However, the versatility of the trust meant that it came to be used increasingly as a means to achieve a framework for future action. Thus trustees were no longer concerned only with land but with investments in stocks, shares, mortgages and other securities which needed to be bought and sold whereas the object of a trust of land was simply to retain it. There was also the development of resulting, constructive and charitable trusts so that Maitland (1936) in commenting on the many uses to which trusts have been put, could describe 'the development from century to century of the trust idea' as 'the greatest and most distinctive achievement performed by Englishmen in the field of jurisprudence'.

MAIN USES TO WHICH TRUSTS ARE PUT TODAY

Some of the main uses are:

(a) Tax-saving
The original reason for the emergence of the modern trust, the avoidance of feudal dues, was to save tax and this is still one of the principal uses of the trust.

Example 4.2

If X has an income of £100,000 a year from investments she will pay tax on the dividends received on the shares. She could set up a trust under which some of the shares are held for her two children, Y and Z. Although the Revenue taxes the beneficial owner of property, in this case Y and Z, they may have no other income and so will not be liable to tax on the dividends.

In addition, favourable tax treatment is given to various types of trust such as accumulation and maintenance trusts established for the benefit of minors (see Chapter 18, but note now the provisions in the 2006 Budget) and the creation of a discretionary trust (see Chapter 5) can be an effective way of avoiding or reducing Inheritance Tax.

(b) To enable land to be held for minors, who cannot themselves hold the fee simple.
(c) To enable funds to be held for purposes, whether charitable, or non-charitable purposes recognised as valid by law e.g. a trust for an animal. However, a charity need not necessarily be a trust. It can be a company or an unincorporated association (see Chapter 14).
(d) To enable investments to be made through unit trusts where trustees buy holdings in companies and then invite members of the public to buy 'units' or shares in the trust fund.
(e) To hold pension funds for employees.
(f) To enable two or more persons to own land. Land held by more than one person has to be held on a trust of land (ss. 34–36 Law of Property Act 1925) and, as married couples normally have the matrimonial home vested in their joint names, it will be held on a trust of land. These are governed by the Trusts of Land and Trustees Act (TLATA) 1996.

(g) To decide disputes relating to the ownership of property by the use of either a **resulting trust** (see e.g. *Barclays Bank* v. *Quistclose* in Chapter 10 and below) or a **constructive trust** (see Chapter 11).
(h) Other uses, for instance the establishment under the National Health Service and Community Care Act 1990 of self-governing trusts to run NHS hospitals and other bodies.

THE CONCEPT OF EQUITABLE OWNERSHIP

In *Westdeutsche Landesbank Girozentrale* v. *Islington LBC* (1996) Lord Browne-Wilkinson set out the essential character of equitable ownership in the following passage which is recognised as an authoritative statement of the law:

'Once a trust is established, as from the date of its establishment the beneficiary has, in equity, a proprietary interest in the trust property, which proprietary interest will be enforceable in equity against any subsequent holder of the property (whether the original property or substituted property into which it can be traced) other than a purchaser for value of the legal estate without notice.'

This passage sets out two vital concepts which need to be appreciated at the outset of any study of the law of trusts:

(a) The beneficiaries acquire a proprietary interest in the trust property. They do not acquire only a personal right to claim damages as for a breach of contract or tort but instead they acquire rights in the trust property itself.
(b) This proprietary interest is not only binding on the trustee but also on third parties into whose hands the trust property comes, with the one exception of a purchaser for value of the legal estate which, comprises the trust property, without notice of the beneficiaries' proprietary interest.

The equitable proprietary interest

There are two points to consider:

(a) What is meant by a proprietary interest?
(b) Assuming that the interest is a proprietary one, what is the significance of it being an equitable one?

The idea of a proprietary interest

There is a fundamental difference between the rights of beneficiaries under a trust and the rights of parties to a contract. A contract creates personal rights which bind the parties but, apart from special cases, as where the Contract (Rights of Third Parties) Act 1999 applies, it does not confer either rights or obligations on third parties. The significance of this is seen when the trustees, for example, wrongfully part with the trust property to others. For example, a trustee, John, may wrongfully take money from the trust fund and give it to his girlfriend, Fifi. The beneficiaries will then have rights against John, for breach of trust, but also against Fifi, from whom they will attempt to recover the money.

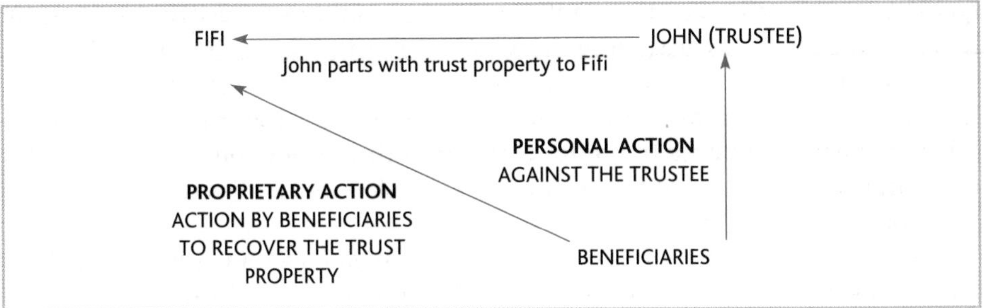

Figure 4.1 Proprietary interest

In the action against Fifi the beneficiaries are not just relying on the relationship between themselves and the trustee but on the proprietary right in the trust property which is conferred on them by the trust. A personal action against John may, in practice, be the easiest way of obtaining redress. John could be compelled to restore the money to the trust. What, though, if John has no money to restore: he may be insolvent. Or he may be untraceable. The personal remedy is then valueless and the proprietary remedy is then the only one available. (Note that the proprietary action may not succeed against Fifi – the fact that the right against her is equitable must be considered – this is considered below. What matters at this stage is that in principle it is available.)

Suppose instead that there is a contract between two parties, John and Fred, under which John agrees to sell Fred his car. John then receives a higher offer for the car from Sarah and sells it to her. Fred can bring a personal action against John for damages for breach of contract, just as the beneficiaries in the above example can bring a personal action against John as trustee. The same objections apply here to a personal remedy: what if John has no money or cannot be traced? The problem here is that the personal remedy is the only one: there was no relationship of trust between John and Fred and so Fred did not obtain any proprietary interest in the car. Anyone who has practised in the field of civil litigation will know that the problem is not usually that your client does not have a good chance of succeeding but whether, if she does win, it will be possible to recover the damages and costs awarded from the other side. This is because the action is a personal one only and dependent on actually getting the sum awarded.

It may be that both a contract and a trust may exist side by side and, if so, the differences between them are graphically illustrated. A good example is *Barclays Bank* v. *Quistclose Investments Ltd* (1970). The implications of this case are dealt with in Chapter 10 but at this stage is important to appreciate the significance of the fact that there was a remedy in the law of trusts as opposed to contract. Rolls Razor was in great financial difficulties. It declared a dividend on its shares but did not have the money to pay it and so Quistclose made a contract to make it a loan for the express purpose of enabling it to pay this dividend. The money was paid into a separate account at Barclays Bank and it was agreed with the bank that the account would 'only be used to meet the dividend due on July 24th 1964'. Before the dividend was paid Rolls Razor went into liquidation and the question was whether Barclays Bank could set the sum in the account off against Rolls Razor's overdraft or whether they held it on trust for Quistclose.

The House of Lords held that there was a trust for Quistclose as the letter clearly indicated that the money was to be used to pay the dividend and for no other purpose. It followed that if for any reason the money could not be used for this purpose then it had to be returned to Quistclose. Accordingly it was held by Rolls Razor on trust for Quistclose.

The significance of the decision was first that, if all had gone well and the loan had achieved its purpose of enabling the dividend to be paid then the relationship would have been simply one of debt and Rolls Razor would have been liable to repay the loan. If it had not done so, a personal action for breach of contract could have been brought. In addition, if the court had held on the facts that there was no trust then the loan arrangement would have applied and Quistclose would have had to join the queue of creditors against Rolls Razor and would probably have had very little chance of ever seeing their money again. What happened, however, was that a relationship of trust was imposed on the existing loan arrangement. Thus, as the money was held on trust for Quistclose, it had an equitable proprietary interest in it which took precedence over any personal claim in the law of debt. Quite simply, in equity the money was theirs.

> *Note 4.2: This case raised a number of issues, some of which are controversial. These are looked at in Chapter 10. You should, for the moment, use this case simply as an illustration of the relationship between personal rights, created here by contract, and equitable proprietary rights.*

> *Note 4.3: Another good example of the relationship between trust and contract is provided by* R v. Clowes *(see Chapter 5).*

The significance of the proprietary interest being equitable

The fact that a trust creates a proprietary interest means that the beneficiaries have an actual property right in whatever is the subject matter of the trust.

Example 4.3

A trust is set up under which Jack holds a car on trust for Belinda. Belinda therefore has a property right in the car. However, it is an equitable and not a legal one. Jack holds the legal right of property in the car as trustee.

If a person has a legal right of ownership in property then this will continue until the legal owner transfers the right to another person. Thus if a painting belonging to me is stolen by X who then sells it to Y, I can recover the painting from Y. The fact that Y did not know that the painting was stolen property is irrelevant.

(There are exceptions to this rule, for example in land law it is possible for a 'squatter' (known as an adverse possessor) to obtain ownership of another's land after possessing it for at least ten years and satisfying other conditions – see the Land Registration Act 2002.) However, any exceptions do not take away from the importance of the basic principle.

In equity the position is different. The rule is that an equitable proprietary interest may be lost if the legal estate is acquired **by a purchaser in good faith for value without notice of the equitable interest**. This is a fundamental rule of equity and must be mastered at the outset of studying the subject.

Thus if in the above example Jack transfers the £1,000 to Albert, who knows nothing of the trust, then although Belinda will have a personal claim against Jack for breach of trust this will be useless if Jack is insolvent or cannot be traced. Will Belinda have a claim against Albert for the money? This will depend on the following:

- Is Albert a **purchaser for value** of the car? If it was a gift from Jack to him then Belinda's rights will prevail as Albert is a volunteer.
- Assuming that Albert was a purchaser for value, was he **in good faith without notice of Belinda's equitable rights**? If Albert was not, then again Belinda's rights will prevail. If, however, Albert had no notice of Belinda's rights then his rights will prevail against those of Belinda.

The central issue is: what is meant by notice? (The words 'good faith' by themselves mean little.) If a purchaser has notice of an equitable interest then she is bound by it. If not, she is not bound. Notice means more than just knowledge and can be:

(a) Actual notice. This is knowledge by the purchaser.
(b) Constructive notice. This is where the purchaser does not have actual knowledge but she would have had actual knowledge had she made the reasonable inquires which a prudent purchaser would have made. In effect, the purchaser **ought** to have known of the interest.
(c) Imputed notice is where the agent of the purchaser has actual or constructive notice. This is then imputed to the purchaser.

It has been said that the doctrine of notice 'lies at the heart of equity' (Lord Browne-Wilkinson in *Barclays Bank* v. *O'Brien* (1994) (see also Chapter 3) and, at this stage, it is useful to have some idea of how it works in practice. An example of **actual notice** is provided by *Barclays Bank* v. *Quistclose* (above). Barclays Bank was bound by the trusts in favour of the creditors and then in favour of Quistclose as it had actual notice of them. As we saw, the letter stating that the loan was only to be used to meet the dividend was sent to Barclays and, as this gave rise to the trust Barclays clearly had notice of it.

Constructive and imputed notice is illustrated by *Kingsnorth Trust Ltd* v. *Tizard* (1986). Mr Tizard was the sole legal owner of the matrimonial home but held it on trust for himself and his wife. (Precisely why it was held on trust is dealt with in Chapter 12.) They had separated but she visited the house every day. Mr Tizard decided to mortgage the house to Kingsnorth Finance and a surveyor from

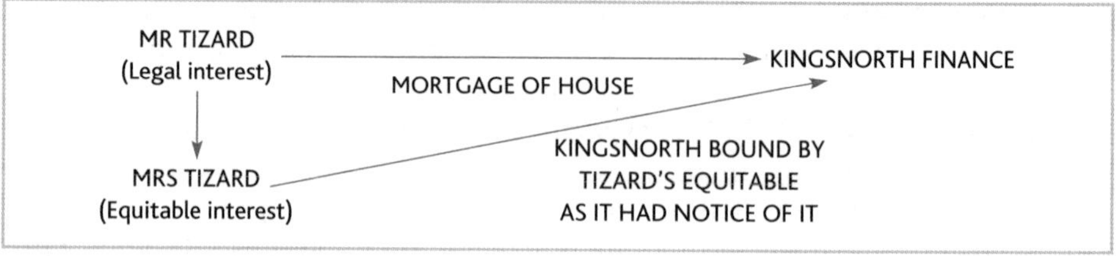

Figure 4.2 Constructive and imputed notice

them came to inspect it. The visit was on a Sunday afternoon, when Mr Tizard knew that his wife would not be there. Mr Tizard told the surveyor that he and his wife had recently separated and that she had no interest in the house. The mortgage was granted but Mr Tizard then absconded with the mortgage money. Kingsnorth Finance sought to sell the house but the wife resisted the claim on the ground that she had an equitable interest in it.

The question was therefore whether Kingsnorth was bound by this interest and it was held that it was. Although Kingsnorth was a purchaser (a lender on mortgage – a mortgagee is a purchaser) and had given value (the mortgage advance) they did have notice of Mrs Tizard's equitable interest. This was because:

(a) The surveyor had constructive notice. Knowing that the Tizards had recently separated he should not have simply accepted at face value Mr Tizard's statement that his wife had no interest in the house but should have made further inquiries.
(b) Given that the surveyor had constructive notice and was employed by Kingsnorth to carry out the survey, Kingsnorth had imputed notice of his constructive notice. This can be seen in Figure 4.2.

THE MAIN TYPES OF TRUST

The main types of trust can be seen Figure 4.3.

The precise circumstances in which certain trusts, especially resulting and constructive trusts, can arise, is a matter of debate, but the following is a brief description of the main ideas behind each of the types of trust. Fuller explanations are given in the relevant chapters.

(a) **Express private trusts** (see especially Chapter 5)
These are expressly created whether by the settlor or the testator to benefit a particular person or persons.
(b) **Resulting trusts** (Chapter 10)
This arises where property has been transferred from one person to another but the beneficial interest results back to the transferor. A resulting trust can arise from the presumed intention of the transferor but this does not explain all cases of resulting trusts.

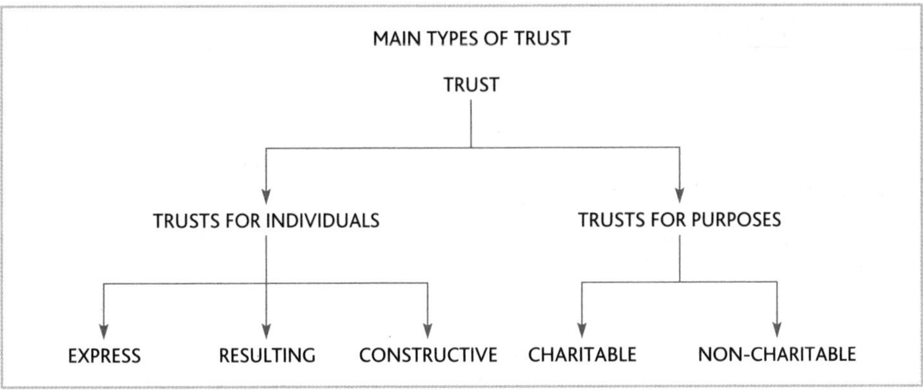

Figure 4.3 The main types of trust

(c) **Constructive trusts** (Chapter 11)
These arise by operation of law. Equity says that in certain instances a person will be compelled to hold it on trust for others. Constructive trusts are increasingly important in practice and are often used to prevent fraud or unjust enrichment by one person at the expense of another.

(d) Charitable (public) trusts (Chapter 14)
These are designed to benefit either society, or a section of it, as distinct from particular persons, as in the case of private trusts. They are therefore more concerned with purposes then with persons.

(e) Non-charitable purpose trusts (Chapter 15)
These, like charitable trusts, are concerned with purposes but for reasons explained in Chapter 15 they are not generally upheld.

Trusts are also classified, not according to their function as above, but in other ways such as completely and incompletely constituted trusts (see Chapter 7) and void and voidable trusts (see Chapter 9). One particular type of trust which it is useful to be aware of at this stage is a **bare trust**. This is where the trustee holds property on trust for an adult beneficiary who is absolutely entitled to the property. It may be, for example, that a person finds it convenient to put property in the hands of a trustee as she is going abroad and in these cases the trustee is often known as the nominee. An example is *Hardoon* v. *Belilios* (1901), where the claimant was employed by share brokers and shares were placed in his name in order to assist in a speculation in shares. The defendant was the absolute beneficial owner of them and it was held that a trust had been created of the shares. In such cases the trustee may have no duties to perform other than to hold the property to the order of the beneficiary.

FURTHER READING

Jones (1997) 'Uses, trusts and a path to privity', 56 CLJ 175. Good on an aspect of the early development of the trust.

Hayton, 'Developing the law of trusts for the 21st century', 106 LQR 87. Essential reading on the possible way forward for the law of trusts.

Kerridge (1994) 'Taxation of trust income', 110 LQR 84. Essential further reading on taxation of trusts, a topic which this book has only been able to glance at.

Simpson (1986) *A History of the Land Law*, Oxford: Oxford University Press. Especially Chapter 8 on the development of the trust.

CHAPTER SUMMARY

- What is a trust?
- History of the development of trusts.
- Split between legal and equitable interest.
- Functions of trusts today.
- Equitable proprietary interest.
- Types of trust.

QUESTION

'The great value of the trust today is in its versatility.' Do you agree?

> *Note 4.4: You will find suggested points for inclusion in this answer in Appendix 2. (You may prefer to complete this question when you have read further about the details of trusts.)*

5 Creating the trust: the three certainties

INTRODUCTION

Three points must be certain for an express private trust to be created.

(a) **Certainty of intention** on the part of the settlor or testator to create a trust.
(b) **Certainty of subject matter** i.e. certainty as to the property which is to form part of the trust.
(c) **Certainty of objects** i.e. certainty as to the beneficiaries of the intended trust.

There are various authorities for these propositions, the best known, but not the first, being Lord Langdale MR in *Knight* v. *Knight* (1840).

REASONS FOR THESE REQUIREMENTS

(a) It is vital that a person is not held to be a trustee of property when in fact an outright gift to them was intended, since a trust creates legal rights and obligations and gives the beneficiaries proprietary interests in the trust property. In Example 5.1 there is no certainty of intention.
(b) As a trust creates legal obligations which can be enforced by the courts, the courts will not uphold a trust when it creates obligations which they cannot enforce because, for example, they are insufficiently clear.

Example 5.1

John by will leaves £1,000 to his sister Susan and may say that he hopes that Susan will throw a good party out of the money for all his old pals. This is an admirable idea but common sense let alone equity says that this is hardly a trust.

Both of these points are brought out by the cases below.

CERTAINTY OF INTENTION

There was a tendency, which persisted until at least *Le Marchant* v. *Le Marchant* (1874), to hold that mere expressions of hope or desire showed sufficient intention but the modern attitude is stricter. In *Re Hamilton* (1895) Lindley LJ said that the courts must look at all the words used by the testator or settlor to see if, on their true construction in the context of the particular gift, a trust was intended. This might involve holding in one case that particular words did not create a trust even though in previous cases similar words have been held to create one. In *Re Steele's Will Trusts* (1948) it was held that a trust was created because the draftsman had used words very similar to those used in *Shelley* v. *Shelley* (1868), which had been held to create a trust, and thus this showed the requisite intention. In both cases the will directed that property should descend through the family passing to the eldest son in each generation and that each eldest son should do everything possible to give effect to this wish. Although this approach is just a particular method of ascertaining intention, it is generally considered that it places too much importance on the precise words used, and indeed it can be seen that the effect of using this rule was that in the later case of *Re Steele* the court imposed a trust despite the use of the word 'wish'. It is suggested that the approach of Lindley LJ is to be preferred.

The use of the word 'trust' itself does not necessarily mean that a trust was intended although it is clearly strong evidence. In *Tito* v. *Waddell (No. 2)* (1977) phosphate was mined on Ocean Island by a British Company under licences from the Crown but in 1920 these licences were vested in Commissioners appointed by the UK, Australian and New Zealand Governments. It was then provided that where land was compulsorily acquired by the Commissioners for mining purposes any royalties or compensation were to be held 'on trust' for the former owners. It was held that this did not create a trust in what Megarry V-C called the 'lower sense' (i.e. an enforceable obligation) but did create one in the 'higher sense' of a moral obligation, in this case owed by the Governments, which was not a matter for the courts. As Lord O'Hagan put it in *Kinloch* v. *Secretary of State for India in Council* (1882): 'There is no magic in the word "trust"'. In the Australian case of *Commissioner of Stamp Duties (Queensland)* v. *Joliffe* (1920) Joliffe paid £900 into a savings bank account in the name of 'Mrs Hannah Joliffe – Edwin Alfred Joliffe – Trustee'. Hannah was his wife. The majority of the court accepted the evidence of Joliffe that he had not intended to create a trust and felt that it could not go behind this. Nevertheless, in practice, the use of the word trust normally decides the matter and indeed in *Joliffe* Isaccs J strongly dissented and held that the name of the account constituted an effective declaration of trust and the court could not go behind this.

The test of intention is undoubtedly subjective in that it asks what the actual intentions of the person were, looking at the words as a whole, rather than concentrating only on particular words. The need for a subjective approach was seen in *Midland Bank plc* v. *Wyatt* (1995) where a husband and wife executed a declaration of trust of the family home in favour of the wife and their daughters. The trust was never acted on and was put in a safe. Evidence was that the document was simply intended to be there 'for a rainy day' when it might be needed to keep the house away from creditors of the husband. The court accordingly disregarded it. (See also Chapter 12.) Nevertheless, as the dissent of Isaccs J in *Joliffe* (above) shows, the use of the word 'trust' may be taken as conclusive proof of that intention. An interesting recent example is *Duggan* v. *Governor of Full Sutton Prison* (2004) where a prisoner claimed that money of his which was taken from him when he entered the prison and placed in an account under the control of the governor was held in trust for him. It was held that it was clear that under rule 43 of the Prison Rules 1999 both ownership and possession of the money passed to the governor and so there was no room for the imposition of a trust as there was clearly no intent to create one. (The purpose of this litigation is not clear as it was accepted that any obligation to invest was limited to investment in an interest bearing account and there was no active investment duty.)

The cases really fall into two headings:

(a) Cases, mainly arising out of wills, where the question was whether there was an outright gift to the beneficiary or whether she was obliged to hold the property on trust.

These cases date mainly from the nineteenth century and in earlier cases 'precatory words', i.e. words indicating hope or request were held to create a trust (see e.g. *Palmer* v. *Simmonds* (1854)). From about this time, however, the attitude of the courts changed and it was increasingly held that words were needed which clearly put the intended trustee under an obligation rather than making a request. The old cases have, however, left an unfortunate legacy by giving the impression that one needs to concentrate on particular words alone.

The newer approach is seen in *Re Adams and the Kensington Vestry* (1884) where a testator left his property to his wife absolutely 'in full confidence that she will do what is right as to the disposal thereof between my children . . .' It was held that no trust was created but there was only a moral obligation on her to provide for the children. Such a case is often known as gift with a motive. This case is often contrasted with *Comiskey* v. *Bowring-Hanbury* (1905) because in both cases the words 'in full confidence' were used but in fact a closer examination of the actual words shows that in *Comiskey* the language was entirely different. Here a testator also left his property to his wife 'in full confidence that she will make such use of it as I would myself and that at my death she will devise it to such one or more of the nieces as she may think fit and in default of any disposition by her thereof by will or testament I hereby direct that all my estate and property acquired by her under this my will shall at her death be divided among my said nieces'. The language is clearly intended to create a binding obligation. As Halsbury LC observed, one significant phrase is 'I hereby direct' and the effect was that the widow would take all the property subject to an obligation at her death to leave it to the nieces but that if she did not then the propriety was to be divided among them anyway.

Straightforward instances of where a trust has not been created are *Re Diggles* (1888) ('it is my desire') and *Re Johnson* (1939) ('I request that') but, as mentioned above, concentration on individual words can give a misleading impression.

(b) Cases other than those arising by will, where the question is usually whether there is an *inter vivos* gift or a trust.

A good example is *Paul* v. *Constance* (1977) where the question was whether money in a bank account in the name of Paul was held in trust for Constance, with whom he cohabited. The account was in his name only because of the embarrassment caused by having an account in two different names and damages received by Paul from an injury at work, together with joint bingo winnings, were paid into it. Paul had said that he wanted Constance to be able to draw on the money and had also said on various occasions that the money belonged to Constance as much as to him. It was held that this was sufficient to create an express trust in her favour. Even less formal words were used in *Gold* v. *Hill* (1998) but they were enough to create a trust. The deceased said to his solicitor 'if anything happens to me you will have to sort things out. Look after Carol and the kids'. (Carol was his mistress.) Although there was obviously ambiguity as to what precisely was intended (possibilities included a gift to Carol, a trust on her or a gift to Carol and the children), Carnwarth J held that the most likely interpretation was a trust to the solicitor for Carol and the children. (This case is also considered in Chapter 8.)

An interesting example of intention, which also shows the interplay of the concepts of contract and trust, is *R* v. *Clowes (No. 2)* (1994). Investors were persuaded by Clowes to part with money apparently for off-shore investments but which was in reality taken by Clowes himself and used to fund an extravagant life-style. The question was whether the money was held on trust by him for the investors or if the relationship between him and them was only one of contract. If it was a trust, then the investors, as beneficiaries, would have a proprietary interest in it and thus by appropriating it Clowes would be guilty of dishonest appropriation of it contrary to s. 5 of the Theft Act 1968. If the relationship was merely one of contract then this would not apply as the investors would not acquire any proprietary interest in it and so there would be no property belonging to another to appropriate. It was held that there was a trust mainly because of the words used in the brochure inviting investments: 'All moneys received are held in a designated clients' account and the clients are the beneficial owners of all securities purchased on their behalf'.

The relationship between contract and trust in this case can be expressed as in Figure 5.1.

Letters of wishes

This is an appropriate place to mention letters of wishes, which are frequently used in practice, often as an adjunct to a will. It may be that a testator has various

DECLARATION OF TRUST ⟶ PROPRIETARY INTREREST ⟶ APPROPRIATION
CONTRACT ⟶ ONLY A PERSONAL INTEREST ⟶ NO APPROPRIATION

Figure 5.1 The relationship between contract and trust

wishes in connection with his property but they are just wishes and are not binding as obligations under a trust are. For example, a testator may wish that his children are educated in a certain faith or may wish that relatives should be able to choose a memento to remember him by. In these cases there is no trust as there is certainty of intention. This is, however, precisely the point. The testator does not intend that there should be a legal obligation and is merely expressing what his own thoughts are. Accordingly, the executors can ignore the wishes but often the letter provides valuable guidance. Letters of wishes and their effect on trustees are considered in Chapter 16.

Effect of a lack of certainty of intention

Where the gift was in a will the donee will take beneficially because no trust was intended (rule in *Lassence* v. *Tierney* (1849)). In other cases, although there may be no trust there may be a contract or some other legal relationship instead.

CERTAINTY OF SUBJECT MATTER

Any property can form the subject matter of a trust, whether it is a chattel, a chose in action, or even a milk quota under EC rules as in *Swift* v. *Dairywise Farms Ltd* (2001), a decision which is worth reading for its analysis of equitable doctrines in the light of modern commercial practices. It is worth making the preliminary point that where there is uncertainty of subject matter this may, particularly in a borderline case, also swing the decision against a finding of certainty of intention. In *Mussoorie Bank Ltd* v. *Raynor* (1882) Sir Arthur Hobhouse observed that 'uncertainty in the subject of the gift . . . throws doubt upon the intention of the testator'.

The subject matter must be certain in four ways.

(a) There must be certainty as to the actual property left on trust. In *Anthony* v. *Donges* (1998) a widow was left 'such minimal part of (the) estate as she might be entitled to . . . for maintenance purposes'. This was held to be too uncertain as no such minimal entitlement exists.
(b) There must be certainty as to how much is left on trust and how much is an outright gift. It not, the donee will take the property absolutely. This happened in *Sprange* v. *Barnard* (1789) where the will gave property to the testatrix's husband 'for his sole use' and then provided that 'the remaining part of what is left, that he does not want . . . to be divided between' members of his family. As the term 'remaining part' was uncertain the husband took absolutely. Another instance of uncertainty is *Palmer* v. *Simmonds* (1854) where the term was 'the bulk of my . . . residuary estate'.
(c) Where the property to be held on trust forms part of a larger whole then there must be certainty as to how much is to form part of the trust. (See below.)
(d) Where the beneficial shares are uncertain. In *Boyce* v. *Boyce* (1849) a testator devised two houses to trustees to convey one to Maria, whichever she should

select and the other to Charlotte. Maria died before making a choice and so the trust in favour of Charlotte failed.

Two final points should be noted:

- Where the subject matter of the trust does not yet exist (i.e. it is future property) then there is no certainty of subject matter. In *Williams* v. *IRC* (1965) an attempt to assign 'the first £500 of the net income which shall accrue to the assignor' on trust failed on this ground.
- Where the trustees are given a discretion this may sometimes enable the court to declare that there is certainty of subject matter. This seems to be the explanation of *Re Golay* (1965) where the testator directed that a Mrs Bridgewater should 'enjoy one of my flats during her lifetime' and 'receive a reasonable income from my other properties'. It was held that the word 'reasonable' provided a sufficiently objective standard to enable the court if necessary to quantify the amount. The case must be regarded as borderline as there was no further assistance given in the will to guide the trustees or the court.

Certainty of subject matter where the goods are not yet ascertained

The issue is in principle the same as in (c) above but is better considered separately as the cases form a distinct group and the matter has caused controversy. The problem can best be appreciated by Example 5.2.

Example 5.2

Clare owes £50,000 and declares that she holds £5,000 of this in trust for Guy. The problem is: which £5,000? Why does it matter? Suppose that Clare spends all her money except for £5,000. She has many creditors and the question is whether the money belongs to Guy or to them. If there is a trust then Guy's claim will succeed as he has a proprietary interest unlike those of the creditors, who have merely a personal one under a contract (see Chapter 4). If there is no trust then the creditors will succeed as Guy will be only the donee of a promised gift.

It may be mentioned that many of the problems here have been caused by failing to observe the relationship between the requirements of certainty and those of constitution of a trust. If the actual £5,000 had been placed in an account specifically set aside for the trust then there would be no problem. It is the failure to set it aside by constituting the trust apart that brings difficulties. In addition, it should be noted that, as in the above example, the contest is often between the intended beneficiary under a trust and creditors.

The first of the modern cases is *Re London Wine (Shippers) Ltd* (1975). Wine was sold to customers but it often remained at the warehouse of the company. It was held that no trust of the wine had been created even though customers received a certificate of titles describing them as beneficial owners of particular wine. Nothing had been done to appropriate the wine to individual customers and the existence of the certificates proved little, as in some cases they were issued before the wine had even been ordered by the company. This was followed by *Re Goldcorp Exchange Ltd (in receivership)* (1994). The claimants had purchased bullion for future delivery from Goldcorp but, although they received a certificate of ownership, no bullion was set aside for them, nor indeed was this intended as the object of the transaction was to enable the owners to sell it when the price had increased. The claim was the same as in *Re London Wine*: were the claimants beneficiaries under a trust so that they had an equitable proprietary interest and therefore had priority over the unsecured creditors? The answer, said the court, was no. Under the law of contract, title to it could not pass because the bullion was unidentified, so also it could not be the subject of a private trust. Again in *Mac-Jordan Construction Ltd* v. *Brookmount Erostin Ltd* (1992) there was no trust of a sum of money retained by the employer of a builder which was to be paid over on confirmation that the work done by the builder was satisfactory. Although the employer was called the trustee, no separate fund of this money was set up and it was held that the builder was not entitled to claim, when the employer became insolvent, in priority to a bank which had a floating charge over the assets of the bank.

The reasoning behind all of these decisions can be broken down into two linked elements:

(a) How can the obligations of a trustee attach to property which is unidentified?
(b) How can the suggested beneficiaries claim in equity against property which is unidentified?

Suppose that, in the above example of Clare and Guy, Clare parts with £5,000 and Guy alleges that this is the £5,000 which belongs to him. How do we know? Does it matter? It may do so as Clare has reduced the total sum out of which Guy can claim. Does it matter if the company, having agreed that I own 50 out of a total of £1,000 bottles, sells 50? Yes, because not all wine is the same. Even if it is all of the same vintage, individual bottles differ in quality.

Suppose again that there is a trust of £5,000 out of £50,000 and Clare has gambled away all but £5,000. Guy alleges that the remaining £5,000 is his and so he can trace this money (see Chapter 20) as he has an equitable proprietary interest in it. How do we know that this is his £5,000?

Against all this is the decision in *Hunter* v. *Moss* (1994) where the defendant, who was the registered owner of 950 shares in a company, executed a declaration that he held 50 of them on trust for the claimant, who was also an employee. The court upheld the trust even though the shares, which were the subject of the trust, could not be identified. The decision is usually explained on the basis that the court distinguished between tangible assets such as wine and intangible assets such as shares, although the court simply referred to a distinction between trusts of chattels and shares. In addition the court relied on an analogy with gifts of shares in a will. Such a gift is valid even though the shares are part of a larger whole e.g. 100 shares out of 1,000 shares of mine in the Hanbury Bank. The problem is that this analogy is false. Although such a gift is valid, the shares are not held by the executors as trustees but as personal representatives until administration of the estate has been completed (*Commissioner of Stamp Duties*

v. *Livingston* (1964)). The result is the beneficiaries in this situation do not have rights as holders of a proprietary interest in the property and so the problems set out above do not apply.

Hunter v. *Moss* has been criticised on the basis that the distinction between shares (or intangible property) and chattels (or tangible property) is a distinction without a difference. Even if there is likely to be less difference between individual shares than there is between individual bottles of wine, is this a satisfactory basis on which to found a distinction between which trusts are valid and which are not? In any case what if some of the shares have been acquired by a forged gratuitous transfer? What is the position if some of the shares have been gambled away? Are they shares belonging to the trust or not? Had a trust been declared of one nineteenth of the shares, this would have undoubtedly been valid as there would then be certainty of the subject matter. As it is the uncertainty makes it impossible to hold that there is a trust.

In support of the decision it has been said that the problem of precisely which shares are subject to the trust can be solved by applying the duty to safeguard the trust property, which means that the trustee is under an immediate duty once the trust is declared to separate those shares which are subject to the trust from the rest of them. If a trustee fails to do this then she has mixed trust property with other assets and would be liable under the tracing rules (see Chapter 20). It could be argued, however, that this confuses two distinct issues: the rules on establishing a trust, with which we are concerned here, and the rules which apply once a trust has been established, such as the duties of trustees. Two less esoteric points are also made: in this case the contest was not between different creditors, as in the other cases, and so holding that a trust existed in *Hunter* v. *Moss* did not give Hunter a preference over others. Additionally, Hunter was the finance director of Moss's company in which the shares were. The managing director already had 50 shares and it was intended to give Hunter the same number.

The cases are a good illustration of the perennial tug in equity between the need not to ignore fundamental principles and the need to do justice. However, it asked why should equity come to the aid of a person who has failed to take what are very simple steps: transfer the shares to Moss. The answer, apparently, was tax considerations and, if we are to argue the point on the basis of general equity, it is then difficult to see why a court should find in favour of Moss.

Effect of a lack of certainty of subject matter

(i) If a settlor has failed to specify the trust property at all then there can be no trust.

(ii) If the settlor has given all the beneficial interest to one beneficiary, subject to a gift over to others of an uncertain amount, then that beneficiary receives all the property. In *Curtis* v. *Rippon* (1820) a testator left all his property to his wife but asked her to make such use of it as should be for the 'spiritual and temporal good' of her children and asked her to remember 'the Church of God and the poor'. As the shares to be taken by the children, the Church and the poor were uncertain, the wife took absolutely. Similarly in *Sprange* v. *Barnard* (1789) the husband took absolutely.

(iii) If the settlor has failed to specify the beneficial shares, as in *Boyce* v. *Boyce*, there will be a resulting trust for the settlor or his estate.

CERTAINTY OF OBJECTS (BENEFICIARIES)

Although it is true to say, as a general principle, that the objects of a private trust must be certain, in fact the degree of certainty required depends on the type of trust. (Note that the rules for certainty of objects in the case of charitable trusts are different also and are dealt with in Chapter 13.)

There are two reasons why some degree of certainty of objects is required:

(a) The practical one that unless the trustees know who the beneficiaries are they cannot distribute the trust property. However, the trustees may from their own knowledge be quite clear who the beneficiaries are but the actual words of the trust may be unclear. For example John may leave all his property to 'my old drinking pals'. His trustee, Bert, knows perfectly well who these are but this is not enough because of reason (b).

(b) The court needs to be able to control the trust. If, for example, the trustees come to the court asking for directions as to who the beneficiaries are then the court needs to be able to give them. Again, it may be individuals who complain to the court that the trustees have not recognised them as beneficiaries when they should have done so. This principle derives from the judgments in *Morice* v. *Bishop of Durham* (1805) where, as Sir William Grant put it: 'There can be no trust over the exercise of which this court will not assume control; for an uncontrollable power of disposition would be ownership, and not trust'. This was approved by Eldon LC, when this case was appealed (1805), who referred to the need for the court to review the administration of the trust if need be and to execute it if the trustee dies. One would think from these statements that the courts would have considerable powers of intervention in the administration of a trust, but, as we shall see in Chapter 16, this is not necessarily so. It should be pointed out in passing that this principle also appears, in the guise of the beneficiary principle, in Chapter 15 in connection with the linked but not identical principle that a trust must have a beneficiary who can enforce it.

It is now necessary to look at the requirements of certainty in the context of particular types of trusts and also powers of appointment.

Powers of appointment

A power may exist under a trust where trustees are given powers to, for example, advance sums of money to beneficiaries as explained in Chapter 18. However, a power of appointment is a different kind of power as it allows the donee of the power to appoint another person as the owner of property. The donee of a power of appointment has, unlike a trustee, no fiduciary duties. Therefore she may decide not to exercise it. Example 5.3 shows how powers of appointment operate.

Example 5.3

Barbara cannot decide the proportion in which her property should be divided among her children, Lucy and Peter. She therefore gives a power of appointment to her husband, Michael. Barbara is the donor and Michael is the donee and Michael is given power to appoint her property among their children Lucy and Peter with a provision that if no appointment is made then they shall take in equal shares. This is known as a gift over in default of appointment. Unlike a trust Michael is not obliged to exercise this power, hence the gift over if he does not. They are discretionary, whereas trusts are obligatory in that the trustees must carry out the trust.

There are two types of powers:

(a) Special, where the donee can only exercise the power in favour of either specified individuals or a specified class, as in this example.
(b) General, where the donee can exercise the power in favour of anyone, including him/herself.

In *Re Gestetner Settlement* (1953) it was held that in the case of powers the test for certainty was whether it could be said with certainty if particular persons were objects of the power. This decision, which did much to clarify and advance the law, was appropriate for powers as the court does not need to exercise the same degree of control; the donee is not obliged to exercise the power and, if not, the gift in default takes over. Thus in the above example Lucy and Peter will take equally if Michael does not exercise the power of appointment. This test was considered and approved in relation to powers in *Re Gulbenkian's Settlement Trusts* (1968).

Fixed trusts

A fixed trust is one where the trust instrument specifies the share which each beneficiary is to take, and thus they have rights of ownership in equity of this share. Here the rule is almost certainly that each beneficiary must be ascertained, i.e. known (*IRC* v. *Broadway Cottages Trust* (1955)). This point is often expressed by saying that it must be possible to draw up a list of all the beneficiaries. The reason is simple: unless the trustee, or the court, knows who the beneficiaries are they cannot carry out their duty of dividing the property. (It had been thought that, in the light of *Re Gestetner* (above), the courts might relax the rules here and bring them into line with those for powers, but this was not so.)

Example 5.4

A testator leaves property to be held on trust for 'the employees or ex-employees of a company or their relatives or dependants *in equal shares*' (my italics). The trustees cannot make a list of all the beneficiaries and so cannot tell what the share of each will be. The trust therefore fails, and the property is held on a resulting trust for the settlor or his estate.

In *OT Computers Ltd* v. *First National Tricity Finance Ltd* (2003) the company instructed its bank to open two trust accounts, one for the payment of customer deposits and the other for the payment of money due to its 'urgent suppliers'. Although that trust for customers was valid, that for urgent suppliers failed through lack of certainty of objects. Although some of the suppliers could be identified, not all of them could. The term 'urgent' was insufficiently clear.

The only caveat which needs to be entered to this refreshingly straightforward point is that in *McPhail* v. *Doulton* (1971) (below). Lord Wilberforce is sometimes held to have expressed the test for certainty in discretionary trusts (below) to include fixed trusts, particularly when he said that a trust should be upheld if there was 'sufficient *practical* certainty' (my italics) for it to be carried out. Although it is sometimes argued that the 'list' requirement does not therefore automatically apply to fixed trusts (see e.g. Matthews 1984), it is almost certainly the case that beneficiaries under a fixed trust must be capable of being listed. (See Martin and Hayton (1984) in reply to Matthews – above.)

Discretionary trusts

Here the trustees have a discretion as to which beneficiaries will receive the trust property and/or the shares which they will receive.

Example 5.5

A testator leaves property to be held on trust for 'the employees or ex-employees of a company or their relatives or dependants'. The similarly worded fixed trust (above) specified that each member of the class should receive an equal share. Here the share is not specified, nor is it specified that each member of the class should receive a portion. It is at the discretion of the trustees.

The idea of a discretionary trust was briefly explored in Chapter 4 when its use in connection with tax saving was mentioned. Here we are concerned with the test for certainty of objects under such a trust.

The modern test for certainty of objects in discretionary trusts was laid down in *McPhail* v. *Doulton* (1970) where Lord Wilberforce in the House of Lords held that it was: 'Can it be said with certainty that any given individual is or is not a member of the class?' (Often known as the **individual ascertainability test**.) The House of Lords, in this case, over-ruled *IRC* v. *Broadway Cottages Trust* (1955) which had applied the same test to discretionary trusts as applies to fixed trusts and held instead that the test for discretionary trusts was the same as that which applies to powers, as laid down in *Re Gulbenkian's Settlements* (1970) (see above).

In *McPhail* the trustees were directed to apply the net income of a fund in making at their absolute discretion grants to the following beneficiaries: 'the officers and employees or ex-officers or ex-employees of a company or their any relatives or dependants'. Under the list principle the trust would have failed as although a list of the officers and employees of the company could doubtless be drawn up, it would not be possible to do so in the case of relatives and dependants. Should this cause the trust to fail?

Following Lord Wilberforce's statement of the individual ascertainability test, the case was remitted to the Chancery Division to decide if the test was satisfied in this case. The High Court and the Court of Appeal held that it was: *Re Baden's Deed Trusts (No. 2)* (1973).

The decision in *McPhail* v. *Doulton*

The problem has been to find a way of reconciling the need for a more relaxed test in discretionary trusts than the 'list' test in fixed trusts, given that discretionary trusts by their nature are more flexible, with the need for a test which gives the courts a reasonable yardstick with which to exercise control if need be. The issue with *McPhail* is simple: the actual wording of the test:

> **'Can it be said with certainty that any given individual is or is not a member of the class?'**

Suppose that in the *McPhail* situation a brother of an employee came to the trustees and said that he was a relative. It could doubtless be proved that he was or was not. But suppose that someone came and said that they were a second cousin twice removed? How could it be said with certainty that she was not a relative? She might be able to show that she probably *was* a relative but how could it be proved that she *was not*?

In *Re Baden* Sachs LJ took a straightforward view: if a person is not proved to be within the class then he is not within it. This, with respect, avoids the issue: the test requires proof of a negative: he was not within the specified class. The fact that he cannot be proved to be actually in the class does not mean that he is not, in fact, within it. Proof of a negative does not follow from lack of proof of a positive. Megaw LJ said that the individual ascertainablity test was satisfied if 'as regards a substantial number of objects, it can be said with certainty that they fall within the trust' even though it cannot be proved whether others fall within it or not. This test has merit, but it is not the individual ascertainability test of Lord Wilberforce. Stamp LJ sought the aid of the principle in *Re Benjamin* (1902) (see also Chapter 17) where the trustees, having done their best to find the beneficiaries, can apply to the court to be allowed to distribute the estate to those of whom they have knowledge. The problem with this is, as pointed out by Martin (1984), that a *Benjamin* order is made where the whereabouts and possibly the continued existence of beneficiaries cannot be ascertained, not where it is uncertain if they ever existed. For instance, it may be certain that I had a second cousin twice removed but it is not known whether she is still alive. A *Benjamin* order is essentially an administrative device, which is not appropriate where, as here, the problem is essentially conceptual.

The root of the trouble seems to be the words 'is not'. Why not then omit them and the test would then simply be 'can there be certainty that any given individual is a member of the class?' The negative requirement did not appear in *Re Gestetner*, which, as we have seen, began the modern development of this branch of equity, and they first appeared in the speech of Lord Upjohn in

Re Gulbenkian. The problem is that if we omit them we then arrive at the one-person test proposed by Denning MR in *Re Gulbenkian* (1968) and rejected by the House of Lords: is it sufficient if it can be said with certainty that any **one** person is a member of the class? This is considered, in the case of trusts for classes, to be too narrow as there might only be one certain member of the class and it has led to other problems, as discussed below.

The real difficulty is that the individual ascertainability test if applied strictly is too near to the 'list' test for fixed trusts. To say that it must be said with certainty if a person is or is not a member of the class comes near to saying that we need to know who is and who is not within it, and the best way of doing this is by drawing up a list. The truth is that we do not have a satisfactory test for deciding the objects of a discretionary trust and so we are left with the *McPhail* one, and must now turn to the other issues raised by it.

The distinction between conceptual uncertainty and evidential uncertainty

If a class of beneficiaries is conceptually uncertain when the *McPhail* test is applied, i.e. persons to whom I am under a moral obligation, then the trust fails. If, however, there is only evidential uncertainty, i.e. 'relatives' or 'dependants' then mere difficulty in adducing evidence to establish who is a member of the class is no objection. Although this is doubtless correct, it may be said that it is a fairly obvious point and the introduction of yet another distinction in an already overcrowded area is unwelcome. Indeed in *Re Tuck's Settlement Trusts* (1978) (below) Denning MR said that he found this distinction 'most unfortunate'.

How should trustees apply the test in McPhail *v.* Doulton*?*

Given that the *McPhail* test, with all its problems, represents the law, how should it be applied in practice by trustees?

Example 5.6

The beneficiaries of a discretionary trust under a will are 'all the relatives of my home town'. Here there is an evidential problem: what is the hometown of the testator? Assuming that this is identified, the trustees must not simply hand out the money, for example, to the first ten residents to come forward. They must find out how many residents there are and, perhaps, devise a scheme for advertising for claims.

The nature of this duty has often been expressed by the courts. Lord Wilberforce in *McPhail* v. *Doulton* pointed out that trustees should not approach their duties in a narrow way. Instead they 'ought to make such a survey of the range ofobjects or possible beneficiaries as will enable them to carry out their fiduciary duty'. In *Re Baden's Deed Trusts (No. 2)* Sachs LJ said that where there is a discretionary trust with very many beneficiaries, the trustees must assess the size of the problem in a businesslike way. In *Re Hay's Settlement Trusts* (1981) Megarry V-C said that a trustee should first appreciate the 'width of the field' and the 'size of the problem' before considering whether a grant was appropriate in individual cases.

One objection to Lord Wilberforce's individual ascertainability test was that, if the trustees for some reason were unable or unwilling to distribute the fund, then the court would need to do so and could only do this by dividing the property equally among the beneficiaries. As these were not all known, this would be impossible. Yet the effect of ss. 36 and 41 of the Trustee Act 1925 (see Chapter 16) is to allow for the appointment of new trustees in such a case and in any event, as Lord Wilberforce observed, although there may be life in the maxim 'equality is equity' in some cases, in others equal division is the last thing that the settlor intended.

Administrative unworkability

In *McPhail* v. *Doulton* Lord Wilberforce said that even though a description of beneficiaries complied with the test he had laid down it might be 'so hopelessly wide as not to form anything like a class', and gave as an example 'all the residents of Greater London'. This principle was applied in *R* v. *District Auditor, ex parte West Yorkshire Metropolitan County Council* (1986) where a trust set up for the inhabitants of the County of West Yorkshire, of which there were about 2,500,000, was held void for administrative unworkability. Although the court accepted that the word 'inhabitants' could be sufficiently certain, without deciding the point, Lloyd LJ held that 'A trust with as many as $2^1/_2$ million potential beneficiaries is . . . quite simply unworkable'. Unfortunately he did not explore this issue further. In *Re Beatty* (1990) Hoffmann J was content to uphold a clause requiring trustees to distribute chattels and money 'among such persons or persons . . . as they think fit' because everyone was an object. The administrative unworkability issue was not discussed.

> ***Note 5.1:*** *The* West Yorkshire *decision is a good example of the inter-relationship between different areas of trust law. The trust was not a valid private trust as it was administratively unworkable and so it could only be valid if it took effect as a trust for charitable purposes, where, as we shall see, the test for certainty is much more relaxed. However, it was not contended that it could be charitable and so it fell into the category of non-charitable purpose trusts, which are normally invalid, as was the case here. Keep these connections in mind for examination purposes.*

An unsolved question is whether a court has the power to declare a trust invalid on the ground that it is capricious, i.e. it does not show any sensible intention on the part of the settlor/testator. There is no doubt that a will is not invalid for being capricious and it is probable that the same principle applies to a trust. In the *West Yorkshire* case (above) Lloyd LJ held that there was nothing capricious about the trust as it was perfectly sensible for the local authority to want to benefit the inhabitants of its area.

In *Re Manisty's Settlement* (1974), which concerned a power, Templeman J observed that the phrase 'all the residents of Greater London' was capricious because it negated 'any sensible intention on the part of the settlor', but in the *West Yorkshire* case Lloyd LJ indicated that the capriciousness point only applied to a power. This seems to be the general view. This is because with a power the duties of the donee of the power are less stringent and so the width of the class is not an issue. Therefore the means of the court controlling wide powers is the capriciousness test.

Test where a condition is attached to a gift

Example 5.7 shows a straightforward situation of a condition attached to a gift.

Example 5.7

Alice by will leaves £100 to her niece Mary 'provided that she shall pass her examinations in Equity and Trusts'. This is clearly a different situation from those which we have been considering: there is no question of making a selection from a number of possible claimants. There is one possible claimant and the question is whether she satisfies this condition.

In *Re Allen* (1953) the gift was to 'the eldest of the sons of A who shall be a member of the Church of England and an adherent to the doctrine of that church'. The Court of Appeal held that this was valid. All that the claimant had to do was to establish that he satisfied the condition.

This straightforward principle has, most unfortunately, been extended from situations where there is just a question of whether a particular person satisfies a condition to those where there is a question of ascertaining the identity of the persons who can satisfy the condition. Emery (1982) distinguishes between:

- a gift to the eldest son of A if that son shall be a member of the Church of England and an adherent to the doctrine of that church, as in *Re Allen*, and
- a gift to the eldest son of A who shall be an adherent etc.

In the first case the gift can only go to the eldest son of A. The test is simply whether he fulfils the condition. In the second case there is a different situation: it is a gift to the eldest son who fulfils the condition. The court will then have to decide what the term 'doctrine of the Church of England' means in order to decide then who will receive the gift. We are then back to the familiar issues of certainty, as in *McPhail* v. *Doulton*.

It is this distinction which the court failed to recognise in *Re Barlow's Will Trusts* (1979), although the fault line may be traced to Denning MR who, in *Re Gulkbenkian*, stated that *Re Allen* was authority for saying that where there is a condition attached to a gift, even where this is uncertain or imprecise, it is still valid so long as at least one beneficiary comes within it. In *Re Barlow*, a testatrix directed her executor 'to allow any member of my family and any friends of mine who wish to do so' to purchase paintings belonging to her. The court held that the trust was valid, even though the words 'family' and, more particularly, 'friends' may have been uncertain because this was not a discretionary trust, where trustees had to 'survey the field' but merely a case of conditions being attached to individual gifts. Thus a gift to a person who did come within the meaning of 'family' or 'friend' would not be invalidated by uncertainty as to whether another person does so. It may, however, be objected that this begs the question: the issue remains that the word 'friends' is uncertain. This was not a case of a gift to one person but a class gift. Suppose that the executors thought that the testator had few friends and so allowed the first three claimants to have all the paintings. It then turned out that the testator had many other friends who were therefore deprived of the chance of acquiring any paintings. Surely the trustees should 'survey the field' and, if so, what would their yardstick be?

Power to cure uncertainty

Trustees, or a third party, may be given a power to decide whether a particular individual is a beneficiary. This power will be valid provided that the question is one of fact. In *Re Tuck's Settlement Trust* (1978) any dispute as to whether a person was of the Jewish faith was to be determined by a Chief Rabbi and that was held to validate the trust. In *Re Tepper's Will Trust* (1987) the gift was to children 'provided that they shall not marry outside the Jewish faith'. The case was adjourned for evidence of the Jewish faith actually practised by the family. However, this may help only where the problem is one of evidential uncertainty. Where there is conceptual uncertainty then it is submitted that the defect is incurable. Thus a gift to 'my old friends' would probably not be saved by allowing trustees to decide who they were. As Jenkins J observed in *Re Coxen* (1948), 'if the testator had insufficiently defined the state of affairs on which the trustees were to form their opinion . . . merely by making their opinion the criteria' this would not save the gift. Nor would it help if the gift stated that 'in case of doubt my wife Anne knows who they are'. Anne may indeed know but how could the court measure her actions if a person alleged that she was a friend but that Anne had excluded her?

Test in purpose trusts

It is probable, although not decided, that the test in *McPhail* v. *Doulton* will apply also to purpose trusts of the kind held valid in *Re Denley* (1969) (see Chapter 15).

Critical approaches to the beneficiary principle: some thoughts

This chapter has taken the view that the beneficiaries need to be defined with at least reasonable precision in order for the court to be able to control the trust and this is the generally accepted view.

However, it is not the only one. Gardner (2003) points out that the courts have increasingly tried to uphold the facilitative aspect of the law of trusts. This means that, wherever possible, their role is to uphold the wishes of the settlor as expressed in the trust, and he gives as instances of this approach both *Re Tuck* and *Re Tepper* (above). In line with this view, Gardner has no difficulty with *Re Barlow* holding that, as long as a description has a recognisable core meaning, it is valid. 'Old friends', he feels, has a large grey area but also a core meaning and, on this basis, the term is sufficiently certain.

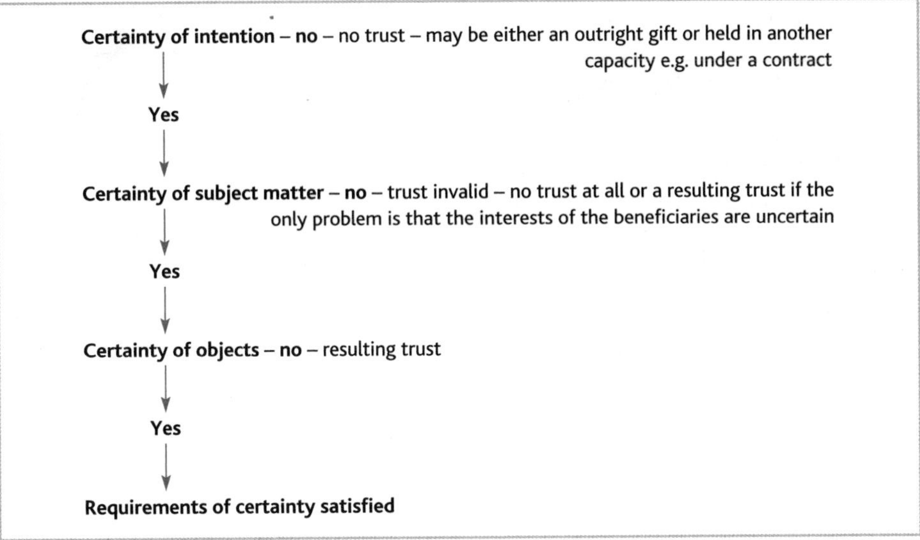

Figure 5.2 The three certainties – a summary

Effect of uncertainty of objects

The property will be held on a resulting trust for the settlor or his estate.

FURTHER READING

Emery (1982) 'The most hallowed principle', 98 LQR 551. A clear investigation of the law on conditions attached to gifts.

Harris (1971) 'Trust, power and duty', 87 LQR 31. Analyses the decision in *McPhail.*

Hayton (1994) 'Uncertainty of subject matter in trusts', 110 LQR 335. Looks at the decision in *Hunter* v. *Moss*.

CHAPTER SUMMARY

- Intention to create a trust.
- Subject matter of a trust.
- Problems where goods are not ascertained.
- Fixed and discretionary trusts.
- Certainty of objects in fixed trusts: list principle.
- Certainty of objects in discretionary trusts: individual ascertainability.
- Conditions attached to gifts.
- Power to cure uncertainty.
- Effect of uncertainty in all three cases: intention, subject matter, objects.

QUESTION

Albert, by will, made the following bequests:

(a) £500,000 to my wife, Jane, and I am confident that she will pay a reasonable sum each year to my Aunt Martha for her maintenance.
(b) £250,000 to my son, John, on trust to use the income for such period as the law allows for the provision of summer outings for the employees and their relatives and/or dependants of my old company, Nuts and Bolts Ltd.

Note 5.2: *You will find suggested points for inclusion in this answer in Appendix 2.*

6 Formalities

INTRODUCTION

A trust must not only comply with the three certainties in order to be valid, it must also comply with any requisite formalities. Before we look at the reasons for this, it is vital to note that this requirement is different from the requirement to use any requisite formalities when property is actually transferred.

Therefore a settlor must:

(a) Execute a written declaration of trust – see this chapter.
(b) Use the appropriate formalities to actually transfer the house (i.e. a deed) – see Chapter 7.

REASONS FOR REQUIRING FORMALITIES

The requirements for formalities was first introduced by the Statute of Frauds 1677 when the requirement for written evidence of a contract for the sale of land was first introduced. The word 'frauds' gives the reason: to prevent someone fraudulently alleging that either a trust of land had been created or that an interest under a trust had been transferred. The relevant parts of the Statute of Frauds were repealed in relation to trusts by the Law of Property Act (LPA) 1925 and replaced by s. 53(1)(b) and (c), which are discussed below. The requirement of written evidence for a contract for the sale of land is now a requirement that the actual contract shall be in writing (s. 2, Law of Property (Miscellaneous Provisions) Act 1989).

Although it is obviously sensible to require writing as a safeguard against fraud, there is no doubt that the area of law described below is ripe for reform. The cases can be extremely complex and the object of the law can be lost sight of entirely. It is good to know that the Law Commission intends to review this topic (Law Commission Consultation Paper 239).

The actual formalities

Declaration of a trust of land

Section 53(1)(b) of the LPA 1925 provides that 'a declaration of trust concerning land or any interest therein must be manifested and proved by some writing signed by some person who is able to declare the same or by his will'.

Example 6.1

Claud is the owner of a house known as 'The Laurels' and says to some friends: 'From now on I am holding "The Laurels" in trust for my children Tim and Tom'. This is not enforceable as there is no writing.

Points to note:

(a) The actual declaration of trust need not be in writing. The words 'manifested and proved' require only written evidence. Section 53(1)(c) does not specify what written evidence is required but it is likely that the cases on s. 40(1) of the LPA 1925 (now repealed) will be a guide here. Section 40(1) required written evidence in cases of contracts for the sale of land (now the actual contract must be in writing), and the courts interpreted this to mean that, provided the main terms of the contract were evidenced by writing, the actual written evidence did not need to be in any particular form. It could be in more than one document, so long as there was evidence to show that they were linked, and the written evidence could have come into existence after the trust was created. In *Gardner* v. *Rowe* (1826) a trust of a lease was granted orally but later a deed was executed stating the trusts. This was held valid.

(b) The signature of the settlor is needed. That of an agent will not suffice because of the words in s. 53(1)(b) 'signed by some person who is able to declare the same'.

(c) The requirement in s. 53(1)(b) applies only to express trusts and not to resulting, implied, or constructive trusts (s. 53(2) LPA 1925). This exception is of great importance as it has enabled the courts to impose a resulting, implied or constructive trust in many cases where there was no written declaration of trust. Good examples are those involving disputes over the beneficial entitlement to the family home and where it is felt necessary to impose a trust to prevent fraud or unconscionable conduct. (See Chapters 10 and 11.) Particularly good instances are *Rochefoucauld* v. *Boustead* (1897) and *Hodgson* v. *Marks* (1971).

(d) Section 53(1)(b) is silent on the position when these requirements are not complied with but it is accepted that this will not make the trust void but only unenforceable, in line with what was the position under s. 40(1) of the LPA (*Gardner* v. *Rowe* (1828)). Therefore it cannot be relied on in any legal proceedings but remains valid unless or until these are brought.

(e) No formalities are required for *inter vivos* declarations of trust of other property. Where the trust is created by will the requirements contained in the Wills Act 1837 as amended by s. 17 of the Administration of Justice Act 1982 must be complied with.

(f) The requirements of s. 53(1)(b) must not be confused with the requirement that once there has been a valid declaration of trust the settlor must, in addition, comply with the necessary formalities to actually transfer the property to the trustees and so constitute the trust. (See Chapter 7.)

Dispositions of equitable interests arising under trusts

Section 53(1)(c) of the LPA 1925 provides that a disposition of an equitable interest or trust must be in writing signed either by the settlor or by his authorised agent.

Points to note:

(a) The actual disposition must be in writing. Written evidence will not suffice. However, the disposition can be contained in more than one document provided that there is evidence to connect them (*Re Danish Bacon Co Staff Pension Fund Trust* (1971)).

(b) The signature of an agent is sufficient.

(c) Section 53(1)(c) does not, by virtue of s. 53(2) of the LPA, apply to resulting, implied or constructive trusts.

(d) Section 53(1)(c) does not require that where an equitable owner makes a disposition of his interest to another (for which writing is of course needed) who is to hold the interest as trustee then the writing must actually contain *details* of the trust (*Re Tyler's Fund Trusts* (1967)).

(e) Failure to comply with s. 53(1)(c) makes the disposition void. This has always been accepted as correct although, as with s. 53(1)(b), the subsection is silent on this point. The accepted view is supported by the word '*must*' in the subsection, and also by the fact that the cases, including two decided by the House of Lords (*Grey* v. *IRC* (1960) and *Oughtred* v. *IRC* (1960) – see below), all proceed on the assumption that a failure to comply with this requirement is fatal to the disposition.

Background to s. 53(1)(c)

(a) The application of s. 53(1)(c) has been complicated by its involvement in cases where settlors have tried to avoid payment of stamp duty or other taxes. Stamp duty is payable on the written instrument by which property is transferred but many settlors have argued that as a particular transaction is not a disposition within the meaning of s. 53(1)(c), no writing is needed and therefore no stamp duty is payable. In any event stamp duty is no longer payable on deeds of gift (s. 82 Finance Act 1985) and so where the transfer is by way of gift there is no longer any tax advantage in not complying with s. 53(1)(c). The subsection applies however in situations other than those concerned

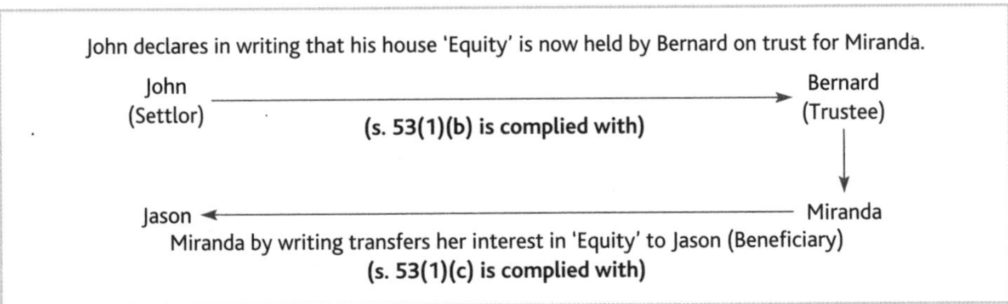

Figure 6.1 Operation of s. 53(1)(b) and s. 53(1)(c) (note that these two subsections operate at different stages)

with taxation and the best way to master this complicated area is to look first at the principles involved rather than at some of the detail of the taxation aspects of the cases.

(b) One way of understanding this area is to keep in mind the policy of s. 53(1)(c) and see whether it is being fulfilled in particular cases. In *Vandervell* v. *IRC* (1967) Lord Upjohn said that the policy was to 'prevent hidden oral transactions in equitable interests in fraud of those truly entitled, and making it difficult, if not impossible, for the trustees to ascertain who are in truth the beneficiaries'. In simple terms the policy is to enable the trustees and beneficiaries to know what is going on.

Application of s. 53(1)(c)

In the following figures, T holds on trust for X absolutely.

In *Grey* v. *IRC* (1960) it was held that such a transaction required writing, although as the trustees are, by definition, involved here it is difficult to see how this accords with Lord Upjohn's policy reason in *Vandervell* v. *IRC*. The court may, however, have been concerned to prevent tax avoidance. The facts of *Grey* v. *IRC* were that the settlor transferred shares to trustees to hold as nominees for him. He then orally directed the trustees to hold the shares on trust for his grandchildren and the trustees later executed a written declaration of trust. The object was to avoid stamp duty: if the oral direction disposed of the settlor's equitable interest in the shares then no duty was payable. However, the court held that as writing was needed for this type of transaction the oral declaration was invalid. The equitable interest was disposed of by the later written declaration of trust which did of course attract stamp duty.

Transfer of the legal estate by a bare trustee to another

A bare trustee, as explained in Chapter 4, is a trustee with no active duties and so can be given directions by the beneficiary to transfer the legal estate.

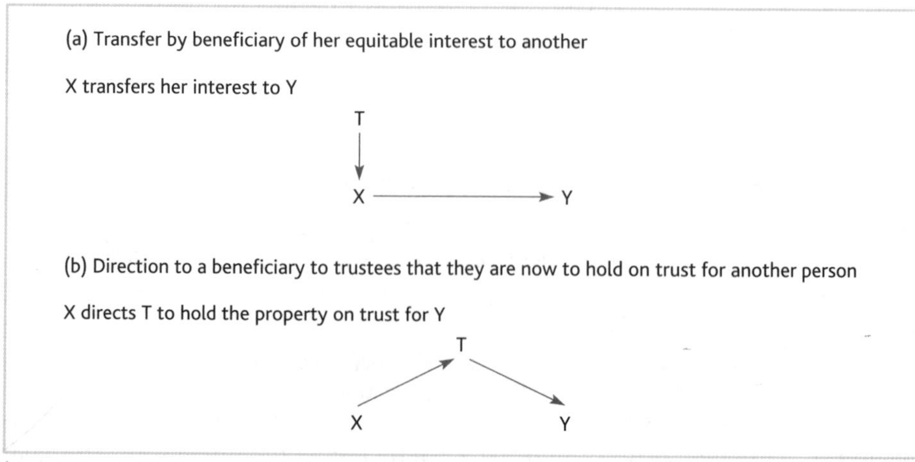

(a) Transfer by beneficiary of her equitable interest to another
X transfers her interest to Y
T
X
Y
(b) Direction to a beneficiary to trustees that they are now to hold on trust for another person
X directs T to hold the property on trust for Y
T
X
Y

Figure 6.2a and b Application of s. 53(1)(c)

Example 6.2

X directs T to transfer shares to Y so that Y becomes absolute owner. A possible form of words could be: 'All my interest in the shares is to go to Y'. The word 'all' could mean that not only the equitable interest in the shares, which belongs to X, but also the legal title to them, which is held by T, should go to Y.

In *Vandervell* v. *IRC* (1967) it was held that this transaction was not caught by s. 53(1)(c) and writing was not needed. Although the equitable interest passes from X to Y, this is done automatically with the transfer of the legal estate and thus there is no separate disposition. (It is interesting that in *Duggan* v. *Governor of Full Sutton Prison* (2004) the same point was made in relation to the transfer of funds owned by a prisoner to the Governor of the prison – see Chapter 5.) In addition, the trustees are necessarily involved and so there is no question of anything being hidden from them. The facts of this case, in so far as they concerned the application of s. 53(1)(c), were that a bank which held shares for Vandervell as a bare trustee transferred them, on his directions, to the Royal College of Surgeons to enable a chair of pharmacology to be endowed. The bank's legal title to the shares and Vandervell's equitable interest in them were accordingly both transferred and so, on the basis of the above reasoning, no writing was needed.

New trusts are declared by the trustee with the consent of the beneficiary

Example 6.3

T declares, with the agreement of X, that he now holds the property on trust for W.

In *Re Vandervell's Trusts (No. 2)* (1974) it was held that this was not within s. 53(1)(c) and so writing was not required. Lord Denning said that, in the context of this particular case, a resulting trust had come into existence to fill a gap in the beneficial ownership and when an express trust was declared, with the assent of the beneficiary under the resulting trust, the equitable interest under that trust automatically ended. It seems that this principle will also apply where equitable interests under express trusts are displaced by the creation of new trusts. The facts were that, taking up the story in *Vandervell* v. *IRC* (above), Vandervell had given Vandervell Trustees Ltd an option to re-purchase the shares from the Royal College of Surgeons but had failed to specify the trusts on which the shares should be held if the option was exercised. In *Vandervell* v. *IRC* it was decided that accordingly the shares would be held on a resulting trust for Vandervell, but this involved him in liability to surtax which this scheme had been trying to avoid. He therefore told Vandervell Trustees Ltd to exercise the option to re-purchase the shares and in *Re Vandervell's Trusts (No. 2)* (1974) the court held that as the shares had been re-purchased with money from a settlement in favour of Vandervell's children, they were held on trust for them. The resulting trust in favour of Vandervell thus ended and, as explained above, no writing was deemed necessary (see *Strauss* (1967)).

It must be emphasised that this principle will apply only where the new trusts are declared by T. If X transferred his equitable interest directly to W then of course there would be a disposition within s. 53(1)(c).

Beneficiary contracts to transfer his equitable interest

This will arise when X contracts with Z to transfer his interest under the trust to him.

The law here awaits clarification, but in *Re Holt's Settlement* (1969) Megarry J accepted that where a contract is specifically enforceable, the purchaser's right to specific performance passes to him as an equitable interest under a constructive trust as soon as the contract is made. Section 53(2) exempts constructive trusts from the formalities required by s. 53(1)(c) and thus no writing is needed. The issue then becomes whether damages would be an inadequate remedy. If so, specific performance is available (see Chapter 2) and there is a constructive trust and no writing is needed. However, in the context of schemes to avoid payment of stamp duty this argument may not succeed as, if it did, avoidance would be extremely simple. A contract would displace the need for a written instrument so that no duty would be payable. It was this conclusion which the court was determined to prevent in *Oughtred* v. *IRC* (1960). Mrs Oughtred and her son both had interests in shares in a private company. Mrs Oughtred's interest was absolute; her son's was reversionary. They orally agreed to exchange their interests and the Inland Revenue Commissioners (IRC) claimed stamp duty on the actual written transfer of the shares. The court held that although in the case of a contract to sell shares in a private company the remedy of specific performance is available because the shares are unique and a constructive trust arises in favour of the buyer, the buyer does not acquire a full beneficial interest until the formal written transfer. This is therefore the disposition and s. 53(1)(c) applies to it. Lord Radcliffe, however, dissented and held that Mrs Oughtred obtained the ownership in equity by virtue of the agreement and this view has been supported by later cases (see *Re Hay* above). The latest case to deal with the matter in depth, *Neville* v. *Wilson* (1997), supports Lord Radcliffe's argument. Here nominees held shares in one company (X) on trust for another (Y). The shareholders of Y agreed to put it into liquidation and to divide the company's equitable interest in these shares amongst themselves. This agreement was not in writing. If the agreement was not effective the interest in the shares would pass to the Crown but the Court of Appeal held that the agreement was effective to transfer the equitable interest to the shareholders by applying the analysis of Lord Radcliffe in *Oughtred*. It is significant that in this case there was no issue of avoiding tax but only the question of whether the shareholders or the Crown obtained the equitable interest (see Thompson (1996)).

As a sub-trust has been created, it can be argued that this is a declaration of trust and so it falls within s. 53(1)(b), in which in any case writing is only needed if it concerns land. However, if X has no active duties to perform and is thus a bare trustee then the effect is that X will have disappeared from the picture and there may be a disposition. On the basis of Lord Upjohn's policy reason in

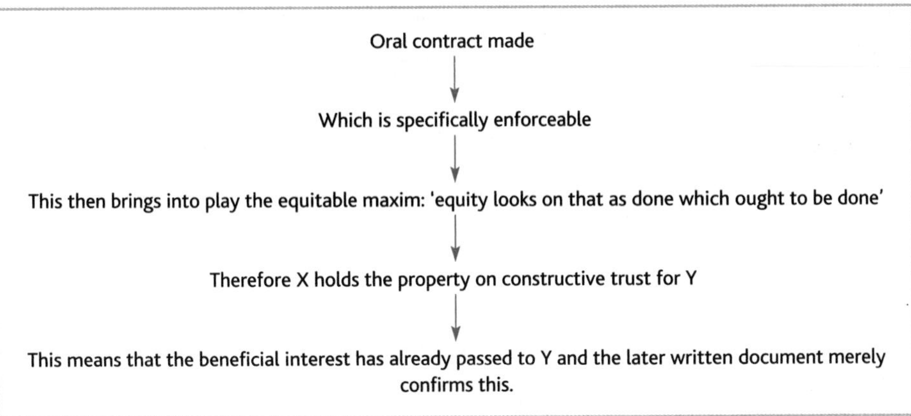

Figure 6.3 The sequence of events in the example based on Lord Radcliffe's dissent in *Oughtred* v. *IRC* and *Re Holt*

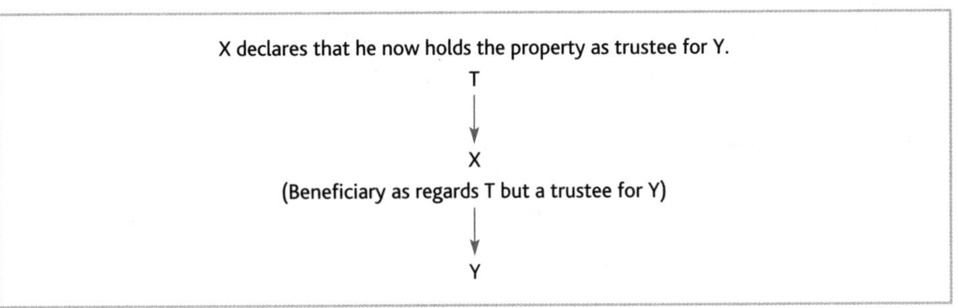

Figure 6.4 Beneficiary declares himself trustee

Vandervell v. *IRC* it is difficult to see how such a transaction can be hidden from the trustees as they will need to be aware of Y's existence.

Beneficiary surrenders his equitable interest

This occurs when X surrenders his interest to T1 and T2.

The position is uncertain but it could be argued, by analogy with *Vandervell* v. *IRC*, that as the legal and equitable titles are now merged there is no disposition.

Beneficiary disclaims his equitable interest

> **Example 6.4**
>
> X, as soon as he becomes aware that he has an equitable interest, disclaims it.

In *Re Paradise Motor Co Ltd* (1968), where the facts were the same way as in the example, it was held that writing is not needed here because 'a disclaimer operates by way of avoidance and not by way of disposition' (Danckwerts LJ).

(i) Beneficiary under a staff pension fund appoints a nominee to receive benefits from the fund

Example 6.5

X, a beneficiary under a staff pension fund, appoints T to receive the money payable by the fund in the event of X's death.

In *Re Danish Bacon Co* (1971) Megarry J doubted if this was a disposition requiring writing but, as explained above, he held that in any event there was sufficient writing.

FURTHER READING

Hayton and Marshall (2005) *Commentary and Cases on the Law of Trusts and Equitable Remedies*, 12th edn, London: Sweet & Maxwell, pp. 70–104.

CHAPTER SUMMARY

- Declaration of trust of land or any interest in land requires writing (s. 53(1)(b) LPA 1925).
- Declaration of trust of other property does not require writing.
- Transfer of the beneficial interest under a trust requires writing (s. 53(1)(c) LPA 1925).
- In certain cases the requirement of s. 53(1)(c) can be avoided (see above).
- In other cases the position is uncertain.

QUESTION

Diane wished to transfer some of her property to her family and friends. She transferred her house 'Fairways' to Jack and Mabel by a properly executed transfer having previously telephoned them and told them to hold the house on trust for her 'near relations'. She telephoned them again and asked them to hold her beneficial share under a trust established by her father for her sister Eileen instead. Lastly she instructed John, her brother, to hold the sum of £10,000, which had been put in a bank account in his name, on trust for her friend Susan.

Diane has now died and Jack, Mabel and John ask your advice on whether they are bound by the trusts set up by Diane.

Note 6.1: You will find suggested points for inclusion in this answer in Appendix 2.

7 Completely and incompletely constituted trusts

INTRODUCTION

In Chapter 5 we looked at the need for certainty in the creation of the trust and in Chapter 6 at the formal requirements needed to create a trust. Here we are concerned with what can be considered the third vital requirement: that the property to be held on trust is actually vested in the trustees.

WHAT DOES THE TERM 'COMPLETELY CONSTITUTED' MEAN?

A completely constituted trust is one where the trust property is actually vested in the trustee/s. It is not sufficient for a settlor merely to intend to create a trust.

The constitution of a trust has important consequences for all parties:

(a) The settlor cannot change her mind and re-claim the property.
(b) The trustees must hold the property in accordance with the terms of the trust.
(c) The beneficiaries can enforce the trust against the trustees (*Paul* v. *Paul* (1882)).

Constitution of a trust is illustrated by Example 7.1:

Example 7.1

X transfers Blackacre to Y to hold on trust for Z. The trust is now constituted and so X cannot claim that Blackacre belongs to him. Y is obliged to hold it on trust for Z and Z can enforce the trust against Y.

WHEN IS A TRUST COMPLETELY CONSTITUTED?

In *Milroy* v. *Lord* (1862) Turner LJ held that:

> the settlor must have done everything which, according to the nature of the property comprised in the settlement, was necessary to be done in order to transfer the property and render the settlement binding upon him. He may, of course, do

this by actually transferring the property to the persons for whom he intends to provide, and the provision will then be effectual, and it will be equally effectual if he transfers the property to a trustee for the purposes of the settlement, or declares that he himself holds it in trust for those purposes; . . . in order to render the settlement binding, one or other of these modes must, as I understand the law of this court, be resorted to, for there is no equity in this court to perfect an imperfect gift.

Note 7.1: The use of the term ***'imperfect gift'****. This can cover two cases:*

(a) Where a person promises an outright gift of property rather than promises to create a trust of it
(b) Where a person promises to give property to others for them to hold as trustees.

The same principle will apply to imperfect gifts in situation (a) as will apply to what are incompletely constituted trusts in situation (b) because generally a trust is created by the settlor without consideration being promised by the beneficiaries. If so, the beneficiaries under a trust have also been promised a gift. Thus whether it is a straight gift as in (a) or a gift in the form of a trust as in (b) equity will not assist a person to obtain it unless any of the rules outlined in this chapter apply.

The judgment of Turner LJ indicates that a trust will be completely constituted when either:

(a) the settlor has vested the legal title to the trust property in the trustee(s) (**Method One**); *or*
(b) the settlor has declared that he now holds the property as trustee (**Method Two**).

In the most recent case on this area, *Pennington* v. *Waine* (2002) (below) Arden LJ considered this whole area and pointed out that the general principles governing the constitution of trusts are, in fact, really an instance of equity following the law (e.g. Methods One and Two) and it is in recognition of exceptions to these rather rigid rules that we can see the influence of equity. Her judgment is well worth reading, as it casts light on what can be a dark area.

In addition, as Turner LJ said above, the property can actually be transferred to those who are to benefit. In this situation there is an outright gift to them and not a trust. As we shall see some of the principles in this chapter can apply to gifts as well as trusts (see below).

Note 7.2: We are concerned here only with inter vivos *transfers because where the trust is created by will, it is constituted by the trust property vesting on the death of the testator in his personal representatives who are then under a duty to vest the property in trustees appointed by the testator.*

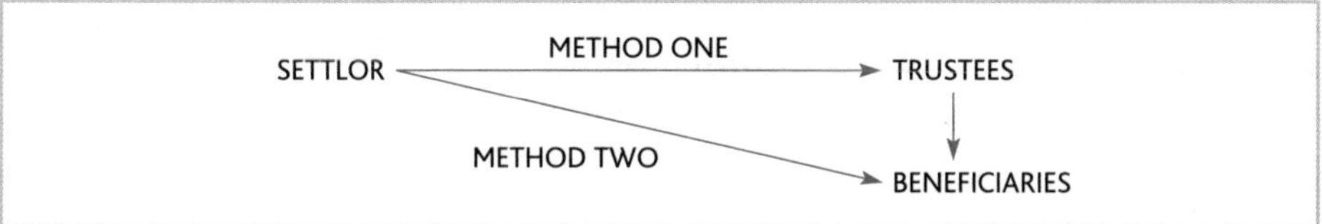

Figure 7.1 Property transferred to trustees – Methods One and Two

Method One: Transferring the trust property to trustees

The method by which trust property is to be transferred to trustees will depend on the type of property in question. Accordingly:

(a) *Legal estates in land* must be transferred by deed (s. 52(1) LPA 1925) and, if title is registrable, then the requirements of the Land Registration Act 2002 must be observed.
(b) *A disposition of an equitable interest* must be in writing (s. 53(1)(c) of the LPA 1925) (see Chapter 6).
(c) *Shares* must be transferred by the form of transfer laid down by ss. 182 and 183 of the Companies Act 1985 together with the stock transfer form prescribed by s. 1 of the Stock Transfer Act 1963 as amended by the Stock Exchange (Completion of Bargains) Act 1976.
(d) *Copyright* must be transferred by writing (s. 90(3) Copyright Design and Patents Act 1988).
(e) *Bills of exchange* must be transferred by endorsement (s. 31 Bills of Exchange Act 1882 and see *Jones* v. *Lock* (1865) below).
(f) *Choses in possession* can be transferred either by:
   (i) delivery to the trustee, coupled with the intention to make a gift; *or*
   (ii) by a deed of gift – this will immediately vest the property in the trustee, even though delivery is later; *or*
   (iii) by contract.

Method Two: Settlor declares that he holds the property as a trustee

In this case there is no transfer of the legal ownership but what does change is the capacity in which the settlor holds the property. Previously he was the absolute and beneficial owner; now he holds as trustee. The clearest way in which this can happen is for the settlor to execute a declaration of trust that he now holds as trustee for particular beneficiaries.

The courts have, however, held a less formal declaration of trust to be effective as in *Paul* v. *Constance* (1977). Here Mr Constance and the claimant lived together, although they were not married. An account was opened in Mr Constance's name only because they would have been embarrassed by having a joint account in different names, and £950 awarded to Constance following an injury at work together with three small joint bingo winnings were paid into it. One withdrawal was made which was for their mutual benefit. At various times Constance said to the claimant: 'the money is as much yours as mine'.

The court held that these words, supported by the evidence of the transactions in the account, established that Constance intended to declare himself a trustee of the money in it for himself and the plaintiff jointly.

> *Note 7.3: The case has been criticised on the ground that it is difficult to see an intention to create an express trust (see Chapter 3). Could it have been better construed as a gift by Constance to himself and Paul jointly? In addition, the case was argued on the basis that there was an express trust. Surely it would have been better considered as an implied or constructive trust?*

However, in other cases the courts have held that on the facts there was insufficient evidence of a declaration of trust. Moreover, they have also applied another principle laid down by Turner LJ in *Milroy* v. *Lord* (1862) that where a gift is imperfect because the donor has not complied with the requisite formalities the courts will not save it by holding that the donor has instead constituted himself trustee of the gift for the donee by making a declaration of trust.

Both these principles are illustrated by *Jones* v. *Lock* (1865). A father, on returning from a business trip, was scolded by his family for his failure to bring a present for his baby son. He therefore produced a cheque made out in his name for £900 and said 'Look you here, I give this to baby', and placed the cheque in the baby's hand. He then took the cheque back but apparently intended to see his solicitor to make provision for the baby. However, he died before he could do this.

The court held that:

(a) There was no gift to the baby because the cheque had not been endorsed (this is no longer necessary: s. 2 Cheques Act 1957).
(b) Nor was there a declaration by Jones that he now held the cheque on trust for the baby. The court said that it would not impose the onerous duties of a trustee on a person unless it was clear that a declaration of trust was intended. Here the father's giving of the cheque to the baby was only symbolic of intention to make proper provision for him.

The baby therefore received nothing.

A similar decision that there was a lack of evidence that the settlor intended to declare himself trustee was reached in *Richards* v. *Delbridge* (1874). Delbridge was a tenant of premises from which he carried on a business. He was assisted in the business by his grandson, Edward Richards, a minor. Shortly before his death he endorsed and signed the following memorandum on the lease: 'This deed and all thereto belonging I give to Edward Bennetto Richards, from this time forth, with all the stock-in-trade'. Delbridge then gave the document to Richards' mother to hold for him. On Delbridge's death there was no mention of the property.

The court held that:

(a) There was no effective transfer of the lease because it was not under seal (this requirement is now in s. 52(1) of the LPA 1925).
(b) There was no declaration of trust. Jessell MR observed that 'for a man to make himself trustee there must be an expression of intention to become a trustee'.

This was not so here: an outright gift was intended, which failed because it was imperfect. (But note *Fletcher* v. *Fletcher* (1844) (see below) where a somewhat lax view of intention was taken.)

Where there is more than one trustee and the trust property has been vested in only one trustee.

This point arose in *T Choithram International SA* v. *Pagarani* (2001) where the Privy Council, on appeal from the Caribbean Court of Appeal, held that the trust would be constituted. The facts were that Mr Paganini, in his last illness, executed a trust deed establishing a foundation which would act as an umbrella for four charities which he had already established. Immediately after he had signed, he stated that all his wealth, including shares in a number of companies, would now belong to the trust. He himself was one of the trustees. He then told his accountant to transfer all his money to the trust but he failed to sign the necessary forms. Apparently he disliked signing these types of documents and had been told that it was not necessary. The companies in which he held shares acted in accordance with the deed by registering the trustees of the foundation as shareholders. After Paganini died, his family claimed that he had not effectively transferred his wealth to the foundation, which accordingly belonged to them.

The Privy Council's decision that the trust was constituted rested on two points:

(a) Had Paganini actually made an effective declaration of trust? He did not use the word 'trust' and his actual words, which were never quite established, appeared to indicate a gift. However, it was held that the context of the words clearly indicated a trust: he intended to give to the foundation and this body was a trust.
(b) Assuming that Paganini had declared himself a trustee (Method Two above), did it matter that the trust property was not vested in the other trustees? The Privy Council held that it did not. Paganini had executed a solemn declaration of trust and it would be unconscionable to allow him to resile (i.e. go back) from this promise. There was no distinction between cases where a person declares himself to be a sole trustee and where (as here) he declares that he is one of a number of trustees. In both cases the trust is constituted.

One might add that, whilst the decision can be supported as an application of *Milroy* v. *Lord*, the more liberal view taken of the requirements for constitution, and the use of the notion of unconscionability, are in line with the approach in *Pennington* v. *Waine* (below) and may signal a more relaxed view of the constitution rules. One could say that the decision in *Paganini* represents a kind of 'third way' between Methods One and Two of constitution of a trust.

Settlor constituting a trust by doing all in his power to do so

Method One (see above) of completely constituting a trust, under which the settlor must transfer the trust property to the trustee, appears to be subject to an exception in certain cases where a trust has been held to be completely constituted when the settlor has done everything which it is in his power to do to transfer the property even though the transfer is not complete until some other person has done a particular act.

The way in which this exception works is shown by Example 7.2.

Example 7.2

X wishes to transfer shares in Z Co., a private company, to Y. X executes the transfer. He has done all in his power. But the transfer is not complete because in the case of a private company its articles can give the directors power to refuse to register the transfer.

The matter first came up in *Re Rose* (1952) where the directors of a private company did in fact register the transfer. The issue here was the time at which the transfer was complete. If this was when Rose executed the transfer then there would be no liability to estate duty because Rose died more than five years after the transfer. If the effective date was the date of registration by the directors then as Rose had died within five years of this, estate duty would be payable. The court held that the effective date was when Rose executed the transfer. It should be noted, however, that the facts of this case did not deal with whether a trust of shares had been completely constituted but the principle in it has applied to this type of situation.

What is the position if the directors refuse to register? Evershed MR in *Re Rose* said that the settlor would hold as trustee for the beneficiaries. But this seems to conflict with Turner LJ's statement in *Milroy* v. *Lord* (1862) that if a gift 'is intended to take effect by transfer, the court will not hold the intended transfer to operate as a declaration of trust' (see below). However, in *Re Rose* (1952), Evershed MR held that this principle only applied where the transfer was incomplete because of failure to comply with the appropriate formalities, as had indeed happened in *Milroy* v. *Lord* itself where a transfer of bank shares was incomplete because the entry in the books of the bank, which was necessary to transfer the legal title, was never made. In the *Re Rose* situation, however, the problem lies not with the transferor but with some third party.

Section 360 of the Companies Act 1985 provides that no notice of any trust, whether express, implied or constructive, shall be entered on the register of shares. In addition, a company is not liable to the beneficiaries for any breach of trust by the trustee. Any dividend declared between execution of the transfer documents and registration will, of course, be paid to the transferor as legal owner but, as he is a trustee, he will hold them on trust for the intended transferee (Evershed MR in *Re Rose* (1952)). The position where the transferee is never registered because of the directors' refusal to do so was not considered in *Re Rose* but the obvious conclusion is that the trust of the shares will continue and so the transferor will be obliged to exercise any voting rights in the interest of the transferee together with any other benefits, such as a rights issue, as well as holding any dividends on trust for him.

It must be noted that although the estate duty provisions dealt with in *Re Rose* no longer exist, the principle remains important because the Finance Act 1986 imposes an Inheritance Tax on gifts made within seven years of death. The tax is chargeable on death but it can also apply to some lifetime gifts.

In *Re Fry* (1945) an intended transfer of shares fell through because the donor had not obtained Treasury consent to the transfer, although it had been applied for. The court held that, as the donor had not done all in his power, the gift remained imperfect. Yet it is difficult to distinguish this case from *Re Rose*. What could the donor do?

It is not clear whether the principle in *Re Rose* applies whenever some act needs to be done by a third party, over which the settlor has no control, or whether it is restricted to certain types of property. Hanbury and Martin (2005a) see the doctrine mainly in terms of shares in private companies but the more general view is that it applies in cases where the actual transfer is out of the settlor's control. Is there any reason why it should not apply to shares in public companies, given that the act of registration of a person as a shareholder is done by the company?

The principle was applied to land registration in *Mascall* v. *Mascall* (1984). Here a gift of land by a father to his son was held to be complete when the father handed over the transfer and the land certificate to the son even though the son had not sent the documents to the Land Registry and had not therefore acquired title (s. 19 Land Registration Act 1925; now the Land Registration Act 2002). It is assumed that the trust pending acquisition by the son here of title was constructive and so no written declaration of trust would be needed (see s. 53(1)(b) and s. 53(2) of the LPA 1925).

The most recent application of the *Re Rose* principle was in *Pennington* v. *Waine* (2002), which did, in fact, involve shares in a private company. It broke new ground as, unlike in *Re Rose* itself, the question involved the constitution of a trust. Mrs Crampton, a shareholder in a private company, told Pennington, a partner in a firm who acted for the company, that she wished to transfer some of her shares to her nephew and she later signed a share transfer form to this effect and gave it to Pennington. He took no further action and the question was whether, on her death, the shares had been transferred to the nephew.

The Court of Appeal held that they had, although the reasoning in the two main judgments differ. Arden LJ upheld *Re Rose* but also held that the fact that there was clear evidence that Mrs Crampton intended an immediate gift of the shares amounted to an assignment of them to the nephew anyway. She held that on the facts it would be unconscionable to allow Mrs Crampton, in view of all that she had done to transfer the shares to the nephew, then to turn round and change her mind and say that they were not his. Clarke LJ's reasoning was more straightforward: there was in fact a perfect gift of the shares as actual delivery of the transfer form was not needed.

Pennington v. *Waine* is also interesting in that it had previously been thought that *Re Rose* itself could be explained on the basis that it was a taxation case and that it would be wrong that liability to estate duty might depend on the tardiness of directors in registering a transfer. Now we have a decision which is not concerned with taxation and which upholds *Re Rose*. (There are several articles on this decision: see e.g. Doggett (2003) and Garton (2003).)

Indirect constitution of a trust

Suppose that the settlor fails to transfer the property directly to the intended trustee but it reaches him by a different, less direct, route. One instance of this is where the trustee becomes the settlor's executor (or possibly administrator).

In *Re Ralli's W.T.* (1964) a testator left his **residuary estate** on trust for his widow for life and then for his daughters, Helen and Irene. Helen had entered into a marriage settlement in which she covenanted to settle future property on volunteers. There was therefore an incompletely constituted trust. However, the trust was constituted by the accident that the claimant was the sole surviving trustee of both Helen's settlement and the testator's will. Accordingly, her share of the residuary estate was vested in him, as both the testator's widow and Helen were dead.

The court held that the claimant held Helen's share on the trusts of the marriage settlement, and not for those entitled under the will. Buckley J said that the claimant 'is at law the owner of the fund and the means by which he became so have no effect upon the quality of his legal ownership'.

The effect of *Re Ralli* can be seen in Figure 7.2.

The basis of the decision in *Re Ralli* is not entirely clear. One is that it is an extension of the rule in *Strong* v. *Bird* (this is discussed below – and note especially the link with *Re Stewart* (1908)), but the other is that provided the trust property reaches the trustees equity is not concerned about the exact route. Be that as it may, *Re Ralli* presents two main difficulties:

(i) Although Buckley J said that he was following the decision in *Strong* v. *Bird* (1874), this decision is based on the intention of the donor. Yet the principle in *Re Ralli* (1964) can operate independently of the donor's intention and, indeed, allow a gift to be perfected by mere chance. In addition, reliance was placed on *Re James* (1935) (see below) which is of doubtful authority.
(ii) The decision subjects a person in the position of the plaintiff here to competing claims of loyalties: to both those entitled to the property under Helen's marriage settlement and those entitled to it under the will as forming Helen's

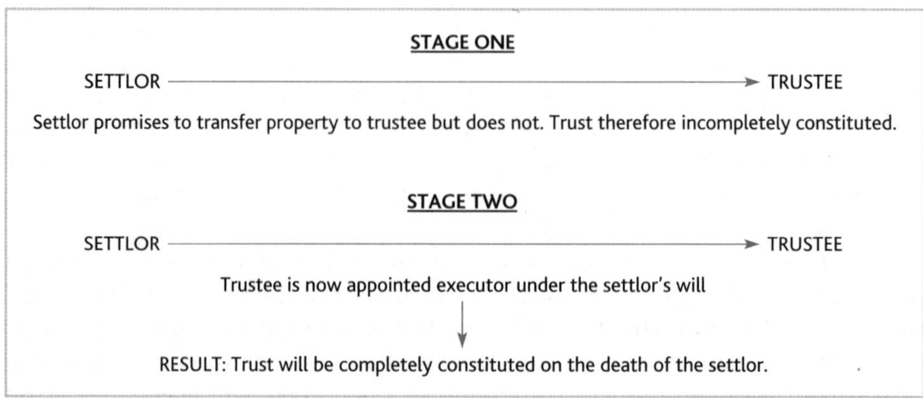

STAGE ONE
SETTLOR
TRUSTEE
Settlor promises to transfer property to trustee but does not. Trust therefore incompletely constituted.
STAGE TWO
SETTLOR
TRUSTEE
Trustee is now appointed executor under the settlor's will
RESULT: Trust will be completely constituted on the death of the settlor.

Figure 7.2 The effect of *Re Ralli*

residuary estate. The court failed to give clear guidance on the position where someone in the claimant's position chooses to favour those entitled under the will.

INCOMPLETELY CONSTITUTED TRUSTS: WHAT IS AN INCOMPLETELY CONSTITUTED TRUST?

A trust is incompletely constituted when it has not been constituted by any of the above methods.

Example 7.3 shows the position where the trust is incompletely constituted:

Example 7.3

X is the owner of Blackacre. He executes a declaration of trust under which Y is now to hold Blackacre on trust for Z. X fails to convey Blackacre to Y. In this case the trust is not constituted and the beneficiary has no rights unless he gives consideration to X. The reason is that 'equity will not assist a **volunteer**' (Lord Eldon in *Ellison* v. *Ellison* (1802)).

However, as Gardner (2003) points out, it is wrong to think of this as a general principle: equity, for example, assists volunteers to obtain injunctions although not specific performance. Even so, in this situation, it has chosen not to do so.

Contracts (Rights of Third Parties) Act 1999

The law in this area, already complex, now requires us to distinguish between the position where any covenant to settle property was made before this Act came into force on 11 May 2000. The position will first be considered on the basis that the Act does not apply, and then on the basis that it does.

Contracts (Rights of Third Parties) Act 1999 does not apply

(a) If the intended beneficiaries have given valuable consideration other than marriage consideration to the settlor they can sue either at common law for damages or in equity to compel the settlor to constitute the trust.
(b) If the intended beneficiaries are within marriage consideration they can sue in equity but not at common law.
(c) If the intended beneficiaries are parties to a deed of covenant with the settlor they may sue upon the covenant at common law and claim damages.
(d) If neither (a), (b) nor (c) applies, the intended beneficiaries have no remedies. As they are volunteers, no assistance will be given by the common law nor by equity for 'there is no equity in this court to perfect an imperfect gift' (Turner LJ in *Milroy* v. *Lord* (1862)).

Always note, however, that once the trust has been completely constituted the above rules do not apply. The beneficiaries, whether volunteers or not, have full rights.

The following examples illustrate the rights of the beneficiary in three different situations:

Example 7.4

S promises T that he will transfer £20,000 to him to hold on trust for B, a volunteer. S fails to do so. The trust is incompletely constituted and as B is a volunteer he cannot either seek damages from S or sue in equity to compel S to transfer the £20,000 to T.

Example 7.5

Assume in the above example that S has entered into a covenant to which B is a party to transfer £20,000 to T on trust for B. Here, although B, as a volunteer, cannot sue in equity to compel S to constitute the trust, he can sue at common law for damages for breach of covenant.

Example 7.6

Assume in the above example that B has provided consideration for S's promise. Again B can sue S to compel him to constitute the trust, although if the consideration is only marriage consideration then only equitable remedies will be available.

It will be seen from the above examples that:

(a) Equity recognises marriage consideration. The common law does not.
(b) The common law enforces promises made in a deed, without valuable consideration. Equity does not.
(c) The common law remedy is damages whereas equity can compel a transfer of property by the remedy of specific performance.

Consideration

The equitable notion of consideration is, in this context, wider than that of the common law. Equity follows the common law rules on consideration and thus good consideration (such as natural love and affection) is not valuable. Nor is past consideration. (See *Re McArdle* (1951), which illustrates not only past consideration but also failure to constitute a trust.) Similarly, the doctrine of privity of contract (see e.g. *Tweddle* v. *Atkinson* (1861)) is recognised by both common law and equity. Equity alone, however, recognises marriage consideration.

Marriage consideration

(a) In order for marriage consideration to be valuable, it must be contained in a settlement made either:
   (i) before and in contemplation of marriage; *or*
   (ii) made after marriage but in pursuance of an ante-nuptial agreement. If it is not made in pursuance of such an agreement then the consideration

(i.e. the marriage) is past. Therefore the issue of the marriage are volunteers. There may be other consideration between the husband and wife but under the doctrine of privity of contract, their issue will not be parties to this.

(b) Who is within marriage consideration?
   (i) the husband, wife and issue of the marriage;
   (ii) more remote issue, e.g. grandchildren (*McDonald* v. *Scott* (1893)).

Illegitimate children, children by a former marriage, children by a possible second marriage or children to which one or both parties stand *in loco parentis* will only be within marriage consideration if their interests are so interwoven with those of the natural children of the marriage that it would be unjust that only the latter should benefit (see *A-G* v. *Jacobs-Smith* (1895)). Next-of-kin are certainly volunteers (see *Re Plumptre's Marriage Settlement* (1910)) below.

The way in which marriage consideration works in the constitution of a trust is shown by Example 7.7.

Example 7.7

X and Y, on their engagement, covenant with the trustees of the marriage settlement that:

(a) X will transfer Blackacre to the trustees.
(b) Y will transfer to the trustees any property she receives on the death of her father to be held on the following trusts:
   (i) for X and Y for their joint lives;
   (ii) remainder to any children of the marriage;
   (iii) in default of issue, to X's next-of-kin.

If X and Y have issue, then as they are within marriage consideration they can apply to the court which can either order Y to settle the property in accordance with the covenant (i.e. transfer it to the trustees) or, if appropriate, simply declare that the property is subject to the trusts of the settlement (as in *Pullan* v. *Koe* (1913) below).

If X and Y do not have issue, then their next-of-kin, e.g. brother, sister, cousins, are volunteers and cannot take any action to compel Y to carry out her undertaking (see *Re Plumptre's Settlement* below).

If X has an illegitimate child, Z, and X and Y have issue, then Z, in order to claim a share in the property which Y undertook to transfer, must prove that his interests are interwoven with those of the issue of the marriage (*A-G* v. *Jacobs-Smith* (1895)). If X and Y have no issue, might Z be able to claim if X and Y were *in loco parentis* to him?

In *Pullan* v. *Koe* (1913) a marriage settlement contained a covenant by a wife to settle certain after-acquired property on the trusts of the settlement. Some of the property was invested in bonds which were at the bank in her husband's name and had therefore not been settled. On the husband's death the court held that the moment that the wife received the property it was subject to a trust enforceable in favour of herself and the nine surviving children of the marriage, as these were within the marriage consideration. In *Re Plumptre's Marriage Settlement* (1910) the facts were similar to those in *Pullan* v. *Koe* (1913) (above) except that the beneficiaries who were seeking to enforce the covenant were not the issue of the marriage, as the wife had died without issue, but the wife's next-of-kin. The court held that, as they were not within the marriage consideration, they were volunteers and thus could not enforce the covenant. A similar case is *Re D'Angibau* (1880).

In *Paul* v. *Paul* (1882) property had been settled under a marriage settlement on the spouses for their joint lives, then to their issue and eventually to the wife's next-of-kin. When it became clear that the spouses would not have any issue, they asked for the capital of the fund to be paid to them. However, in contrast to *Re Plumptre* (above), the court held that as the trust had been constituted the next-of-kin had enforceable rights and the fact that they were volunteers was immaterial.

Beneficiary a party to a deed of covenant

If one of the intended beneficiaries is a party to a deed of covenant then although equity will give him no assistance he may still bring an action for damages at common law and the fact that he is a volunteer is immaterial. Equity will not intervene to frustrate such an action unless fraud or undue influence (see Chapter 3) is involved.

In *Cannon* v. *Hartley* (1949) a father covenanted on the breakdown of his marriage to make provision for a daughter by settling certain property on her. The daughter was a party to the deed and was thus held able to obtain damages at common law when the father refused to settle the property.

> *Note: One obstacle to actions on covenants is that they may be barred by lapse of time. This was the case in* Pullan v. Koe *(1913) (see above) but such an action was not necessary as the trust was completely constituted.*

Action by trustees

As *Cannon* v. *Hartley* (1949) illustrates, a party to a deed of covenant may sue on it at common law. If the beneficiaries are not volunteers, the trustees can sue on a covenant to which the trustees are parties and to ensure that the property is settled (*Pullan* v. *Koe* (1913)). What if the beneficiaries are volunteers? In many cases of incompletely constituted trusts, trustees have been parties to covenants (see *Re Plumptre's Settlement*). Can trustees then sue and obtain damages at common law even though the intended beneficiaries, as volunteers, cannot do so? Any damages could then be held in trust for the beneficiaries.

> *Note 7.4: An action in equity would of course not be possible (*Re Plumptre *(1910) above).*

However, the courts have discouraged such actions. In *Re Pryce* (1917) there was a marriage settlement where the ultimate beneficiaries were the next-of-kin of the wife, who were volunteers. The husband had died and the wife did not want the covenant to be enforced. It was held that the trustees ought not to take steps to enforce the covenant by bringing an action for damages. In *Re Kay* (1939) the court went further by directing them not to do so. *Re Cook* (1965) is a slightly weaker authority as the decision was simply that the intended beneficiaries could not compel the trustees to take proceedings. It should be said, though, that these are all decisions at first instance and in none of them did the trustees actually attempt to sue: they simply sought the directions of the court on what they should do.

One problem, if trustees were allowed to sue, is the measure of damages which they would be awarded. It is the beneficiaries, not the trustees, who need to be compensated and on this basis damages awarded to the trustees should be nominal. Yet in *Re Cavendish Browne's Settlement Trusts* (1916), trustees were awarded a sum which was equivalent to the value of the property which had been covenanted to settle. However, the case pre-dates *Re Pryce* (1917) and the other cases above. In addition, in this case, unlike the others above, the property was actually in existence at the date of the covenant. This seems, however, a very slight ground on which to distinguish them and the better view is that the line of cases beginning with *Re Pryce* represent the current law.

If substantial damages are awarded, then for whom should they be held? One argument is that instead of being held for the beneficiaries they should be held on a resulting trust for the settlor because as the settlor has not yet fully constituted the trust he considers the trustee as holding on a resulting trust for him meanwhile. As the settlor (or his estate) would be the defendants to such an action, it would presumably be dismissed as being circuitous (see *Snelling* v. *Snelling* (1973)). This point was not considered in *Re Cavendish Browne*.

The Contracts (Rights of Third Parties) Act 1999 does apply

This Act was, as is well known, passed to reduce the effect of the doctrine of privity of contract, which prevented a third party from enforcing a contract. The object of the Act is to allow a third party to enforce it when that contract was made for his benefit. Section 1 provides that a third party may, in his own right, enforce a term of a contract if that contract expressly provides that he may, or if the term purports to confer a benefit on him. This will not, however, apply, if it appears on a proper construction of the contract that it was not intended that the third party should benefit. The third party must be identified by name in the contract, or as a member of a class, or as answering a particular description but need not be in existence when the contract is made. Finally, and most importantly for our purposes, it is clear from s. 7(3) that the word 'contract' includes both simple contracts and also special contracts, i.e. those entered into by deed. Thus, it will apply where there is a covenant to settle.

If the third party does have a right of action, then he may have any remedy which would be available had he been a party to the contract and was bringing an action for breach. Thus, both common law and equitable remedies may be claimed. There is doubt as to whether a third party could obtain specific performance as he is a volunteer and in *Cannon* v. *Hartley* a volunteer who was a party to a deed was unable to do so. As Hanbury and Martin (2005b) point out, why should a third party claiming under the Act be in a better position than an actual *party* to a deed? The probability is, therefore, that a third party cannot obtain specific performance.

Leaving this issue aside, the Act changes the position as in *Re Pryce*, where, it will be recalled, the next-of-kin were unable to compel the trustees to bring an action for damages. Under the Contracts (Rights of Third Parties) Act the next-of-kin would be able in their own right to sue for damages provided that the conditions in the Act are satisfied. If a trustee does sue and obtains damages on behalf of the beneficiaries, then if those beneficiaries also sue under this Act, s. 5 provides that the court will reduce the damages awarded to them to take into account the sum awarded already to the trustees.

Trusts of the benefits of covenants

Can there be a trust of the right to sue on a covenant to transfer property, i.e. a trust of a chose in action? In *Fletcher* v. *Fletcher* (1844) a father entered into a voluntary covenant with trustees to pay £60,000, in the events which happened, to his sole surviving illegitimate son. Although the trustees refused to sue, the court held that the son could claim the money either by suing in his own name in equity or by using the name of the trustee in order to sue at common law. The reason given was that the covenant to pay the money was held on a completely constituted trust for the son even though the trust of the actual £60,000 was never constituted. The difficulty is that there is no evidence that the settlor ever intended that such a trust should be created. In later cases, such as *Re Schebsman* (1944), much stronger evidence of intention has been required. An agreement between a company and one of its employees that the company would pay sums of money to him, and after his death to his wife and child, was held not to make the employee a trustee for them. Here again there was a promise to pay money but no trust was found. Nor did the idea of a trust find favour in *Jackson* v. *Horizon Holidays Ltd* (1975). In addition, the assumption in *Fletcher* v. *Fletcher* that the son could compel the trustees to sue is contrary to the line of authority beginning with *Re Pryce* (above). The only way of distinguishing it from these cases is to say that *Fletcher* v. *Fletcher* involved existing property, whereas the other cases involved after-acquired property but this is scarcely satisfactory. It may be better to regard *Fletcher* v. *Fletcher* as being confined to its own particular facts and it may be regretted that this case, which lay in obscurity for many years, was ever exhumed.

Trusts of future property

These are shown by Example 7.8.

Example 7.8

X purported to convey, by voluntary settlement, the property which she would inherit under the will of her brother (*Re Ellenborough* (1903)). This is future property because the settlor does not, and indeed may never possess it, if, for instance, the will is altered.

Contracts to convey such property are valid and even if there is a voluntary covenant it is enforceable by a beneficiary who is a party to it (*Cannon* v. *Hartley* (1949)). The position is exactly the same as if the property was present property. However, what happens if, as in *Re Ellenborough* there is a mere voluntary settlement, i.e. an incompletely constituted gift? There cannot be a valid declaration of trust because there is no subject matter and it is probable that the principle in *Fletcher* v. *Fletcher* (see above) does not apply.

Four cases need to be considered:

(a) The settlor later receives the property and then declares that he holds it as trustee. This will now constitute the trust because although the initial declaration of trust was invalid through lack of subject matter this defect has now been cured by the subsequent declaration of trust.
(b) The settlor receives the property and transfers it to the trustees. This can be considered as a fresh declaration of trust so as to constitute the trust.
(c) The property reaches the trustees by a different route as in *Re Ralli* (1964). Here it may well be that the trust is constituted on the authority of *Re Ralli*.
(d) The settlor, when he receives the property, declines to transfer it, as happened in *Re Ellenborough* (1903). Here the court refused to compel the transfer. In effect the decision was based on the fundamental principle that, as the trust had not been constituted, because initially the settlor could not do this as she did not possess the property, and in addition, the intended beneficiaries were volunteers, the court would not assist them.

EXCEPTIONS TO THE RULE THAT EQUITY WILL NOT PERFECT AN IMPERFECT GIFT

The rule in *Strong* v. *Bird* (1874)

The rule states that if an incomplete gift is made during the donor's lifetime and the donor has appointed the donee his executor, then the vesting of the property in the donee completes the gift. The rule may be said to rest upon the donor's intention, unlike that in *Re Ralli* (1964) (see above), and also upon convenience because, as the whole of the estate has vested in the donee as executor, there would be no point in the donee suing himself (see Walton J in *Re Gonin* (1979)).

In *Strong* v. *Bird* X borrowed £1,100 from Y, his stepmother, who lived in his house, and who paid £212 10s a quarter for board. It was agreed that the debt should be paid off by X reducing Y's rent by £100 a quarter until the debt was

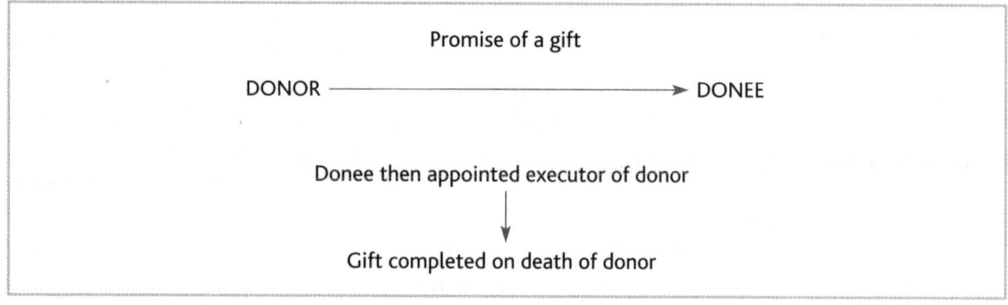

Figure 7.3 Equity will not perfect an imperfect gift

repaid. This happened for two quarters but Y then generously said that in future she would pay the full rent, which she did until her death. X was her executor and it was held that this appointment of X extinguished the remainder of the debt which X owed to Y.

Although the case involved a gift, the principle in it can apply also to a trust, e.g. X appoints Y and Z his trustees and promises to convey Blackacre to them on trust for W. He also appoints Y and Z his executors. X dies without having executed a deed of conveyance but his appointment of Y and Z as executors will vest the legal estate in them on trust for W.

The common law regarded the appointment of a debtor as executor as extinguishing the debt because it assumed that the creditor, by making the appointment, intended this to be so. Equity took a different view: it required the debtor to account to the estate for the debt so that the money was available to pay off creditors or available for the beneficiaries. The significance of *Strong* v. *Bird* was that here equity followed the common law and allowed the appointment of the debtor to extinguish the debt. The reason for this was the stepmother's continuing intention to release the debt.

However, equity struck out on its own in *Re Stewart* (1908) when the rule in *Strong* v. *Bird* was extended from cases of forgiveness of debts to those where there has been an incomplete transfer of property to a person who is also appointed executor under the will of the transferee. The effect is that the transfer may now be valid. It is here that the rule is one of equity alone. The deceased handed an envelope containing a letter from his brokers saying that notes had been bought together with a bought note (i.e. evidence of the purchase). The envelope did not, however, contain the actual notes and so there was an incomplete transfer. The wife was one of the executors and it was held that she was entitled to the bonds. Parry and Clark (2002) convincingly criticise this decision on the ground that the wife received the bonds in her fiduciary capacity as one of the executors and yet was able to receive a benefit from them by keeping them.

Nevertheless the decision in *Re Stewart* has been accepted in later cases and was applied in the difficult decision in *Re Ralli* (above).

Conditions for the rule to apply

(a) The rule will apply even though there are other executors, because the entire legal estate vests in each executor (*Re Stewart* (1908)).

(b) In *Re James* (1935) the rule was extended to **administrators**. An imperfect gift of real property made by a donor to his housekeeper was perfected when she had herself appointed as one of two administrators of his estate. The difficulty is that this decision makes the perfection of a gift rest upon the mere fortuitous chance that the donee was appointed administrator and has nothing to do with the donor's intention. In *Strong* v. *Bird* (1874) itself the rule was said to apply only to an executor and in *Re Gonin* (see below) Walton J would only have followed *Re James* with the greatest reluctance. As *Re James* is a decision at first instance the point remains open in the higher courts.
(c) The donor must intend to make an immediate *inter vivos* gift. An intention to make a testamentary gift is not enough (*Re Stewart* (1908)).
(d) There must be a *continuing* intention to make the gift. In *Re Gonin* (1979) a mother wished to leave her house to her daughter but thought that she could not do so because the daughter was illegitimate. Instead she wrote a cheque for £33,000 in the daughter's favour which was found after her death. The cheque could not be cashed as the mother's death terminated the bank's authority to pay it but the daughter, as administratrix, claimed the house under the rule in *Strong* v. *Bird*. The court held that even if the rule applied to administratrices, there was no continuing intention on the mother's part that the daughter should have the house. Instead, the giving of the cheque indicated that she should have the money instead.

The requirement of a continuing intention will likewise not be met if the donor, having intended to give property to X, later gives or lends it to Y (*Re Freeland* (1952)) or, indeed, once again treats the property as his (*Re Wale* (1956)). In neither case will X's appointment as executor or administrator perfect the gift.

See Kodlinye (1982) for a survey of the Rule in *Strong* v. *Bird*.

Donatio mortis causa (gifts in contemplation of death)

The principle of a *donatio mortis causa* (*donatio* for short) derives ultimately from Roman law but in its modern form its origin can be traced to the Statute of Frauds 1677. Previously it had been possible to make a will orally but the Statute imposed such stringent conditions on these that they passed out of use. One condition was that the will had to have been made in the last illness of the testator but there were others, such as that there had to be three witnesses present and it had to be put in writing within three days of its making. The idea of allowing the validity of a disposition made in the testator's last illness was taken up by equity, which used the doctrine of *donatio mortis causa* in order to mitigate the effect of this part of the Statute of Frauds. Thus this doctrine can be seen as another example of equity finding the means to mitigate what it felt was the severity of a statute. The practical effect is that a person is able to leave property on their death without complying with the formalities in the Wills Act 1837, and so the effect of a *donatio* is very similar to that of a secret or half secret trust. (See Chapter 8.) It should be noted that property, which is the subject of a *donatio*, could also be taken to satisfy the debts of the deceased, although only as a last resort when the assets of the estate are insufficient to pay debts.

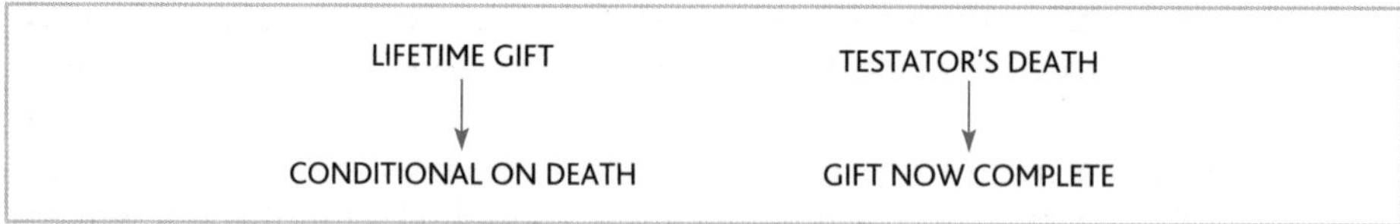

Figure 7.4 The operation of a DMC

A DMC operates in the way shown in Figure 7.4.

In *Re Beaumont* (1902) Buckley J described a *donatio mortis causa* as a gift of an amphibious nature. This is because it is neither a gift ***inter vivos*** nor a legacy. It is not an ***inter vivos*** gift because by definition these are gifts between the living. A *donatio* only takes effect on death. It is not a legacy, as it does not form part of the testator's estate. Instead it is the delivery of property in contemplation of the donor's death, and which is conditional on death and only takes effect on death.

The relationship between a will and a *donatio* is shown by Example 7.9.

Example 7.9

John has left his car by will to Jack. On his deathbed John gives it to Alice under a valid *donatio mortis causa*. The car does not belong to Alice until John's death but immediately on John's death the car does belong to Alice and so it does not form part of John's estate which is left by will. Accordingly Alice gets the car and not Jack.

In *Re Craven's Estate* (1937) Farwell J laid down three conditions for an effective *donatio* to which a fourth must be added: that the property is capable of passing by *donatio*. In practice, one would consider the fourth condition first of all.

The conditions are:

(a) There must be a clear intention to make a gift which will automatically be complete on death, but the gift may be revoked either expressly by the donor or revoked by implication should he recover. This is often expressed shortly by saying that the gift must not be absolute but only conditional on death.

However, the fact that the gift is conditional on death need not be expressly stated but may be inferred from the circumstances (*Re Lillingston* (1952)). Thus in *Northcott* v. *Public Trustee* (1955) the donor handed over her Post Office Savings Bank Book to her aunt and said 'I want you to have it now'. At the time she was dangerously ill and indeed she died the next day. It was held that there was a valid *donatio*, despite the use of the word 'now', which, by itself, indicated an absolute gift. The point seems to be that, where the donor is near death, then the courts may be prepared to imply a condition that the gift is conditional on death even though conditional words are not present and indeed the actual words used point in themselves to an absolute gift. One cannot expect precision of language from a person *in extremis*. Logically, if a person is *in extremis* and there is no hope of recovery, then there is no question of the gift being merely conditional on death as death is certain, and so there is not a valid DMC. This point was taken in the Scottish case of *Lord Advocate* v. *McCourt* (1893) but it does seem to take logic a stage too far as the effect is that the more certain death is, the less likely a *donatio* will be valid. In the two recent Court of Appeal decisions on *donatio*, *Woodard* v. *Woodard* and *Sen* v. *Hedley* (below), the donors were both clearly in the last stages of illness but the point that the gifts could not be conditional was not made.

If the gift is revoked, then the donee holds the gift as trustee for the donor. A gift will be revoked by the donor recovering dominion over it (*Bunn* v. *Markham* (1816)) or by the donee predeceasing the donor (*Tate* v. *Hilbert* (1793)) but not where the donor takes the property back for safe custody (*Re Hawkins* (1924)). However, as explained above, a *donatio* will not be revoked by the subject matter of the gift being bequeathed to another person by will because the donee's title is complete on death whereas the bequest only takes effect later (*Jones* v. *Selby* (1710)). However, in this case it was held that a *donatio* may be satisfied by a legacy to the donee, an example of the equitable doctrine of satisfaction (see Chapter 3).

(b) *The gift must be made 'in contemplation of the conceived approach of death'* (Lord Eldon in *Duffield* v. *Elwes* (1827))

The words 'conceived approach of death' mean that death is contemplated as an actual possibility in the relatively near future. Therefore, the donor must have been doing more than merely contemplating the fact that he is not immortal but, on the other hand, he need not be *in extremis* or in his last illness. In *Cain* v. *Moon* (1896) Russell CJ said that the gift must have been made 'in contemplation, though not necessarily in expectation, of death'. This seems to be a useful distinction. A person can make a valid *donatio* even though he has not, for instance, only been given a matter of hours to live. What seems to be required is that the donor should believe his death to be impending for some reason (Farwell J in *Re Craven's Estate* (1937), and in practice a *donatio* will often be made when the donor is very ill. In *Thompson* v. *Mechan* (1958) death from the ordinary risks of air travel was held to be insufficient, but contemplation of death from a surgical operation or active service in time of war is probably enough (see *dicta* in *Agnew* v. *Belfast Banking Co.* (1896)). If this requirement is satisfied then it is immaterial that death occurs from some other cause. In *Wilkes* v. *Allington* (1931) the donor was suffering from incurable cancer but in fact died in an even shorter time from pneumonia. A gift made was held valid.

In *Re Dudman* (1925) it was held that a gift in contemplation of suicide was not a valid *donatio* because suicide was then a crime. Since the passage of the Suicide Act 1961, under which this is no longer so, the position is doubtful. If, however, a gift is made in contemplation of death from some other cause but in fact the donor commits suicide there is a valid *donatio* (*Mills* v. *Shields (No. 1)* (1948)).

(c) *The donor must part with dominion over the subject matter of the gift.*

This is the vital feature of a *donatio*; the law will not accept mere words: there must be some act of handing over the goods or, where this is not possible, some other delivery such as the keys to a car (*Woodard* v. *Woodard*

(1995) – below). In older cases it was often said that 'dominion' over the goods must be transferred but this concept was never clearly explained and now in *Sen* v. *Headley* (1991) Nourse LJ helpfully said that the test was whether the 'ability to control' had been transferred. This covers not only keys to a car but also the keys to a box where the deeds of house are kept (*Sen* v. *Hedley* – below). However, as Borkowski (1999) points out, it would be better to use the word 'right to control'.

The case law can be divided as follows:

- *Chattels.* The donor must hand over the chattel itself or the means of obtaining control of it, such as the key to the box where it is. On the other hand, in *Re Craven's Estate* (1937) Farwell J said that this would not be sufficient if the donor retained a duplicate key (but see *Woodard* v. *Woodward* below), nor will it be enough if the donor parts with the box but not the key to it (*Re Johnson* (1905)). In *Woodard* v. *Woodard* (1991) the deceased, having already allowed his son to use his car and given him the keys, said to him on his deathbed in hospital 'You can keep the keys, I won't be driving it (the car) any more'. It was held that this was a valid *donatio*. The parting with the keys was enough and there was no need to have parted with the car's log book as this is not a document of title. The fact that the deceased may have had a second set of keys at home was irrelevant because he could not use them unless he made a miraculous recovery which would, in any case, revoke the gift, and it did not matter either that the son was already in possession of the car as a **bailee**.
- *Choses in action.* As physical delivery is not possible the donor must part with a document which would have to be produced in any action on the chose, even though the document does not pass the legal ownership. (If it does, the gift is perfect and there is no need to worry about whether there is an effective *donatio*.) Instances of where a particular document has been held to be sufficient are: a bank deposit passbook; a post office Savings Bank Book (both in *Birch* v. *Treasury Solicitor* (1951)); National Savings Certificates (*Darlow* v. *Sparks* (1938)); and a building society passbook (*Griffiths* v. *Abbey National BS* (1947)).

(d) *The property must be capable of passing by donatio.* For various reasons, certain types of property have been held to be incapable of passing by *donatio*. The main instances are:

- *The donor's own cheque or promissory note.* The reason for the exclusion of cheques is that the donor's death terminates the bank's authority to pay on it (*Re Beaumont* (1902)). A holder for value may sue, but in this case there will, by definition, have been a contract and the rules on *donatio* will be inapplicable. A possible exception to this rule is where a cheque is paid immediately after death before the banker has been told of the death and closed the account (*Tate* v. *Hilbert* (1793)). In this case there would be a *donatio* of the money represented by the cheque and not of the cheque itself. A promissory note is only a gratuitous promise to pay. There seems however no reason why a cheque drawn on another's account, but negotiated to the donor, cannot be the subject of a valid *donatio*.

- *Stocks and shares*. In *Re Weston* (1902) the court held that a certificate of building society shares could not be the subject of a valid *donatio* and in *Moore* v. *Moore* (1874) the same principle was applied to railway stock. This latter decision was based on *Ward* v. *Turner* (1752) which appeared to decide that South Sea Annuities could not be the subject of a valid *donatio* although it is probable that the decision turned upon the manner of the transfer and so *Moore* v. *Moore* is of doubtful authority. In *Staniland* v. *Willott* (1852) shares in a public company were held to be capable of being the subject of a valid *donatio*. There seems to be no authority on shares in private companies. This particular area is in need of clarification: there seems no good reason why a certificate of building society shares cannot be the subject of a valid *donatio* (*Re Weston* above) and yet a building society passbook can be (*Griffiths* v. *The Abbey National BS* above).

> *Note 7.5: If there has been a complete transfer of the subject matter of the* donatio, *such as the handing over of a chattel, then the* donatio *will be complete on death. If some further action is necessary to complete the transfer, as where a bank deposit book has been handed over, then prior to the completion of formalities the personal representatives of the donor will hold the legal title on trust for the donee.*

Can land be the subject of a valid donatio?

In *Duffield* v. *Elwes* (1827) Lord Eldon held that there could be a valid *donatio* of a mortgage security by delivery of the mortgage deeds and a bond but underlying his judgment was an assumption that the absolute estate could not have passed by delivery of the title deeds. Accordingly it was believed that land could not be the subject of a valid *donatio* and this principle was applied by the Supreme Court of New South Wales in *Bayliss* v. *Public Trustee* (1988). However, in *Sen* v. *Headley* (1991) the Court of Appeal has held that land can indeed be the subject of a valid *donatio* and that in such a case the land will be held on a constructive trust for the donee pending the actual transfer. The deceased had lived with the plaintiff as man and wife for some years and on his deathbed he managed to put the keys to his house into the claimant's handbag and later said 'The house is yours, Margaret. You have the keys. They are in your bag. The deeds are in the steel box'. The court held that as all the other requirements for a valid *donatio* were satisfied, there was a valid *donatio* of the house. Parting with dominion over the deeds could amount, in principle, to parting with dominion over the land itself and here this was so, especially as there was no practical possibility of the deceased ever returning home. It was possible for land to pass by *donatio* because on a *donatio* a constructive trust arose. Lord Eldon in *Duffield* v. *Elwes* (1827) had recognised that such a constructive trust could arise by operation of law and thus the formalities requirements of what is now s. 53(1)(b) of the LPA 1925 do not apply because a constructive trust of land can arise without the need for written evidence (s. 53(2) LPA 1925). As Nourse LJ observed, the constructive trust has been 'a ready means of developing our property law in modern times and that . . . process is a continuing one' (see also Chapter 11). A close parallel can be observed here with secret trusts (see Chapter 8) which also take effect under a constructive trust and which are also ways of making a transfer without complying with the formalities prescribed for the making of wills. What would have been the position though if the land had been registered? Would the handing over of the Title Information Document have been sufficient?

Proving a *donatio*

There are no clear rules of evidence as to how a *donatio* must be proved. This might seem surprising given that there is the obvious temptation on the part of an unscrupulous person who is present at the bedside of a dying person to allege that a *donatio* was made to them. The courts do look very carefully at the evidence but there have been cases (e.g. *Sen* v. *Headley*) where the court accepted the uncorroborated evidence of the donee that there had been a *donatio* to them.

The future of *donatio mortis causa*

Nourse LJ in *Sen* v. *Hedley* observed: 'Let it be agreed that the doctrine (of *donatio mortis causa*) is anomalous'. Moreover, he later said 'Every such gift (by *donatio*) is a circumvention of the Wills Act 1837'. Here are the issues in a nutshell: the doctrine of *donatio* is undoubtedly anomalous and, moreover, it operates in direct contradiction to a statutory provision. This latter point has never bothered equity much and indeed the same objection could be made to the doctrine of secret and half secret trusts. It has been suggested (see the discussion in Borkowski) that the doctrine could be confined to property below a certain value. The fixing of an arbitrary upper limit seems wrong in principle and a better idea could be to have a presumption against a *donatio* unless it could be shown that the donor had no reasonable alternative means of disposing of the gift.

Proprietary estoppel

An imperfect gift may be perfected by the operation of this doctrine as shown in Example 7.10.

Example 7.10

X owns a piece of land and says to Y 'You can have it as a market garden'. Y takes over the land and develops it as a market garden but the land is never conveyed to him. X later attempts to turn Y out.

Here the gift is imperfect because of the lack of a conveyance but the injustice of allowing a person in X's position to rely on this may be remedied by the doctrine of proprietary estoppel. This, in brief, applies where one party (X) encourages another (Y) to act to his detriment by infringing some legal rights of X's while under a mistaken belief as to his own rights. This encouragement may be either positive or mere acquiescence.

The doctrine is considered in more detail in Chapter 10.

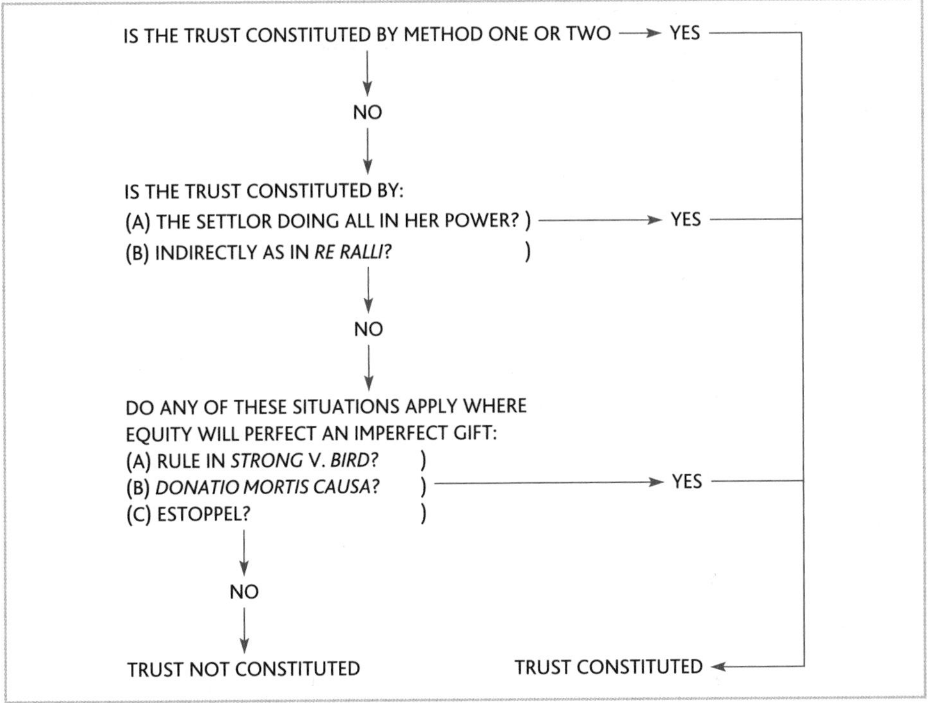

Figure 7.5 Summary of the rules on constitution of a trust

Statutory exceptions to the principle that an imperfect gift cannot be perfected

(a) As a minor cannot hold a legal estate in land (s. 1(6) LPA 1925) a conveyance of such an estate to him is by itself imperfect. However by s. 27(1) of the Settled Land Act (SLA) 1925 such a conveyance operates as an agreement for valuable consideration to execute a settlement in the minor's favour and meanwhile to hold the land in trust for him.

(b) A settlement, which fails to comply with the requirements of the SLA, may be perfected by the trustees, at the request of the tenant for life or the statutory owner, executing a principal vesting deed.

FURTHER READING

Borkowski (1999) *Deathbed Gifts*, London: Blackstone Press. Contains a summary of every significant case on this area as well as being a fascinating account of this branch of the law.

Doggett (2003) 'Explaining *Re Rose*; the search goes on', 62 CLJ 263. Looks at recent cases in this area.

Garton (2003) 'The role of the trust mechanism in the Rule in *Re Rose*', Conv. 364. Another look at recent cases.

Halliwell (2003) 'Perfecting imperfect gifts and trusts: have we reached the end of the Chancellor's foot?' Conv. 192. Yet another look at the recent cases.

Kodilinye (1982) 'A fresh look at the Rule in *Strong* v. *Bird*', Conv. 14. A useful account of the origin and development of this rule.

CHAPTER SUMMARY

- Two methods of constituting a trust.
- Method One: transfer of trust property by settlor to trustee(s).
- Method Two: settlor declares herself a trustee.
- Position of beneficiaries where trust not constituted.
- Indirect constitution – *Re Ralli*.
- Cases where the settlor can only do what is in her power to do.
- Three cases where equity will perfect an imperfect gift.

QUESTION

Fred had been told by his doctor, Mark, that he had an incurable illness and had only three months to live. He summoned three close friends, Barbara, Michael and Catherine, to see him and told them that as they had been faithful friends he would like to give them each something.

(a) He handed over his share certificates in Midland Optical Illusion Co to Barbara.
(b) He handed over a cheque for £2,000, drawn in Michael's favour, to Michael.
(c) He said to Catherine: 'The title deeds to my house are in that strong box over there. Here is the key to it. The house is now yours'.

Two weeks later Fred was killed in a plane crash. His will left all his property to Steve.

Advise Barbara, Michael and Catherine as to their entitlements, if any, to Fred's property.

> *Note 7.6: You will find suggested points for inclusion in these answers in Appendix 2.*

8 Secret and half-secret trusts: mutual wills

INTRODUCTION: SECRET AND HALF-SECRET TRUSTS

A secret trust arises where a will states that property is left to a beneficiary as an absolute gift, but the testator has agreed with the beneficiary that the beneficiary is to hold the property as trustee. There is therefore no mention in the will of any trust.

A **half-secret trust** arises where property is left by will to a beneficiary and the will states that the beneficiary is to hold on trust but the terms of the trust are not declared in the will. Instead the terms of the trust are agreed between the testator and the beneficiary. Therefore here the will mentions the existence of a trust but not the terms of the trust.

Example 8.1
Example of a secret trust

A clause in John's will states: 'I leave £1,000 to Albert Smith absolutely'. However, John had told Albert that he was to hold the £1,000 on trust for John's friend, Sarah. This is a secret trust as the will makes no mention of it and it appears to be an absolute gift.

Example 8.2
Example of a half-secret trust

A clause in Barbara's will states: 'I leave £1,000 to Steve Jones on trust'. Barbara had told Steve that he was to hold the £1,000 on trust for Michael. This is a half-secret trust as the fact that it is a trust in mentioned is the will but not the details.

The will may not use the term 'trust'. This does not prevent there from being a trust: the test, as always in deciding intention to create a trust, is whether a person is put under the obligations of a trustee. For example, the words above may read: 'I leave £1,000 to Steve Jones to carry out the purposes which I have mentioned to him'. This can still be a half-secret trust provided that there is sufficient certainty of intention to create a trust. This is the kind of point which a good examination candidate will pick up: Taking the words used in the will, do they show sufficient intention?

This chapter will first explain the requirements for the validity of these trusts and will then consider the basis on which equity enforces them and the reasons why they are used.

REQUIREMENTS FOR THE VALIDITY OF A SECRET TRUST

In *Ottaway* v. *Norman* (1972) Brightman J held that the following requirements must be proved:

(a) **The intention** of the testator to subject the primary donee (i.e. the intended trustee) to an obligation in favour of the secondary donee (i.e. the intended beneficiary). In *Kasperbauer* v. *Griffith* (2000) Peter Gibson J emphasised that all three certainties must be satisfied.
(b) **Communication** of that intention to the primary donee.
(c) **Acceptance** of the obligation by the primary donee either expressly or by acquiescence.

Although this basis has been criticised because it suggests that a testator could, as it were, 'contract out' of the Wills Act, there seems little doubt that these requirements must in themselves be present, although taken together it may be argued that they do indeed give the impression of contracting out of the Wills Act. It is now proposed to examine each requirement in turn.

The intention of the testator

The principle here is the same as with any form of trust: there must be certainty of intention. Mere precatory words are not enough (see *Knight* v. *Knight* (1840) and Chapter 5). It is illustrated in the context of secret trusts by *McCormick* v. *Grogan* (1869). A letter from the testator to the sole beneficiary gave details about an intended secret trust but said 'I do not wish you to act strictly on the foregoing instructions, but leave it entirely to your own good judgment to do as you think I would, if living, and as the parties are deserving'. It was held that these words did not impose a trust. Similarly in *Re Snowden* (1979) the testatrix left the residue of her estate to her brother and there was evidence that she wanted him to 'split it up as he thought best' although there was also evidence that she wanted him to divide it equally between her nephews and nieces. It was held that this evidence did not establish the existence of a trust. A recent example is *Margulies* v. *Margulies* (2000). Here the testator had intended to disinherit one of his sons (X) but then wrote letters to his solicitor which were evidence that he had changed his mind. He wrote to X that the solicitor and another son were 'aware of my wishes and added that "I hope that you will find it possible to communicate with them in the future since they, as well as I, have your best interests at heart"'. It was held that these words did not amount to a trust. As Nourse LJ observed: 'Wishes are suggestive of language in precatory, not imperative form. In *Gold* v. *Hill* (1998) (below) the words used were 'look after Carol and the kids' and these were sufficient.

What types of obligation can be imposed?

A secret trust normally imposes an obligation to hold property on trust for another but the obligation on the trustee can be to make provision for beneficiaries after his own death. Thus in *Re Gardner (No. 1)* (1920) a wife left property to her husband for his life and thereafter to be held on a secret trust for certain beneficiaries. (The death of one of these beneficiaries before the wife was the cause of the litigation in *Re Gardner (No. 2)* (1923) (see above).) In *Ottaway* v. *Norman* (1972) the testator left his bungalow to her housekeeper but there was a secret trust whereby she should leave it, together with certain other property, by will to the testator's son and his wife.

Communication of the testator's intention

The fact that he is to hold the property on trust, and the details of the trust, must be communicated to the legatee before the testator's death (*Wallgrave* v. *Tebbs* (1855)). It does not matter whether communication is before or after the will and it can be made through the testator's authorised agent (*Moss* v. *Cooper* (1861)). If the existence of the trust is not communicated to the intended trustee until after the testator's death then he will take beneficially, as happened in *Wallgrave* v. *Tebbs* (1855), unless he had accepted the position of a trustee, in which case it would be fraudulent for him to take beneficially, and he will hold on a resulting trust for the testator's estate.

What is the position where the existence but not the detail of the trust is communicated before the testator's death? In *Re Boyes* (1884) it was held that the legatee held on a resulting trust for the testator's estate. As the legatee had been told of the existence of the trust it would be fraudulent for him to take beneficially. However, it appears that the secret trust can be enforced if the legatee is not actually told its details *before* the testator's death but is told where to find them *after* his death, for example, by the testator giving him a sealed envelope with the details. In *Re Keen* (1937) Lord Wright drew an analogy with the case of a ship 'which sails under sealed orders', and is therefore 'sailing under orders though the exact terms are not ascertained by the captain till later'. However, *Re Keen* did not in the end turn on this precise point which can still, to some degree, be considered open.

(a) *Position where the testator intends to impose a secret trust on more than one person, but does not communicate the trust to all persons.* In *Re Stead* (1900) Farwell J distinguished between where a gift is made to joint tenants and to tenants in common. He held that:

  (i) If the gift is made to tenants in common then any secret trust imposed will only be binding on those to whom it is communicated. The rest take beneficially.

  (ii) If the gift is made to joint tenants then if the secret trust is communicated and accepted by some joint tenants before the will is made then all are bound. If, however, the communication and acceptance take place after the will but before the testator's death then only those joint tenants to whom the trust was communicated and accepted are bound. The others take beneficially. This is what happened in *Re Stead* (1900).

Example 8.3

X leaves property by will to Y and Z in equal shares and tells Y (but not Z) that both Y and Z are to hold in trust for W. Y and Z are tenants in common because the words 'in equal shares' are words of severance (*Payne* v. *Webb* (1874)). Thus Y is bound by the trust but Z is not.

Example 8.4

X leaves property by will to Y and Z and tells Y, but not Z, that Y and Z are to hold the property on trust for W. Y and Z are joint tenants because there are no words of severance. Thus whether Z is bound depends on if X communicated the secret trust in favour of W to Y before he made his will. If he did, then Z is bound. If he did not, Z is not bound and takes beneficially.

The position can also be illustrated as in Figure 8.1.

These rules in *Re Stead* (1900) do not seem to rest on any clear principle and Perrins (1972) has persuasively argued that the decision is not supported by the cases upon which Farwell J relied. Instead, the correct rule is that enunciated in *Huguenin* v. *Baseley* (1807) that 'no man may profit by the fault of another'. The question to be asked is whether the gift (as in the above example) to Z was **induced** by Y's promise that both he and Z would hold the property in trust for W. The practical significance of this, according to Perrins (1972), is that if the secret trust is communicated to and accepted by Y after the will is made, then it will become very difficult to show that the gift to Z (and Y) in the will already made was induced by Y's subsequent promise. Thus Z is likely to take beneficially.

(b) *Position where the trust is communicated but a later addition or alteration to it is not.* In *Re Cooper* (1939) a testator communicated a secret trust in respect of £5,000 which he had left to trustees but failed to tell them of a later codicil increasing the sum to £10,000. The extra £5,000 was held to go on a resulting

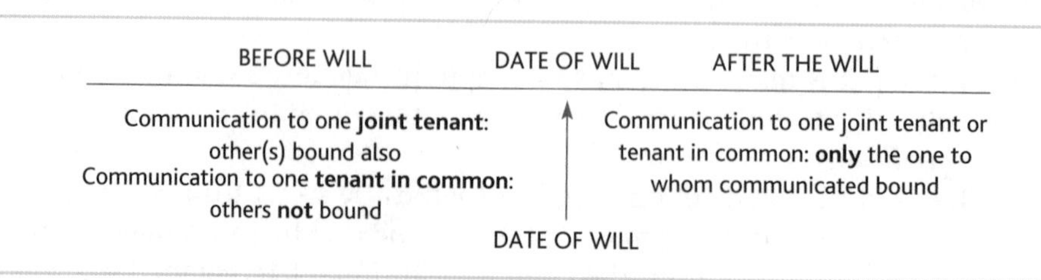

BEFORE WILL
DATE OF WILL
AFTER THE WILL
Communication to one joint tenant: other(s) bound also
Communication to one tenant in common: others not bound
Communication to one joint tenant or tenant in common: only the one to whom communicated bound
DATE OF WILL

Figure 8.1 Communication of the testator's intention

trust for the testator's estate. Greene MR observed that it might have been different had the later codicil stipulated a lesser sum or if there had been a trifling difference (or if the testator had said '£5,000 or whatever sum I may hereafter choose to **bequeath**'). In each case the trustees would probably be bound by the sum in the codicil.

Where the secret trustee predeceases the testator the position is probably as stated in *Re Maddock* (1902) where Cozens-Hardy LJ said *obiter* that the trust would fail because the existence of the trust depends on the personal obligation imposed on the trustee. The same may apply if the trustee disclaims.

Acceptance of the trust

In *Wallgrave* v. *Tebbs* (1855) it was held that the testator could accept the trust if he either 'expressly promises, or by silence implies, that he will carry the testator's intention into effect'.

REQUIREMENTS FOR THE VALIDITY OF A HALF-SECRET TRUST

The rules on the testator's intention and on acceptance of the trust which apply to secret trusts (see above) apply also to half-secret trusts.

Communication of a half-secret trust

Here the position is different from that in secret trusts and, to make matters worse, the law here is confused. There are three possible rules:

Rule 1. Communication must be in accordance with the terms of the will so that if the will says 'on trusts the details of which have been communicated by me' then a communication after the will would be invalid.

Rule 2. The will itself must not refer to the possibility of a future communication.

Rule 3. Communication must, irrespective of what the terms of the will are, occur before or at the time of the making of the will.

Thus if Rule 1 applies, communication can be before or after the will, provided that it is in accordance with the terms of the will, whereas if Rule 2 applies, communication must be at or before the making of the will and in addition the will itself must not allow for the possibility of a later communication. Thus even if communication was before the will, then if Rule 2 applied it would not be valid if the will itself allowed for the possibility of communication after the will.

In *Johnson* v. *Ball* (1851) the will referred to a letter which had been signed containing trusts and yet in fact communication was after the will. It was held that, in accordance with Rule 1, communication was invalid as being inconsistent with the terms of the will. In *Blackwell* v. *Blackwell* (1929), which was the first case to definitely establish the validity of half secret trusts, the trusts had been communicated before the will and the will itself referred to a previous communication by the use of the words 'indicated by me to them'. Thus on both Rules 1, 2 and 3 above, communication was valid. The main source of confusion is *Re Keen* (1937). A testator gave £10,000 to trustees to hold on trust and to be 'disposed of by them among such person, persons or charities as may be notified by me to them . . . during my lifetime'. One of the trustees had previously been given a sealed envelope containing the name of the beneficiary which he did not open until after the testator's death, although he was aware that it contained the beneficiary's name. The Court of Appeal held that, had the rules on communication been complied with in other ways, the fact that the envelope was not opened until after the testator's death would not have made communication of the trust invalid. However, communication was invalid and Wright MR gave the following reasons for this:

(a) The words 'to be notified by me' indicated a future communication and this was invalid because the testator would be giving himself power to make dispositions after he had made his will which were informal rather than by a duly attested codicil. (This was an application of Rule 2 above.)
(b) The actual communication was before the will and was thus inconsistent with its terms which indicated a future communication (application of Rule 1 above).

In *Re Spence* (1949) the issue was decided on the basis of Rule 1. Here the testator left property to four persons 'to be dealt with in accordance with *my* wishes which I have made known to them'. As he had not communicated with all of them it was held that communication was inconsistent with the terms of the will and thus ineffective. In *Re Bateman's Will Trust* (1970) the will used the words 'shall be stated by me' in referring to the time of communication of the details of the trust and it was held that, in accordance with Rule 2, this was invalid although there was no evidence about whether communication had already been made. In the Irish case of *Re Prendiville* (1990) the court restated the rule in Irish law (*Re Browne* (1944)) that there is no difference in the rules on communication of both secret and half-secret trusts and therefore communication of a half-secret trust can take place at any time up to the testator's death. Thus in *Re Prendiville* the court refused to follow *Re Keen* although on the facts of *Re Prendiville* it was not clear when communication had taken place. It may be noted that in most American states and also in some Australian jurisdictions the rule is the same as for secret trusts: communication can be up to the time of death. A good recent example is the Australian case of *Ledgerwood* v. *Perpetual Trustee* (1997) where Young J held that communication could take place after the date of the will.

It is often said that the correct rule is Rule 3, that communication must be at or before the making of the will, although none of the cases was decided on this point alone. The true rule is still an open question in the House of Lords and possibly in the Court of Appeal, also in view of the uncertainty of the precise ratio of *Re Keen* (1937). Rule 3 itself rests on an observation in *Blackwell* v. *Blackwell* (1929) by Viscount Sumner, who said that 'A testator cannot reserve to himself a power of making future unwitnessed dispositions by merely naming a trustee and leaving the purposes of the trust to be supplied afterwards'. This was, however, *obiter*, because, as we saw above, communication here was before the will. There was *dicta* to the same effect by Parker V-C in *Johnson* v. *Ball* (1851).

The problem is that both Rules 1 and 2 are concerned with the relationship between the communication of the trust and the terms of the will. The justification which Wright MR gave for Rule 1, which was that the testator should not give himself a power to make future unwitnessed dispositions, is questionable in view of the clear rule that secret trusts operate *dehors* the will.

Rule 3 seems to depend on the probate doctrine of incorporation by reference under which a testator can incorporate a document into his will that has not been duly executed. This is, however, subject to the requirement that the document must already be in existence at the date of the will and also be referred to in the will as being already in existence. Thus in *Re the Goods of Smart* (1935) the will directed the trustees to give specified articles to 'such of my friends as I may designate in a book . . .' This was invalid as the will referred to a future document and did not refer to it already being in existence at the date of the will.

It is difficult to see why the rules for secret and half-secret trusts should be different and it is to be hoped that the courts will change these rules so that they are the same for both types of trust. One telling reason in favour of having the same rule is the simple one that, as a will can be revoked at any time until death and thus does not take effect until then, why should any other document, such as one containing details of secret or half-secret trusts, be subject to rules which insist that validity is to be decided at an earlier date?

On the assumption, which represents the majority view today, that the correct rule is Rule 3, then the communication requirements for a valid secret and half-secret trust can be summarised as in Figure 8.2.

A codicil to a will, in the absence of any contrary intention on the part of the testator, has the effect of republishing that will. Accordingly the date of the will is now the date of the codicil with the result that, at the date of the codicil, the testator will have made a new will together with the alterations in the codicil (*Re Champion* (1893)). If a testator executes a will where there is a half-secret trust and subsequently communicates the details of that trust to the trustee, then communication may be invalid as being after the will. If, however, that testator then executed a codicil to his will then communication would automatically have now been made before the will and so communication would be valid. There is no rational principle here and it is suggested that this is another reason for applying the same rules on communication of a secret trust to half-secret trusts also.

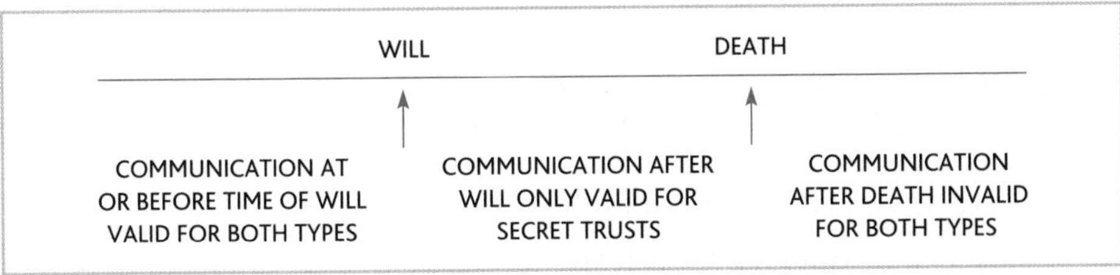

Figure 8.2 Effect of a later codicil on the time of communication

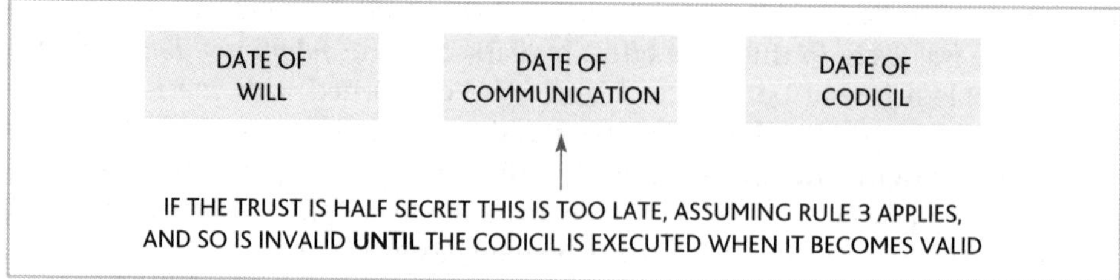

Figure 8.3 Half-secret trusts and Rule 3

BASIS ON WHICH EQUITY ENFORCES SECRET AND HALF-SECRET TRUSTS

The origin of the equitable jurisdiction to enforce secret trusts dates from immediately after the passage of the Statute of Frauds in 1677 which imposed formal requirements even on oral wills of more than £3 in value and also on declarations of trusts of land. What seems to have happened soon after is that testators started to attempt to avoid these provisions by leaving property to a particular person but to impose a trust on them to hold it for the benefit of others. The first reported case is *Thynn* v. *Thynn* (1684).

There are three possible explanations for why the courts enforce secret and half-secret trusts:

Prevention of fraud

This appears to have been the original justification. The courts felt that, if they were to allow devices such as these, which disregarded statutory provisions, a compelling reason was needed which could only be found in the need to prevent fraud and this is clearly seen in the judgment of Guildford LC in *Thynn* v. *Thynn* (above).

Example 8.5

X leaves property absolutely by will to Y but tells Y that he is to hold it as trustee for Z. If Y is able to disregard X's wishes because of the lack of compliance with the statutory formalities and so keep the property himself he would be using a statute (i.e. the Wills Act) as 'an engine of fraud'; something which equity has always striven to prevent.

The clearest statement of the principle is found in the speech of Lord Westbury in *McCormick* v. *Grogan* (1869): 'the jurisdiction which is involved here is founded altogether on personal fraud'.

There are two problems with this principle:

(i) A jurisdiction based on fraud is indeed a reason why the intended trustee should not take beneficially but is not by itself a reason why the secret or half-secret trust should be enforced in favour of the beneficiaries. A resulting trust in favour of the testator's estate would achieve the desired result. A possible way round the difficulty is to give the word fraud a wider meaning as fraud on the beneficiaries through their not receiving their entitlement under the trust. The point seems to have been recognised by Lord Buckmaster in *Blackwell* v. *Blackwell* (1929): 'the trustee is not at liberty to suppress the evidence of the trust . . . in fraud of the beneficiaries'.

(ii) The notion of the prevention of personal fraud as a justification breaks down altogether in the case of half-secret trusts where, because of their existence being declared in the will, there is no possibility of the intended trustee taking beneficially. The will states that he is a trustee. The reason for this problem is that the validity of half-secret trusts was not accepted until *Blackwell* v. *Blackwell* in 1929, after the fraud theory had been established.

In *Re Snowden* (1979) Megarry V-C, whilst recognising that these are cases where fraud is involved, held that 'it is now clear that secret trusts may be established where there is no possibility of fraud'. The fraud theory, as the sole justification of the enforcement of these trusts, no longer seems to be tenable.

Valid declaration of *inter vivos* trust

The modern view is that secret and half-secret trusts are enforced simply because the testator validly declared an *inter vivos* trust and on the testator's death this trust became completely constituted by the property vesting in the trustee. Their essence is therefore the acceptance by the legatee of a personal obligation. Thus Lord Warrington in *Blackwell* v. *Blackwell* said: 'what is enforced is not a trust imposed by the will but one arising from the acceptance by the legatee of a trust communicated to him by the testator on the faith of which acceptance the will was made or left unrevoked'. Even so, there are problems with this theory particularly in connection with the observance of the formalities provisions (see below). However, the theory does account for not imposing a resulting trust because the effect of this would usually be that the testator's family received the property which, if the testator had intended to benefit a mistress or an illegitimate child, would run counter to the obligations imposed on the legatee.

Remedial constructive trust

In the New Zealand case of *Brown* v. *Pourau* (1995) Hammond J held that the old fraud theory should no longer be used as a justification for secret trusts. Instead it should be based on the remedial constructive trust with the result that the legatee will hold the property on a remedial constructive trust to give effect to the (secret) trust placed on him. Remedial constructive trusts are discussed in Chapter 11.

The whole basis on which secret trusts are enforced has most recently been examined by Critchley (1999), who concludes that the fraud theory is still a possible justification for their enforcement but only if certain conditions are met.

WHY ARE SECRET AND HALF-SECRET TRUSTS USED?

There are two main reasons why testators may chose to use secret or half-secret trusts:

(a) A will is a public document and a testator may not wish a particular bequest to be known. An obvious example is a bequest to a mistress of whose existence his family was unaware.
(b) In the case of a secret trust the testator, having made his will, can then alter its terms at any time before his death simply by communicating with the trustee. This advantage does not apply to half-secret trusts (see *Re Keen* (1937) below).

The effect of these trusts is to enable a testator to avoid the formalities required by the Wills Act 1837 (as amended by s. 17 of the Administration of Justice Act 1982). An instruction to a trustee of a secret or half-secret trust can, on the other hand, be oral or, even if it is in writing, there is no need to comply with the requirements of the Wills Act. Thus in *Re Young* (1951) the beneficiary under a half-secret trust had witnessed the will in which the existence of the trust was declared. The rule that a witness to a will cannot normally take a legacy (Wills Act 1837 s. 15) was held not to apply here because the beneficiary did not take by virtue of the gift in the will but by virtue of the half-secret trust. The result would, of course, have been the same had the trust been secret. This point is often expressed by saying that secret and half-secret trusts take effect *'dehors'* (outside of) the will.

Attestation of a will by a trustee of a half-secret trust should not affect the validity of the legacy and therefore of the trust because he is not a beneficiary on the face of the will (*Cresswell* v. *Cresswell* (1868)). However, a trustee of a fully secret trust does take beneficially on the face of the will and the position where he attests is uncertain. The principle in *Re Young* (1951) may apply so that the legacy and therefore the trust are saved or it may be held that the legacy is ineffective and so the trust fails through lack of subject matter.

In *Re Gardner (No. 2)* (1923) one of the beneficiaries under a secret trust predeceased the testatrix but it was held that the share of the deceased beneficiary did not lapse but passed to her personal representative. However, had the gift been made by will her share would have lapsed and fallen into residue. Although this decision clearly illustrates the point that secret and half-secret trusts operate '*dehors* the will', it has been doubted in most of the leading textbooks and may well be wrong. Romer J explained his decision on the basis that the beneficiary acquired an interest as soon as the trustee had accepted the secret trust, but this conflicts with the principle that a beneficiary acquires no interest under a trust until it has been completely constituted (see *Milroy* v. *Lord* (1862) and Chapter 7). It is impossible to reconcile these two propositions and thus it is doubtful if *Re Gardner* would be followed.

SECRET AND HALF-SECRET TRUSTS IN SITUATIONS OTHER THAN WILLS

Intestacy

Although the case law is concerned with secret trusts arising under wills, there is no reason why they cannot arise under intestacy.

Example 8.6

Amanda says to her sister, Dawn: 'I am thinking of making a will but I really haven't the time or money to see a solicitor about it. As you are my only relative you will get everything on my death but I want you to hold my property on trust for the following friends of mine, each of whom is to have an equal share'. Amanda then tells Dawn the names of the friends who are to benefit. Dawn agrees to this.

There seems no reason why a secret trust should not arise in these circumstances. (See *Sellack* v. *Harris* (1708).)

On an inter vivos transfer of property

Can a secret or a half-secret trust arise on an *inter vivos* transfer of property? In *Re Tyler* (1967) Pennycuick J indicated that they can only arise where the transfer is by will although it is not clear why this should be so. In *Gold* v. *Hill* (1998) the doctrine of secret trusts was applied to a nomination under which the deceased nominated Gold to receive benefits payable on his death under an insurance policy. The deceased told Gold that he was going to Nigeria on work which could be risky and that 'If anything happens to me you will have to sort things out – you know what to do – look after Carol [his mistress] and the kids. Don't let that bitch [his wife] get anything'. It was held that this created Gold a constructive trustee of the proceeds of the policy by analogy with the doctrine of secret trusts. In the Australian case of *Russell* v. *Scott* (1936) a secret trust arose when a joint bank account was opened in the names of A and B, with money contributed by A only, but with the intention that any money remaining at A's death should belong to B. Although the court did not describe this as a secret trust the effect was the same as if a trust had been declared by A (see Critchley (1999)).

Standard of proof required

In *Re Snowden* (1979) Megarry V-C indicated that there were two possible standards of proof required to establish the existence of a secret or half-secret trust:

(i) If fraud is alleged then a high standard is required. In *McCormick* v. *Grogan* (1869) Lord Westbury had referred to the need 'to show clearly and most distinctly' that the intended trustee acted *in malo anima* (in bad faith).
(ii) If there is no fraud then the standard is the ordinary civil standard of proof required to establish the existence of a trust, i.e. a balance of probabilities.

OTHER RULES APPLICABLE ONLY TO HALF-SECRET TRUSTS

(a) The trustee cannot take beneficially if the intended trust fails. Unlike secret trusts (see *Wallgrave* v. *Tebbs* (1855) above) the trustee of a half-secret trust cannot take beneficially if the trust fails because of lack of compliance with the communication requirements. As he has been named as trustee he will hold on a resulting trust for the testator's estate. An interesting but as yet unresolved issue is the position where he is himself the residuary legatee.

(b) Where the trustee under a half-secret trust predeceases the testator the probability is that the trust will not fail (*Re Smirthwaite's Trusts* (1871)), the basis of this rule probably being the maxim that a trust does not fail for want of a trustee. The trustee's personal representatives would then become trustees.

QUESTIONS APPLICABLE TO BOTH SECRET AND HALF-SECRET TRUSTS

(a) Can the trustee take beneficially under the trust?

 (i) The will may make it clear that the trust does not apply to the whole of the legacy and that therefore a person is a trustee of only part and a legatee of another part. It may be, however, that the legacy is conditional on the person performing his obligations as a trustee (see *Irvine* v. *Sullivan* (1869)).

 (ii) The will may not refer to a beneficial gift to the trustee who may however seek to prove such a gift by reference to extrinsic evidence. In *Re Rees* (1950) the court refused to allow evidence to be admitted that the trustees were intended, after certain payments had been made, to hold any surplus for themselves. The court appeared to find that a trust was imposed on the whole amount and so refused to allow evidence that would conflict with this by giving the trustees a gift of part. It may have been influenced by the fact that the trustee was the testator's solicitor, who had drafted the will. In *Re Tyler's Fund Trusts* (1967) while finding on the facts that no beneficial gift was intended in this case, Pennycuick J confessed that he found difficulty with *Re Rees* and it seems that in principle extrinsic evidence is admissible unless it is clear from the will that the *whole property* is to be held on trust, as in *Re Rees*.

(b) Are secret and half-secret trusts express or constructive?

If these trusts are express, then do the requirements of s. 53(1)(b) of the LPA 1925 apply so that written evidence is required? If they are constructive, then such evidence is not required (s. 53(2) LPA 1925).

The point is uncertain although in *Ottaway* v. *Norman* (1972) a secret trust of land was upheld despite the lack of written evidence. It may well be that, if the rationale of these trusts is the prevention of fraud, they are constructive. However, as they are created by the express declaration of the trustee, they may also be express although presumably not subject to the requirements of the Wills Act. In the New Zealand case of *Brown* v. *Pourau* (1995) (see above) it was held that these are constructive trusts.

MUTUAL WILLS

Mutual wills are where two people (usually husband and wife), having mutually agreed that the same person(s) should have their property after they are both dead, make separate wills, usually in which they leave property to each other, but which have the essential characteristic that there is a gift to the same agreed beneficiary. Each party's will is often in similar terms but there seems no reason why this should always be so. Note that the parties do not *have* to be husband and wife (*Walpole* v. *Orford* (1797)).

Example 8.7

A husband, George, and wife, Mary, agree that George will make a will in which he will leave £10,000 standing in a bank account in his name to Mary for life with remainder to the X charity, and that Mary will make a will leaving £10,000 to George for life with remainder to Y charity. If George is the first testator to die, then Mary will receive the £10,000 but will only have a life interest and will then hold it on trust for the X charity. To allow Mary to take the £10,000 but not to require her to hold the remainder on trust for X charity would be a fraud on George as well as on the X charity. The same will apply if Mary dies first.

In practice a mutual will is often less complex: it leaves the whole estate, or the residuary estate, of the testator to the survivor with a proviso that after their death it shall pass to their children.

In *Re Dale* (1993) Morrit J held that the doctrine of mutual wills could also apply where the second testator (Mary in the above example) receives no personal benefit under the will of the first testator (i.e. George). The first testator has performed his part of the agreement by making his will in the manner promised in it and so it would be a fraud on him to allow the second testator to ignore that agreement. In this case the testators were parents who had made identical wills in favour of their two children leaving them their property equally. After the death of the father, the mother made a new will in which one child, the plaintiff, would inherit only £300 and the other, the defendant, would inherit all the rest.

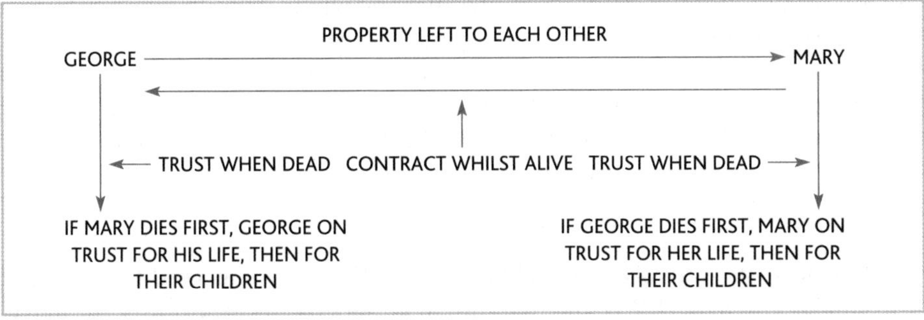

Figure 8.4 A mutual will

The court held, on a preliminary issue, that the doctrine of mutual wills applied, under which, the mother having died, the defendant would hold the mother's estate as trustee for both the plaintiff and the defendant in equal shares.

If the wills are not mutual then the doctrine will not apply, as in *Goodchild* v. *Goodchild* (1997) where, although the husband and wife had executed identical wills, there was no evidence that this was as a result of an agreement not to revoke them. However, the court felt that as the mother had left the estate to the father in the, albeit mistaken, belief that he would be legally bound by their agreement that the property would ultimately go to their son, this created a moral obligation on the father. Thus the court could award the son maintenance out of the estate under the Inheritance (Provision for Family and Dependants) Act 1975. As the son was an adult and able to look after himself, this would not normally have been ordered but the existence of the mother's belief tipped the scales in his favour.

While George and Mary are still alive the situation is one of contract: the revocation by either of them without notice to the other of a will made in pursuance of the agreement will be a breach of contract and damages will be payable by the party in breach. Thus in *Healey* v. *Brown* (2002) it was emphasised that when there is a lifetime disposition in breach of the agreement then the duty crystallises. An action for breach can be brought by the survivor, as a party, and possibly also by a beneficiary if the Contracts (Rights of Third Parties) Act 1999 applies and if the agreement was entered into on or after 11 May 2000, as the Act does not apply to contracts entered into before this date. (The Act is dealt with in more detail in Chapter 7 but, briefly, the agreement must be capable of being construed as conferring a benefit on the third party.) The same applies if the breach consists of a refusal by a party to make a will. If the breach becomes apparent only after the death of a party, when it is found that he has not left a will in accordance with the agreement, then damages can be recovered from his estate as in *Robinson* v. *Ommanney* (1883). However, it is not clear how damages would be calculated in these cases. In *Re Parkin* (1892) Stirling J referred to the possibility also of an action for specific performance to complete the transfer of the property. However, no action can be brought to restrain the actual revocation of the will because wills are always revocable (*Re Hey's Estate* (1914)). It is doubtful whether an action in contract can be brought where the will is revoked by the marriage of one of the testators. Marriage automatically revokes a will (Wills Act 1837, s. 18) and thus it could be argued that the will is revoked by operation of law and not by the voluntary act of a party. Yet surely marriage is a voluntary act? An action can obviously not be brought where the parties have, by mutual agreement, agreed to end the contract, nor can the intended beneficiaries bring an action unless the Contracts (Rights of Third Parties) Act 1999 applies.

Liability of the survivor: trust

The law of trusts is involved at a slightly later stage when, as Lord Camden put it in *Dufour* v. *Pereira* (1769), 'he that dies first, does by his death carry the agreement on his part into execution. If the other then refuses, he is guilty of a fraud

. . . and becomes a trustee of course'. Once the first testator has died, leaving an unrevoked will made in pursuance of the agreement, then 'the survivor will be treated as holding the property on trust to apply it so as to carry out the effect' (of the mutual will) (Clauson J in *Re Hagger* (1930)). Similarly, in the recent case of *Healey* v. *Brown* (2002) it was emphasised that the duty 'crystallises on death'. Thus in the above example if George dies first, then Mary holds his £10,000 in a bank account on trust for the X charity. If, however, George has broken the agreement by executing a new will revoking the one made under the agreement, then on George's death no trust was in existence, although, as explained above, there may be contractual remedies. Suppose that Mary, after George's death, herself makes a new will in different terms? Although, as mentioned above, she cannot be restrained from making a new will, her personal representatives will still hold her property that was the subject of the agreement on trust for the intended beneficiary. It should finally be noted that there is some authority for saying that the trust arises at a later stage only when the survivor receives the benefit under the first will, which would accord with the notion of these trusts being constructive (see below). Yet even if this is so, the trust will relate back to the death of the first to die.

Proof of an agreement

Merely because, for instance, a husband and wife have made wills in similar terms does not by itself mean that they have made an agreement in the terms which we have been discussing. An agreement must be proved on the ordinary civil standard of a balance of probabilities. In *Re Oldham* (1925) wills were made by a husband and wife in similar terms but there was no evidence of any agreement not to revoke them and, in addition, they had left their property to each other 'absolutely'. The evidence of intention to make mutual wills was held to be insufficient. On the other hand, in *Re Cleaver* (1981) an elderly couple who had married late in life made wills in each other's favour and in default of survival to the testator's three children in equal shares. They then each reduced the interest of one child to a life interest after the testator's death. The testatrix made a will in similar terms. Although the testatrix made two later wills in different terms it was held that evidence of mutual wills was established by the similarity of the original wills, the fact that both then reduced the interest of one child, and the conformity of the testatrix's will made after her husband's death with the previous one.

The express terms of the will may clarify which property is included in the trust but if they do not then:

(a) The trust undoubtedly includes property received by the survivor from the estate of the first to die.
(b) It must also include all property owned by the survivor at the time of the first death (*Re Hagger* (1930)).
(c) Does it include property acquired by the survivor after the first death? The position is doubtful but in *Re Cleaver* (1981) Nourse J said that the survivor

> could enjoy the property as absolute owner, unless, of course, the will only gave him a life interest, 'subject to a fiduciary duty which, so to speak, crystallised on his death, and disabled him only from voluntary dispositions *inter vivos*', i.e. in this context dispositions made in bad faith. Thus it seems that the survivor must not, for example, go on a world cruise with the money but is restricted to using the money for ordinary living expenses. Yet as the existence of mutual wills is often not known until after the death of the survivor, the beneficiaries might not have any remedy in practice.

A trust arising from mutual wills cannot be express but there is a difference of opinion among textbook writers as to whether it is either a resulting (or implied) trust or a constructive trust. In *Re Cleaver* (1981) the court held that the trust is constructive.

Secret trusts and mutual wills

Both of these doctrines uphold forms of testamentary disposition which do not comply with the provisions of the Wills Act and the factual similarities can be close. *Ottaway* v. *Norman* (1972) could have been decided on the principles of mutual wills but for the lack of evidence of any agreement and so was decided on the basis of secret trust. There is also, as we have seen, evidence for considering both doctrines as imposing constructive trusts.

Mutual wills and joint wills

Although a will jointly made by two parties is obviously different from mutual wills, the same principles apply in that the survivor of joint testators will also be bound by a trust. Joint wills are rare in practice.

FURTHER READING

Critchley (1999) 'Instruments of fraud: testamentary dispositions and the doctrine of secret trusts', 115 LQR 631. A useful look at the whole area.

Meager (2003) 'Secret trusts: do they have a future?' Conv. 203. Interesting research showing that secret trusts are important in practice.

Perrins (1972) 'Can you keep half a secret?' 88 LQR 225. Demonstrates that the principles in *Re Stead* rest on a tenuous historical basis.

CHAPTER SUMMARY

- Secret trust does not appear on the will.
- Half-secret trust: only the fact of the trust appears on the will – not the details.
- Different rules on communication of secret and half-secret trusts.

- Mutual wills are where the two testators make wills, usually but not necessarily, leaving property to each other, but always where there is a gift to the same beneficiary.

QUESTION

Edward made a will in 2000 in which he left £50,000 to Charles and Susan, his brother and sister. In 2001 Edward said to Charles: 'I know that you will not forget Amy, my old friend'. Charles made no reply. Susan was not told of this request. In 2002 Edward died and afterwards Susan found a letter addressed to her in which Edward said 'I trust that you will give £5,000 to Amy'.

Advise Amy, Charles and Susan on their entitlements, if any, under Edward's will.

Would it make any difference to your answer if Edward's will had stated that he left '£50,000 to Charles and Susan to be used for purposes which I will communicate to them' and the other facts were the same?

Note 8.1: You will find suggested points for the answer to this question in Appendix 2.

9 Void and voidable trusts

INTRODUCTION

The intervention of the courts in these cases has usually been justified on the ground of public policy, except where the object of the trust is to contravene an already established rule of statute or common law. This is in itself controversial. What does 'public policy' mean? Where the object of the trust is to break a rule of law it is clearly void but the term 'public policy' is one used by the courts to strike down a trust which is not *per se* illegal. Thus in *M'Caig* v. *University of Glasgow* (1907) the testator's will provided that the income of his estate should be devoted to the building of statutes of himself and his family and also building artistic towers at various sites on his estates. This was held void on other grounds but Lord Killachy said that in any event it would have failed as being contrary to public policy as 'if it is not unlawful, it ought to be unlawful, to dedicate by testamentary disposition, the whole income of a large estate . . . to objects . . . which have no other purpose or use than that of perpetuating at great cost, and in an absurd manner, the idiosyncrasies of an eccentric testator'. This comes close to saying that, because the court considers the gift to be utterly useless, it shall fail. There is a tendency for the courts today to be much more cautious before expressing such sentiments and the main interest of this subject lies more in other areas.

WHERE CONTRAVENTION OF PUBLIC POLICY WILL INVALIDATE A TRUST

(a) Trusts which promote an unlawful activity as in *Thrupp* v. *Collett* (1858) where a bequest to pay the fines of poachers was held void.
(b) Capricious or useless trusts as in *Brown* v. *Burdett* (1882) where a testatrix devised a house on trust to block up all but four of the rooms. These provisions did not even have the merit of tax avoidance, because window tax was abolished in 1851, and they were held void.

Unlawful conditions

The power of the courts to strike down a trust where a gift depends on an unlawful condition is again an example of public policy as it is the courts who often decide if a condition should be held to be unlawful.

(a) Conditions which tend to restrain marriage completely are void are but partial, restraints are not, e.g.:
   (i) Conditions against marrying a person born in Scotland or of Scottish parents (*Perrin* v. *Lyon* (1807));
   (ii) Conditions only applying to second or subsequent marriages or requiring consent to marriage (*Re Whitings Settlement* (1905)). The point that the withholding of such consent may then make the condition a total restraint on marriage is as yet unexplored by the courts.

(b) Conditions designed to induce a future separation of husband and wife are void (*Westmeath* v. *Westmeath* (1834)) but trusts contained in a deed of separation where the parties have already decided to separate are valid (*Wilson* v. *Wilson* (1849)).

(c) Conditions designed to induce a separation of a parent from child are void (*Re Boulter* (1922)). In *Blathwayt* v. *Lord Cawley* (1975) an attempt was made to extend the principle to conditions relating to the religious upbringing of children. It was held that a condition in a settlement which provided for the forfeiture of a person's interest if he became a Roman Catholic was not void, the court stressing the importance of the principle of freedom of testamentary disposition. It was also held that the clause on its construction did not apply to the facts of the case. Lord Wilberforce's speech in the House of Lords contains an interesting discussion of public policy in this area and is considered below.

(d) Conditions restraining the alienation of property given to a beneficiary absolutely are void (*Re Brown* (1954)), although this point needs to be considered in relation to protective trusts (see Chapter 11).

CONSEQUENCES OF ILLEGALITY

(a) Trusts which are unlawful (see above) fail and so in *Brown* v. *Burdett* (1882) the court held that the house was not disposed of by the will. There will thus be a resulting trust for the settlor. If the trust is only partly unlawful, e.g. one object is lawful, the other is not, then it may be possible to sever the unlawful part and enforce the rest if it is possible to ascertain the part of the trust property which was to be held on unlawful trusts (*Mitford* v. *Reynolds* (1848)). In addition, these trusts will often be invalid as non-charitable purpose trusts (see Chapter 15).

(b) Unlawful conditions: A distinction is drawn here between conditions precedent and subsequent. A condition precedent is one where the gift will not take effect unless the condition is fulfilled while a condition subsequent is one where the gift, having already vested, will be forfeited unless the condition is complied with.

   There are three rules:
   (i) If a condition subsequent is void the gift remains valid, i.e. Blackacre to X until he marries. If this condition is void (see above) then even if X marries he can keep Blackacre.

(ii) If a condition precedent attached to a gift of **realty** is void then the gift fails, e.g. Blackacre to X unless at the time he is married. There will be a resulting trust for the settlor.

(iii) If a condition precedent attached to a gift of personalty is void then the gift fails if the condition was '*malum in se*' (illegal in itself), e.g. to X provided that he shall first have killed Y. Once again there will be a resulting trust for the settlor. If the condition was only '*malum prohibitum*' (illegal only by statute or against public policy), then the gift is valid and passes unfettered by the condition. Although the law on what '*malum prohibitum*' can consist of is not entirely clear, a possible example would be a condition imposing a restraint on marriage. In *Re Piper* (1946) part of the testator's residuary estate was to be held for such of four children as attained the age of 30 and did not live with their father. (Their mother had divorced their father before the date of the will.) It was held that the gift was void as *malum prohibitum* as it was against public policy to bring about the future separation of parent and child but Romer J found the distinction between *malum in se* and *malum prohibitum* difficult. The Law Commission (1999) has now recommended that it should be abolished.

THE LAW ON DISCRIMINATION AND CONDITIONS IN TRUSTS

Many trust deeds were drawn up when there was no legal prohibition against discrimination. Indeed, the first example of such laws was in the Race Relations Act 1976 and the Sex Discrimination Act 1975. These statutes have themselves been added to and now discrimination is also prohibited on grounds of disability (Disability Discrimination Act 1995), sexual orientation (Employment Equality (Sexual Orientation) Regulations 2003 and religion and belief (Employment Equality (Religion and Belief) Regulations 2003). Age discrimination will be prohibited from December 2006.

As will be seen from their titles, some of these laws only apply to employment but although others, such as the Race Relations Act also apply to, for example, the provision of goods and services, none of them applies to private trusts. Thus, it is still perfectly possible to have in law a private trust which restricts its benefits to, for example, persons of a certain sexual orientation. The relationship between conditions in private trusts which discriminate and the general law was considered by Lord Wilberforce in *Blathwayt* v. *Lord Cawley* (1975). It will be recalled that the case concerned a condition under which an interest would be forfeited if a person became a Roman Catholic. He observed that it could have been argued that such a prohibition was against public policy. However, he resisted this suggestion partly on the ground that it conflicted with another fundamental principle, that of freedom of testamentary disposition. Put simply, a testator is free to leave his/her property in any way he/she chooses. This decision was itself in 1976 and it may be that the courts today would take a different view. (It should be noted that his words contrast very strongly with the view of Lord Killachy in *M'Caig* v. *University of Glasgow* referred to at the beginning of this chapter.)

The position in relation to charitable trusts differs somewhat and is considered in Chapter 13.

EFFECT OF EUROPEAN CONVENTION ON HUMAN RIGHTS ON CONDITIONS IN PRIVATE TRUSTS

The other issue is the effect of the European Convention on Human Rights (ECHR) (now incorporated into UK law by the Human Rights Act (HRA) 1998) on discriminatory provisions in trusts. The ECHR sets out various rights, such as Respect for Private and Family life (Art. 8), Freedom of Thought, Conscience and Religion (Art. 9) and The Right to Marry (Art. 12). In addition, Art. 14 contains a prohibition on discrimination in the exercise of rights under the ECHR on the ground of sex, race, religion and political or other opinions. However, Art. 1 of the First Protocol to the ECHR provides that the right to peaceful enjoyment of possessions is a fundamental right.

The ECHR does not apply directly to private trusts, enforcement being rather indirect. In brief, it only applies directly to public bodies (s. 6 HRA) but in addition the courts must take into account the decisions of the European Court of Human Rights (s. 2 HRA).

Thus the picture in relation to private trusts is complex, as Example 9.1 shows:

Example 9.1

Jane is a beneficiary under the will of her Uncle Jack. This provides that Jane is to inherit half of his estate provided that at the date of his death she is unmarried and that she has not cohabited with anyone. If she becomes a member of the Liberal Democratic Party and/or an agnostic at any time whether before or after his death she will forfeit her inheritance.

It will be seen that these provisions are in conflict with Art. 8, Art. 9, Art. 12 and Art. 14, yet Uncle Jack owns the property which he is leaving Jane and so it could be argued that if these conditions are declared invalid then Art. 1 of the First Protocol is infringed. Moreover, no action could be brought before the courts alleging breach of the ECHR as Uncle Jack is not a public body. Finally, it may be noted in passing that an argument based on general public policy considerations would fail in view of the remarks of Lord Wilberforce in *Blathwayt* v. *Lord Cawley* (above).

The most that can be said is that in time the total effect of both anti-discrimination law and the ECHR will be to induce a climate in which discriminatory clauses in even private documents will be considered unacceptable.

Note 9.1: The position in relation to charitable trusts is considered in Chapter 13.

TRUSTS AND THE RULES CONCERNING PERPETUITY, INALIENABILITY AND ACCUMULATIONS

The law has always taken the view that property should not be tied up for too long a time. This has led to the following rules, which not only apply to interests under trusts but also to other interests in land. As the Law Commission points out (Report No. 251, 1999), the justification for these rules is 'the need to place some restriction on how far one generation can control the devolution of property at the expense of generations to follow'.

The rule against perpetuities

(a) The **common law rule**. This rule is directed against trust, or other property, vesting at a remote time in the future. As its operation is not confined to trust property, a detailed consideration of the rule is found in books on land law. A general statement of the rule is that 'an interest must vest, if it vests at all, within some life or lives in being or twenty-one years thereafter'. The following examples show the operation of the rule.

Example 9.2

Property is left on trust for X if he qualifies as a barrister. This is valid because, if X is to qualify, he must do so within a life in being (his own here).

Example 9.3

Property is left on trust for the first child of X to qualify as a barrister. This is void because X may have a child born after the date of the execution of the trust instrument who may qualify as a barrister more than 21 years after the date of X's death, X being the life in being. This may be highly improbable, but the point is that it is possible.

The effect of the rule can also be explained in this way by reference to these examples.

(b) The effect of the **Perpetuities and Accumulations Act 1964**. This Act only applies to dispositions coming into effect after 15 July 1964. In the case of such a disposition one must first look at the common law rule (see (a) above).

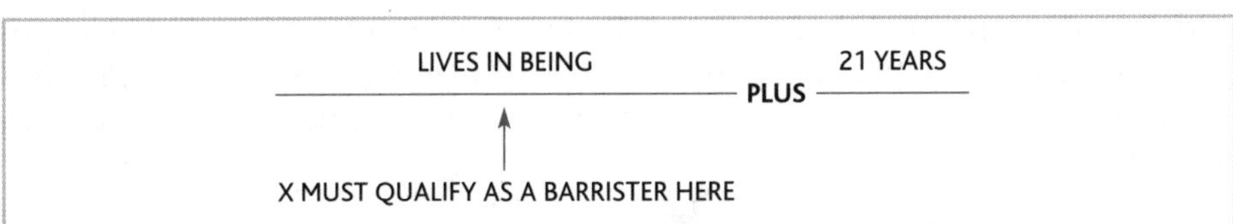

Figure 9.1 Diagram of Example 9.2

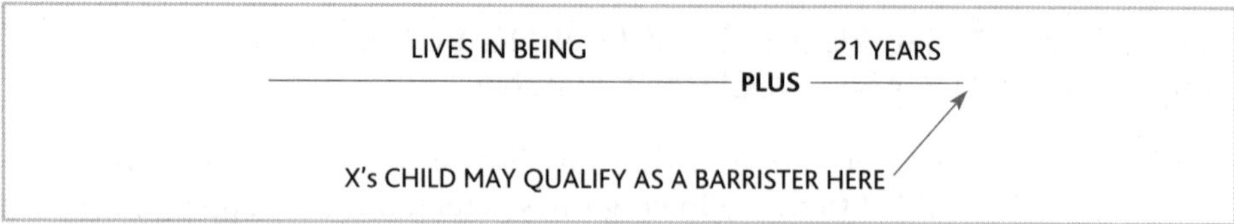

Figure 9.2 Diagram of Example 9.3

If the disposition is void under the common law rule then one considers whether it can be saved by the application of the rules in this Act.

(i) Section 1 of the Act allows a settlor to specify a perpetuity period of a maximum of 80 years rather than the common law period.
(ii) Section 3(1) of the Act provides that where a disposition is void under the common law rule then rather than declaring it void one must 'wait and see' whether in fact the interest does vest outside the common law rule perpetuity period. If so, it will of course be void; if not, it will be valid.

The effect of this Act is shown by Example 9.4, which should be contrasted with the examples above showing the operation of the common law rule.

Example 9.4

Property is left on trust to the first child of X to become a barrister. Under the 1964 Act one must wait and see whether in fact a child of X's does become a barrister within the perpetuity period rather than simply declaring the gift void because of the perhaps remote possibility that it might not do so.

The rule against inalienability (rule against perpetual duration)

This rule is not concerned with the time at which an interest must vest but at the tying up of capital and income for an excessive time. It provides that if the capital fund must be kept intact (i.e. inalienable) beyond the perpetuity period then the trust will be void. The perpetuity period here is the common law one, the general opinion being that the 1964 Act does not apply here (see s. 15(4)). The main application of this rule is to non-charitable purpose trusts and it is considered further in Chapter 15.

The rule against accumulations

This rule is directed at trusts which require the income to be accumulated (i.e. added to the capital), rather than distributed, for an excessive period. Sections 164–166 of the LPA 1925 provide that a settlor may not direct in an *inter vivos* settlement that income should be accumulated for longer than one of the following periods:

(a) The life of the settlor.
(b) 21 years from the death of the settlor.

(c) The minority of any person(s) living or *en ventre sa mère* at the death of the settlor.
(d) The minority of any person(s) who would be entitled to the income directed to be accumulated if they were of full age.

Section 13 of the Perpetuities and Accumulation Act 1964 added the following two periods, one of which can also now be chosen in instruments coming into effect after 15 July 1964:

(e) 21 years from the date of the making of the settlement.
(f) The duration of the minorities of person(s) living or *en ventre sa mère* at the date of the making of the settlement.

Where the settlement is created by will then the permitted accumulation periods are:

(a) 21 years from the date of the testator's death.
(b) The minorities of any person(s) living or *en ventre sa mère* at the testator's death.
(c) The minorities of any person(s) who would under the will be entitled to the income directed to be accumulated if they were of full age.

The settlor or testator can choose which of the above periods are to apply. If none is chosen, then the period is:

(a) In an *inter vivos* settlements, the life of the settlor.
(b) In settlements created by will, 21 years from the date of the testator's death.

If a longer period than those specified is selected then the direction to accumulate is invalid if the specified period exceeds the common law perpetuity period. Otherwise it is only invalid as to the excess beyond the authorised period. The court in this case will select one of the authorised periods (above) most appropriate to the settlor's intentions.

At the end of whatever period applies the accumulated income must be distributed.

Possible changes

The Law Commission, in its Report No. 251 (1999) proposes that there should be major changes to these rules, pointing out that they are 'needlessly complicated'. The proposals are:

- The rule against perpetuities should only apply to interests and rights under wills and trusts.
- In the case of perpetuities there should be one fixed period of 125 years, which is about the maximum achievable under the present law (i.e. the combination of lives in being plus 21 years). This period would be subject to the wait and see principle.
- The rule against accumulations should be abolished except in relation to charitable trusts.

TRANSACTIONS DESIGNED TO KEEP PROPERTY FROM CREDITORS

Introduction

The idea behind these transactions is shown by Example 9.5.

Example 9.5

X has business debts of £100,000. He has a house and £100,000 in a bank account and in order to keep these from his creditors he transfers the house and the money to Y, his brother, on trust for X's wife with the intention that X himself will still be able to enjoy it.

The following sections consider how the law treats such a transaction.

Note 9.2: The fundamental rule is that if such a transaction is unlawful then it is voidable.

Section 423 of the Insolvency Act 1986

This applies whether or not the debtor has been adjudged bankrupt and empowers the court to set aside transactions entered into at an undervalue if satisfied that they were made for certain purposes.

(a) *What is an undervalue?* This is where the person entering into a transaction with another either:
   (i) makes a gift to him or receives no consideration or receives from him significantly less consideration than he himself provides; *or*
   (ii) makes it in consideration of marriage.

   The effect is that a transaction for adequate consideration cannot be set aside even if the transferee knew that it was made with the intention to defraud creditors.

   A good example of the term 'undervalue' is provided by *Agricultural Mortgage Corporation plc* v. *Woodward* (1995). A farmer was insolvent and there was a mortgage on his farm of £700,000. He tried to prevent his main creditor from gaining the farm by granting his wife a protected agricultural tenancy at the full market rent of £37,250 per annum but it was held that this was still a transaction at an undervalue. The wife received the benefits of her home being safeguarded, the ability to continue the family business and the fact that she gained the surrender value of her tenancy, which gave her a 'ransom' surrender value against the creditor.

(b) *What purposes?*
   (i) putting assets beyond the reach of a person who is making or may make a claim against him;

(ii) otherwise prejudicing the interests of such a person in relation to the claim which he is making or intends to make.

Therefore the court must be satisfied that there was an intention to defraud in either of the above ways. The application to the court can be made by the victim of the transaction or, where the debtor is bankrupt, by the trustee in bankruptcy, the official receiver, or by the liquidator or administrator if the bankrupt is a corporation. There is no time limit for an application.

The court can order property transferred by the transaction now set aside to be vested in any person, either absolutely or for the benefit of those on whose behalf the application is made. Similar orders can be made in respect of the proceeds of sale of the property, or property acquired with such proceeds. Persons who acquire the property set out in s. 423 in good faith and for value and without notice of the circumstances, from a person other than the debtor, are protected.

In *Moon* v. *Franklin* (1996) the defendant, an accountant, who was being sued for professional negligence, gave £65,000 to his wife and transferred a house, previously jointly owned by them, into his wife's sole name. It was found that, although at the time these transactions were made the defendant was about to receive a substantial sum from the sale of his practice which could have explained them, there was no doubt on the facts that they were caught by s. 423: they were at an undervalue and made for the defendant's purpose of putting his assets beyond the reach of his creditors.

Note 9.3: See Miller (1998) for a review of this section.

Section 339 of the Insolvency Act 1986

This, unlike s. 423, only applies where an individual has been adjudged bankrupt. It permits the trustee in bankruptcy, in a case where an individual bankrupt has entered into a transaction at an undervalue, to apply for an order restoring the position to what it would have been but for the transaction. Undervalue here has the same meaning as in s. 423 (above) but, unlike s. 423 there is no requirement here that the transaction must have been entered into to achieve certain purposes. Thus intention to defraud is irrelevant. See *Re Densham* (1975) and *Re Abbott* (1982) (Chapter 12) on the effect of s. 42 of the Bankruptcy Act 1914 (to some extent the predecessor of s. 339) in disputes over ownership of the family home.

Section 340 of the Insolvency Act 1986

This enables the court, at the request of a trustee in bankruptcy, to make orders arising out of preferences given by the bankrupt to creditors, sureties or guarantors. A preference is any transaction which puts that person in a better position than he would otherwise have been. The court can make an order restoring the position to what it would have been but for the preference.

Time limits for applying under s. 339 and s. 340 of the Insolvency Act 1986
Section 341 provides:

(a) A two-year time limit, beginning from the date of presentation of the bankruptcy petition, in transactions at an undervalue except that the period is five years where the individual was insolvent at the time of the transaction or became insolvent in consequence of it.
(b) A six-month time limit in the case of preferences which are not undervalues except that where the preference is given to an associate, e.g. a spouse, other relative, or partner, the trustee has two years to apply.

There are similar provisions protecting third parties as apply in orders made under s. 423.

Insolvency of a company: ss. 238–241 of the Insolvency Act 1986

These contain similar provisions to those in s. 339 and s. 340 in cases where a company has gone into liquidation or an administration order has been made although the time limits are slightly different.

Other provisions dealing with fraudulent transfers

(a) Section 37 of the Matrimonial Causes Act 1973 enables a spouse (X) who has brought proceedings against the other spouse (Y) for financial relief under the Act to apply to the court for an order setting aside any disposition made by that spouse (Y) with the intention of defeating her claim.
(b) Sections 10–13 of the Inheritance (Provision for Family and Dependants) Act 1975 contain similar provisions enabling the court to review dispositions made by the deceased within six years of death, other than those made for full valuable consideration with the intention of defeating applications for relief under this Act.

OTHER CASES OF ILLEGALITY IN THE LAW OF TRUSTS AND PROPOSALS FOR CHANGE

This chapter has concentrated on certain instances of illegality but there are others, principally in connection with transfers for illegal purposes which can give rise to a resulting trust, which will be looked at in Chapter 10. In addition, the jurisdiction of equity is influenced by the maxim that 'he who comes to equity must come with clean hands'.

The Law Commission (Consultation Paper 154 (1999)) recommended that the present rules on the effect of illegality on both trusts and contracts, which it described as complex and obscure, should be replaced by the giving of a discretion to the courts to decide if a claim to a remedy should be barred by illegality. There would be a number of factors to be considered: the seriousness of the illegality; the knowledge and intention of the party claiming relief; if denying the claim would deter the illegality and/or further the purpose of the rule which made the transaction illegal and if denying the claim would be proportionate to the illegality.

These proposals would be especially relevant in cases such as *Tinsley* v. *Milligan* (1993) (see Chapter 10).

FURTHER READING

Keay (2003) 'Transfers to defeat creditors: The problem of purpose under s. 423 of the Insolvency Act 1986', 67 Conv. 272. Useful account of an important area often neglected.

CHAPTER SUMMARY

- Objects of trust void on grounds of public policy – what is public policy?
- Void conditions: conditions precedent and subsequent.
- Effect of the law on discrimination and the Human Rights Act.
- Rules against perpetuities and accumulations.
- Transactions designed to defeat the claims of creditors: Insolvency Act 1986, s. 423 (transactions at an undervalue), s. 339 and other statutory provisions.
- Proposals for reform.

QUESTION

'The jurisdiction of the courts to strike down trusts on grounds of public policy rests on no clear principle and is in urgent need of clarification and updating by the courts.'

Do you agree?

Note 9.4: You will find suggested points for inclusion in this answer in Appendix 2.

Part Three

RESULTING TRUSTS, CONSTRUCTIVE TRUSTS: TRUSTS OF THE HOME

The common feature of both resulting and constructive trusts is that, unlike express trusts, they are not created by the express agreement of the parties as evidenced in a trust deed, or some other writing or, except in the case of trusts of land or an interest in land (s. 53(1)(b) LPA 1925), orally. Although this much is clear, the exact nature of both these trusts and their relationship to each other has been the subject of considerable debate. Both types of trusts have been used by the courts in the last 50 years in creative ways which have added much to the influence of equity on the regulation of everyday life, but, as often in English law, the exact foundations on which these trusts operate is still uncertain, although they have the common feature that they are both implied by the courts.

A most useful indication to the differences between express trusts, on the one hand, and both resulting and constructive (which he calls imputed trusts) trusts on the other, is provided by Moffat (1999), who observes that there are three distinctions between them:

(a) Functional. Express trusts are often employed as a planning device but imputed trusts are ways of resolving disputes over ownership or entitlement to property.

(b) Formal. Express trusts must comply with certain formalities such as s. 53(1)(c) of the LPA (see Chapter 6). Imputed trusts are not affected by these (s. 53(2) LPA).

(c) Substantive. Express trusts arise because of some expression of intention by a property owner but imputed trusts arise by operation of some legal rule. As Moffat points out, this particular distinction breaks down in cases of disputes over the family home where intention plays a significant role.

10 Resulting trusts

INTRODUCTION

A resulting trust gets its name from the Latin verb *resalire* (to jump back) and this identifies the essential feature of the trust: that the beneficial interest results to, or jumps back to, the settlor who created the trust. The basis of an action founded on a resulting trust is that one is seeking to recover one's own property. The idea is strange: a person (X) gives property to another (Y) and then Y ends up holding it on trust for X.

BASIS OF THE RESULTING TRUST

The prevailing orthodoxy used to be that there were two types of resulting trust:

(a) Automatic resulting trusts, where there was a resulting trust independent of the intentions of the settlor, as where the settlor has failed to specify the beneficial interests and so there is either a lack of certainty of objects or no objects at all (see Chapter 5).
(b) Presumed resulting trusts, as where a person transferred property to another without consideration but where no words of gift were used. These, which are dealt with in this chapter, were considered to arise from the presumed intention of the transferor.

This division was proposed by Megarry J in *Re Vandervell's Trusts (No. 2)* (1974) but this was disapproved of by Lord Browne-Wilkinson in *Westdeutsche Landesbank Girozentrale* v. *Islington LBC* (1996), who saw resulting trusts as arising from the common intention of the parties. However, the use of the phrase 'common intention' has also been the source of confusion. Nor is it felt by many (e.g. Chambers 1997) that it is justified from the facts of cases which often show that the transferee is unaware of the actual transfer as in *Re Vinogradoff* (1935). Here the testatrix had transferred an £800 War Loan which was in her own name into the joint names of herself and her four-year-old daughter. It was held that the daughter held it on a resulting trust for the testatrix, on principles dealt with more fully below. In addition, in cases of beneficial entitlement to the family home the leading case of *Lloyds Bank plc* v. *Rosset* (1990) identifies a common intention as a necessary requirement but rests these cases on the notion of a constructive trust. (See Chapter 12.) Moreover, as a study of the cases in Chapter 12 will show, the search for a common intention has led to situations where it is arguable that the courts have found an intention on flimsy evidence (see e.g. *Eves* v. *Eves* (1975)). In short, common intention has become an instrument of judicial activism.

Another test for the existence of a resulting trust is suggested by Chambers, who proposes that all resulting trusts should be considered as arising from the presumption of the **lack of** any intention by the transferor to pass any beneficial interest to the transferee when the transferee has not provided the entire consideration for the property. Thus, as Chambers points out, the resulting trust operates to return specific property to the transferor because he/she did not intend to benefit the transferee. The effect is that, unless this presumption is rebutted, a resulting trust arises by operation of law. Chambers would then see resulting trusts as being the major vehicle by which equity contributes to the law of unjust enrichment, a concept which is touched on in this book in connection with a breach of trust (see Chapter 20).

The problem is to decide what happens to the beneficial interest: Lord Reid in *Vandervell* v. *IRC* (1967) argued that this remains with the transferor (or donor) throughout and so equity is simply recognising a fact. This view is now no longer generally held and instead it is considered that on any transfer only the legal interest passes to the transferor and where the resulting trust arises from that transfer then a new equitable interest then arises which is held for the transferee. (See Chambers (above) and Millett (1998).)

Lord Browne-Wilkinson in *Westdeutsche* then argued that a resulting trust only came into existence when the conscience of the transferee was affected by becoming aware that he had received property from which he was not intended to benefit. This has been forcefully criticised by Chambers, who gives this example: suppose that A gives money to B by mistake and B gives it to C who has no notice of A's mistake. A's right to recover the money from C would depend on whether B had notice of the mistake before he gave it to A. Why should notice matter? Surely, Chambers argues, the trust should respond to A's lack of intention to benefit the recipient and does not depend on notice. Accordingly the resulting trust comes into existence as soon as the property is transferred.

Another issue is the extent to which a resulting trustee is subject to any of the duties of a trustee. A resulting trustee does not assume office as a result of voluntarily agreeing to do so and, of course, there is no trust instrument. Even so, in some cases a resulting trustee will owe fiduciary duties. For example, suppose that property is transferred to X to hold on trust for 'all my old drinking pals'. As we saw in Chapter 5, this is invalid through lack of certainty of objects and so X is a resulting trustee with a fiduciary duty to hold the property for the settlor or his estate.

SITUATIONS WHERE A RESULTING TRUST ARISES: A SUMMARY

(a) Purchase of property in another's name or where there is a voluntary transfer.
(b) Where the settlor has failed to specify the beneficial interests or where the settlor's intentions with regard to the disposal of the trust property cannot be carried out, either fully or at all.
(c) In a commercial context.

The concept of a resulting trust appears at various points in the law of trusts and so normally they are considered in their context in different parts of the book. Note particularly the discussion of resulting trusts in Chapters 8, 12 and 20. The remainder of this chapter will deal with specific forms of resulting trust.

Purchase of property in the name of another or in the joint names of the purchaser and another

Where a person pays the purchase money for property and either has it put into another's name, or that of himself and another jointly, then it is presumed that the other holds the property on trust for the person who paid for it (*Dyer* v. *Dyer* (1788)). The principle of 'he who pays, owns' is important in questions arising as to ownership of the family home and is considered further in Chapter 12. However, it can apply in other situations and an attempt was made in *Savage* v. *Dunningham* (1974) to apply it to an informal flat-sharing arrangement. The tenancy agreement was in the defendant's name but the rent and other expenses were shared equally between the claimants and the defendant. The claimants, on this basis, claimed an interest by way of resulting trust when the defendant purchased the flat but the court refused to equate payment of rent with payment of actual purchase money.

Voluntary transfer

Where there is a voluntary transfer (i.e. a gift) of personalty to another or into the joint names of the transferor and another, there is a presumption of a resulting trust for the transferor. In *Re Vinogradoff* (1935), as explained above, a grandmother transferred an £800 War Loan into the joint names of herself and her granddaughter and it was held that after the grandmother's death the granddaughter held it on trust for her estate. There is no clear authority on the corresponding position where land is involved.

Presumption of advancement

The above rules are only presumptions. They can be rebutted by evidence of a contrary intention on the part of the transferor, as in *Standing* v. *Bowring* (1885), where the plaintiff transferred Consols into the joint names of herself and her godson with the express intention that the godson should have them absolutely if he survived her. In certain situations equity goes further and holds that there is a **presumption of advancement (or gift)** which displaces the presumption of resulting trust. However, here also the intention of the transferor is paramount and can be used to rebut the presumption of advancement in which case the presumption of resulting trust applies (see Example 10.1 below).

Situations where there is a presumption of advancement

There is a presumption of advancement where a transfer is made from a father to a child and from a husband to a wife. In addition the presumption probably applies where a transfer is made to a child by a person standing *in loco parentis* to it, i.e. a person who has taken on the duty of father of a child to make provision for that child (Jessel MR in *Bennett* v. *Bennett* (1879)). This can apply to any relative or other person who, because the parents are unable or unwilling to do so, has taken on the duty of looking after the child and can also apply to the father of an illegitimate child (*Beckford* v. *Beckford* (1774)). There is statutory presumption of gift in relation to an engagement ring, even though no marriage takes place (s. 3(2) of the Law Reform (Miscellaneous Provisions) Act 1970).

There is no presumption of advancement where a transfer is made from a wife to a husband, or where she pays the purchase money for property and has it put in his name, and thus a resulting trust will arise. Nor is there a presumption between a mother and a legitimate child because, according to *Re De Visme* (1863), a woman is under no obligation to maintain her children. This seems a strange view in present day conditions and it is likely that, in practice, a presumption of a resulting trust could easily be rebutted here as was recognised by Jessel MR in *Bennett* v. *Bennett* (1879). In the Australian case of *Nelson* v. *Nelson* (1995) a presumption of advancement did apply when a mother transferred property into the names of her children. Presumptions of advancement are illustrated by Example 10.1.

Example 10.1

X is the father of Y. He opens a bank account in Y's name and X puts £1,000 into it. There is a presumption of advancement here. However, X may bring evidence to show that he still regarded himself as owner of the money and so try to establish that Y holds the £1,000 on a resulting trust for him.

If X is Y's mother then the presumption of advancement may not apply and there will be a presumption that Y holds the £1,000 on trust for X. However, the presumption can be rebutted by evidence that a gift was intended.

Rebutting the presumption of advancement

As mentioned above, the presumption can be rebutted by evidence of a contrary intention but three points should be noted:

(a) In *Shephard* v. *Cartwright* (1955) it was held that a person wishing to bring evidence to rebut the presumption, i.e. to show that no gift was intended, cannot bring evidence of matters arising *after* the transaction to support this contention. However, such evidence is admissible if an action is brought *against* him. Thus, in the above example, suppose that X sought to bring evidence of a letter written by him to Y *after* the bank account had been opened stating that he (X) still regarded that money as his, the rule in *Shephard* v. *Cartwright* would prevent that evidence being admitted.

(b) In *Lord Grey* v. *Lady Grey* (1677) Lord Finch C said that acquiescence by a child, in whose name a purchase has been made, of the receipt of the rents or income from it by his father does not rebut the presumption of advancement. If the child is an infant it is natural that the father should receive the money. If he is an adult it is an act of good manners by him not to dispute the receipt of them by the father. Again, however, evidence of a contrary intention may be given. In *Warren* v. *Gurney* (1944) retention of the title deeds by the father with a declaration, contemporaneous with the transfer, that a gift was not intended, was enough to rebut the presumption.

Presumptions of advancement and evidence of fraudulent conduct

In a number of cases a party's claim, either to a share in property under a resulting (or constructive) trust or a claim to rebut a presumption of advancement, has been based on evidence which itself discloses some illegality. To what extent is this evidence admissible? If it is not admissible, the other party may obtain an absolute right to property purchased, at least in part, with money belonging to the party who is relying on the evidence of illegality. If it is admissible, what then of the maxim that 'he who comes into equity shall come with clean hands'?

In *Gascoigne* v. *Gascoigne* (1918) a husband who was in debt to moneylenders took a lease of land on which he built a house with his own money but he put the lease into his wife's name with the object of protecting the property from his creditors. His later claim that the wife held as trustee for him was dismissed because he was not allowed to rebut the presumption of advancement in his wife's favour by bringing evidence of his fraudulent conduct. In *Tinker* v. *Tinker* (1970) the conduct involved was not in fact fraudulent at all. A husband put the matrimonial home into his wife's name in case a business venture which he was considering might fail. The court held that he could not claim that his wife held as trustee for him because he was an honest man and must be taken to have intended that the house should belong to his wife so that he could truthfully say that it was her property. In *Sekhon* v. *Alissa* (1989) a mother and daughter both contributed to the purchase of a house which was conveyed into the daughter's name alone because if the mother's name had been on the title there would have been a capital gains tax liability on any future sale since the mother already owned a residence. The court held that the presumption of a resulting trust for the mother was rebutted. The fraudulent purpose had not been carried out, as the house had not been sold, and in any case she had only considered the tax issue in general terms. A similar decision was *Tribe* v. *Tribe* (1996). Here a landlord served notices on a tenant requiring him to undertake substantial repairs to two properties. The tenant therefore reduced his assets by transferring shares in a family company to his son for a sum which was not paid and so claimed that he could not afford the repairs. In fact the repairs were carried out anyway and the deception need not have been made. The son claimed the shares on the basis that the apparent gift gave rise to a presumption of advancement but the court held that the father could rely on his intention, which was to make a gift. Although this intention was tainted by illegality this had not been carried out.

In *Tinsley* v. *Milligan* (1993) the issue was not a possible claim by creditors but a claim to a beneficial share in a house because of contributions made to its purchase. The parties were in a same-sex relationship and the house was in the claimant's name only in order to facilitate a fraudulent claim to housing benefit by the defendant. The court held that the claimant held the house on a constructive trust for both her and the defendant in equal shares. In the Court of Appeal it was held, by a majority, that there was no rigid rule that whenever property was put into another name for an illegal or immoral purpose this always prevented the owner from recovering it. The 'public conscience' test was applied under which the court must weigh the consequences of granting, or not granting, relief. In the House of Lords, the majority held that the issue of illegality was irrelevant: the defendant's claim was made out by proving the existence of a common understanding concerning ownership (see Chapter 12) and she had no need to refer to the reason why the house was conveyed into the claimant's name alone.

The reasoning of the House of Lords has been much criticised but has been followed, although without much enthusiasm, by the Court of Appeal. In *Silverwood* v. *Silverwood* (1997) X authorised the withdrawal from her account of money which was then put by her son into another account in the names of his children. X meanwhile began to receive income support which she would not have qualified for had she not made the withdrawal. On X's death her executor claimed that the children held the money on a resulting trust for her. The Court of Appeal agreed that it could not be proved that X knew of any illegal purpose. Even if she had known the outcome would probably have been the same as her claim was not based on any illegal purpose but simply on straightforward resulting trust principles. One can see why Nourse LJ in *Silverwood* considered that the principle in *Tinsley* was a 'straightjacket'.

The High Court of Australia declined to follow *Tinsley* v. *Milligan* in *Nelson* v. *Nelson* (see also above). A mother transferred property into the names of her children so that she would qualify for a defence service loan on a property which she was buying. A presumption of advancement arose between her and the children (see above) and this was not rebutted. The court favoured a broader approach to the question of whether the fraudulent purpose was relevant and held here that the mother would be sufficiently penalised under the penalties imposed under the Act which she had sought to circumvent. To prevent her from enforcing a resulting trust would not, on the facts, be justified.

The Law Commission has reviewed this area of transfers for an illegal purpose and has made recommendations which were set out at the end of Chapter 9. One effect would be to clarify the *Tinsley* v. *Milligan* principle.

Presumptions of advancements today

These presumptions have been criticised especially when a party has tried to use them in a dispute over entitlement to interests in the family home (see Chapter 12) and there is no doubt that they are losing their force. A good example of

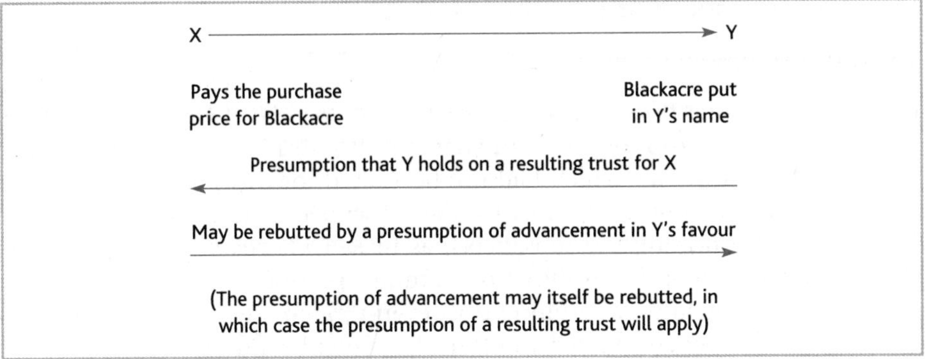

Figure 10.1 The issue of presumption of advancement

where the presumption was rebutted is *McGrath* v. *Wallis* (1995). A father contributed most of the purchase price of a house which was put in his son's name so that a mortgage could be obtained. It was held that the presumption was rebutted: the reason for putting the house in the son's name was clear and there was no reason why the father, who was only 63 at the time, should want to give the house to his son. This case could have been better decided on the basis of what the respective intentions of the parties were: the issue of presumption of advancement seemed to get in the way.

Joint bank accounts

When a husband and wife have a joint bank account then the presumption of advancement can apply. Thus where both have paid into the account and the husband dies then the money will be presumed to belong to the wife, unless the presumption is rebutted. A more realistic situation may be to hold that there is a presumption that the money was intended to be held by them as joint tenants so that whether the husband or wife dies first the money will belong to the survivor. In *Jones* v. *Maynard* (1951) it was suggested that if the husband buys investments in the wife's name with money from the account then the wife will be entitled to them. It would be interesting to know if the same applies if the wife buys them for the husband?

Failure by the settlor to specify the beneficial interests

Where a trust fails for lack of certainty of objects (beneficiaries) there is a resulting trust (see Chapter 5). Again in *Vandervell* v. *IRC* (1967) (see Chapter 6) Vandervell had given Vandervell Trustees Ltd an option to purchase shares which he had transferred to the Royal College of Surgeons but had failed to specify the trusts on which the shares were then to be held. There was thus a resulting, or what Lord Wilberforce called an automatic trust, for Vandervell. The beneficial interest, he said, could not 'remain in the air' therefore 'it remains in the settlor'.

Failure to dispose of the beneficial interest

There are two possible consequences:

(a) *Resulting trust for the settlor.* In *Re The Trusts of the Abbott Fund* (1900) a fund had been subscribed for the maintenance of two deaf and dumb ladies and it was held that money which had not been used for this purpose went, after their death, on a resulting trust for the subscribers. There can, of course, be problems in locating the subscribers, as in *Re Gillingham Bus Disaster Fund* (1958), where money left over from a fund to care for those disabled in an accident was held on a resulting trust even though a good deal of the fund came from street collections and thus the subscribers were untraceable (this case, and others on this topic, are dealt with in greater detail in Chapter 14).

(b) *Absolute gifts to the beneficiaries.* In *Re Osaba* (1979) it was held that where a trust had been created for the maintenance of two women and the education of the third then on the death of the first two and the completion of the third's education the property belonged absolutely to the third. The court approved of the principles laid down in *Re Sanderson's Trust* (1857) that where money is given and a purpose is assigned for it then there is a (rebuttable) presumption that the purpose is only the motive for the gift and thus the gift is absolute. Even so, it may be that *Re Abbott* (1900) was correctly decided on the construction basis that a resulting trust was intended.

Resulting trusts in a commercial context

Trusts used to give security for loans: the '*Quistclose* trust'

The following examples show the relationship between the concept of loan and the concept of a trust.

Example 10.2

X lends £1,000 to Y. This relationship is simply one of a loan creating a debt. Y becomes insolvent. Whether X will get his £1,000 back will depend on the extent of Y's liabilities. X will have to take his place along with Y's other creditors.

Example 10.3

X lends Y £1,000 for a specific purpose, e.g. to repay Z. Here the relationship is also one of loan but may in addition create a trust i.e. Y holds the £1,000 on trust for the purpose of repaying Z but if that purpose cannot be carried out then a secondary trust arises under which Y holds the £1,000 on a resulting trust for X. The advantage to X is that if Y becomes insolvent the £1,000 will not be part of his general assets but will be earmarked specifically to repay X. Thus X gets his £1,000 back in preference to Y's general creditors.

This point arose in *Barclays Bank* v. *Quistclose Investments Ltd* (1970). The facts were set out in Chapter 4, but briefly, a firm, Rolls Razor, which was in financial difficulties, borrowed money from Quistclose for the specific purpose of paying a dividend on its shares. However, before the dividend was paid Rolls Razor went into liquidation and it was held that the loan was held on a resulting trust for Quistclose and could not be claimed by the bank, which had notice of the trust, and which wished to set the loan off against the firm's overdraft. The effect was to give the respondents preference over the firm's general creditors. Had there been no trust and the action had been brought in contract for debt then Quistclose would not have had such a preference.

Problems with the* Quistclose *type of trust

(a) The *Quistclose* decision dealt only with the situation where money was lent for a purpose which could not be carried out at all. What if:
   (i) the loan was used for the intended purpose?
   (ii) the loan had only partly been used for the intended purpose?

   In *Re EVTR* (1987) the appellant lent £60,000 to a company to assist it in purchasing new equipment. The company made an agreement to purchase this but then went into liquidation before it was due for delivery. Thus in effect situation (ii) above applied. The court held that the *Quistclose* principle applied and that the £60,000, less agreed deductions, should be held on a resulting trust for the appellant. Had the contract for the purchase of the equipment been completed and the money entirely spent (i.e. situation (i) above applied) then, as Dillon LJ observed, no trust would have arisen and the appellant would have merely been an unsecured creditor.

(b) Who are the beneficiaries under a *Quistclose* trust? Were the shareholders in *Quistclose* beneficiaries? What are their rights?

   The rights of beneficiaries await clarification. However in *Carreras Rothmans Ltd* v. *Freeman Mathews Treasure Ltd* (1985) the court rejected an argument that a *Quistclose*-type trust did not exist because the beneficiaries had no enforceable rights at all. The claimants, cigarette manufacturers, had engaged the defendants as advertising agents and when the defendants got into financial difficulties the claimants paid sums into a special bank account to enable the defendants to pay off their creditors. The claimants were held entitled to an order that the money should be applied for those creditors because the money was held on trust for them. The court quoted from Megarry V-C in a similar kind of case, *Re Northern Developments (Holdings) Ltd* (1978), where he observed that beneficiaries under this type of trust do not obtain a full beneficial interest but the benefit which they obtain is the assurance that their debts will be paid in an orderly manner. Megarry V-C likened this to the type of purpose trust recognised as valid in *Re Denley's Trust Deed* (1969) (see Chapter 15) where, in this case, the beneficial interests are in suspense.

What if the loan in *Quistclose* had been made to pay the borrower's other creditors? Would a trust have been created for them? Peter Millett, as he then was, (1985) argued that it did not, on the basis that the lender was the sole beneficiary in this type of trust. In support of this argument he cites earlier cases where a trust for a lender had been held. Chambers, however, sees the *Quistclose* trust in a wider context. He argues that a *Quistclose* trust should not be limited to situations where money is loaned to be used to pay creditors and there is a trust for the lender but it can be used whenever money is paid to another on condition that it be used for a particular purpose. This purpose can be anything which 'creates an enforceable restriction on the recipient's use of the money'.

In *Twinsectra Ltd* v. *Yardley* (2002) Lord Millett modified his earlier view (Millett 1985) that an express trust arises for the borrower in *Quistclose*-type cases and instead he analysed the situation as one where a trust automatically arises in favour of the lender but this is defeated by the exercise by the lender of the power to apply the money for the specified purpose. Where there is no express trust of the money declared by the lender, then a resulting trust will arise in his favour. He was persuaded by the argument of Chambers (1997) (see above) that a resulting trust arises where there is a lack of any intention by the transferee (the lender here) to pass beneficial interest to the transferor (the borrower here).

Trusts where payment has been made in advance for goods

X pays £2,000 to Y Co, a mail-order firm, for goods. Y goes into liquidation before the goods are supplied. What right does X have to the return of the money? As with the *Quistclose*-type cases, a trust may be imposed here in order to give a person the right to the return of his money in preference to the general creditors.

In *Re Kayford Ltd* (1975) sums paid in advance by customers to a mail order company when ordering goods from it was paid by the company into a separate account and it was held that a trust had been created of the money for the customers. However Megarry J stated that 'different considerations may perhaps arise in relation to trade creditors' and so the *Re Kayford* principle is probably confined to private customers. Even here the customers may have difficulty in tracing their money, unless it has been paid into a separate account, and will not have to use the rules in *Re Hallett's Estate* (1880) and *Clayton's Case* (1816). (See Chapter 20.)

Accordingly, although *Re Kayford* is certainly an addition to consumer protection in this area its value is probably limited. In *Re London Wine (Shippers) Ltd* (1975) (see Chapter 5) it was held that the company did intend to become a trustee of the wines which it had sold to customers because it had referred to purchasers of the wine as 'the beneficial owner' and used the term 'your wine' although the claim for a trust failed through uncertainty of subject matter.

FURTHER READING

Chambers (1997a) *Resulting Trusts*, Oxford: Oxford University Press. Essential reading but the views expressed have not found universal acceptance. A good place to start in view of the clarity of the exposition.

Glister (2004) 'The nature of Quistclose Trusts. Classification, reconciliation', CLJ 632. Another contribution to the growing literature on this.

Millett (1985) 'The Quistclose Trust: Who can enforce it?', 101 LQR 269. Note that Millet's views have changed since this article was written but it is still a useful starting point.

Millett (1998) 'Equity's place in the law of commerce', 114 LQR 214. Deals with the *Quistclose* trust as well as other areas.

Swadling (1996) 'A new role for resulting trusts', 16 LS 110. Useful survey of this area.

Swadling ed. (2004) *The Quistclose Trust: Critical Essays*. Oxford: Hart Publishing. Gathers together a variety of views.

CHAPTER SUMMARY

- Resulting trusts return the beneficial interest in the property to the settlor who created the trust.
- Resulting trusts arise where property is purchased in another's name.
- Presumption of a resulting trust may be rebutted by a presumption of advancement.
- Problems where the transfer giving rise to the alleged trust is made for a fraudulent purpose.
- Resulting trusts arise where the settlor fails to specify the beneficial interests.
- '*Quistclose* trust' arises in circumstances where a loan is made for a purpose which fails. It may also arise in other cases.

QUESTION

Do you consider that the *Quistclose* trust should have any place in modern equity?

Note 10.1: You will find suggested points for inclusion in this answer in Appendix 2.

11 Constructive trusts, proprietary estoppel and protective trusts

INTRODUCTION

This chapter first links two examples of equitable intervention that have much in common: the constructive trust and estoppel. Although generalisations are notoriously risky in this area, it can be said that in both cases equity is reacting to a set of circumstances and, whilst in one the solution is the imposition of a trust, in the other it is the granting of a broad-based remedy. However, it will be seen that constructive trusts can themselves be seen as a remedy and the interplay between constructive trusts and estoppel as performing a remedial function has led to much debate. This theme will also be explored in the next chapter (Trusts and Home). Protective trusts are considered here as they are another example of equity reacting to a particular type of circumstances, in this case the likely event being the possible bankruptcy of a beneficiary.

CONSTRUCTIVE TRUSTS

These have been defined by Millett (1998) as arising 'whenever the circumstances are such that it would be unconscionable for the owner of the legal title to assert his own beneficial interest and deny the beneficial interest of another'. The difficulty has always been in going further and giving a clearer indication of when a constructive trust may arise. One problem is that, in cases involving the family home, a constructive trust has been said to rest on the common intention of the parties (see Chapter 12) and secret trusts (Chapter 8) can also rest on intention, in this case that of the testator. If this is so then it is very difficult to find any clear conceptual basis for constructive trusts as intention plays a part in resulting trusts (as we saw above) and obviously express trusts arise from the intention of the settlor.

If trusts of the family home and secret trusts are left out of the equation then some ideas become clearer. It is then true that a constructive trust has nothing to do with intention, whether express or implied, and such a trust is imposed by law. The other clear point which can be made is that a constructive trust will be imposed when the conscience of the owner of property is affected in such a way that equity insists that he/she should hold it for the benefit of another.

It has often been said that it would be wrong to go beyond this type of statement. This is because, as Edmund Davies LJ put it in *Carl Zeiss Stiftung* v. *Herbert Smith & Co* (1969), 'Its boundaries have been left perhaps deliberately vague so as not to restrict the court by technicalities in deciding what the justice of a particular case may demand'.

Note 11.1: Examples of constructive trusts are to be found in other chapters, e.g. Chapter 8 (secret trusts), Chapter 12 (trusts of the family home) and Chapter 20 (liability of recipients of trust property).

Situations in which a constructive trust has been imposed: a summary

(a) Profits made by a person in a fiduciary position.
(b) Where a statute has been used as an 'instrument of fraud'.
(c) The remedial constructive trust.

The topic of liability where a stranger intermeddles with trust property is considered in Chapter 20 (breach of trust) as this is linked to other possible situations of a breach.

Profits made by a person in a fiduciary position

Meaning of fiduciary

A fiduciary need not be an express trustee. Various relationships have been held to be fiduciary such as those between a company director and a company, employer and employee, solicitor and client and principal and agent. There is no definition of fiduciary and Mason (1977) has, in a well-known phrase, described the fiduciary relationship as a 'concept in search of a principle'. A useful description often quoted is that a fiduciary 'is, simply, someone who undertakes to act for or on behalf of another in some particular matter or matters' (Finn 1977).

The search for a wide ranging principle has, as Mason points out, been inhibited by the fact that labelling a relationship as fiduciary 'unleashes equitable remedies'. The result is that, for example, in the *Quistclose* case (see Chapters 4 and 10) the imposition of a fiduciary relationship, on what had appeared to be one of lender and borrower, led to the lender having an equitable proprietary interest in the subject matter of the loan (i.e. the money lent) and was able to have a prior claim over the borrower's creditors.

In *Bristol and West Building Society* v. *Mothew* (1996) Millett LJ held that the 'distinguishing obligation of a fiduciary is the obligation of loyalty. This core liability has several facets. A fiduciary must act in good faith; he must not make a profit out of his trust; he must not place himself in a position where his duty and interest may conflict; he may not act for his own benefit or the benefit of a third person without the informed consent of his principal'.

English law has traditionally restricted the relationship to the types of categories set out above. However, in Canada the courts have been more adventurous. In *Norberg* v. *Wynrib* (1992) the doctor–patient relationship was categorised as fiduciary so that when a doctor prescribed a drug in return for sexual favours the courts held that he was liable not only for assault and battery but also for equitable compensation (see Chapters 3 and 20). In *M(K)* v. *M(H)* (1992) the relationship between a child abuser and his daughter, who was his victim, was also fiduciary.

General principles

Persons in a fiduciary position must not use that position to make an unauthorised benefit for themselves. If they do so, they will be a constructive trustee of those profits. The rule is a strict one and, as the cases show, can be harsh. It was held to apply in *Keech* v. *Sandford* (1726) even though the trustee had not acted fraudulently nor deprived the trust of any benefit. Here a trustee (X) of a lease of a market was granted a renewal of the lease in his own name because the landlord did not wish to renew it on trust as the beneficiary was a minor who could not be bound by the usual covenants. It was held that X held the renewed lease on trust for the minor.

The decision in *Keech* v. *Sandford* has led to a stream of case law on the general question of the extent of when fiduciaries are, and are not, entitled to use opportunities for their own benefit. However, Oakley (1997) contends that the decision should be viewed very much as a creature of its own time and place. He observes (at p. 235) that at that time charitable and other public bodies were restricted in the length of leases which they could grant and so leases were often renewed as a matter of right. Accordingly, a failure to renew was depriving the trust of a grant of a lease which it had a right to expect. Be that as it may, the principle in *Keech* v. *Sandford* was restated in *Bray* v. *Ford* (1896) by Lord Herschell thus: 'It is an inflexible rule of a Court of Equity that a person in a fiduciary position . . . is not, unless expressly authorised, entitled to make a profit; he is not allowed to put himself in a position where duty and interest conflict' (this principle is discussed in more detail in Chapter 16).

The rule also applies where a person making the profit is not a trustee but is in a fiduciary position (see *Boardman* v. *Phipps* (1967) and *Industrial Development Consultants Ltd* v. *Cooley* (1972) (below)) but will not apply if no such relationship can be found. In *Swain* v. *Law Society* (1982) the Law Society was held not to be in a fiduciary position when negotiating a compulsory insurance scheme on behalf of all solicitors so as to make it liable to account for the commission made because the Law Society was acting in a public capacity and so no question of trust law, being private law, arose.

The principle in *Keech* v. *Sandford* and *Bray* v. *Ford* was applied in *Boardman* v. *Phipps* (1967), where the appellants were a solicitor to a trust (Boardman) and one of the beneficiaries (Phipps). The trust owned a substantial holding of shares in a company and the appellants were dissatisfied with its performance. They obtained information, through this connection with the trust, about the company's affairs and as a result they decided to obtain control of the company by purchasing the remainder of its shares. Having done this they reorganised it and made considerable profits for themselves. The trust could not have bought the shares without seeking the sanction of the court and it did not consider doing this. The appellants were held liable to account to the trust for the profits made because they were constructive trustees as they had used the trust shareholding to acquire the necessary information about the company and in addition the respondent beneficiary had not been kept fully informed of the situation. However, the appellants had acted in good faith throughout and so should be allowed 'liberal payment' for their skill in the negotiations which had resulted in the trust acquiring a considerable benefit. Lord Upjohn, however, forcefully dissented and observed that 'the appellants have bought for themselves and with their own money shares which the trustees never contemplated buying and they did so in circumstances fully known and approved of by the trustees'.

This decision has been strongly criticised. There was no doubt that the appellants were in a fiduciary relationship towards the trust, out of which they obtained the opportunity to make a profit. What is disputed is whether they were in a position where their duty as fiduciaries and their personal interest might conflict. Lord Cohen in the House of Lords stressed that there could be a conflict if Boardman had been asked his advice by the trustees about the wisdom of their acquiring a majority shareholding in the company. However, it has been pointed out (e.g. by Oakley – above), that if this had happened Boardman could quite simply have declined to act on the ground of a conflict of interest. In any event, there was little likelihood that the trustees would wish to do this as they had already considered this possibility and decided against it. On a simpler level, the trustees declined to take advantage of an opportunity presented to them to make a profit by acquiring extra shares and when others did so the trust was then allowed to take *their* profit. One idea is that this decision, which was based on the use of information, could have been better treated as one of a possible breach of the equitable duty of confidence (see Chapter 3).

Company directors as fiduciaries

Company directors must not make a profit from their position. If they do, they will be held liable to account for the profit to the company. In *Regal (Hastings) Ltd* v. *Gulliver* (1942) Regal Ltd (R) set up a subsidiary (X Ltd) to acquire the leases of two cinemas. The owner of the cinemas was only prepared to lease them if the share capital of X Ltd was fully subscribed and, because the resources of R only permitted it to subscribe for part of the share capital, the directors of R then subscribed for the rest. The directors subsequently made a profit from their shares and were held liable to account for this to the company. As in *Boardman* (1967) they had acted in good faith and here the company, as with the trust in *Boardman*, did not intend to buy the shares. The result in both cases was to provide a windfall: for the company in this case and for the trust in *Boardman*.

In *Industrial Development Consultants Ltd* v. *Cooley* (1972) the defendant was a director and general manager of the claimant company. He attempted, on the company's behalf, to interest a Gas Board in a project but the Gas Board, having declined to deal with the company, offered the project to the defendant personally. He was held liable to account to the company for the profit he had made and unlike the parties in the above two cases he had not acted in good faith: he had obtained his release from the claimants so as to take up the contract by falsely stating that he was ill.

A less rigorous view was taken in *Queensland Mines Ltd* v. *Hudson* (1978) where the defendant, the managing director of the claimant company, had obtained licences for the claimant to develop some mines. When the claimant found itself unable to do so the defendant, with the claimant's full knowledge, took the licences himself and developed them. He was not held liable to account for profits made because he had not deprived the claimant of any opportunity and had kept the claimant fully informed. It is, however, difficult to reconcile this decision with *Boardman* and *Regal*. Another example of a less inflexible attitude is found in another Australian decision, that of *Warman International* v. *Dwyer* (1995). The claimants held an agency for the distribution of Italian gearboxes and the manufacturer of them then suggested a joint venture where the gearboxes would actually be assembled in Australia. The claimants rejected this idea but an employee of theirs then took it up and formed a joint venture with the defendants and as a result the defendants ended their relationship with the claimants. The claimants claimed that the whole of the goodwill of the joint venture was held on trust for them. The Australian High Court held that a distinction should be drawn between where a fiduciary acquires a specific asset (e.g. as in *Keech* v. *Sandford*), and where a business is acquired and operated, as in *Boardman* v. *Phipps*. In the latter case it was held that it might be inequitable to compel the 'errant fiduciary' to account for the whole of the profit and instead allow him/her a proportion of the profits. This is what occurred here and so an account of the first two years' profit was ordered on the basis that the conduct of the defendant had caused the manufacturers to terminate their agency with the claimants earlier than they would have done. Even here an appropriate allowance had to be made for the effort and skill of the defendant and the manufacturer, as in *Boardman* v. *Phipps*. The difference between this decision and *Boardman* was, of course, that here the liability to account only applied to a proportion of the profits whereas in *Boardman* it applied to all of them.

A more straightforward case is *Guinness plc* v. *Saunders* (1988) where after the takeover of Distillers plc by Guinness the sum of £5.2 million was paid to a company controlled by Ward, a director of Guinness, for Ward's services in connection with the takeover. As this payment had not been disclosed to the Board of Directors of Guinness (pursuant to s. 317 of the Companies Act 1985) Ward held this sum on a constructive trust for Guinness even though the other directors as individuals were aware of the payment.

In *O'Sullivan* v. *Management Agency and Music Ltd* (1985) an exclusive management agreement made between the claimant, at that time a young and unknown composer, and one of the defendants was held to have been made through undue influence and thus to be voidable (see Chapter 3). Although the defendants were liable to account to the claimant for their profits, as they were in a fiduciary position, they were allowed reasonable remuneration including a small profit element because their skill and labour had made a significant contribution to the claimant's success. In *Guinness plc* v. *Saunders* (1990) (see above) Ward argued that he was entitled to a *quantum meruit* for the services he had rendered in connection with the takeover bid. The court refused this and distinguished *Boardman* v. *Phipps* on the ground that the fiduciary there had taken a risk with his own money whereas here Ward, by contracting with the company for his services, had simply taken the company's property.

Receipt of bribes by a person in a fiduciary position

In *A-G for Hong Kong* v. *Reid* (1994) it was held that where persons receive bribes in breach of their fiduciary duty then they become a constructive trustee of them. Here, Reid, a Crown prosecutor, took bribes and then used them to buy land. It was held that, when he had taken the bribes, he became under an immediate duty to pay them over to his principal (i.e. his employer) and so the bribes were the property of his employer in equity. Thus the employer was entitled to claim the profits from the bribes when they were invested. Although this decision clearly has much to commend it on the level of ensuring that a person who takes bribes does not benefit by simply investing them, it also has the result that where a person has taken bribes and invested the proceeds the employer can claim these. Thus if the person is bankrupt, as here, the employer is in a better position that the unsecured creditors of that person.

Position of an agent of trustees

In *Lee* v. *Sankey* (1872) Bacon V-C held that an agent of trustees, such as a solicitor or banker, is not liable as such as a constructive trustee in respect of trust property in his possession and so he is not liable to an action by the beneficiaries. However, he can become a constructive trustee if property is transferred to him in breach of trust and he either has the necessary knowledge or if he assumes the character of a trustee (see *Mara* v. *Browne* (1896)). In *Dubai Aluminium Co Ltd* v. *Salaam* (2002) the House of Lords laid down principles to be applied where it is sought to make the partner liable for the acts of another partner who dishonestly assisted in a breach of trust. Here a dishonest partner had drafted and signed bogus consultancy agreements involving over $50 million. The claimant was the victim of this fraud, and it was held that the firm was liable as, although the acts were not authorised, they were so closely connected with the acts which the dishonest person was authorised to do that he was acting in the ordinary course of business when he committed the acts. Therefore the firm was vicariously liable.

■ Where a statute has been used as an engine of fraud

A constructive trust can be imposed to enforce an oral agreement in a case where written formalities are required by the LPA 1925 if to insist on those formalities would amount to fraud. In *Rochefoucauld* v. *Boustead* (1897) the claimant had mortgaged land but was having difficulty in repaying the mortgage. The defendant bought the land and orally agreed to hold it as trustee for the claimant. However, he treated the land as his own. The court held that the claimant was entitled to an account of profits made on the land because although the trust in the claimant's favour, not being in writing, did not satisfy the requirements of what is now s. 53(1)(b) of the LPA 1925 (see Chapter 6), it would be a fraud on the defendant's part to take the profits for himself.

This principle was followed in *Bannister* v. *Bannister* (1948) where the defendant sold a cottage to the claimant subject to an oral agreement that she could continue to live there. When the claimant subsequently brought an action claiming possession of the cottage, relying on the absence of writing, the court held that he held the cottage on trust for the defendant to permit her to occupy it for her lifetime. Again, in *Hodgson* v. *Marks* (1971) the owner of a house sold it to her lodger (Evans) on the oral understanding that the house would continue to be hers. Evans then sold the house to Marks, who took without notice of the agreement. The court held that the house was held on trust for Mrs Hodgson, who thus remained the beneficial owner in equity and so had an overriding interest under what was s. 70(1)(g) of the Land Registration Act 1925 (now s. 3(2) of the Land Registration Act 2002) which bound Marks.

A difficulty here is deciding which type of trust was created. In *Rochefoucauld* the court appeared to be simply enforcing the express trust which existed in the claimant's favour and to be saying that the formalities provisions (here s. 53(1)(b) of the LPA 1925) can be disregarded where to do otherwise would lead to fraud. In *Hodgson* the trust was categorised as a resulting trust, which by s. 53(2) is exempted from the formalities requirements, and only in *Bannister* was it held to be a constructive trust, to which s. 53(2) also applies. It is suggested that the exact category in which the trust is fitted does not greatly matter as it is the principle which is important.

The courts do not always, however, impose a trust where a failure to comply with a statutory requirement can lead to injustice. In *Midland Bank* v. *Green* (1981) an option granted by a father to his son to purchase a farm had not been registered as required by the Land Charges Act 1972 and the father, having changed his mind about the sale, then carried out a 'sham' sale to his wife so that the son's option was then defeated. The son's claim failed, Lord Wilberforce observing that 'it is not fraud to rely on legal rights conferred by an Act of Parliament'. In *Sen* v. *Headley* (1991) (see Chapter 8) the court imposed a constructive trust so as to give effect to a *donatio mortis causa* of land where the actual transfer did not comply with the statutory formalities.

The new model constructive trust

In a series of cases in the 1970s Denning MR sought to develop what he called 'a constructive trust of a new model' (*Eves* v. *Eves* (1975)). The existence of a fiduciary relationship was not required to found such a trust: instead one would be imposed 'whenever justice and good conscience require it . . . it is an equitable remedy by which the court can enable an aggrieved party to obtain restitution' (Denning MR in *Hussey* v. *Palmer* (1972)). The main areas in which the new model constructive trust have been used are in disputes over the home (see Chapter 12) and the enforceability of contractual licences.

CONTRACTUAL LICENCES

The problem

A licence to use land is not the same as a lease. It does not give an estate or interest in the land but simply a right to use the land, e.g. to a lodger or to guests at a party. Such a licence, if contractual, is binding on the grantor and equity may enforce it by an order of specific performance (see *Verrall* v. *Great Yarmouth BC* (1981) see Chapter 2) and injunction, although, as with all equitable remedies, these are discretionary.

Suppose that the grantor sells the land. Is the licence binding on the transferee? In *Binions* v. *Evans* (1972) Denning MR held that a contractual licence could give rise to a constructive trust which can bind a transferee except a bona fide purchaser of the land without notice. Mrs Evans was the widow of an employee and her husband's employers agreed that she could continue to live rent free in the cottage they had occupied provided she kept it in good order. The employers later sold the cottage to the respondents. They had notice of Mrs Evans' rights and indeed they paid a lower price as a result of her being in occupation. There would have been no difficulty had the court simply imposed a constructive trust on the Binions on the ground that it would be unconscionable for them to assert their rights when they had purchased expressly subject to those rights. However, Denning MR based his decision, not on their unconscionable conduct, but on the need for a contractual licence to be binding on third parties. Thus he held that the respondents (the Binions) held the contractual licence on a constructive trust for Mrs Evans who thus continued to hold the land under the original agreement. (The other two members of the Court of Appeal held instead that Mrs Evans had become a life tenant under the Settled Land Act 1925, which meant that she could sell the cottage, which was certainly not what had been intended.)

The principle in *Binions* v. *Evans* (1972) was followed in *Lyus* v. *Prowsa Developments Ltd* (1982) where the claimant contracted with developers to buy a plot of land with a house to be built on it, but before the house was built or the contract completed the developers went into liquidation. The bank mortgagees then sold the land, which was later re-sold, and in both cases it was a term of the contract that the property was sold subject to the claimant's agreement. It was held that the purchasers held the land on a constructive trust for the claimants who were entitled to specific performance of it. A further example in this area is *Re Sharpe* (1980).

Difficulties with the new model constructive trust

In both *Binions* v. *Evans* (1972) and *Lyus* v. *Prowsa* (1982) the constructive trust was treated as a remedy, i.e. to enable a particular result to be achieved, such as allowing Mrs Evans to remain in the cottage. In one way the use of constructive trusts as remedies is not new: *Keech* v. *Sandford* (1726) could be viewed in this way. What is new is that, as in *Binions* v. *Evans*, the constructive trustee's obligations are really those of a licensor of land and he/she is only made a constructive trustee in order make the licence binding on him/her. This leads to another odd result: the licensor (i.e. the Binions), by virtue of the constructive trust, continues to have a personal interest in the matter, unlike the normal case of trusteeship. Moreover, there was no actual trust property in *Binions* v. *Evans*: what was held on trust was just a legal concept: a contractual licence. Finally, the fact that here the trust was a remedy and nothing else is seen by the fact that, instead of protecting Mrs Evans by imposing a trust, Denning MR could have granted an injunction restraining the Binions from evicting her in breach of their agreement not to do so.

There are two further and more general objections to the new model constructive trust:

(i) To look at a constructive trust as a remedy and not as a substantive institution is wrong because, even though constructive trusts have always been remedies in one sense (see above), they have also been substantive trusts because the property is trust property and therefore if the trustee becomes bankrupt the beneficiaries take priority over the trustee's creditors.
(ii) More fundamentally, the idea of imposing a constructive trust whenever justice requires leads to uncertainty. As Mahon J memorably observed in the New Zealand case of *Carly* v. *Farrelly* (1975): 'No stable system of jurisprudence can permit a litigant's claim to justice to be consigned to the formless void of individual moral opinion'. Note that this issue is explored further in a specimen examination answer in Appendix 3.

The idea of the new model constructive trust is generally out of favour. In trusts of the family home the law is now firmly based on the common intention of the parties and, although, as we shall see in Chapter 12, this has caused difficulties, there is no intention at present of returning to the approach of Denning MR and the new model constructive trust. In cases of contractual licences, the Court of Appeal in *Ashburn Anstalt* v. *Arnold* (1989) held that a contractual licence does not create an interest in land.

The new model constructive trust was firmly rejected by the Court of Appeal in *Halifax Building Society* v. *Thomas* (1995). The defendant obtained a loan to buy a flat by a fraudulent misrepresentation and, when he fell into arrears the mortgagee sold it. After it was sold there was a surplus and the mortgagee claimed this on the ground that there was a constructive trust in its favour as the defendant should not gain from his fraud. The court held that this was wrong. A constructive trust could only be imposed where there was a fiduciary relationship between the parties and here there was none. In effect the court declined to impose a trust simply because it seemed that this was necessary to prevent what might be considered unconscionable behaviour.

The future

Nevertheless the idea of a remedial constructive trust is not entirely dead. The decision in *A-G for Hong Kong* v. *Reid* (1994) that, for the first time, bribes are subject to a constructive trust may have heralded a different approach.

In *Westdeutche Landesbank Girozentrale* v. *Islington LBC* (1996) Lord Browne-Wilkinson observed that 'the remedial constructive trust, if introduced into English law, may provide a more satisfactory way forward' (than resulting trusts). However, in *Re Polly Peck International plc (No. 2)* (1998) the Court of Appeal firmly rejected the idea of imposing a remedial constructive trust. Here the applicants, who owned land in Cyprus, claimed that they were entitled to a remedial constructive trust of the profits which subsidiaries of Polly Peck had made from their land after it had initially been wrongfully appropriated by the Government of Northern Cyprus. The object of the claim was to give them a proprietary remedy which would give them priority over the creditors of Polly Peck. The Court of Appeal, in rejecting their claim, pointed to the difficulty in imposing a remedial constructive trust. As Nourse LJ pointed out, you cannot grant a proprietary right to A, who has not had one before, without taking one away from B. Moreover, he considered Lord Browne Wilkinson's remarks in *Westdeutche* '**obiter dicta** and tentative'. The future of the remedial constructive trust thus remains uncertain.

PROPRIETARY ESTOPPEL

Proprietary estoppel was briefly explored in Chapter 7 in the context of imperfect gifts. However, it would be wrong to see estoppel merely in this context. The doctrine has a vitality of its own and it will be seen that it can apply in a variety of situations. As Denning MR, who used the doctrine of estoppel with enthusiasm, said in *Amalgamated Investment and Property Co* v. *Texas Commerce International Bank Ltd* (1982): 'The doctrine of estoppel is one of the most flexible and useful in the armoury of our law'.

In *Willmott* v. *Barber* (1881) Fry LJ held that the following points need to be proved to succeed in a plea that there is promissory estoppel:

(a) The claimant must have made a mistake as to his legal rights.
(b) The claimant must have either expended some money or done some act on the basis of this mistaken belief.
(c) The defendant, who owns the legal right which the claimant argues that it would be inequitable for him to enforce, must have known of the existence of his own right which is inconsistent with the right asserted by the claimant.
(d) The defendant must have known of the claimant's mistaken belief as to his rights.
(e) The defendant must have encouraged the claimant in his expenditure of money or acts which he has done, either by direct encouragement or by abstaining from asserting his legal right.

Although these 'five probanda', as they are often known, were referred to with approval by Scarman LJ in *Crabb* v. *Arun DC* (1976), they are now felt to impose too much of a straightjacket on estoppel. For example, there may be no mistaken belief yet there seems to be a clear case of estoppel. In *Taylor Fashions Ltd* v. *Liverpool Victoria Trustees Co Ltd* (1981) Oliver J emphasised that the basis of the doctrine is whether the assertion of strict legal rights would be unconscionable and that detailed criteria for the operation of the doctrine would be inappropriate. This simpler formula seems preferable.

A good example of estoppel is *Inwards* v. *Baker* (1965). A father suggested to his son that he should build a bungalow on land owned by the father. The son did so, although there was no formal conveyance to him, and on the father's death it was held that the son could remain in the bungalow for as long as he wished. In *Pascoe* v. *Turner* (1979) the claimant and defendant lived in the claimant's house but the claimant told the defendant that 'the house is yours and everything in it'. Relying on this she spent, to the claimant's knowledge, a substantial part of her small savings on repairs and improvements. When the claimant sought to remove her from the house the court held that the claimant should convey the house to her (see Chapter 12 for further instances of the use of estoppel linked to a constructive trust to resolve disputes of this kind).

The idea of detriment

This generally means that the person seeking to rely on an estoppel must have altered his position in some way in reliance on the encouragement of the other, as occurred in the above two cases. In *Greasley* v. *Cooke* (1980) it was held that detriment need not involve expenditure on the land. Here the defendant had moved into the claimant's property initially as a servant but had then cohabited with the owner's son and after the owner's death had stayed on and cared for the owner's family. She had never received payment because she was led to believe that the house was her home for life. It was held that she could remain for as long as she wished. Denning MR went further and suggested that detriment was not even a requirement and that it was sufficient if it would be inequitable for the other party to go back on his word. However, in *Coombes* v. *Smith* (1986) it was held that this remark only meant that where a party has acted in a way that appears to be to their detriment following assurances from the other there is a rebuttable presumption that these acts were done in reliance on the assurances. This is important, as often in a close relationship there will be a lack of firm evidence as to the effect of a particular promise.

An interesting example is *Wayland* v. *Jones* (1995). Here the claimant (X) and the deceased (Y) were cohabitees and X helped Y in a café which he ran as well as acting as his chauffeur and general companion. Y promised to leave X both a house and the business but only received a car and some furniture. The interest of the case lies in the connection between the promise of Y and X's conduct. The Court of Appeal held that once it is established that there was a promise as to ownership and it is possible to infer that (in this case) Y's promise induced X's conduct then the onus shifts to Y to show that X did not rely on the promises. In this case this could only be done by proving that X would have stayed in the relationship even if the promise had been withdrawn.

In *Re Basham* (1987) it was held that the belief which the other party has encouraged does not have to relate to existing rights and specific assets. The claimant and her husband had lived with her stepfather, helping him to run his house and buying carpets for it, encouraged by the stepfather's frequent statements to the claimant that the house would be hers on his death. He died intestate but it was held that the claimant was entitled to the house. It was sufficient that the belief related to the acquisition of a future right.

Estoppel and promises to leave gifts in wills

In *Taylor* v. *Dickens* (1998) the testatrix told her gardener that she was going to leave him her house by will and, as a result, he no longer accepted any wages for his work. She then left the property elsewhere but the gardener's action based on estoppel failed in the ground that, in the cases of promises to leave gifts in wills, there was in effect an additional requirement that the promisor created or encouraged a belief in the mind of the other that the promisor would not change that part of the will in which the gift was given.

It was widely felt that this was too rigid a requirement and the position was soon changed by the decision of the Court of Appeal in *Gillett* v. *Holt* (2000). The claimant had worked for the defendant on his farm since he left school at 16 in 1956 and the essence of his claim was that the defendant had on at least seven occasions promised to leave him the farm business and had executed a will leaving him his entire estate. The claimant argued that he had acted on these promises to his detriment and that as a result the defendant was estopped from going back on them even though he had subsequently executed a will leaving his property to someone else.

The evidence of detriment was based on the relationship between the claimant and the defendant which went beyond that of employer and employee. The claimant, for example, lived at the farm for some time and the defendant at one stage talked of adopting him; the defendant was shocked when the claimant announced that he was getting married. The claimant gradually became increasingly useful on the farm and became the farm manager. He and his family lived in a house owned by a company controlled by the defendant and, in effect, they provided the defendant with a surrogate family, even deferring to his wishes about the education of their children. The claimant received a lesser wage than he would have done elsewhere and did not apply for other jobs where he might have expected a higher wage. Finally, in 1992, after 36 years, the relationship began to cool and in 1994 the defendant executed a new will leaving all his property elsewhere.

The Court of Appeal did not accept that a promise to leave by will must be considered revocable. As Robert Walker LJ put it '. . . the inherent revocability of testamentary dispositions . . . is irrelevant to a promise or assurance that "all will be yours"' (one of the phrases used by the defendant). In other words, although a testator can revoke a will, this will not affect an estoppel arising out of a promise *not* to revoke it. As a result, although the second will in this case remained valid, the claimant was entitled to the house which he had occupied together with some land and £100,000 and so this property would, on the death of Gillett, be held on trust for the claimant by the person to whom the property had been left under the second will.

How should the rights be given effect to?

The principle is that if the equity is established by proving estoppel then the court has a discretion on how it must be satisfied. It is often said that the court must seek to do the minimum equity between the parties and this may mean that the claimant receives nothing as he has already received enough to do justice to his claim. A good example is *Sledmore* v. *Dalby* (1996), where a promise to leave a house had been relied on as the claimant had made various improvements to it but the equity had already been satisfied as the claimant had already lived in it rent free for 18 years.

In *Inwards* v. *Baker* (1965) the son was given a licence to remain but problems with the enforceability of licences against third parties (see above) may have been the reason why in *Pascoe* v. *Turner* (1979) (see below) a conveyance of the legal estate was ordered. In *Dodsworth* v. *Dodsworth* (1973) the court refused to allow the parties to remain in the property for the rest of their lives because this would make them tenants for life under the Settled Land Act, which was more than had been intended. (A tenant for life can sell the property.) Instead, the parties were allowed to remain until, in effect, their expenditure on the house constituting the reason for estoppel had been reimbursed. A recent interesting example of estoppel is *Parker* v. *Parker* (2003), which concerned an unsuccessful claim under estoppel by the Earl of Macclesfield to remain in the ancestral home of Shirburn Castle. (See Thompson (2003).)

Proprietary estoppel and other doctrines

Proprietary estoppel and promissory estoppel

Proprietary estoppel differs from the doctrine of promissory estoppel as developed in *Central London Property Trust Ltd* v. *High Trees Houses Ltd* (1947) because proprietary estoppel can found a claim where none existed before whereas promissory estoppel is considered as a 'shield not a sword' (Birkett LJ in *Combe* v. *Combe* (1951)). However, in *Amalgamated Investment & Property Co Ltd* v. *Texas Commerce International Bank Ltd* (1982) Denning MR considered that all types of estoppel were really aspects of the principle that a person will not be allowed to go back on an assumption created if it would be unjust to do so.

Proprietary estoppel and the former doctrine of part performance

The former doctrine of part performance used to enable a contract for the sale of land to be enforced despite the absence of writing on the basis that one party had partly performed the agreement. This doctrine was abolished by the Law Reform (Miscellaneous Provisions) Act 1989, which now requires all contracts for the sale of land to be made in writing. It might have been thought that the doctrine of estoppel would be the obvious replacement for part performance but in *Yaxley* v. *Gotts* (2000) the Court of Appeal decided that the correct basis was the imposition of a constructive trust. This was because s. 2(5) of the 1989 Act provided that s. 2 did not affect the operation of 'resulting, implied or constructive trusts'.

Here the claimant, Mr Yaxley, was a builder who intended to buy a house in order to renovate it and let it as flats. However, he could not raise the necessary capital and so he made an arrangement with the second defendant, Mr Brownie Gotts, under which Mr Gotts would buy the house but Mr Yaxley would get the ground floor flat, which he was to convert into two, in return for converting the flats on the other floors and acting as Mr Gotts' managing agent for all the flats in the house. The agreement was not in writing, partly at least because the parties were friends, although there was evidence that Mr Yaxley did ask for a written agreement and was assured that one would be prepared, although it never was. An additional factor was that the property was actually purchased by Mr Alan Gotts, the first defendant, who was the son of Brownie Gotts. As often happens, the belief of the parties that there was no need to make a formal agreement turned out to be mistaken, because there was a disagreement three years later as a result of which Mr Yaxley was excluded from the house.

The Court of Appeal held that, as there was an agreement between the parties which showed a 'common intention' on the basis of *Lloyds Bank* v. *Rosset* (1990) (see Chapter 12), this was sufficient to impose a constructive trust. As the decision rested on intention the court clearly needed to give effect to this and the county court judge had found that there was an agreement that Mr Yaxley should in some sense 'own' the ground floor flat and this finding was not challenged on appeal. Nor was there any challenge to the remedy, which was that his equitable entitlement would be satisfied by the grant of a long lease (in the event, for 99 years) of the flat.

The relationship between proprietary estoppel and part performance is shown by Example 11.1.

Example 11.1

X orally agrees that Y can have Blackacre to use as a smallholding. Y enters on Blackacre and erects various buildings on the land and generally improves it. X then claims Blackacre relying on the lack of writing. Whereas before Y's acts in partly performing the agreement (erection of buildings, etc.) might enable the court to hold that they were sufficient acts of part performance, the court will now impose a constructive trust so that X holds Blackacre on such a trust for Y.

Proprietary estoppel and constructive trusts

Estoppel has been linked to the concept of the constructive trust in cases involving the family home (see Chapter 12) and so the obvious question is whether they are distinct areas of equity or if it is simply, as it were, just a case of two labels for the same contents. In *Lloyds Bank* v. *Rosset* (1990) Lord Bridge referred to the 'agreement and detrimental conduct' cases as giving rise to a constructive trust or proprietary estoppel and the family home cases such as *Pascoe* v. *Turner* and *Burrows and Burrows* v. *Sharp* (1991) were based firmly on estoppel. This topic is considered further in Chapter 12.

The distinction between the concepts of a constructive trust in this type of situation and estoppel is also brought out by *Gillett* v. *Holt*. In these types of cases a constructive trust rests on a common intention (see *Yaxley* v. *Gotts* (above) and also Chapter 12 and especially *Lloyds Bank plc* v. *Rosset*) but in cases of estoppel the object is to prevent a party from suffering detriment. However, in the High Court in *Gillett* Carnwarth J emphasised the need for a 'mutual understanding . . . between promisor and promisee, both as to the content of the promise and as to what the promisee is doing, or may be expected to do, in reliance on it'. The Court of Appeal rejected this. It held that with estoppel the initial promise is made without consideration and it is the reliance on it which makes it irrevocable. The search for mutual understanding is an irrelevance.

> *Note 11.2: For an interesting exploration of personal liability in estoppel cases see Bright and McFarlane (2005).*

PROTECTIVE TRUSTS

The object of a protective trust is to restrain spendthrift beneficiaries. Indeed, in the USA a similar type of trust is called a 'spendthrift trust'. The mechanisms used are a determinable life interest with a discretionary trust should that interest determine. Accordingly property will be settled on trust, e.g. for X for life until he becomes bankrupt or voluntarily alienates his interest or any other event occurs which would entitle a third party to the income. Thus if X attempts to mortgage the trust property to repay his debts his interest will then be forfeited so that instead of a mortgagee becoming entitled to trust property the discretionary trusts will come into operation.

Section 33 of the Trustee Act 1925 provides that a reference in a settlement to 'protective trusts' will bring the protective trusts in s. 33 into operation. The discretionary trusts specified here are that the income from the settlement is to be applied at the trustee's discretion for the maintenance, support or benefit of any of the following:

(a) The principal beneficiary and any spouse, children or more remote issue of his, *or*
(b) The principal beneficiary and the persons who would, if he were dead, be entitled to the trust property or the income where there is no spouse or issue in existence.

The principal beneficiary is the same person as the life tenant whose interest was forfeited and so the result is that whereas before he was absolutely entitled to the income from the trust his entitlement is now at the trustee's discretion.

Section 33(1) expressly provides that an advancement of capital made under an express power or under s. 32 of the Trustee Act 1925 (see Chapter 18) shall not cause a forfeiture of an interest. Likewise, in *General Accident Fire and Life Assurance Corporation Ltd* v. *IRC* (1963) it was held that a life tenant's interest was not forfeited when part of his income was diverted by a court order to his former wife.

FURTHER READING

Bright and McFarlane (2005) 'Proprietary estoppel and proprietary rights', 66 CLJ 449 Conv. 14. Useful survey of the whole area.

Finn (1977) *Fiduciary Obligations*, Cambridge: Cambridge University Press. A standard work.

Oakley (1997) *Constructive Trusts*, 3rd edn. London: Sweet & Maxwell. An excellent survey of the whole area.

Wells (1999) 'A restrictive approach to proprietary estoppel in the Court of Appeal', 63 Conv. 462. Considers *Gillett* v. *Holt*.

CHAPTER SUMMARY

- Constructive trusts imposed on those who make a profit out of their fiduciary position.
- Constructive trusts imposed where a statute was used as an engine of fraud.
- New model constructive trust.
- Estoppel: representation – detriment – remedy?
- Protective trusts.

QUESTION

Is it possible to arrive at a satisfactory description of what a constructive trust is and what it does?

Note 11.3: You will find suggested points for inclusion in the answer at Appendix 2.

12 Trusts and the home

INTRODUCTION

The legal background

All of the following examples, except one, refer to situations dealt with in this chapter, and the one which does not is included for the purposes of comparison.

Example 12.1

An elderly brother (Arnold) sells his own house and moves in with his sister (Maud). He uses the money from the sale of his house to pay for essential repairs to his sister's house.

Arnold claims a share in the house.

Example 12.2

Jack and Jill are getting married and their respective parents each provide 50 per cent of the deposit on the house which they are buying.

Their parents claim a share in the house.

Example 12.3

Steve and Mike are partners and they each contributed 50 per cent of the cost of the house in which they live. The house is in Steve's name.

Mike claims a share in the house.

Example 12.4

Laurie and Anastasia are married but are now going through a divorce. The family home is in Anastasia's name.

Laurie claims a share in the house.

Example 12.5

Fred and Mollie are not married and their house is in Fred's name.
Mollie claims a share in the house.

Example 12.6

Take Example 12.4, but now Laurie and Anastasia are not seeking a divorce but the dispute is between them and a third party, for example, a mortgage lender. Anastasia has taken out a loan secured by a mortgage without the knowledge of Laurie and she cannot repay it. The lender is seeking to repossess the house and the question is what, if any, interest in the house does Laurie have as against the lender.

All of these situations are commonly met with today. Clearly equity is involved in all but one of them. (Which are the odd ones out? (See below.)) This is because the legal title to the house is held by one party and so the only way in which the other party can claim a share is in equity by arguing that the house is held on trust for them and so they have a beneficial share. What is the way forward? If there is a trust document which clearly states that the party claiming has a share then that should end the matter but often there is not. The result is that the courts have tried to find a solution based on resulting trusts, constructive trusts and estoppel.

The situations where the law of trusts does not provide the answer are Examples 12.3 and 12.4. Where the parties are married and a divorce is sought then, under the Matrimonial Causes Act 1973, the court has very wide powers to allocate the assets of the couple and this includes power to make orders as to the entitlement to the family home. Accordingly, the law of trusts plays no direct part here. In *Mossop* v. *Mossop* (1988) it was held that the Matrimonial Causes Act does not apply to disputes between engaged couples which will therefore be governed by the rules set out in this unit.

Note 12.1: In Example 12.3 the position has recently changed because, under the Civil Partnership Act 2004, where a civil partnership between members of the same sex (see ss. 1 and 3) has been registered (see s. 2) then, if there is a dispute between the partners about entitlement to property the court shall, under s. 66, make any order with respect to the property as it thinks fit. This language is very similar to that used in matrimonial legislation (see (i) above) and so the court will apply principles from matrimonial law and not trust law in future between same sex partners.

Note 12.2: Where the parties are married, s. 37 of the Matrimonial Proceedings and Property Act 1970 may be of use in these situations. It provides that where a spouse or fiancée makes substantial contributions to improvement of property then this entitles them to such a share in the property as seems just to the court. However, s. 37 merely declares the law and does not enunciate any new principle.

Thus, we can say that the one situation where the law of trusts is not involved in disputes over the home is on divorce or (in future) on the breakup of a civil partnership.

The social background

There are three main reasons why this area has become one of the most significant in the whole of the law of trusts:

(i) The rise in owner occupation. 100 years ago, most people leased their houses but now nearly 70 per cent of houses are owner occupied and only around 10 per cent are rented. (See Social Trends 30 (2000), quoted in Tee (1998), from which these and other data quoted here are taken.)
(ii) The rise in house prices, which has meant that the home is usually the most valuable asset which a family has.
(iii) The extent to which couples have rights in the home. 100 years ago, if the couple did own their home, it would almost certainly be in the name of the man. In 1984, 74 per cent of new mortgages were taken out by couples although this was the high point: this figure declined to 56 per cent in 1998 and by comparison 39 per cent of mortgages were taken out by single people in 1998, with those granted to single women doubling between 1984 and 1998. In addition, not only did couples increasingly share the legal ownership, but, more significantly for the law of trusts, women are now far more likely to have contributed to the cost of acquisition, even if they are not actually owners.

THE RESPONSE OF THE LAW OF TRUSTS

Assuming that it is to the law of trusts that we must turn to find a solution to disputes over entitlement to the home, how does it respond? This initially depends on how the parties have arranged the matter. There are the following possibilities:

(a) The parties may hold the legal title to the home in both their names, in which case they will be legal joint tenants. Here there may be an express declaration of trust which provides that the parties are to hold the property as beneficial joint tenants.
(b) The property may be held in the name of only one party but there is an express declaration of trust which sets out the beneficial entitlement of both parties. This must either be in writing or be evidenced in writing (s. 53(1)(b) LPA 1925).
(c) Where the property is, unlike in (a) above, in the name of one party only but, unlike (b), there is no express declaration of trust. This situation, which is clearly undesirable in practice, nevertheless often happens and it is here that equity has had to apply the concepts of resulting and constructive trusts. The

requirement that a declaration of a trust of land must be in writing does not apply to resulting or constructive trusts (see LPA s. 53(2)) and so the fact that an agreement is oral is no bar to its enforcement. It is with this area that the remainder of this chapter will be largely concerned.

SUMMARY OF THE POSITION WHERE THERE IS NO EXPRESS DECLARATION OF TRUST

The present approach of the courts is based on giving effect to any **common intention** which the parties had with regard to entitlement to the home. This is the approach currently favoured by the English courts (see e.g. *Lloyds Bank plc* v. *Rosset* (1990), the present leading authority).

However, as the law is still in a state of some flux, it is a good idea to first take a historical approach to see how it reached its present position.

THE COURT OF APPEAL IN THE 1970s

Eves v. *Eves* (1975) – a case study in judicial attitudes

This well-known case is an excellent illustration of the way in which judges, on the same set of facts, are able to decide cases involving disputes over the home either on a general basis of what is equitable or, alternatively, on the basis of common intention.

The facts are perhaps the best known of all cases in this area. The claimant, aged 19, lived with the defendant and they intended to marry when she had obtained a divorce from her husband. They found another house and the defendant told her that, although it was to be a house for themselves and their children, it would have to be put into his name only as the claimant was under 21. This untrue statement was, he later admitted, simply just an excuse to avoid putting it into joint names.

The claimant did not pay towards anything to the cost of acquisition but she did a great deal of work to it by, for example, wielding a 14lb sledgehammer to break up concrete and in general renovating what was a dilapidated house. The relationship broke up and the claimant claimed that the house was held on trust for him and her.

Denning MR in the Court of Appeal held that, having regard to the defendant's conduct at the time in telling the claimant that it was to be their joint home, it would be inequitable to allow him to deny her a share in the house. He quoted his judgment in *Cooke* v. *Head* (1972): 'Whenever two parties by their joint efforts acquire property for their joint benefit, the court may impose or impute a constructive or resulting trust'.

Browne LJ and Brightman LJ also held in her favour but on different reasoning. They accepted that there was an arrangement that the house would be in joint names and they found that there was a link between this arrangement and the work which the claimant did on the house. On this basis she was entitled to a share.

Criticisms of this approach

The conclusion that there was common intention has been strongly criticised: Clarke (1992) tellingly analyses the situation: 'I am about to move into a new house with my girlfriend. She wants to have a share in the property. I do not want her to have a share. I find some excuse which fobs her off. Surely this is not agreement: it is disagreement'. The truth seems to be that the judges were determined to find that she was entitled to a share and used the notion of agreement as a convenient tool which was ready to hand.

The uncertainty which the approach of Denning MR could lead to was, however, criticised at the time, as this trenchant passage from the judgment of Bagnall J in *Cowcher* v. *Cowcher* (1972) shows: 'In any individual case the application of [established rules of law] may produce a result which appears unfair. So be it: in my view that is not an injustice . . . in determining rights, particularly property rights, the only justice that can be attained by mortals . . . is justice that flows from the application of sure and settled principles . . .'

Moreover, the point has often been made that in property matters, where the rights of third parties, such as purchasers, may be involved, it is vital that questions of beneficial entitlement to property should be settled according to clear rules. In addition, heed should be taken of the 'note of caution' sounded by Griffith LJ in *Bernard* v. *Josephs* (1982), who observed that one reason why a man and woman might decide to live together without marrying is to preserve their independence and the court should beware of always making the same assumptions and drawing the same inferences as it would in the case of a married couple.

A final point of criticism of the wider approach of the Court of Appeal is that it does not seem appropriate where a third party is involved. In *Hussey* v. *Palmer* (1972) the claimant was invited by her son-in-law and daughter to live with them and she paid for an extension to be built for her to live in. When she left she was held to be entitled to repayment of the sum left on a constructive trust on the ground that the defendant (the son-in-law) could not conscientiously keep the money himself. The effect was to give her an interest in the house. Would it have been better to have treated the transaction as a loan?

The vital point, when reading this chapter, is to be aware that the present state of the law is controversial and there are other solutions then the one currently favoured.

THE PRESENT STATE OF THE LAW

Concepts used by the courts

In giving effect to their decisions the courts have used the concepts of:

(i) resulting or implied trust;
(ii) constructive trust;
(iii) estoppel, which has been linked with the imposition of a constructive trust in e.g. *Grant* v. *Edwards* (1986) and *Lloyds Bank plc* v. *Rosset* (1990).

The courts have often observed that it matters little, if at all, whether the trust which is imposed is called a resulting, implied or a constructive trust (see e.g. Lord Diplock in *Gissing* v. *Gissing* (1971) and below). However, the fundamental difference between a resulting and a constructive trust in this context is that if a resulting trust is held to have arisen when a party is claiming on the basis of contributions, then the extent of their beneficial share will be in proportion to their contributions. If a constructive trust is imposed, then the courts have a wider discretion as to the extent of the shares. The detailed implications of this are considered later but, for now, the type of trust in these cases will be referred to as a constructive trust, in line with the words of Lord Bridge in *Rosset*.

The final point is that, once the courts have decided that a party is entitled to a share, they then need to decide the extent of that share.

It is worth keeping in mind that here are two issues, which need to be kept separately:

(a) Does the party get a share at all?
(b) If so, what is the size of that share?

The 'common intention approach' to the problem

This approach is the one currently taken by the courts and its origin is found in *Pettitt* v. *Pettitt* (1970) and *Gissing* v. *Gissing* (1971), two cases involving disputes over entitlement to the matrimonial home. Although, as mentioned above, these disputes are now dealt with under the Matrimonial Causes Act 1973, the requirement that there must have been a common intention that the party whose name was not on the conveyance should have some entitlement was upheld by the Court of Appeal in later cases involving cohabitees and others, as explained below.

In *Lloyds Bank plc* v. *Rosset* (1990) Lord Bridge, following the approach of the Court of Appeal in *Grant* v. *Edwards* (1986), gave an authoritative statement of what is the present law: He held that in the absence of any express declaration of trust the court must consider:

(a) Has there at 'any time prior to acquisition, or exceptionally at some later date, been any agreement, arrangement or understanding between them (the parties) that the property is to be shared beneficially'. Such a finding can, he said, be based only on evidence of express discussions. Once such a finding has been made 'it will only be necessary for the partner asserting a claim to a beneficial interest' to show that he or she acted to his or her detriment 'or significantly altered his or her position in reliance on the agreement in order to give rise to a constructive trust or a proprietary estoppel'. (These are referred to in this chapter as 'agreement and detrimental conduct cases'.)
(b) In sharp contrast there was, said Lord Bridge, the situation where no agreement or arrangement can be found. Therefore 'the court must rely entirely on the conduct of the parties' as the basis from which to infer a common intention to share the property beneficially and as to the conduct relied on to give rise to a constructive trust. Here, direct contributions to the purchase price

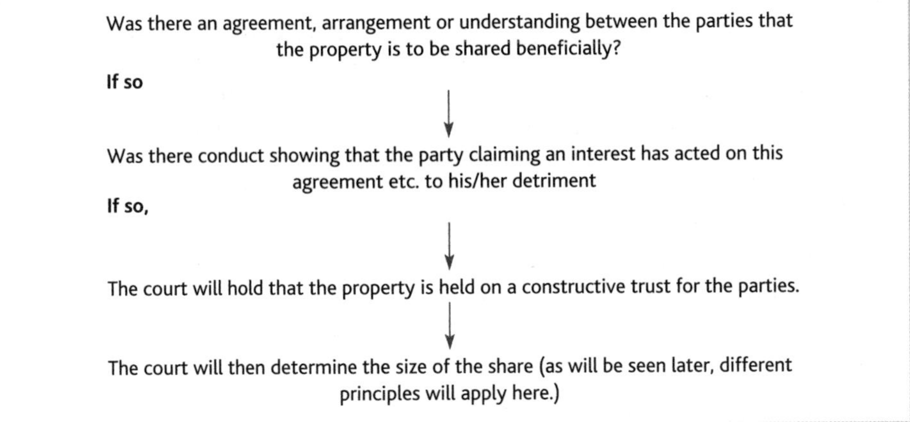

Figure 12.1 Agreement and detrimental conduct cases (situation (a) in *Rosset*): a summary

'whether initially or by payment of mortgage instalments will readily justify the inference of a constructive trust' but 'it is at least extremely doubtful whether anything less will do'. (Referred to in this chapter as 'direct contribution cases'.)

If, however, the answer to these questions is no, then it is necessary consider the situation in Figure 12.2.

If the answer to this question is also no, then the party claiming has no entitlement to any beneficial interest in the property.

Cases involving the application of situations (a) and (b) will now be considered.

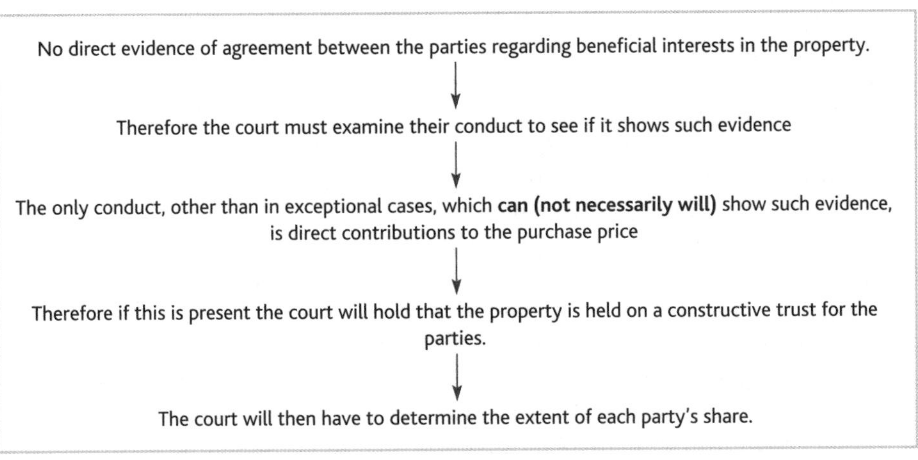

Figure 12.2 Direct contribution cases (situation (b) in *Rosset*): a summary

Agreement and detrimental conduct cases considered in detail

The fundamental problem in this area is that of finding any evidence at all of the common intentions of the parties, given that they have not made them plain by any declaration of trust, which is precisely why this part of the law exists. Very often the question of who owns the property and in what shares will be the last thing on their minds. Thus in *Hammond* v. *Mitchell* (1991), Waite J observed that the parties were 'too much in love at this time either to count the pennies or pay attention to who was providing them'. In theory, there are two separate elements: common intention and evidence that it was acted on to the detriment of the party claiming. As Nourse LJ put it in *Grant* v. *Edwards*: would the party have done what he/she did but for the agreement (i.e. their common intention)? Yet in fact the elements of common intention and detrimental reliance are often confused, as we shall see.

Grant v. *Edwards* (1986) also concerned cohabitees where again the house was conveyed into the man's name only, the excuse being that if the woman's name was on the title deeds it would prejudice her position in divorce proceedings pending against her husband. The woman made substantial contributions to housekeeping and general expenses, although the man paid off the mortgage and the court held that her contributions amounted to acting to her detriment sufficient to raise an estoppel. Common intention was found from the man's excuse which was again held to be just a trick to prevent the agreement being formalised.

Note: Although this case and *Ungarian* v. *Lesnoff* (below) predated *Rosset*, they are still of relevance as in *Grant* v. *Edwards* Nourse LJ put forward principles to decide beneficial entitlement which are in essence the same as in *Rosset*.

In *Ungarian* v. *Lesnoff* (1989) the defendant gave up a promising academic career in Poland and surrendered her rent controlled flat in order to live with the claimant in England. The claimant paid for the home which was in his name although the defendant made considerable improvements to it. The court held that proof of a common intention was provided by the defendant having given up her career and flat, together with conversations at the time indicating an agreement, and her subsequent acts amounted to acting to her detriment. Vinelott J held that detrimental acts (e.g. the improvements here) need not refer only to the house and could therefore include the other acts of the defendant.

In *Hammond* v. *Mitchell* (1992), the defendant, a former Bunny Girl, was held to be entitled to a beneficial interest in the house, which was registered in the claimant's name and where they had lived for eleven years, on the basis of discussions which amounted to an understanding that she would be so entitled. In particular the claimant had said to her: 'Don't worry about the future because when we are married it will be half yours anyway . . .' In addition he had told her that the house was to be conveyed into his sole name for tax reasons. She had acted to her detriment by supporting her husband's speculative business ventures which could have led to loss of the house. The basis of this decision is extremely flimsy: there was no evidence that the woman had consented to what the man said and so no evidence of common intention. Yet one was found. How could she have acted to her detriment on the basis of a common intention of which she was ignorant?

A recent example is *Chan Pu Chan* v. *Leung Kam Ho* (2001), where the defendant promised the claimant that he would leave his wife for her and bought a house in which he promised her a share. This was the evidence of common intention and detrimental reliance was found in the help that she gave him in running his business.

An instance of where common intention was argued but failed is *Springette* v. *Defoe* (1992), where the issue was not whether a party should receive a share but its extent. The problem was that there was no evidence that the parties had ever discussed their respective interests and Steyn LJ observed that 'Our trust law does not allow a party's rights to be affected by telepathy'.

A final and vital point is that Lord Bridge stressed that any evidence of common intention must exist prior to acquisition or exceptionally at some later date. Therefore the normal rule is that the beneficial interest must be ascertained from consideration of the intentions of the parties at the date of acquisition which will usually mean the date of purchase of the house. This was reaffirmed in *Turton* v. *Turton* (1987).

Direct contribution cases considered in detail

Here, as held in *Lloyds Bank* v. *Rosset* (1990), only direct contributions to the purchase price will suffice, and Lord Bridge seemed to virtually close the door on any other way in which a share could be acquired under this head by saying that 'as I read the authorities it is at least extremely doubtful if anything less will do'.

In *Buggs* v. *Buggs* (2003) the often overlooked point was made that, even though there may be direct financial contributions, these must be referable to a common intention to acquire a beneficial interest in the property. X sought a declaration that she was entitled to a share in a flat which had been bought for the mother of her former husband, Y. It was held that, although she had undoubtedly contributed to a common pool from which the mortgage was paid, there was no intention that either X or Y was to acquire a beneficial interest. Instead, it was intended that the whole family unit should benefit from the investment in the flat and not X and Y personally.

In *Springette* v. *Defoe* (1992) the court treated the discount allowed to a local authority tenant exercising a statutory right to buy as a direct contribution, and in *Le Foe* v. *Le Foe* (2001) the wife had made indirect contributions to the cost of the mortgage payments on the family home and this was held to be sufficient. It is unlikely, in view of Lord Bridge's words in *Rossett* (above), that where one party has paid all the household expenses to free the income of the other party to pay the mortgage that this indirect contribution will suffice. However, in *Burns* v. *Burns* (1984) Fox LJ considered that this would be sufficient (although of course his remarks pre-date *Rosset*): 'If there is a substantial contribution by the woman to family expenses, and the house was purchased on a mortgage, her contribution is, indirectly, referable to the acquisition of the house since, in one way or another, it enables the family to pay off the mortgage instalments'. The Law Commission Paper 'Sharing Homes' (2002) recommended that indirect contributions of the kind mentioned by Fox LJ should suffice and there may be scope for the law to move forward here. As things stand, this remains probably the most controversial aspect of this area of the law.

Where a claimant cannot bring her claim under either the 'agreement and detrimental conduct' head or the 'direct contribution' head

Here the claim will fail. The best known instance of this is probably *Burns* v. *Burns* (1984). The parties were cohabitees and the house was in the defendant's name. The claimant made no direct contribution to the purchase price but brought up their two children, looked after the house and, when she began work, she started to pay some bills and did some decorating. The court held that these acts were insufficient to establish any common intention about ownership. Nor, applying *Rosset*, had she made a direct contribution to the cost of acquisition. The details of this case repay careful study, for it is when the present law is criticised that the situation here is what critics have in mind.

A slightly more recent example of a failure to establish a beneficial interest is found in *Ivin* v. *Blake* (1993). Here a house was bought for the mother but was put into the name of her son as it was believed that the mother could not obtain a loan. The mother, however, paid both the deposit and the mortgage instalments. The sister, who lived in the house until the mother's death, claimed that she was entitled to a beneficial share but as there was no evidence that she had contributed to the purchase of the house, her claim failed.

Presumptions of advancement in this area (see Chapter 10)

These play little part, being regarded as outmoded. In *Pettitt* v. *Pettitt* (1970), for example, Lord Reid could see little reason for applying the presumption in the case of a husband who spends money on improving his wife's property. He therefore would not accept an argument that the husband must be regarded as having made a gift to her in accordance with the presumption of advancement. In *Calverly* v. *Green* (1984) Murphy J felt that these presumptions should be discarded altogether.

Determining the size of the share

Position before the decision in *Oxley* v. *Hiscock*

Until the decision in *Oxley* v. *Hiscock* (2004) (below) there were three approaches:

(a) The traditional rule was that if a resulting trust is imposed then property should be held for each party in proportion to their contributions but if a constructive trust is imposed the court has a more general discretion. Thus where the claim is based on direct contributions to the purchase price then the resulting trust principle will apply and they will be entitled to shares in proportion to their contributions unless there is evidence of a common intention to the contrary (*Springette* v. *Defoe* 1992). Where the claim is based on a common intention (agreement and detrimental reliance cases) the court must look for some evidence of what share the parties intended each should have.

(b) The exact opposite approach is that of Lord Diplock in *Gissing* v. *Gissing* (1971), who suggested that the parties are taken to have agreed that when the property was acquired their shares were not to be quantified then, but would be left to be decided when the relationship ended on the basis of what is fair.

(c) The approach in *Midland Bank plc* v. *Cooke* (1995). The court held that, even where the claim is based on direct contributions, it has a discretion to award the parties shares which do not correspond to their contributions but are assessed on a wider principle, as distinct from the approach in *Springett* v. *Defoe*. The problem is to find a principle for this wider approach. In *Cooke* the Court of Appeal held that it was that the court must undertake a survey of the whole course of dealing between the parties relevant to their ownership and occupation of the property to determine 'what proportions the parties must have assumed to have intended (from the outset) for their beneficial ownership'.

Here the house was bought in the name of the husband with a mortgage of £6,450, the balance coming from the husband's savings and a wedding present of £1,100 from his parents to both of them. The husband subsequently took out a later mortgage and the question was one of the wife's rights as against the mortgagee. It was held that, although her actual contribution (half of the wedding present) only gave her a 6.47 per cent share on strict resulting trust principles, in cases of direct contributions the court can look at all the circumstances to find the true intentions of the parties. Here there was evidence that they intended to share equally in other matters, such as the profits of the business and the bringing up of their children. In addition, the house had been put into joint names after the mortgage and the wife had helped to maintain and improve it. This led the court to infer that the parties intended that they should each have a 50 per cent share in the house.

The significance of *Oxley* v. *Hiscock*

This was a fairly standard case of a claim by a cohabitee to a share in equity of the home. However, the actual decision of the Court of Appeal may point the way to a change in judicial attitudes in this whole area.

Mrs Oxley met Mr Hiscock in 1985 and at that time she was a secure tenant of a house. Mr Hiscock moved in with her and, when she exercised her right to buy the property was conveyed into her sole name, although he contributed £25,200 towards the price by way of a mortgage to her. Later this house was sold and another property was bought which was conveyed into his name. The £25,200 lent on mortgage was used as part of Mr Hiscock's contribution to the purchase and he made further cash contributions. Mrs Oxley also contributed and the rest of the price was found by a mortgage. The relationship ended and the usual question arose as to their beneficial shares in the property.

The Court of Appeal held that they each had a beneficial share as they had both made a financial contribution and this was evidence of a common intention on the lines of *Lloyds Bank* v. *Rosset*. Although there was still the need for a detrimental reliance, as a constructive trust is involved, this was easily inferred from the making of the financial contribution. As for the extent of the beneficial shares, Chadwick LJ found the reasoning in Cooke to be the least satisfactory of the possibilities as he found it artificial to attribute an intention to the parties at the outset of their relationship when they had clearly given no thought to the matter. Instead he proposed that the test should be the simple one of what 'would be a fair share for each party having regard to the whole course of dealing between them in relation to the property?'

This was in effect the reasoning which was applied in the earlier case of *Drake* v. *Whipp* (1996), where the woman provided 40 per cent of the purchase price of a barn which was bought for conversion into a house. The man provided the rest and they both contributed to the actual conversion both with their labour and financially. Although the woman's contribution in financial terms was 19.4 per cent it, was held that, as there was no direct evidence of their intentions regarding their shares, the court could assess her share as 40 per cent.

However, in a subsequent decision to *Oxley* v. *Hiscock*, *Curley* v. *Parkes* (2004), the law has been thrown into doubt once more (Dixon 2005). The claimant was a former partner of the defendant in whose name the house was. He had both made a lump sum payment towards the acquisition of the house which they had shared and had contributed to a joint account out of which mortgage repayments were made. It was held by the Court of Appeal that, as both these payments were made after the acquisition of the house, they could not count towards a claim under a resulting trust.

This is a confusing and unsatisfactory decision although there was a decision to the same effect in *Carlton* v. *Goodman* (2002). The source of the trouble appears to have been the decision in the county court that, as there was no evidence that there was any common intention about beneficial ownership, any claim had to be based on a resulting and not a constructive trust and the decision that in a resulting trust any beneficial interest arises once and for all when the property is purchased. Subsequent contributions to the repayment of the mortgage are not contributions to the purchase price but go to discharging the debt owed to the mortgagee. This seems to be a surprisingly restrictive view of the part played by mortgage repayments in establishing a beneficial interest and it is significant that *Lloyds Bank* v. *Rosset* was not mentioned at all. The emphasis placed on the concept of a resulting trust contrasts with the emphasis on constructive trusts in *Oxley* v. *Hiscock*.

What may happen in future is that, assuming that *Curley* v. *Parkes* is regarded as confined to situations where the claim rests only on a resulting trust, the wider discretion which the courts now have to decide on the exact extent of a party's beneficial interest may in time lead to that discretion being applied to deciding whether a party should have any share at all. This would mean the *Rosset* principles could be eroded. Indeed the judgement of Chadwick LJ in *Oxley*, with its realisation that search for common intention in cases of ascertaining the extent of the shares is a chimera, could with equal force be applied to a search for common intention with regard to whether party has a share at all. We are really back to the criticisms of *Eves* v. *Eves* 30 years ago (see above). The use made by Chadwick LJ of the principle of estoppel in reaching his decision is discussed below.

Entitlement to share in any increase in value

In *Turton* v. *Turton* (1987) it was held that where a person is entitled to a share in the home then they are entitled to share proportionately in any increase in its value and that the date for assessing that value is the date when it is realised. This will normally mean, in the case of a house, the date when it is sold. In *Protheroe* v. *Protheroe* (1968) it was held that where a party is entitled to a share in a property held leasehold then they are also entitled to share in the value of the freehold reversion if this is purchased.

How to give effect to a beneficial interest which a party has

In *Bull* v. *Bull* (1955) it was held that in these cases the parties are, in the absence of a contrary intention, tenants in common in equity and the legal estate is held on what was then a trust for sale but is now a trust of land. Thus the Trusts of Land and Appointment of Trustees Act 1996 (TLATA) governs the position and, in particular, s. 12 gives rights of occupation to any beneficiary if the purpose included giving him this right, but there will not be a right to occupy if the land is either unavailable or unsuitable for occupation by him. The right of occupation may be restricted or excluded under s. 13 and the trustees may impose reasonable conditions on occupation by a beneficiary. Under s. 14 any person interested may apply for a sale of the property, and if the court then orders a sale the proportion of the selling price which they will receive will depend on the extent of their beneficial interest as determined by the court.

The principles under which the court can order a sale are set out in s. 15 of TLATA, which provides that the court must have regard to:

(a) The intentions of the person who created the trust.
(b) The purposes for which the property was held.
(c) The welfare of any child who occupies or who might reasonably be expected to occupy the property.
(d) The interests of any secured creditor or beneficiary.

There was a considerable body of case law on the predecessor of s. 15, s. 30 of the LPA 1925. In *Mortgage Corporation Ltd* v. *Shaire* (2001) Neuberger J (see Pascoe 2000) said that it was likely that Parliament intended to tip the scales 'more in favour of families and against banks and other chargees' (i.e. by comparison with s. 30). Nevertheless, the cases under s. 30 can still be referred to, albeit with caution. An interesting recent one is *Bank of Baroda* v. *Dhillon* (1998), where it was held that a bank could obtain an order for sale of the matrimonial home even though the wife had an overriding interest under what was then 70(1)(g) of the LRA 1925 (now Sch. 3 para. 2 to the LRA 2002) which bound the bank. The crucial factor was that the children were grown up and after the sale W would still have enough money for other accommodation.

An early case on s. 30, but one which is probably still good law, is *Re Buchanan-Wollaston's Conveyance* (1939), where land was bought by co-owners to prevent it from being built on. One later wished to sell but the others did not. As the original purpose remained, the court refused to order a sale.

A series of cases have dealt with disputes on a divorce. In *Jones* v. *Challenger* (1961) a sale was ordered where there were no children resident in the home but other earlier cases decided on s. 30 should now be discarded and the criteria in s. 15 of TLATA used instead together with the remarks in *Shaire*. In *Re Evers's Trust* (1980) the court considered that the underlying purpose may include the provision of a home for children also so that their interests must be considered and this clearly accords with the remarks in *Shaire*. (The Family Law Act 1996 now deals with the sales of matrimonial homes.)

> *Note 12.3: In* Ungarian v. Lesnoff *(1989) the court held that the woman became a tenant for life under the Settled Land Act 1925, which gave her the power to sell the house, even though it was accepted that the intention was only that she would be able to live in it for the remainder of her life. Such a finding is not possible anyway now as, since the Trusts of Land and Trustees Act 1996, it is not possible to create new strict settlements.*

Terminology in this area

Much confusion has been caused by the use of the terms resulting trusts, constructive trusts and proprietary estoppel to deal with what often appears to be the same point: how to protect the beneficial interest of a person in property when that person is not the legal owner. A particularly good example of this confusion is the recent decision in *Curley* v. *Parkes* (above). The source of this is, on one level, the words of Lord Diplock in *Gissing* v. *Gissing* (1971): 'A resulting, implied or constructive trust . . . it is unnecessary for present purposes to distinguish between these three classes of trust'. These words have often been criticised and, on another level, are perhaps evidence of a deep-seated reluctance on the part of English judges to grapple with doctrinal issues. Be that as it may, this confusion has led to unfortunate divergences in the cases.

In *Springette* v. *Defoe* (1992), where a right was claimed because of contributions to the cost of acquisition, the court proceeded on traditional resulting trust principles and referred to *Dyer* v. *Dyer* (1788). As the parties had made unequal contributions to the purchase price and there was no evidence of express discussions that they had intended to hold equally, their shares were in proportion to their contributions. Yet in *Lloyds Bank* v. *Rosset* (1990) Lord Bridge, also discussing the type of case where direct contributions are made, used the term 'constructive trust' although in the type of case where there is an express agreement supported by detrimental reliance he used the terms 'constructive trust or proprietary estoppel'. The distinction between a resulting and a constructive trust seems to be important where the party in whose name the house is becomes bankrupt and the other party seeks to assert his claim against trustee in bankruptcy. In

Re Densham (1975) it was held that a constructive trust which had been imposed, and which gave the woman a half share, was void as against the trustee in bankruptcy as being a 'transaction at an undervalue' (see s. 423 of the Insolvency Act 1986 – Chapter 9). However, the interest was based on a resulting trust, which gave the woman a ninth share, being the amount she had contributed to the purchase, and was not a transaction at an undervalue and was thus binding on the trustee in bankruptcy. The reasoning was that an interest under a resulting trust is earned while that under a constructive trust is, in a sense, given to a party by the court so as to achieve justice (see also *Re Abbott* (1982)). However, it seems unfortunate that such an important consequence can hinge on a categorisation which often depends on the language used by individual judges.

Estoppel

The concept of estoppel has been explained in Chapter 11 but the principle may be briefly restated as follows: where one party (X) encourages another (Y) to act to his (Y's) detriment, or at least acquiesces whilst Y acts to his detriment, then X may be required to give effect to the expectations in which he encouraged Y.

Estoppel can clearly be a useful tool in deciding disputes arising over beneficial interests in the home, and indeed Lord Bridge in *Rosset* coupled it with a constructive trust (see above). However, the courts have not, in recent years, applied estoppel as an independent cause of action and it is doubtful if the addition of the words 'proprietary estoppel' in *Rosset* really added anything. The question here is whether estoppel has any part of its own to play in this area.

It has been argued that there is no difference between the terms constructive trust and proprietary estoppel. They both require a common intention and detrimental reliance. However, it is argued to the contrary that with a constructive trust the court is simply recognising something which already exists because of what the parties have done, yet with proprietary estoppel any interests will only operate prospectively, from the date of the court order. (*Re Sharpe* (1980)). Moreover, whereas the starting point for the imposition of a constructive trust seems to be to ensure that the common intention of the parties is given effect to, the idea behind estoppel is that of preventing a party from suffering detriment.

An example of estoppel in the context of rights in the home is provided by *Pascoe* v. *Turner* (1979). The claimant and defendant co-habited in a house which was registered in the name of the claimant only. When their relationship ended, the claimant told the defendant that the house and everything in it was hers and, in reliance on this, she spent her own money on repairs and improvements and, most importantly, the claimant knew this. Accordingly, he could be said to have encouraged her in the expectation that she would obtain an interest. It was held that the only way to ensure that the defendant would be secure for her lifetime would be to order that the house be conveyed into her own name.

Another instance is *H* v. *M* (2004). Here the claim was by the wife's parents to beneficial ownership of a farm which had originally been owned by W's parents but was then put in the names of W and H as the parents were in financial difficulties. The parents, however, continued to live there. They made some contribution to the cost of acquisition of the farm by W and H but the case was decided on pure estoppel principles. The court held that there had never been any intention that the parents should be the beneficial owners of the farm after the sale to H and W and, although they had spent considerable sums on its restoration, they had not acted to their detriment in any way. This was because the sale by them to W and H of the farm had meant that they were able to continue there and so, in effect, any equity in their favour was satisfied.

In one of the most recent cases to come before the Court of Appeal, *Oxley* v. *Hiscock* (2004) (above), Chadwick LJ, when discussing the law on ascertaining the extent of the beneficial interests, used estoppel language: 'The court makes such order as the circumstances require in order to give effect to the beneficial interest in the property of the one party, the existence of which the other party (having the legal title) is estopped from denying'. His intention was, presumably, to move away from the language of the common intention constructive trust.

Where estoppel is the basis of the claim the court has discretion, if estoppel is found, to make such an order as is necessary to do the minimum equity between the parties, and this may mean not granting the party who succeeds in claiming estoppel the remedy which is asked for. (See *Sledmore* v. *Dalby* – Chapter 11.) In *Burrows and Burrows* v. *Sharp* (1991) Mrs Sharp agreed with Mr and Mrs Burrows, her granddaughter and her husband, that they would pay the mortgage on her council flat, thus enabling Mrs Sharp to purchase it in return for the Burrows inheriting the flat on Mrs Sharp's death and making a home for Mrs Sharp's physically handicapped daughter. The arrangement broke down and the court ordered Mrs Sharp to refund the Burrows' expenditure. The alternative, to give them the right to live in the house together with Mrs Sharp and her daughter, was not practicable as the relationship between them had broken down. The court considered that an order to refund their expenditure was the minimum needed to satisfy the equity as the Burrows, by starting to pay off the mortgage, had undoubtedly acted to their detriment.

Nevertheless, the present law is still based in the *Rosset* principles and at present a claim based only on estoppel would be likely to fail unless either of the two ways of claiming in *Rosset* are made out. Estoppel can be seen as an integral part of the Rosset principle, as it underpins the notion of detriment, rather than an independent cause of action except perhaps in special cases.

OTHER APPROACHES TO THE PROBLEM OF IDENTIFYING AND QUANTIFYING THE BENEFICIAL INTERESTS IN THE FAMILY HOME

The approach of the courts in other Commonwealth countries

The distinctive feature of the approaches adopted by the courts of Canada, Australia and New Zealand has been the search for a wider basis on which to rest the jurisdiction of the courts as opposed to that adopted in *Rosset*. The approaches of each country differ in detail, however, and each will be examined.

Canada

The leading case is *Pettkus* v. *Becker* (1980). The parties, an unmarried couple, Mr Pettkus and Miss Becker, lived together in a property which was in Mr Pettkus' name. They had, in fact, through their joint efforts, acquired several properties from which their bee-keeping business was run and the legal titles to all of them were in his name. One farm had been bought out of his savings but this was only possible because Miss Becker had paid all their living expenses out of their joint earnings. She had also contributed to the running of the farm and, for example, although only herself weighing 87lb, had lifted a beehive weighing 80lb. (Shades of the sledgehammer in *Eves* v. *Eves*!) The court held that there was no claim on the basis of a resulting trust as there was no common intention (note that in *Rosset* this was labelled a constructive trust) but that there could be a constructive trust claim.

Dickson J, who delivered the majority judgment, held that 'The principle of **unjust enrichment** lies at the heart of the constructive trust'. In matrimonial (which, in this context, clearly includes disputes between unmarried couples) cases he suggested that there are three requirements to be satisfied before an unjust enrichment can be said to exist: an enrichment, a corresponding deprivation and absence of any juristic reason for the enrichment. Gardner (1993) observes that there was no clear explanation of precisely how Mr Pettkus was enriched but one possible explanation was that Miss Becker's labours with the beehive increased the profits he was able to make from the honey. The element of deprivation meant that Mr Pettkus must have been enriched by the work of Miss Becker, which was certainly the case as he had the benefit of 19 years' labour on the farm by her. Finally, the absence of any juristic basis really means, as Gardner observes, that the enrichment was unjust. This requirement was explained by Dickson J as follows: 'Where one person in a relationship tantamount to spousal prejudices herself in the reasonable expectation of receiving an interest in property and the other person in the relationship freely accepts benefits conferred by the first person in circumstances where he knows or ought to have known of that reasonable expectation, it would be unjust to allow the recipient of the benefit to retain it'. The court then ordered that the parties should share equally both the farm and all other assets acquired by them jointly.

A later case, *Peter* v. *Beblow* (1993), shows the application of this principle to the provision of domestic services by the woman as 'housekeeper, homemaker and step-mother' and the court ordered that, as these services were an enrichment to the man the home should be transferred into the woman's name.

Australia

Here the leading case is *Baumgartner* v. *Baumgartner* (1987). The situation was the familiar one of where an unmarried couple pooled incomes to meet their living expenses and the purchase of a house which was, however, put in the man's name. They separated and the court held that the woman was entitled to a 45 per cent share, corresponding to the amount of pooled income which she had contributed. The *ratio* of the decision was unconscionability: given that this by itself does not get us far, the court referred to *Muchinski* v. *Dodds* (1985), where Deane J referred to the principle of joint endeavour: this means that where there is a joint endeavour which has failed and one party has contributed money or other property to the endeavour which it was not intended that the other should retain, then equity will not permit him to do so. Here there is still some requirement of common intention but in *Baumgartner* there was a finding on the facts that there was no common intention that the woman should share the property. Other later cases have failed to follow through the logic of requiring common intention or, to put it another way, an intention that the endeavour should be joint. Thus in *Hibberson* v. *George* (1989) the man told the woman that she was to have no interest in the house but this did not stop the court from holding that there was a joint endeavour. Finally, *Baumgartner* has been criticised on the ground that it does not offer significant guidance on how the parties' interests in the property are to be apportioned. (See Oakley 1996, pp. 288–98.)

New Zealand

The decision in *Gilles* v. *Keogh* (1989) is based on yet another concept, that of meeting the reasonable expectations of the parties. The parties were unmarried and the home was bought in the name of the woman who also paid for it. All outgoings came from their pooled earnings and the man worked on improving the house and garden. They then bought another house with the proceeds of the sale of the first and this was also put into the woman's name. Two mortgage repayments came from their joint account. The man later claimed a share but the court held that he was not entitled to this. The judgments are based on the principle that the claimant had an expectation of an interest, that this was shared by the other party or at least that they did nothing to discourage the idea. Here the woman had always made it clear that the house was to be her own and so the man could not reasonably have had an expectation to the contrary. Although this may seem to be focusing on the question of intentions and so not really advancing the argument much, Gardner (1993) points out that in other New Zealand cases the approach is slightly different. Although the principle of reasonable expectations is used, the courts have used an objective test of whether a reasonable person in the claimant's position would have expected an interest (see e.g. Cooke P in *Hayward* v. *Giordani* (1983)), and this has been followed in later cases such as *Lankow* v. *Rose* (1995). There has also been some support for proprietary estoppel as the correct basis but in *Phillips* v. *Phillips* (1993) Lord Cooke, as President of the New Zealand Court of Appeal, felt that this was not appropriate. The picture in New Zealand is thus not really clear.

Statutory intervention

The De Facto Relationships Act, a New South Wales Statute of 1984, attempted to put the law on cohabitees' rights on a statutory footing. The basis of the jurisdiction is whether it would be just and equitable to make an order. The statute allows the court to make orders adjusting the interests of *de facto* partners in property having regard not only to financial but also non financial contributions, such as contributions made in the capacity of homemaker or parent, and including contributions made by a child, whether a child of the partners or another child accepted by one or both of the partners into the household. The court can make an order provided that there is a child of the parties to the application or that the applicant has made substantial contributions of the kind referred to above or that the applicant has care and control of a child of the respondent and failure to make the order would result in serious injustice to the applicant. In addition, no order can be made unless the *de facto* relationship has lasted for at least two years.

The Property Relationships Legislation (Amendment) Act 1999 extends the categories to which the legislation applies to either *de facto* relationships or any close personal relationships between two adult persons, whether or not they are related by family, who are living together and one or each of them provides the other with domestic support and personal care (s. 5). This includes both same and opposite sex relationships as well as relationships such as brother and sister.

The leading case on whether an order should be made adjusting the interests of the parties is *D* v. *McA* (1986). Powell J proposed a four-stage test:

- Identify and value the interest of the parties.
- Decide if contributions of the kind referred to in the statute have been made.
- Have the claimant's contributions already been recognised and compensated?
- If not, then what order should be made so that these contributions will be recognised and compensated?

THE FUTURE

It seems unlikely that the law will remain in its present state of being entirely governed by the law of trusts. The different interpretations of the courts, the narrowness of the *Rosset* principle, and the confusion which all this has led to, is really evidence of a failure to find any clear principle on which case law can be founded. Having said this, it would be wrong to discard the *Rosset* principles too lightly, because as Dixon (2005) observes: 'there is little doubt that for a while it brought a measure of clarity to the law concerning the informal acquisition of interests in land via the well worn doctrines of resulting and constructive trusts'. However, it is likely that a statutory solution will ultimately be found, at least in some cases. In 2000 the Law Society recommended that the courts should have power, on the breakdown of a non-marital cohabitative relationship, to make a financial award or reallocate rights in property. Whilst this is a start it does not take account of the variety of situations where a person may acquire rights in property as indicated by the examples at the start of this chapter. The Law Commission (2002) investigated the possibility of legislative reform but disappointingly concluded that it was not possible to devise a satisfactory scheme 'for the destination of shares in the shared home which can operate fairly and evenly across all the diverse circumstances which are now to be encountered'. However, along with various suggested changes to the approaches of the courts (see under 'Direct Contributions', above), it did also recommend that 'further consideration should be given to the adoption – necessarily by legislation – of broader based approaches to personal relationships . . .'. This could be done, it suggested, by, for example, registration of civil partnerships. The fact that registration of civil partnerships for same-sex relationships is now possible under the Civil Partnership Act 2004 will make it likely that pressure will then be exerted to extend the concept of registering a civil partnership to opposite-sex relationships and this will bring with it power to regulate property matters in the same way as is done when there is a divorce. Even so, there will remain cases where either the parties have not registered their partnership or where this is not possible, as where a brother and sister each make contributions to the cost of acquisition of property which is then held in the sister's name. It is possible that legislation could be framed which could cover all eventualities but this seems to have disappeared from the agenda for the moment and so it seems that the law of trusts will continue to play a part in the area of the home, albeit possibly a reduced one. That being so, the question is whether the *Rosset* principles will continue to hold sway or if there will be a move to a wider jurisdiction, possibly based on the approaches in Commonwealth cases. It is noteworthy that in practice the effect of the Rosset principles may be lessening (see e.g. the decision in *H* v. *M* (above) where *Rosset* was not mentioned and the remarks in the discussion of *Oxley* v. *Hiscock* (above)). Indeed, in this latter case, Chadwick LJ observed that it may be that one day the House of Lords will decide to solve the problems either by giving estoppel a larger role, 'or even by following the recent trend in other Commonwealth jurisdictions towards more generalised principles of unconscionability and unjust enrichment'.

Note 12.4: See appendix at the end of this chapter for the Law Commission's latest consultation paper.

FURTHER READING

Dixon (2005) 'Resulting and constructive trusts of land; the mist descends and rises', 69 Conv. 79. Discusses *Oxley* v. *Hiscock* and other recent cases.

Gardner (1993) 'Rethinking family property', 109 LQR 263. Although somewhat dated, still useful.

Law Commission (2002) Discussion Paper 'Sharing homes'.

Law Society (2000) Law Reform Advisory Committee, *Matrimonial Property*.

Pascoe (2000) 'S. 15 of the Trusts of Land and Appointment of Trustees Act 1996: a change in the law?', 64 Conv. 315. Although this area is usually dealt with in more detail in land law, it is relevant to an understanding of the law on trusts of the home and this article provides a useful starting point.

Rotherham (2004) 'The property rights of unmarried cohabitees: a case for reform', 68 Conv. 268. Excellent general survey.

CHAPTER SUMMARY

- Equitable interest in the home may be acquired under an express trust or an implied trust.
- Two ways in which an interest may be acquired under an implied trust.
- The court has a wider discretion in deciding the size of the share.
- How to give effect to a beneficial interest.
- Role of estoppel.
- Different approaches e.g. other Commonwealth courts.

QUESTION

Paul, a bachelor, is the freehold owner of 'The Laurels', a large detached house. He meets and becomes friendly with Samantha, a model, who owns a small flat. Paul suggests to Samantha that she gives up her flat and moves in with him and that she should give up her job so that she will have time to look after the house. Samantha agrees. She gives Paul £5,000 from the proceeds of sale of her flat to help pay off the mortgage on 'The Laurels'. Paul says to her: 'If anything happens to me, this house is yours you know'.

After about a year Paul meets Marianne, another model, and suggests that she comes to live at 'The Laurels'. He says to Samantha: 'Off you go. You've got no rights here you know'.

Advise Samantha.

> *Note 12.5: You will find suggested points for inclusion in the answer in Appendix 2.*

APPENDIX

Law Commission Consultation Paper 179: Cohabitation: The Financial Consequences of Relationship Breakdown.

The Law Commission has now begun the process of seeing if in fact it is possible to replace the provisions of the law of trusts and estoppel mentioned in this chapter by a statutory framework. The consultation period ends on 30 September 2006, to be followed by a final report by August 2007. This means that we are some way from change in this area but there is a strong possibility that eventually a statutory framework will emerge. The following is a very brief summary.

The paper deals with opposite-sex or same-sex couples who live together in intimate relationships, and does not include relationships between blood relatives or caring relationships. Views are sought on how the qualifying relationship can be defined and on whether the scheme should just include couples with children. It is proposed that the scheme should only apply to those who share a joint household.

The heart of the proposals is the proposed statutory scheme. This is based on:

(a) economic advantage (the retention of some economic benefit arising from contributions made by the other party during the relationship); or
(b) economic disadvantage (economic sacrifices made as result of that party's contribution to the relationship or resulting from continuing child care responsibilities following separation).

The significant difference from the present law is that contributions are defined much more widely than just financial ones. There is a proposed filter (which may be controversial) that a claim to financial relief cannot succeed unless it would be substantially or manifestly unfair not to provide a remedy. Finally, the orders available to the courts would be the same as on a divorce.

13 Charitable trusts

Note 13.1: The law on charities will change considerably if the Charities Bill 2005 becomes law. Part One, which deals with the regulation of charities, is incorporated into this chapter, and the other remainder, which deals with regulation of charities, is dealt with in Chapter 14. The position at the time of writing (January 2006) is that the Bill has passed through the House of Lords and it is anticipated that it will soon go to the Commons. Look at the website for this book for details of when the Act is in force and further details of changes which it makes to charity law.

INTRODUCTION

Charities play a vital role in society. The Charity Commissions' Annual report for 2004–5 shows that there were 189,531 registered charities and that 6,279 new charities were registered in the year ending March 2005. The main charities had a total income in 2004–5 in excess of £36 billion and there were over 900,000 charity trustees. Charities employed 600,000 paid staff.

Sources of charity law

The statute law on charities is now largely contained in the Charities Act 1993, which has consolidated most of the Charities Act 1960, the Charities Act 1992, the Charities Act 1985 and the Charitable Trustees Incorporation Act 1872. However, certain sections of the 1960, 1985 and 1992 Acts remain in force. When the Charities Bill 2005 becomes law the Charities Act 1960 will be repealed and so will parts of the Charities Acts 1992 and 1993. Charity law can also be found in decisions both of the courts and also of the Charity Commissioners, because the Commissioners decide on applications for registration as a charity (see below).

Advantages of charitable status

Since this chapter is concerned with the requirements which a trust must satisfy in order to be charitable, one needs to be aware at the outset of the advantages of charitable status. There are considerable fiscal advantages, comprising exemptions from various taxes provided that the income of the charity is applied for charitable purposes, e.g. income tax, corporation tax, and capital gains tax. Charities are liable to value added tax but various items are zero-rated such as the sale by a charity of donated goods. A charity is entitled to 80 per cent relief from council tax and the local authority may increase this to 100 per cent. A familiar advantage is that under the gift aid scheme (which replaced deeds of covenant) a charity can reclaim income tax paid at the basic rate when the gift was made by a UK taxpayer.

There are also the following advantages from the point of view of validity:

(a) The objects of a charitable trust need not be certain. Thus, as we saw in Chapter 5, while the objects of private trust must be certain, and thus a gift for 'benevolent purposes' would fail, a gift for 'charitable purposes' would be valid. In cases such as this, the courts may establish a scheme for the application of the funds to particular charitable objects, and the Charity Commissioners have similar powers, conferred by s. 16 of the Charities Act 1993. The powers of the Commissioners are dealt with in Chapter 14.

(b) Although charitable trusts are trusts for purposes rather than individuals, the absence of ascertainable beneficiaries who can enforce them does not affect their validity because it is the Attorney-General who enforces charitable trusts. Under s. 33 of the Charities Act 1993 charity proceedings can be brought by the charity or its trustee, the Attorney-General, or 'by any person interested' which, in *Richmond upon Thames LBC* v. *Rogers* (1988), was held to include a local authority in the case of a local charity. However, individuals who may benefit from the charity have no *locus standi* to enforce it and so, in *Hauxwell* v. *Barton-upon-Humber UDC* (1974), the Attorney-General was substituted for two individuals. In addition, s. 32 of the Charities Act 1993 gives the Charity Commissioners concurrent powers with the Attorney-General in the enforcement of charitable trusts (see Chapter 14 and also *A-G* v. *Cocke* (1988) (Chapter 20) for another aspect of this issue).

(c) Charitable trusts are subject to the rule against perpetuities, in that a gift to a charity must vest within the perpetuity period. Therefore if there is a gift to an individual followed by a gift (a gift over) to a charity, the gift to the charity will fail if it vests or might vest outside the perpetuity period. However, a gift to one charity with a gift over to another charity is valid even though the gift to the second charity may take place outside the perpetuity period (*Christ's Hospital* v. *Grainger* (1849)).

Types of charitable organisations

Charities do not need to exist under the form of a trust, although many of them do. They can exist in other forms as follows:

(a) *Charitable corporations*. The corporation will almost invariably be a company limited by guarantee, and the advantage of corporate status is that the company, as a legal person, will have legal rights and liabilities rather than the trustees. On the other hand, it may well be felt in the case of small trusts that the expense and trouble of complying with the statutory formalities outweighs this advantage. In addition there are specific charitable corporations, such as universities, established either by Royal Charter or Statute. Section 35(4) of the Companies Act 1985 provides that in the case of a charitable company, a person dealing with the company, who knows that a transaction is *ultra vires* the company, cannot enforce that transaction against it whereas it is uncertain whether this applies in the case of other companies. It should be noted that the Charities Bill 2005 proposes a new form of organisation, a 'charitable incorporated organisation', which will avoid dual regulation under both charity and company law.

(b) *Unincorporated associations.* These will normally be run by a chairperson and committee and their basis, as with all unincorporated associations, is that of a contract between their members. Such an organisation has the advantage of flexibility and may be suitable for small charities.

(c) *Other types of organisations,* e.g. societies registered under the Friendly Societies Act.

All forms of charitable organisation, whether or not they are trusts, are, in general, governed by the same rules. Thus references to charitable trusts in this chapter should, unless otherwise indicated, be taken to include other forms of charitable organisations. Indeed, s. 96 of the Charities Act 1993 defines a charity as '*any* institution, whether corporate or not, which is established for charitable purposes'.

Registration as a charity

Most charities are required, whatever form the charity takes, to register with the Charity Commissioners, although certain charities are exempt (see Chapter 14). The advantage of registration as a charity is that the organisation is conclusively presumed to be a charity (s. 5(1) Charities Act 1960) and so the privileges of charitable status outlined above can be claimed.

The fact that an organisation is not included on the register of charities does not mean that it is not a charity but it does mean that in order to claim the above privileges it will have to prove to the relevant authorities, such as HM Revenue and Customs, that it *is* a charity.

HISTORY OF DEFINITIONS OF CHARITY

Whether or not a trust is charitable is a question of law. The settlor's or testator's opinion as to whether the purpose is charitable is irrelevant except that the court will not 'defeat on doubtful evidence the avowed benevolent intention of a donor' (Lord Simonds in *National Anti-Vivisection Society* v. *IRC* (1948)).

The traditional doctrine is that, in order to be charitable, a gift must fall within the spirit and intention of the preamble to the Charitable Uses Act 1601. Although repealed in 1888 by the Mortmain and Charitable Uses Act, the effect of this celebrated preamble has been preserved by s. 38(4) of the Charities Act

1960. The preamble sets out the following charitable purposes (which are given a modernised format).

- The relief of aged impotent and poor people.
- The maintenance of sick and maimed soldiers and mariners, schools of learning, free schools and scholars in universities.
- The repair of bridges, ports, havens, causeways, churches, sea-banks and highways.
- The education and preferment of orphans.
- The relief, stock or maintenance for houses of correction.
- The marriage of poor maids.
- The supportation, aid and help of young tradesmen, handicraftsman and persons decayed.
- The relief or redemption of prisoners or captives.
- The aid or ease of any poor inhabitants concerning payment of fifteens, setting out of soldiers and other taxes.

However, in *Scottish Burial Reform and Cremation Society* v. *Glasgow City Corporation* (1968), Lord Wilberforce said: 'it is now accepted that what must be regarded is not the wording of the preamble itself but the effect of decisions given by the courts as to its scope . . .' The process was well described by Lord Reid in the same case when he observed that the courts first used to seek an analogy between an object mentioned in the preamble and the object in the case before them. They then went further, and were satisfied if they could find an analogy between an object already held to be charitable and the object in the case before them. This process is shown by the fact that religion receives only a passing mention in the above list, in the reference to the repair of churches, but it emerged as one of the main heads of charity.

Lord Macnaghten in *Commissioners for Special Purposes of the Income Tax* v. *Pemsel* (1891) gave a simpler definition laying down that charity comprised four principal divisions:

(a) Trusts for the relief of poverty.
(b) Trusts for the advancement of education.
(c) Trusts for the advancement of religion.
(d) Trusts for other purposes beneficial to the community, not falling under any of the preceding headings.

DEFINITION OF CHARITY PROPOSED BY THE CHARITIES BILL 2005

Charitable purposes recognised under the Charities Bill 2005 in outline

> *Note 13.2: The original definitions of charitable purposes were amended in the House of Lords partly as a result of the recommendations of a Joint Committee of both houses. The list below is that agreed by the House of Lords.*

Now all of the above definitions are to be swept away and, under clause 2 of the Charities Bill the following charitable purposes will be recognised by law:

(a) Prevention or relief of poverty.
(b) The advancement of education.
(c) The advancement of religion. Religion includes a religion which involves more than one god and a religion which does not involve belief in a god.
(d) The advancement of health or the saving of lives (including the prevention or relief of sickness, disease or human suffering).
(e) The advancement of citizenship or community development (including rural or urban regeneration, promotion of civic responsibility, volunteering, the voluntary sector or the effectiveness or efficiency of charities).
(f) The advancement of the arts, culture, heritage or science.
(g) The advancement of amateur sport (this is defined as a sport which involves physical skill and exertion).
(h) The advancement of human rights, conflict resolution or reconciliation or the promotion of religious or racial harmony or equality or diversity.
(i) The advancement of environmental protection or improvement.
(j) The relief of those in need, by reason of youth, age, ill-health, disability, financial hardship or other disadvantage (including providing accommodation or care).
(k) The advancement of animal welfare.
(l) The promotion of the efficiency of the armed forces of the Crown.
(m) Any other purposes that:
    (i) are not listed but are currently charitable under charity law;
    (ii) any purposes analogous to any purpose currently charitable or listed above; and
    (iii) any purpose analogous to a purpose recognised as charitable after the Bill is passed.

The intention is that there shall be no change to the current interpretation of terms currently used in charity law and so it is not intended that this change will result in activities becoming charitable where they were not before, but the exception is (g), because amateur sport as such was not recognised as charitable. Instead the aim is clarity and bringing the categories up to date so that they accord with the types of activities which charities registered today engage in. A good example is category (i): environmental protection or improvement does not exist as a specific head today and is simply included under the fourth head of trusts for the general benefit of the community. Now it will have a category of its own. Another example is animal welfare charities, which until now have appeared to rest on the strange basis that the benefit to be considered is that of those caring for the animals. This is now corrected with the specific acknowledgement of animal welfare as a head of charity.

Before going further, it should be made clear that two other requirements must be satisfied for a trust to be charitable:

(a) **It must have an element of public benefit.**
(b) **It must be exclusively charitable.**

Public benefit under the Charities Bill 2005

The presumption of public benefit is removed and so the effect is that all charities must demonstrate that their purposes are for public benefit. This will cause interesting arguments: for example, churches and other places of worship have always been assumed to be for the public benefit (see below e.g. *Neville Estates Ltd* v. *Madden* (1962)) but this will now have to be proved. However, public benefit is given the same meaning as it currently has in charity law, and so existing case law is still relevant, so that the change may be one of form rather than substance. The Joint Committee has recommended that criteria for deciding public benefit should be included in the Bill (some principles for deciding public benefit have already been agreed between the Home Office and the Charity Commission).

In the discussion which follows the topic of public benefit will be discussed where possible in connection with each head, although in the case of some of the new heads added by the Charities Bill, there may be no authority as yet.

CHARITABLE PURPOSES UNDER THE CHARITIES BILL IN DETAIL

> *Note 13.3: The classification under the Charities Bill will be adopted on the basis that it is virtually certain that the Bill will come into force.*

Trusts for the relief of poverty

Meaning of poverty

In *Re Coulthurst* (1951) Evershed MR explained that 'poverty does not mean destitution, . . . it may not unfairly be paraphrased for present purposes as meaning persons who have to "go short" in the ordinary acceptation of that term . . .' Accordingly, in this case a gift for the widows and orphans of deceased employees of a bank was upheld as charitable and gifts to persons of 'limited means' (*Re Gardom* (1915)) or 'moderate means' (*Re Clarke* (1923) 'or needy persons' (*Le Page* v. *Payne* (1954)) have all been upheld as charitable. Nor is there any objection to poverty being defined in terms of minimum income qualification, provided, of course, that the qualifying threshold is at an appropriate level. Thus in *Re De Carteret* (1933) a trust was upheld which provided for the payment of annual allowances to widows or spinsters whose income was between £80 and £120 a year, although the crucial point here was that a preference was to be given to widows with dependent young children.

In this area, as always when the courts have dealt with the meaning of charity, there are decisions which are difficult to reconcile. In *Re Sanders Will Trusts* (1954) a gift to provide 'dwellings for the working classes and their families' was not held to be charitable because the expression 'working classes' did not denote poor persons. In *Re Niyazi's Will Trusts* (1978) a gift to be used for 'the construction of or as a contribution towards the cost of a working men's hostel' in Famagusta, was held charitable, although Megarry V-C admitted that it was 'desperately near the borderline'. He felt that whereas the term 'dwellings' as in *Re Sanders* indicated ordinary houses, the term 'hostel' indicated 'somewhat modest accommodation', especially when prefixed by the term working-men and the fact that there was an acute housing need in Famagusta. There was additional evidence that the accommodation was likely to be used by the poor.

A gift which, on the other hand, fell clearly outside the scope of charity was that in *Re Gwyon* (1930) where a fund to provide 'loose fitting breeches, gathered in at the knee' (i.e. knickers) for boys in Farnham was not charitable because boys of affluent parents could have benefited.

Requirement of public benefit

This requirement scarcely existed in poverty cases, in contrast to the position with the other heads of charity. The explanation seems to be that in a line of cases beginning with *Isaac* v. *Defriez* (1754) the courts have held valid a trust for 'poor relations' or a similarly narrow class and in *Oppenheim* v. *Tobacco Securities Trust Co Ltd* (1951) Lord Simonds in the House of Lords said that it would be unwise to 'cast doubt on decisions of respectable antiquity in order to introduce a greater harmony into the law of trusts as a whole'. Thus in *Dingle* v. *Turner* (1972) a trust fund to pay pensions to poor employees of a certain company was held charitable. Now, however, the Charities Bill 2005 requires that trusts for the relief of poverty must have an element of public benefit.

Trusts for the advancement of education

Meaning of education

Education includes the provision of schools, universities and other similar institutions, together with ancillary purposes, such as the payment of teachers and administrative staff (*Case of Christ's College, Cambridge* (1757)). However, education includes much more than this. In *Re Shaw's Will Trusts* (1952) Vaisey J said that it included 'not only teaching, but the promotion or encouragement of those arts and graces of life which are, after all, perhaps the finest and best part of the human character'. On this basis he held charitable a gift by the widow of George Bernard Shaw to provide what Vaisey J described as 'a sort of finishing school for the Irish People'. In *Royal Choral Society* v. *IRC* (1943) Lord Greene MR emphatically rejected the argument that education meant only teaching a class. It did not, he said, mean only the teaching of painters and the training of musicians but, as in this case, the 'purpose of raising the artistic taste of the country' by the performance of choral works. (Under the Charities Bill, the area of arts festivals and other similar events will come under head (f): the advancement of the arts, heritage and science.) However, where the purpose is propaganda, rather than education, then it will not be charitable. Thus in *Re Shaw* (1952) a gift in George Bernard Shaw's will for research into a new phonetic alphabet was not charitable partly because one object was to persuade the public that a phonetic alphabet would be a good thing. Another reason why the gift failed was that it aimed merely at the increase of knowledge, which is not necessarily by itself education.

The principle that education requires not only the acquisition of knowledge but also its spreading in some way has been applied in many cases. In *Beaumont* v. *Oliveira* (1869), for instance, a gift to the Royal Geographical Society was held charitable because the society aimed at the 'diffusion' of geographical knowledge.

In *Re Besterman's Will Trust* (1980) Slade J likewise emphasised that a trust for research will only be charitable if, in addition to the subject of that research being useful, there is the intention to disseminate it. In *Re Hopkins' Will Trusts* (1964) a gift to be applied towards finding the Bacon-Shakespeare manuscripts was held charitable because the result of any discovery was intended to be published and the research was in itself valuable as being designed to improve the literary heritage.

The principle that knowledge must have an educative value lies behind the decision in *Re Pinion* (1965), where a studio and its contents were given to trustees to enable them to be used as a museum. However, Harman J stigmatised the contents as 'a mass of junk'. (Under the Charities Bill a museum will come under head (f) (advancement of arts, heritage and science) but the public benefit hurdle, as shown by this case, will remain.) On the same principle Vaisey J, *in Re Dupree's Deed Trusts* (1945), although holding that the playing of chess by boys and young men aged under 21 was educational, was concerned about a slippery slope leading from chess to draughts, then to bezique through to bridge and whist and, by another route, to stamp collecting and the acquisition of birds' eggs.

Requirement of public benefit

> *Note 13.4: The cases below were of course decided under the present law, where there is a presumption of public benefit in trusts for the advancement of education. Under the Charities Bill 2005 public benefit will need to be proved and readers might care to consider whether the decisions in any of these cases would now be different, although a major shift in judicial attitudes is unlikely.*

A clear example of where this requirement was not met is *Re Compton* (1945), where a trust for the education of the children of three named families was held not to be charitable. In *Oppenheim* v. *Tobacco Securities Trust Co Ltd* (1951) a trust was held not charitable where it was to provide for 'the education of children of employees or former employees of the British American Tobacco Co Ltd or any of its subsidiary or allied companies' even though the number of employees exceeded 110,000. Lord Simonds held that the fact that the group was large did not make the trust charitable if the connection between its members was based on some personal tie, whether it was membership of a particular family as in *Re Compton* (1945) or employment by a particular employee or employees, as here. Lord MacDermott dissented, holding that there was the intention to benefit a class of substantial size and importance in such a way that the interests of the class as a whole were advanced. He felt that the question should always be one of degree, depending on the facts of each case and pointed to the difficulties of applying the rule laid down by Lord Simonds: was a distinction to be drawn between those employed in a particular industry, with a number of firms, before it was nationalised (presumably the public) and those employed when it was nationalised (presumably not the public because the relationship depended on the connection with one employer)? In *Dingle* v. *Turner* (1972) (see above) Lord Cross (with whom all the other Law Lords concurred) agreed with Lord MacDermott although this was *obiter*.

In *Re Koettgen's Will Trusts* (1954) the trust was for the promotion of commercial education for those who could not afford to pay for it themselves with a preference to be given of up to 75 per cent of income to employees of a particular firm. This was held charitable because the gift to the primary class contained the necessary element of public benefit. If a particular group had had an absolute right to part of the money, or if the trust had been phrased the other way round, so that there was a preference for the public in the absence of qualified applicants from employees of the firm, then it would not have been charitable. Even so, in *IRC* v. *Educational Grants Association Ltd* (1967) Pennycuick J found 'considerable difficulty' with *Re Koettgen* (1954) and thought that a trust for the public with a preference for a private class as a trust for both charitable and non-charitable objects. There seems no doubt that if the percentage is greater than in *Koettgen* then the trust will not be charitable, for example, if the trust provided that the preference for employees was 80 per cent. In the IRC case the defendant was a corporation established for the advancement of education which was financially supported by payments made by the Metal Box Co Ltd and some of its employees. In one year between 75 per cent and 85 per cent of income had been paid towards the education of children connected with this company and the court held that, although it was conceded that the trust was established for charitable purposes, these payments were not charitable. The fact was, as Pennycuick J put it, that between 75 per cent and 85 per cent of income had been spent for the benefit of children by virtue of a private characteristic: their connection with the Metal Box Co Ltd.

The court was, in effect, applying the *Oppenheim* decision here but the difficulty with that decision remains: suppose that 50 per cent or 25 per cent of the funds had been applied solely for their children? Would the payments then have been charitable? A better course might be to say that trusts such as those in the above cases are not charitable because their purposes are not charitable since they are essentially trusts for the purposes of a particular organisation, rather than base the decision on the requirement of public benefit.

Trusts for the advancement of religion

Religion includes a religion which involves more than one god and a religion which does not involve belief in a god.

Under the present law, there is no explicit recognition that religions which either involve belief in more than one god or no god at all can be charitable, although, we will see, the Charity Commissioners have accorded charitable status to these religions and so have the courts. For example, in *Varsani* v. *Jesani* (1999) the court dealt with an application to apply the property of a Hindu sect *cy près*. *Cy près* is dealt with in Chapter 14, but the point here is that the sect was charitable.

Meaning of religion

The term 'religion' includes not only Christianity but certainly also Judaism (*Straus* v. *Goldsmid* (1837)) and, though there is no authority on other religions such as Islam and Buddism, regulations which were made under the Charities Act 1960 assumed that religions other than Christian were charitable. In addition, places of non-Christian worship (such as Sikh temples) were given Council Tax exemption as charities. Moreover, in *Varsani* v. *Jesani* (1999) (above) it was accepted that a Hindu sect was charitable. The redefinition of religion in the Charities Bill (see above) puts this matter beyond doubt. The Unification Church has been registered but the Church of Scientology has not. The law does not distinguish between different branches of the Christian Church. Thus while the main branches of Christianity, such as Anglicanism, Roman Catholicism, Methodism, the Baptists and the Quakers, are obviously charitable, charitable status is accorded to sects which are small and may be considered eccentric. The leading case here is *Thornton* v. *Howe* (1862), where a trust for the publication of the works of Joanna Southcote, who styled herself as the mother of the second Messiah, was held charitable even though the judge considered them foolish. More recently, in *Re Watson* (1973) a gift to provide for publication of the works of a retired builder, who belonged to a small group of fundamentalist Christians, was held charitable even though expert evidence considered them to have no intrinsic value. The point was that the group genuinely held these beliefs which were undoubtedly religious in character.

In *Funnell* v. *Stewart* (1996) the High Court held that a gift to a group to be used to further faith healing work was charitable. The group held weekly religious services, which were only open to members of the group, but also held faith healing services which were open to the general public. The court regarded the faith healing services as charitable as they had a religious element and a sufficient element of public benefit was assumed. Under the Charities Bill the presumption of public benefit is removed and so in future public benefit in this type of case will have to be proved. In *Re Hummeltenberg* (1923) a gift for the training of spiritualist mediums was held not charitable. Although faith healing is of course not the same as spiritualism, it can be argued that *Funnell* v. *Stewart* is an instance of a wider approach by the courts to the question of charitable status for groups of these kinds.

Distinction between religion and ethics

However, the law does insist on some form of theistic belief. In *Re South Place Ethical Society* (1980) the society's objects were the 'study and dissemination of ethical principles and the cultivation of a rational religious sentiment'. Dillon J held that these were not concerned with the advancement of religion because 'Religion as I see it is concerned with man's relations with God, and ethics are concerned with man's relations with man'. However, he did hold that the objects were educational and thus charitable. Similarly in *United Grand Lodge of Ancient*

Free and Accepted Masons of England and Wales v. *Holborn Borough Council* (1957) the objects of freemasonry were not held to be charitable. Donovan J stressed the importance of the word 'advancement' of religion. It was held that masonry did not involve any religious instruction or programme of persuasion. Its precepts, laudable though they might be, were essentially directed towards the leading of a good moral life even though masonry also insists on belief in a supreme creator.

Gift must be for the advancement of religion

In the *United Grand Lodge* case, Donovan J said that 'to advance religion means to promote it, to spread its message ever wider among mankind'. As he then pointed out, this is done in a variety of ways, and examples of where a gift has been held to be for the advancement of religion are gifts for the maintenance of places of worship and of particular parts of the building such as a stained glass window (*Re Raine* (1956)) and the spire (*Re Palatine Estate Charity* (1888)), and gifts for the clergy such as the payment of stipends (*Re Williams* (1927)) and for the relief of aged, sick and infirm clergy (*Re Forster* (1939)).

A gift for missionary work was held in *Scott* v. *Brownrigg* (1881) not to be charitable because it was too wide but gifts for the promotion of 'God's work' have been held charitable on the assumption that they were to be used for the advancement of religion (see e.g. *Re Barker's Will Trusts* (1948)). A gift to a bishop, vicar or other minister of religion without any specific purpose being mentioned is valid because the gift must be used for the religious purposes inherent in the trustee's office but if purposes are mentioned they must be charitable. Thus in *Farley* v. *Westminster Bank Ltd* (1939) it was held that the words 'parochial work' in a gift could allow it to be used for purposes not strictly charitable.

Requirement of public benefit

> *Note 13.5: The same point applies as was made above in connection with trusts for the advancement of education. Here also the removal of the presumption of public benefit may mean that cases decided under the old law would now be decided differently, although it is unlikely that there will be a major change in the attitudes of the courts.*

It appears that this requirement can be met in one of two ways:

(i) By providing religious activities which are available to the public. It is on this basis that a trust for the provision of church buildings will be of public benefit and also a trust for other religious activities such as the publication of literature or missionary work. In *Re Hetherington* (1989) it was held (following *Re Caus* (1934)) that a trust for the celebration of masses was charitable because 'the public celebration of a religious rite edifies and improves those who attend it'. The fact that the masses could be said in private was not a bar to charitable status as there was, in effect, one purpose, the saying of masses, capable of implementation in two different ways. One, public masses, is charitable, the other, private masses, is not. The court applied the principle that where a gift has a single purpose which could be performed by either charitable or non-charitable means, it should be construed as a gift to be performed by charitable means. However, in *Gilmour* v. *Coats* (1949) a gift to a community of strictly cloistered and enclosed nuns was not held charitable because the benefit conferred on the public by their prayers was, per Lord Simonds, 'manifestly not susceptible of proof'. In addition, the possibility that the public might have been edified by the nuns' example of self-denial was too vague and intangible. Yet it will be recalled that in *Re Watson* (1973) (above) works of no intrinsic religious value were held charitable, the element of public benefit presumably being satisfied on the basis that the books had been distributed. The contrast between the cases is strange.

(ii) By the presence among the public of persons who have to be edified by attendance at a place of worship. In *Neville Estates Ltd* v. *Madden* (1962) a trust for the advancement of religion among members of the Catford Synagogue was held charitable on this basis even though the services at the synagogue were only open to those on its list of members. Had the services at the convent in *Gilmour* v. *Coates* (1949) been open to the public then that part of their activities might have been charitable although even so gift might have failed on the ground that their activities were not exclusively charitable.

Advancement of health or the saving of lives, including the prevention of sickness, disease, or human suffering

In *Re Resch's Will Trusts* (1969) a private hospital was held charitable despite the fact that it did not operate for profit, its charges were not low. Gifts for ancillary purposes, such as the training of doctors and nurses or the provision of extra facilities for patients, will also be charitable, as will gifts for the treatment and/or investigation of particular diseases or conditions such as drug addiction (*Re Banfield* (1968)) or blindness (*Re Lewis* (1955)).

Advancement of citizenship or community development (including rural or urban regeneration, promotion of civic responsibility, volunteering, the voluntary sector or the effectiveness or efficiency of charities)

The object here seems to be to make it clear that trusts which, for example, encourage volunteering, are charitable.

Advancement of the arts, culture, heritage or science

This will cover, for example, museums and arts festivals. Until now, these trusts, although undoubtedly charitable, have not been specifically charitable and have sometimes sat rather uneasily under education. *Re Pinion* (1965) (above) could have come under this head but for the lack of public benefit.

Advancement of amateur sport

> *Note 13.6: As mentioned above, this is the one area which is not charitable under the present law but will be charitable when the Charities Bill is in force.*

Sports for the young, including not only chess but also useful activities such as those undertaken by the Boy Scouts Movement (*Re Webber* (1954)) were previously held to be charitable. In *IRC* v. *McMullen* (1981) a trust to provide facilities for pupils at schools and universities to play association football or other games or sports was held charitable. Hailsham LC held that the education of the young should not be limited to 'formal instruction'. He quoted with approval Eve J in *Re Mariette* (1915) who observed that education means the development of the body as well as the mind. However, playing games is not by itself educational and thus, said Lord Hailsham, a trust for physical education of those other than the young might not be charitable. The Charities Bill now widens this category and proposes that all amateur sports will qualify for charitable status provided that the sport involves physical skill and exertion.

Advancement of human rights, conflict resolution or reconciliation or the promotion of religious or racial harmony, equality or diversity

As the Amnesty case (*McGovern* v. *A-G* (1982) – see below) shows, activities of this kind can easily come within the definition of political trusts and so lose their charitable status. Presumably these trusts, in order to remain charitable, will need to concentrate on research and activities such as the actual promotion of mediation and conciliation.

Advancement of environmental protection or improvement

The National Trust was recognised as charitable in 1916 by the decision in *Re Verrall* and in *A-G (NSW)* v. *Sawtell* (1978) a bequest to preserve native wild life was upheld as charitable.

The relief of those in need by reason of youth, age, ill health, disability, financial hardship or other disadvantage, including the provision of accommodation or care to these persons

A specific example here is the charity 'Motability', which provides transport for the disabled and, more generally, charities for the young, the old, the disabled and for the other purposes mentioned above.

It includes the relief of suffering caused by disasters (*Re North Devon and West Somerset Relief Fund Trusts* (1953)), which can include not only relief from factors such as damage to property, which might itself cause poverty, but also relief from bereavement and personal injury. Also included are gifts to found childrens' homes (*Re Sahal's Will Trust* (1958)), but not, apparently, to purchase amenities which may be considered luxurious, such as TVs (*Re Cole* (1958)). What would be considered a luxurious item today?

The advancement of animal welfare

This has always been held charitable but the grounds for doing so have been uncertain. Now this is clarified by the Charities Bill and the decision in *Re Grove-Grady* (1929) has, thankfully, gone. Here the Court of Appeal emphasised that a trust for animals will only be charitable if human beings are involved in some way. The good of the animals themselves is apparently not enough. In this case the object of a trust was to provide an animal sanctuary and to keep a staff of employees to ensure that no human beings should molest or destroy any of the animals there. As Russell LJ put it, 'Beyond perhaps hearing of the existence of the enclosure the public does not come into the matter at all'. By contrast, in *Re Murawski's Will Trust* (1971) an animal sanctuary of a more usual kind, providing care and shelter, was held charitable. A difficult decision is *Re Wedgwood* (1915), where a gift to be applied to ensure that animals were humanely slaughtered was held charitable. Lord Cozens-Hardy held that the gift 'tended to promote public morality by checking the innate tendency to cruelty' yet this somewhat vague principle is not easy to square with *Re Grove-Grady*. It certainly seems that in *Re Wedgwood* the distinction between 'charitable object' and 'public benefit' (see above) was not drawn.

The promotion of the efficiency of the armed forces of the Crown

This is already recognised as charitable, for example, the promotion of the efficiency of the armed services (e.g. *Re Stephens* (1892) – teaching of shooting in the Army).

Any other purposes that:

(i) are not listed but are currently charitable under charity law. One instance specifically mentioned here is the Recreational Charities Act 1958 and this is dealt with in full below;
(ii) any purposes analogous to any purpose currently charitable or listed above; and
(iii) any purpose analogous to a purpose recognised as charitable after the Bill is passed.

Some examples from the previous law which do not seem to fit into any of the above examples are:

Gifts to the fire service and the police

The police (*IRC* v. *City of Glasgow Police Athletic Association* (1953)) and the fire services (*Re Wokingham Fire Brigade Trusts* (1951)).

Gifts to localities

In *Goodman* v. *Saltash Corporation* (1882) Selborne LC held that a gift 'for benefit of the inhabitants of a parish or town or of any particular class' of the is charitable. It thus appears that the purpose for which the gift is given could b for benevolent purposes which, in other contexts (see below), are not treated as charitable. In *A-G* v. *National Provincial and Union Bank of England* (1924) it was held that this principle will not be extended although it will be followed in similar cases. However, in *Williams' Trustees* v. *IRC* (1947) Lord Simonds appeared to expressly reject the test by holding that 'if the purposes are not charitable *per se* localisation of them will not make them charitable'. However, in *Peggs* v. *Lamb* (1994) two bodies concerned with the provision of income to the freemen of the Borough of Huntingdon and their widows were considered charitable on basis of the reasoning in *Goodman* v. *Saltash Corporation* (1882).

Under the previous law the requirement of public benefit was subjected to a stricter test in cases under the fourth head than in others and it will be interesting to see if this approach is followed by the courts when dealing with the new head, which is in effect a replacement for the fourth head. It is submitted that this would be mistaken as there is now one clear test of public benefit for all charities and there is no longer a presumption of public benefit in cases of education and religion. It is suggested, therefore, that the old cases on public benefit under the fourth head can in general be disregarded.

However, one guide for public benefit may survive into the new law. This is the idea of 'a class within a class'. In *IRC* v. *Baddeley* (1955) (see above) Lord Simonds doubted whether the requirement would be satisfied 'if the beneficiaries are of a class of persons not only confined to a particular area but selected from within it by reference to a particular creed'. Thus even had the purposes of the gift in this case been charitable, it would have failed as possibly being limited to actual or potential Methodists in a certain area. (There was doubt as to the precise term of the trust.) It was a gift to a class within a class. The point was put more vividly by Stamp QC in argument in the Court of Appeal in the case and quoted by Lord Simonds: 'Who has ever heard of a bridge to be crossed by impecunious Methodists?'

A good example here is the Recreational Charities Act 1958. This was passed as a result of the decision of the House of Lords in *IRC* v. *Baddeley* (1955) which cast doubt on the previous assumption that recreational trusts were charitable by holding that a trust for the 'moral, social and physical well-being of persons resident in East Ham and Leyton was not charitable'. Accordingly s. 1 provides that it shall be charitable 'to provide, or assist in the provision of, facilities for recreational or other leisure-time occupation, if the facilities are provided in the interests of social welfare . . .'

Section 1(2) provides that the facilities will only be treated as being provided in the interests of social welfare if either:

> '(a) The facilities are provided with the object of improving the conditions of life for the persons for whom the facilities are primarily intended *and*
>
> (b) (i) those persons have need of such facilities as aforesaid by reason of their youth, age, infirmity or disablement, poverty or social or economic circumstances;

or (ii) the facilities are to be available to the members or female members of the public at large'.

Section 1(1) further provides that the Act does not affect the principle, i.e. the requirement, of public benefit.

In *IRC* v. *McMullen* (1981) the phrase 'social welfare' was examined. Walton J in the High Court said that it connoted some element of relief from deprivation, especially because of the words in s. 1(2)(a) 'improving the conditions of life' but Bridge LJ in the Court of Appeal disagreed. Social welfare need not be limited to the deprived: 'Hyde Park improves the conditions of life for residents in Mayfair as much as for those in Pimlico or the Portobello Road'. In *Guild* v. *IRC* (1992) the House of Lords agreed with the approach of Bridge LJ. Lord Keith observed that 'persons in all walks of life and all kinds of social circumstances may have their conditions of life improved by the provision of recreational facilities of a suitable character'. Thus the phrase 'social welfare' covered either 'those who suffer from some sort of social deprivation' (s. 1(2)(b)(ii)) or others provided that in the latter case the facilities are available to the public at large. The court accordingly held that a gift of residue to a sports centre was charitable. The gift also referred to 'some similar purpose in connection with sport' and, by a 'benignant approach' the court held that this was intended to be for purposes similar to those of the sports centre and so this part of the gift was also charitable.

Another example of charitable activity which may now come under this head is the relief of suffering caused by disasters (*Re North Devon and West Somerset Relief Fund Trusts* (1953 above)), and gifts to found a children's home (*Re Sahal's Will Trust* (1958 above)).

POLITICAL TRUSTS

A trust where the main object is to achieve a political purpose is not charitable.

Meaning of 'political purpose'

Slade J in *McGovern* v. *A-G* (1982) said that it included trusts to:

(i) further the interests of a particular political party;
(ii) procure changes in the laws of either the United Kingdom or a foreign country;
(iii) procure a reversal of Government policy or of particular decisions of governmental authorities whether in the United Kingdom or in a foreign country.

Examples of political purposes

Furthering the interests of a particular political party

In *Re Hopkinson* (1949) a testator gave the residue of his estate to found an educational fund to advance adult education with particular reference to a programme of education put forward by the Labour Party. Vaisey J held that this gift was for political propaganda and thus not charitable. Similar decisions have been reached on trusts for the support of the Conservative Party (*Bonar Law Memorial Trust* v. *IRC* (1933)) and the Liberal Party (*Re Ogden* (1933)), although here the trust was upheld on other grounds.

If, however, the trust is for the advancement of education, or some other charitable purpose, then there will be a valid charitable gift even though there may be some connection with political purposes. In *Re Hopkinson* (1949) the court was unwilling to adopt this construction of the gift, holding that the trust was dominated by the political purpose, but in *Re Scowcroft* (1898) a gift with political overtones was upheld as its main purpose was charitable. Here a gift for a village club and reading room 'to be used for the furtherance of Conservative principles and religious and mental improvement, and to be kept free from intoxicants and dancing' was held valid. The explanation of this decision may, however, be that it pre-dates the notion that political purposes cannot be charitable, which really began with Lord Parker's speech in *Bowman* v. *Secular Society* (1917).

A more recent application of the principle found in *Re Scowcroft* (1898) is *Re Koeppler's Will Trusts* (1986). Here a gift which was uncertain in its precise terms was construed as being for the purposes of the Wilton Park project which involved conferences on issues of current political debate but which did not involve the propagation of political opinions or any activities of a party political nature. Instead, the object of the project was a genuine attempt to find and disseminate the truth and accordingly the gift was held to be for the advancement of education.

Procuring changes in either the law, or reversals of government policy or government decisions

In *National Anti-Vivisection Society* v. *IRC* (1948) the main object of the society was found to be the total abolition of vivisection with, in consequence, the repeal of the relevant legislation, now the Animals (Scientific Procedures) Act 1986. It was therefore held not to be a charitable body.

In *McGovern* v. *A-G* (1982) a trust was established by Amnesty International with four main objects:

(a) The relief of prisoners of conscience and their relatives.
(b) Seeking the release of such prisoners.
(c) The abolition of torture or inhuman treatment or punishment.
(d) Research into human rights and the dissemination of the results of that research.

Although objects (a) and (d) were held by themselves to be charitable, objects (b) and (c) involved attempting to procure changes in the law and the reversal of government decisions, whether in the United Kingdom or abroad. The trust was therefore held not to be charitable, there being no possibility of severing the charitable from the non-charitable objects (see *Salusbury* v. *Denton* (1857) below).

A university or college students' union is a charitable body, as it is connected with the advancement of education. Accordingly, a students' union must not use its funds for political purposes, as in *Baldry* v. *Feintuck* (1972), where the use of union funds to campaign for free school milk to be restored was held to be political (see also *A-G* v. *Ross* (1985)). In *Webb* v. *O'Doherty* (1991) an injunction was granted to restrain a students' union from spending money in support of a campaign against the Gulf War. The court distinguished between campaigning by seeking to influence public opinion, which is not charitable, and mere discussion of political issues, which can be charitable. In the New Zealand case of *Re Collier* (1998) a trust in a will to promote world peace where the testator was encouraging soldiers to lay down their arms was political and in *Southwood* v. *A-G* (1998) a trust to educate the public in militarism and disarmament was not charitable as the main purpose was to promote pacifism and to challenge the policies of governments. The message behind these decisions seems to be that where a trust has a flavour which could be political, then the courts will look carefully to see whether the trust has a particular message to promote which is not charitable. The rule that campaigning for a change in the law is not a charitable object has been criticised on the ground that no objection seems to be taken to charities campaigning *against* a change in the law, such as the campaign of the Lord's Day Observance Society against changes to Sunday trading legislation.

Reasons why political purposes are not held to be charitable

Reasons given by Slade J In *McGovern* v. *A-G* (1982)

(i) The courts cannot judge if a change in the law is for the public benefit because it will not normally have evidence before it to enable it to do this.
(ii) Even if the court does have such evidence, to hold that a change in the law is desirable would usurp the function of the legislature.
(iii) In the case of trusts campaigning to secure the alteration of foreign laws, not only would there be the evidential problem referred to at (i) above, but the enforcement of such a trust might prejudice the relations of this country with that of the foreign country concerned.

In *National Anti-Vivisection Society* v. *IRC* (1948) Lord Simonds gave a fourth reason:

(iv) That the Attorney-General, as the 'guardian of charity' could not be expected to ensure the performance of a trust whose object was to alter the law in a way contrary to the wishes of the government. Yet it may be said, with respect, that this confuses the executive with the judicial functions of the Attorney-General's office. Now that s. 32 of the Charities Act 1993 gives the Charity Commissioners powers to take proceedings in the enforcement of trusts, the validity of this reason could however be affected although the Attorney-General's consent will still be needed (see also *A-G* v. *Gouriet* (1977)).

Attitude of the Charity Commissioners

Some charities have found difficulties when engaging, for example, in campaigns which may have a political flavour to them. The Charity Commissioners, in their

Annual Report for 1981, pointed out that a charity can help the Government to reach a decision on a particular issue by providing information and argument, provided that the emphasis is on rational persuasion but, on the other hand, the boundary between education and propaganda must not be crossed and any research must be objective and balanced. In their 1997 Report the Commissioners gave further guidance. They emphasised that any political activity must be in furtherance of and ancillary to the objects of the charity and within its powers. On this basis, charities may, for example, respond to Government proposals contained in Green and White Papers and may inform and educate the public on issues relevant to the charity. They can engage in campaigning, provided that they do so on the basis of reasoned arguments and can advocate a change in the law if they believe that this would help in furthering the activities of the charity.

If the Charities Bill 2005 becomes law, political trusts will still not qualify for charitable status but the advancement of human rights, conflict resolution and reconciliation will be a specific head of charity. However, as mentioned above, their activities must not cross the boundary into political trusts.

THE OBJECTS OF THE TRUST MUST BE EXCLUSIVELY CHARITABLE

Meaning of 'exclusively charitable'

This is the one area of the law on charitable status to be unaffected by the Charities Bill 2005.

In order to qualify as a charity the trust must be exclusively charitable so that a gift to it will inevitably be used for charitable purposes. Where there are two objects, one undoubtedly charitable, the other not necessarily so, then the trust will not be charitable. Thus in *IRC* v. *City of Glasgow Police Athletic Association* (1953) one of the association's purposes, to promote the efficiency of the police, was charitable, but another purpose, to provide recreational facilities, was not and therefore the association was not charitable. Similarly, in *IRC* v. *Baddeley* (1955) (see above), where property was to be used 'for the promotion of the religious, social and physical well-being of persons . . .', the inclusion of the word 'social' prevented the purposes from being charitable.

Where the non-charitable purposes are only ancillary or incidental to the charitable purposes

In this situation the inclusion of non-charitable purposes will not prevent the trust from being charitable. In *London Hospital Medical College* v. *IRC* (1976) a students' union, whose primary purpose was to further the educational purposes of a college, was charitable, even though it also conferred personal benefits on union members. This principle has even been held to allow the provision of an annual dinner to trustees on the ground that this would assist in the better administration of the trust (*Re Coxen* (1948)).

Gifts for charitable and/or benevolent purposes

Where a gift is given for 'charitable and benevolent' purposes (*Re Best* (1904)) or 'charitable and deserving objects' (*Re Sutton* (1885)) then the gift is charitable because charity is an essential qualification. But if the word 'or' is used instead of 'and' there is an alternative, and all of the funds could be used for non-charitable purposes. Thus in *Chichester Diocesan Fund and Board of Finance* v. *Simpson* (1944) the words 'charitable or benevolent' meant that the gift was not charitable. The point can be summed up by saying that 'and' in these cases means that the words are to be construed conjunctively whereas 'or' means that they are to be construed disjunctively.

Severance

Where trustees are obliged to apply part of the property for a charitable purpose and part for a non-charitable purpose then the court can sever the two parts and allow the charitable part to stand on its own. In *Salusbury* v. *Denton* (1857) a fund was to be used partly towards the foundation of a charity school and partly for the benefit of the testator's relatives. The court severed the two parts and, as the size of each part had not been specified, it was held, on the principle that 'equality is equity', that they would be divided equally. Severance would not, of course, be possible if the gift could, at the discretion of the trustees, be applied wholly for non-charitable purposes.

CHARITABLE TRUSTS (VALIDATION) ACT 1954

The Act was passed as a result of concern about cases such as *Chichester Diocesan Fund* (1944) (above). The Act provides that if the terms of a trust coming into operation before 16 December 1952 allow property to be applied either exclusively for charitable purposes or for non-charitable purposes then the terms shall be treated as if they allowed the property to be applied only for charitable purposes. Thus, had the *Chichester Diocesan Fund* case been subject to the Act, the word 'benevolent' would have been ignored and the word 'charitable' would have applied to the whole of the gift. Although the Act does not apply to the terms of trusts coming into operation after 16 December 1952 its effects can still be felt in trusts coming into force before this date.

FURTHER READING

Chesterman (1979) *Charities, trusts and social welfare*, London: Weidenfeld & Nicholson (now out of print). As the title indicates, sets the law of charities in its social context. Still interesting, especially in view of the Charities Bill 2005.

Fletcher (1996) 'Charities for the advancement of education', 112 LQR 557. Useful on *Funnell* v. *Stewart* and *Re Hetherington*.

Warburton (1997) 'Charities, members, accountability and control', 61 Conv. 372. Very valuable article on some contemporary issues.

CHAPTER SUMMARY

- Advantages of charitable status.
- Types of charitable organisation.
- Four heads of charity under the existing law.
- Proposed new definition of charity under the Charities Bill 2005.
- Requirement of public benefit.
- Political trusts.
- Must be exclusively charitable.

QUESTION

Helen made the following bequests in her will:

(a) £10,000 to campaign against the closure of village schools
(b) £5,000 to encourage the playing of cricket among promising young players. In the selection of such players a preference shall be given to pupils of my husband's old school.

Consider the validity of these bequests as charitable gifts.

Would your answer be different if the provisions of the Charities Bill 2005 were in force?

> **Note 13.7:** *You will find suggested points for inclusion in this answer in Appendix 2.*

14 Failure of charitable gifts: administration of charities

Note 14.1: This chapter deals with those parts of the Charities Bill 2005 which are concerned with the administration of charities (Parts 2, 3, and 4).

INTRODUCTION

A charitable gift may fail where the charity to which it was made has ceased to exist, or indeed has never existed. Failure of objects in the case of a private trust brings into operation a resulting trust for the settlor or his estate (see Chapter 5). In the case of charities the law strives to ensure that the gift is still devoted to its charitable purposes by the doctrine of *cy-près* (see below). First, however, it is necessary to examine three situations where the courts have held that the gift has not failed at all.

CONTINUATION OF THE CHARITY IN ANOTHER FORM

If the charity no longer exists as a separate entity but instead has been amalgamated with other charities, it may be possible to say that the particular charity to which the gift was made is continuing. In *Re Faraker* (1912) a testatrix bequeathed a legacy to 'Mrs Bailey's Charity, Rotherhithe', the object of which was to benefit poor widows. However, the charity had been amalgamated with others with the object of benefiting the poor in general of Rotherhithe. The court held that the amalgamated charities were entitled to the gift. In *Re Roberts* (1963), however, a gift was made to the Sheffield Boys' Working Home which by then had ceased to exist and most of its assets had been transferred to the Sheffield Town Trust. It was held that the *Re Faraker* principle could not apply as the purposes of the Sheffield Town Trust were different. However, a *cy-près* scheme was ordered.

GIFT FOR THE PURPOSES OF AN UNINCORPORATED ASSOCIATION

An unincorporated association has no legal existence as such. This principle causes much difficulty in the case of non-charitable gifts (see Chapter 15). However, with charitable gifts the fact that the gift was to an unincorporated association can be a positive advantage, because as the gift could not have been to the association due to its lack of a legal existence, it must be instead for its purposes, and provided that these are still continuing the gift has not failed. The point was taken in *Re Finger's Will Trust* (1972), where a testatrix left shares of her residuary estate to various charities, two of which had ceased to exist at the date of her death. One of these was an unincorporated association and, as it was held that the gift was for charitable purposes, and these purposes were still being carried on, a scheme would be ordered to give effect to the gift. The other charity was a corporation and so, as the gift was to the corporation itself and not for its purposes, the gift failed. However, it was possible to apply it *cy-près*.

INCORRECT DESCRIPTION OF THE INSTITUTION

Provided that it is still possible to identify the institution the gift will not fail. In *Re Spence* (1978) the gift was to 'The Blind Home Keighley' instead of 'Keighley and District Home for the Blind', but the gift here failed on other grounds (see below).

Cy-près doctrine

Assuming that neither the *Re Faraker* (1912) nor the *Re Finger* (1972) solution is possible and so the gift has failed, *cy-près* application can be ordered. This doctrine enables the court (or the Charity Commissioners) to make a scheme to apply the gift for purposes as near as possible (*cy-près*) to the donor's original intention.

Cy-près application is possible provided that:

(a) the donor showed a general charitable intention;
(b) the gift failed within the meaning of s. 13 of the Charities Act 1993.

General charitable intention

(a) *Subsequent failure of the gift.* The requirement of a general charitable intention need not be satisfied where the charity ceases to exist **after** the testator's death (a case of subsequent failure), because the property would already have vested in the recipient and so it can be applied *cy-près*. In *Re Slevin* (1891) money was left to an orphanage which existed at the testator's death but ceased to exist before the money was paid over. *Cy-près* application was ordered. In practice, the principle in *Re Slevin* will only be of use if the charity ceases to exist between the date of the testator's death and the time when his/her estate is to be distributed.

(b) *Initial failure of the gift.* Most situations, however, concern initial failure of the gift, i.e. the institution was not in existence at the date of the testator's death. In such cases a general charitable intention must be found. In *Re Lysaght* (1966) Buckley J said that such an intention would exist where there was 'a paramount intention on the part of the donor to effect some charitable purpose', as distinct from a situation where 'the donor means his charitable intention to take effect but only if it can be carried into effect in a particular specified way'. This he called a particular (often called a specific) charitable intention. The distinction is neatly illustrated by *Re Henry Wood Memorial Trust* (1966). After the Queens' Hall was destroyed in 1942 an appeal was launched in 1944 to build a new concert hall. In 1946 a trust deed was executed with wider purposes: to foster musical appreciation among the public and, in particular, to build a concert hall. Insufficient funds were, however, subscribed and it was held that money given in response to the appeal was given for specific charitable purposes (i.e. the building of the hall) but the money given in response to the trust deed was given for wider purposes which showed a general charitable intention. (The court then ordered an inquiry into how much had been collected in response to the trust deed as distinct from the earlier appeal.)

It can be very difficult to find evidence to show that a testator had a general intention to benefit charity as distinct from an intention to benefit one particular charity and it is easiest to look at this topic under the following headings:

(i) *Gift is only for the purposes of a particular institution.* If that institution has ceased to exist before the testator's death then *cy-près* application is not possible because there is no general charitable intention. Thus, in *Re Rymer* (1895) there was a gift to a seminary which had ceased to exist and in *Re Spence* (1978) there was a gift to an old people's home which had likewise ceased to exist. In both cases no general charitable intention was found and so the gifts were held on resulting trusts for the testators' estates.
(ii) *Gift is for a purpose represented by a particular institution.* In *Re Roberts* (1963) the gift to the Sheffield Boys' Home could be applied *cy-près* because the gift was not so connected with the home as such that it ended when the home did. Whether a case falls into this category or (i) above is a question of fact. In *Re Finger* (1972) (see above) the gift to the corporation, the National Council for Maternity and Child Welfare, was held to show a general charitable intention partly because the council co-ordinated the activities of other bodies over a fairly wide field.
(iii) *Gift to an institution which has never existed.* In *Re Harwood* (1936) a gift to the Belfast Peace Society, which had never existed, was applied *cy-près* because the testator showed a general intention to benefit societies whose object was the promotion of peace. However, the mere fact that an institution has never existed is not always evidence of a general charitable intention and in *Re Koeppler's Will Trusts* (1986) *Re Harwood* was doubted on the ground that promotion of peace was political and not charitable.

(iv) *Gift to several institutions*. A gift to several charitable institutions with similar objects may show a general charitable intention so that if one of them either does not exist, or no longer exists, this gift may be applied *cy-près*; see Megarry V-C in *Re Spence* (1978), where he described this as 'charity by association'. However, where there are several charitable gifts together with a non-charitable gift which has failed, the inclusion of the non-charitable gift may negate the presumption of general charitable intention. In *Re Jenkins' Will Trusts* (1966) the testatrix bequeathed her residuary estate to six charitable institutions together with the British Union for the Abolition of Vivisection which was not charitable. The court held that the mere inclusion of a non-charitable gift among charitable gifts did not imply that the non-charitable gift was intended to take effect as a charitable gift. In *Re Satterthwaite's Will Trusts* (1966) the testatrix left her residuary estate to a number of animal welfare organisations, which were charitable, an anti-vivisection society, which was not charitable, and also to the London Animal Hospital, which had never existed. It was held that this last gift could be applied *cy-près* as there was a general charitable intention. *Re Satterthwaite* was decided 12 days earlier than *Re Jenkins*, in which it was not cited and with which it is difficult to reconcile. A possible explanation is that the London Animal Hospital had never existed as a charity and so the principle in *Re Harwood* (1936) (see above) applied.

(v) *Gift for purposes*. A gift for purposes rather than an institution can be applied *cy-près* if there is a general charitable intention. In *Biscoe* v. *Jackson* (1887) a gift to provide a soup kitchen and cottage hospital 'for the parish of Shoreditch' was held to show such an intention to provide for the sick and poor of the parish.

Removal of conditions

Where a particular condition attached to a trust is preventing the carrying out of the main purpose of the trust, the *cy-près* doctrine may be used to remove the condition on the ground that its existence makes the carrying out of the trust impossible. In *Re Dominion Students' Hall Trust* (1947) a colour bar was removed from the constitution of a company which maintained a hostel for students and one of whose objects was to promote 'community of citizenship' among members of the Commonwealth.

The same principle has been applied where the recipient of a gift will not accept it with a particular condition attached. In *Re Woodhams* (1981) a condition attached to scholarships to two music colleges, limiting applicants to boys from two named children's homes, was removed because the colleges would otherwise have declined the gifts on the ground that the restriction was impractical. In *Re Lysaght* (1966) a gift to the Royal College of Surgeons (RCS) to hold on trust to found medical studentships contained a condition stating, *inter alia*, that the students should not be of the Jewish or Roman Catholic faith. The RCS refused to act as trustee unless this condition was removed, which it was. Where

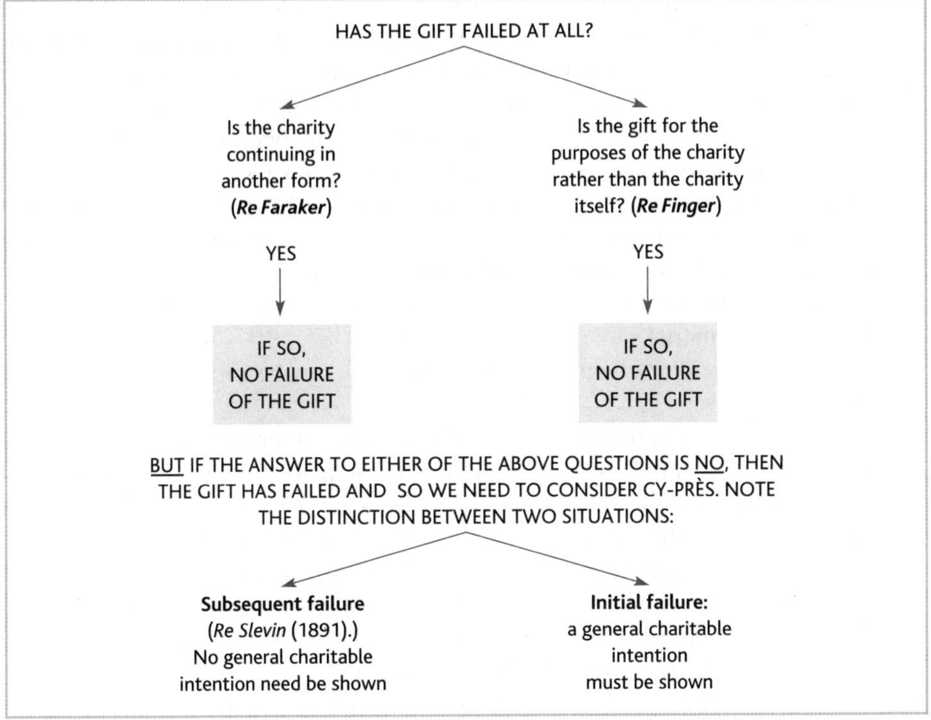

Figure 14.1 Summary of the position where there is a possible failure

a trustee declines to act the court will normally appoint another trustee but here it was held essential to the carrying out of the trust that the RCS should act as trustee.

A general charitable intention must, of course, also be found in these cases. In *Re Lysaght* (1966) it was held that the general charitable intention was the foundation of medical studentships, and in *Re Woodhams* (1981) it was the fostering of musical education.

Impossibility

Even though general charitable intention was shown, property could not be applied *cy-près* unless it was impossible or impracticable to carry out the trust. These words were generously construed (see e.g. *Re Dominion Students' Hall Trust* (1947) above). Where, however, a purpose was very difficult to fulfil, the *cy-près* doctrine did not apply, however inconvenient this might be (see *Re Weir Hospital* (1910)).

However, s. 13 of the Charities Act 1993 has considerably widened the jurisdiction of the courts and the Charity Commissioners to approve a *cy-près* scheme. It provides that property can be applied *cy-près* in the following situations:

(a) Where the original purposes in whole or in part have either been fulfilled as far as they may be or cannot be carried out according to the directions and the spirit of the gift. The Charities Bill 2005 proposes that in addition the courts will have to consider the social and economic circumstances prevailing at the time of the application (clause 12). In *Re Lepton's Charity* (1972) a gift was made by will in 1715 of land to be held on trust to pay out of the rents £3 a year to the minister of a chapel and the 'overplus of the profits' to the poor of the town. In 1715 the total income was £5 a year. The land had been sold and the resulting investments yielded £791 a year. The court held that the basic intention could no longer be carried out and so a scheme was ordered whereby the minister received £100 a year.

(b) Where the original purposes provide a use for only part of the property, e.g. if a surplus remains.
(c) Where the property given and other property can be more effectively used together.
(d) Where the original purposes were laid down by reference to some area which has ceased to be a unit for some other purpose (e.g. changes in local government boundaries) or by reference to a class of persons or area which has ceased to be suitable. In *Peggs* v. *Lamb* (1994) the court applied this rule so as to enlarge a class of beneficiaries from the freemen of the Borough of Huntingdon and their widows to all the inhabitants of the Borough. It was still possible to ascertain the spirit of the gift because although there was no founding document, the spirit could be inferred.
(e) Where the original purposes have wholly or partly either:
    (i) been adequately provided for by other means;
    (ii) ceased as being useless or harmful to the community or ceased in law to be charitable; *or*
    (iii) ceased in any other way to provide a suitable and effective method of using the property, e.g. if the original benefits are now provided by public bodies, or if the charity has been removed from the Register of Charities. It was held in *Re Lepton* (1972) that this could also have been a ground for that decision. It was applied in *Varsani* v. *Jesani* (1999), where a Hindu sect had split into two groups and so the property of the sect was divided between two new groups.

In *Re JW Laing Trust* (1984) a donor, who had settled shares, required both capital and income to be distributed within ten years of his death but the recipients, who did not wish to receive large amounts of capital, applied to dispense with this requirement. The court held that s. 13 of the Charities Act did not apply. It referred only to objects of the trust and this was an administrative matter, but the court did agree to the application in the exercise of its inherent jurisdiction.

In *Oldham BC* v. *A-G* (1993) the council wished to sell lands, which had been given to it on trust for use as playing fields, to developers and to acquire a new site for the playing fields. The court held that none of the provisions in s. 13 applied so as to allow a *cy-près* scheme but the court did have a general jurisdiction to authorise the sale of charity lands where this would benefit the charity.

Where there has been an initial failure of the gift, a general charitable intention will need to be shown for s. 13 to apply, although if there is only a subsequent failure, i.e. if the property has already been dedicated to charity (see *Re Slevin* (1891) above) no general charitable intention need be found.

Anonymous donors

Section 14 of the Charities Act 1993 provides that property given for specific charitable purposes which fail can be applicable *cy-près* even though there is no general charitable intention provided that either:

(a) It belongs to donors who cannot be identified or found after:
   (i) the prescribed advertisements and inquiries have been published and made; and
   (ii) the prescribed period beginning with the publication of those advertisements has expired, or

(b) it belongs to a donor who has inserted a disclaimer in the prescribed form of his right to have the property back.

Trustees will be under no liability with respect to claims made after the period prescribed in (a)(ii) above. If the trustees then make a scheme to apply the property *cy-près* it will still be possible for a donor, who could not previously be identified or found, to claim provided that he does so within six months of the scheme being made. The scheme must specify the total amount of the property which belonged to such donors and if the aggregate amount claimed by them exceeds the total set aside for this purpose then the Charity Commissioners may direct that each claimant should receive only a proportion of his claim. Property is conclusively presumed to belong to donors who cannot be identified or found if it consists of:

(a) proceeds of cash collections made by collecting boxes or other means not adapted for distinguishing one gift from another; *or*

(b) the proceeds of any lottery, competition, entertainment, sale or similar money-raising activity.

The donors of prizes or articles are entitled either to their return or to the proceeds of sale. The court can also direct by order that property can be treated as belonging to donors who cannot be identified when either:

(a) it would be unreasonable, having regard to the amounts likely to be returned to the donors, to incur expense in returning the property; *or*

(b) it would be unreasonable, having regard to the nature, circumstances and amount of the gifts involved and to the lapse of time since they were made, for the donor to expect the property to be returned.

Clause 14 of the Charities Bill 2005 proposes an additional power to apply gifts *cy-près* where the 'solicitation' (e.g. the charity appeal) specifically states that any property given in response to it will, in the event of the charity purposes failing, be applicable for *cy-près* purposes generally unless the donor declares otherwise at the time of making the gift.

ADMINISTRATION OF CHARITIES

Note 14.2: The present law will first be considered, as it may be some time before that part of the Charities Bill 2005 dealing with the regulation of charities comes into force. The new regime proposed by the Charities Bill will then be looked at.

Present law

The Charity Commissioners are established by Act of Parliament, the principal statute now being the Charities Act 1993. Their general function is to promote the effective use of charitable resources encouraging better methods of administration, giving charity trustees information and advice, and investigating and checking abuses. They have the following principal specific functions:

(a) To decide whether a trust or institution is charitable and can be registered as a charity. Appeals against their decision lie to the High Court.
(b) To make schemes and orders to enable charity property to be more effectively used, e.g. *cy-près* schemes. There is a concurrent jurisdiction with the High Court here.
(c) To give consent to legal proceedings relating to charities.
(d) To give advice to charity trustees on any matter affecting the performance of their duties. A trustee who then acts in accordance with this advice is deemed to have acted in accordance with the trust unless the trustee knows, or should know, that the advice was given in ignorance of material facts. In *Mills* v. *Winchester Diocesan Board of Finance* (1989) it was held that the Commissioners do not owe any duty of care in negligence when giving advice.
(e) To authorise dealings with charity property where the trustees would not otherwise be able to do so, e.g. authorisation of a sale of land.
(f) To make and bring into effect common investment schemes for charities under which different trusts can pool their funds for investment purposes.

The Charities Act 1992

This Act, most of which is now incorporated in the Charities Act 1993, has strengthened the powers of the Charity Commission in a number of ways. Some of the main examples are:

(a) The Commissioners can now act in the affairs of a charity where either there has been misconduct or mismanagement in a charity's administration or it is necessary or desirable to act so as to preserve charity property. Previously the Commissioners could act only if both these requirements were satisfied. Action which can be taken includes suspending or removing trustees and other officials and appointing a receiver and manager of the charity's property (s. 18).
(b) Certain persons are disqualified from acting as charity trustees such as those convicted of any offence involving fraud or dishonesty (s. 72).

(c) All registered charities must submit annual statements of account to the Commission with the exception of companies which must make a return instead to the Registrar of Companies (s. 42).
(d) The annual income limit below which charities are exempt from registration is now £1,000. (This sum can be altered by regulations made the Secretary of State.) (See s. 3.)
(e) The Commissioners may direct that any registered charity change its name if the name under which it is registered may mislead the public about the true nature of the charity's purposes or if it is necessary to order such a change to prevent one charity exploiting another's name.

Small charities

Section 74 of the 1993 Act enables the trustees of small charities (those with a gross income not exceeding £5,000 in the last financial year and which do not hold land on trust for the purposes of the charity) to resolve to transfer the property to other charities. At least two-thirds of the trustees must agree and they must be satisfied that the purposes of the charity which is to receive the property are as similar as is reasonably practicable. Alternatively, the trustees may agree to modify any or all of the objects by substituting new objects if they consider that the charity's resources are no longer being effectively applied and that the new objects are as similar to the old ones as practicable.

After the trustees have passed a resolution to achieve either of the above purposes it must be sent to the Charity Commissioners. In addition, public notice of the proposals must be given. If the Commissioners agree, the objects are deemed to be altered. In effect, therefore, the Act provides for a shorter and simpler *cy-près* procedure in these cases.

Section 75 allows trustees of charities with a permanent endowment (i.e. capital) which does not include land and a gross income in the last financial year of £1,000 or less to resolve to spend the capital as income. However, the trustees must first consider if the powers under s. 74 would be more appropriate. A two-thirds majority of the trustees is needed and the Commissioners must agree.

Local authorities and charities

Section 76 of the 1993 Act allows county and district councils to maintain an index of local charities and under s. 77 they can review local charities and make recommendations to the Commissioners, e.g. to modernise their objects or merge them. Local authorities can also draw the Commissioners' attention to cases where charities have become 'lost', i.e. there do not appear to be any trustees although the charity has money in a bank account, and they also have the right to be represented on some local charities.

Regulation of charities under the Charities Bill 2005

The Charity Commission will become a statutory corporation with objectives, functions and duties defined in the new Act. It will be required to produce an annual public report and to hold an annual public meeting. The general functions of the Commission are to determine charitable status, to promote better administration of charities, to investigate misconduct and to disseminate information to the public and to the Government. These provisions have been the subject of some criticism on the ground that they do not impose any express requirements on the Commission to act in accordance with the Human Rights Act and the general principles of natural justice. The Joint Committee recommends that there should be a requirement that the Commission should use its powers proportionately, fairly and reasonably.

- There will be a new Charity Appeal Tribunal allowing an appeal from all formal decisions of the Commission by, essentially, any interested party and this will include the Attorney-General acting in the public interest. The tribunal may reverse a decision or send it back to the Commission with directions. A further appeal can be made to the High Court, but only with consent and on a point(s) of law.
- All charities must be registered but:
  (a) The compulsory registration figures will be increased to an income of £5,000 and not £1,000. Charities below this figure will be able to register voluntarily.
  (b) There will no longer be a requirement that a charity must register if it possesses a permanent endowment or uses or occupies land.
- There will be two categories of exempt charities:
  (a) Those subject to a regulator, other than the Charity Commission, which has agreed to take responsibility for charity law regulation.
  (b) If there is no suitable regulator, the charity will be subject to regulation by the Charity Commission but for an initial transitional period this will only apply to charities with an income over £100,000.
- The category of excepted charities will be abolished and these charities will now have to register, although initially there will be an income threshold.
- The Commission will have greater powers to make schemes where charitable appeals have failed and the Bill will contain powers allowing promoters of appeals, when appealing for funds, to also invite donors to declare that if the appeal fails their donations should be returned to them. If the donor does not make such a declaration, or if the donor cannot be found, then the funds can automatically be applied *cy-près* for charitable purposes, i.e. there is no need to obtain the sanction of the Charity Commission or the court. (These new powers should be compared with the existing ones in s. 14 of the Charities Act 1993.)
- The Commission will have new powers to require charities to take specified action in the best interests of a charity or the specified application of charitable property.
- There are new detailed powers in connection with the audit of the accounts of charities.
- A new, and potentially most useful provision, is that a charity may become a Charity Incorporated Organisation (CIO), which will enable a charity to have

a legal structure which combines registration as a company and registration as a charity. This will avoid the present position under which a charity as a company limited by guarantee is regulated by both company and charity law. A CIO can be created as a new entity or an existing charity can be converted into a CIO. This should be most attractive to many charities which at present function as companies limited by guarantee.

- There is a new power for all charity trustees to be remunerated out of the charity's funds for goods or services they provide to the charity. Reasonable remuneration must be paid and there are detailed provisions and safeguards governing the exercise of this power.
- The Charity Commission will have power to relieve trustees, auditors and independent examiners from liability for a breach of trust or duty, provided they acted honestly and reasonably and ought fairly to be excused for the breach. This is in line with s. 61 of the Trustee Act 1925, which applies to private trusts (see Chapter 20).
- There are detailed provisions allowing the trustees of small unincorporated charities to transfer all the charity's property to another charity, to amend their objects and to modify their administrative provisions. In addition, small charities have powers to spend their capital endowment and there are detailed new rules designed to assist with mergers between charities.

> *Note 14.3: Part 3 contains detailed provisions designed to regulate fundraising by charities and other similar organisations.*

FURTHER READING

See the list for Chapter 13.

CHAPTER SUMMARY

- Where charity is continuing in another form.
- Where charity is an unincorporated association.
- Conditions for *cy-près* to apply.
- Administration of charities.

QUESTION

Arthur, a lecturer in Equity and Trusts, died in 2005 and left the following bequests in his will:

(a) £50,000 for the Fund for Distressed Equity Lawyers, a registered charity.
(b) £25,000 to his old school, Hanbury College for Boys.
(c) £10,000 to the St Wulstans's Hospital.

After the date on which Arthur made his will but before his death, the Fund for Distressed Equity Lawyers was wound up and its assets were transferred to the Distressed Lawyers Benevolent Association, which is also a registered charity. Hanbury College amalgamated with the Lower Wick School for Girls in 2000 and the St Wulstan's Hospital never existed, although there was a St Wilfrid's Hospital.

Advise the executors of Arthur's will on what should be done with these bequests on the assumption that they are for valid charitable objects.

> *Note 14.4: You will find suggested points for inclusion in this answer in Appendix 2.*

15 Non-charitable purpose trusts

INTRODUCTION

Look at the following examples. They may help you in understanding the nature of non-charitable purpose trusts.

Example 15.1

X transfers property to Y for him to hold as trustee for Z. This is a straightforward private trust where property is to be held on trust for a particular beneficiary and it is of course valid.

Example 15.2

X transfers property to Y for him to hold as trustee for charitable purposes. This is not a trust for particular persons and is therefore not a private trust. Instead it is a trust for purposes and, as we saw in Chapter 14, because those purposes are charitable, the trust is valid even though there are no identifiable beneficiaries.

Example 15.3

X transfers property to Y to hold 'for the maintenance of good relations between nations . . . the preservation of the independence of the newspapers and similar purposes'. This is also a trust for purposes rather than persons but here the purposes are not charitable.

Non-charitable purpose trusts are generally void, although there are exceptions to this rule, and it is with these trusts that this chapter is concerned.

Why are trusts for non-charitable purposes generally held to be void?

The origin of the rule that trusts for non-charitable purposes are generally void is sometimes said to be the dictum of Grant MR who said in *Morice* v. *Bishop of Durham* (1805): 'there must be somebody in whose favour the court can decree performance'. In fact, however, this was a trust which failed through lack of certainty of objects. It is more accurate to say that the basis of the rule is found in the beneficiary principle: a trust must have a beneficiary who can enforce it. As Harman J said in *Re Wood* (1949): 'a gift on trust must have a *cestui que trust*'. The problem is really one of control. If there is no one who can take action in the case of, for example, maladministration of trust funds, then there is not really a trust at all but an absolute gift to the supposed trustee. The point was made by Roxburgh J in *Re Astor* (1952): 'it is not possible to contemplate with equanimity the creation of large funds devoted to non charitable purposes which no court and no department of state can control or, in case of maladministration, reform'. Charitable trusts can be enforced by the Attorney-General rather than by a beneficiary (see Chapter 14) and so are subject to control. A trust for non-charitable purposes, rather than persons, has no beneficiary who can enforce it and the settlor will not be allowed to do so. These trusts are sometimes known as trusts of imperfect obligation because of this lack of beneficiaries who can enforce them. Examples are *Re Astor's Settlement Trusts* (1952), of which the terms were given in Example 15.3 above, and *Leahy* v. *A-G for New South Wales* (1959) where a testator left a sheep station on trust for 'such order of nuns of the Catholic Church or the Christian Brothers as my executors and trustees shall select'. The gift was not charitable because some of the orders of nuns were contemplative (see *Gilmour* v. *Coats* (1949) – Chapter 14) and it would therefore have been held to be an invalid purpose trust had it not been saved by a New South Wales statute which allowed charitable trusts to be applied only in favour of the charitable parts.

Despite this apparently fundamental objection to trusts for non-charitable purposes, the law did not become finally settled until *Re Astor* in 1952. Until then it was arguable that there was no absolute principle that these trusts were void and, in particular, that these trusts were not subject to the perpetuity rules (see below). A good example is *Re Drummond* (1914), where a trust was upheld where the objects were the Old Boys of Bradford Grammar School and to acquire premises for a clubhouse. These objects may have been worthy but they were certainly not charitable. Since the decisions in *Re Astor* and *Leahy* v. *A-G for New South Wales* (1959) the law has been tightened so that there is now a general principle that these trusts are void, subject to certain exceptions. This change in attitudes has had two consequences:

(a) It inevitably means that some of the earlier cases need to be treated with a degree of reserve.
(b) It has presented equity with a problem. Is there any reason why these trusts should be void and, if not, is there any way forward so that these trusts can, at least in some circumstances, be enforced? This chapter will look at the cases where attempts have been made to find a way forward and will also consider other avenues which could lead to enforcement.

Valid non-charitable purpose trusts

In the following exceptional cases trusts for non-charitable purposes have been held valid.

(a) **Tombs and monuments.** A trust for the building or maintenance of a tomb or monument has been held valid as in *Re Hooper* (1932), where a testator made a gift for the care of some family graves and monuments and a tablet in a church window. Such trusts can be charitable and therefore valid where they are for a tomb which can be regarded as part of the fabric of the church (*Hoare* v. *Osborne* (1866)) or for the maintenance of the churchyard as distinct from a particular tomb (*Re Vaughan* (1886)). However, in all cases the trust must comply with the requirement of certainty of objects (see Chapter 5). This requirement was not met in *Re Endacott* (1960), where a testator left money to a parish council to 'provide some useful memorial to myself' which was held much too wide and uncertain. Although the court in *Re Endacott* did not doubt any of the earlier cases, it is clear that it does represent the stricter approach indicated in *Re Astor*.

(b) **Animals.** Trusts for the care of specific animals are valid as in *Re Dean* (1889), where money was left for the maintenance of the testator's horses and hounds. A trust for the maintenance of animals in general can be charitable (see Chapter 14). However, trusts to not only maintain but also *to breed from* the testator's animal would be void.

(c) **Miscellaneous.** A trust for the saying of masses was originally void as being for 'superstitious uses' but in *Bourne* v. *Keane* (1919) they were upheld but without consideration of the beneficiary issue, possibly on the assumption that they would be said in public. Trusts for the saying of masses in public would be charitable (*Re Hetherington* (1989) and see Chapter 14). It would be strange if the gift specifically provided that the masses were only to be said in private but if they were actually said in private then the trust would probably also be valid. This would be on the basis that the gift for the saying of masses provided stipends for the priests saying them and so assisted in the endowment of the priesthood (Browne-Wilkinson V-C in *Re Hetherington* (1989) and see also Chapter 14). In *Re Khoo Cheng Teow* (1932) a trust for the performance of non-Christian private ceremonies was upheld but in *Re Endacott* (1960) Evershed MR said that these categories should not be extended. It is sometimes said that in *Re Thompson* (1934) the court held that a trust for the promotion of fox hunting was valid. In fact, the case concerned a gift to be applied to the promotion of fox hunting with a gift of residue to Trinity Hall, Cambridge. The issue was whether the trust was void as there was no beneficiary but the court held that it was not as the purpose was sufficiently certain. A trust for the promotion of fox hunting would now be void now anyway in view of the Hunting Act 2004.

It should be noted that in all these cases these are 'trusts of imperfect obligation' as there is no means of compelling the trustee to perform the trust, nor often of knowing if he/she has done so.

Valid non-charitable purpose trusts and the rule against inalienability

The trusts in the above cases must comply with the rules against inalienability. These were set out in detail in Chapter 9 and it will be recalled that the inalienability rule is concerned with the tying up of money for an excessive time. As such they are applicable to non-charitable purpose trusts which could tie up a fund to be used, for example, 'to maintain and breed from the testator's cats', indefinitely. The effect is that such a trust will be void unless from the beginning it is certain that persons will have become absolutely entitled by the end of a period of time. (It should be noted that the 'wait and see' provisions of the Perpetuities and Accumulations Act 1964 do not apply to purpose trusts (see s. 15(4)). The question is then: in what period of time must this occur? The general view is that the 80-year period probably does not apply but it is argued strongly by Maudsley (1979) that, on a close analysis of s. 15(4), it does as the subsection refers to 'the perpetuity period' and it is logical that this should be the same period as in the rest of the Act, i.e. 80 years. However, the general view is that the 80-year period does not apply to non charitable purpose trusts and the period is usually felt to be 21 years because the lack of individual beneficiaries means that there can be no lives in being. However, in *Re Khoo Cheng Teow* (1932) the court accepted a period of 21 years plus royal lives. Nevertheless, the courts within these limits have tried to see that otherwise valid purpose trusts do not fail on the ground of falling foul of the perpetuity rules. A striking illustration is *Re Haines* (1952), where judicial notice was taken of the doubtful proposition that a cat cannot live for more than 21 years. The courts assume that monuments will be erected within the perpetuity period (*Mussett* v. *Bingle* (1876)) and trusts which are to continue 'for so long as the law allows' will be construed as lasting for 21 years (*Pirbright* v. *Salwey* (1896)). In *Re Dean* (1889) a gift of an annual sum for 50 years if any of the testator's horses and hounds should live so long was held valid and the perpetuity point was ignored.

Trusts expressed for a purpose but which are really for the benefit of individuals

Given that, apart from the above cases, English law appeared to set its face against recognising non-charitable purpose trusts, the bold decision of Goff J in *Re Denley* (1969) appeared to offer a way forward. Here he was able to construe what appeared to be a trust for purposes as one for individuals. A plot of land was conveyed to trustees 'for the purpose of a recreation or sports ground primarily for the benefit of the employees of the company' and also for the benefit of such other persons as the trustees might allow. This was held valid as a trust for the employees because they were entitled to the use of the land. This decision has, however, been difficult to classify. Was the trust one for individuals, in which case there is no problem, or is it a kind of hybrid trust, being partly private and partly for purposes? A useful companion case to *Re Denley* is the older one of *Re Smith* (1914), where a gift to a small identified community of Franciscan Friars at Clevedon was upheld. Here there could be no doubt that this was a beneficial gift to the friars as there was no air of a purpose trust at all: but the same cannot be said of *Re Denley*.

In *Re Grant's Will Trusts* (1979) Vinelott J had no difficulty in holding that the *Denley*-type trust was a private trust. He saw no distinction in principle between a 'trust to permit a class defined by reference to employment to use and enjoy land' and 'a trust to distribute income at the discretion of trustees among a class'. The problem is that this is not how Goff J saw the position in his judgment in *Re Denley*. His judgment expressly distinguished between two kinds of purpose trust:

(a) those where the benefit 'is so indirect or intangible' that no individual who may benefit has the right to apply to the court to enforce it, and
(b) those where, as here, there are individuals who can apply.

It has been said that Goff J concentrated too much on the fact of benefit rather than whether particular persons were beneficiaries and that this has muddied the waters (see Matthews 1996). Could the rule in *Saunders* v. *Vautier* (1841) (see Chapter 19) apply to allow the beneficiaries (if they could be identified) to end the trust and claim the trust property? If they could, then the purpose of the trust is defeated and this brings us back to the point that this seems to be a trust for purposes as well as individuals. In addition, Goff J himself acknowledged the difficulty which could arise where there were differences between the beneficiaries over the purposes for which the sports club could be used. Could the court settle a scheme? He felt that it could not, as this was not a charitable trust. One could say that this comparison with a charitable trust is precisely the point: it was a trust for purposes but these were not charitable. Also, who could bring an action for breach of trust? Certainly the employees could, but the trust envisaged others as being beneficiaries. Be that as it may, in *Re Lipinski's Will Trusts* (1976) Oliver J accepted the decision in *Re Denley* saying that it accorded 'both with authority and common sense'. The truth is probably that, although *Re Denley* is suspect from the theoretical point of view, it made good sense on the facts.

GIFTS TO UNINCORPORATED ASSOCIATIONS

Definition of an unincorporated association

In *Conservative and Unionist Central Office* v. *Burrell* (1982) Lawton LJ said that an unincorporated association exists where two or more persons are 'bound together for one or more common purposes, not being business purposes, by mutual undertakings, each having mutual duties and obligations, in an organisation which has rules which identify in whom control of it and its funds rests and upon what terms and which can be joined or left at will. The bond of union members . . . has to be contractual'.

There are many examples of these, such as local clubs and societies, where there is no point in forming a company as the formalities would be too burdensome. Even larger bodies, such as county cricket clubs and football clubs are sometimes unincorporated, with any property such as the club ground being held by trustees, although the trend is towards incorporation.

The problem with gifts to these associations

With the exception of a trade union (see s. 2 of the Trade Union and Labour Relations Act 1974), an unincorporated association cannot hold property and so

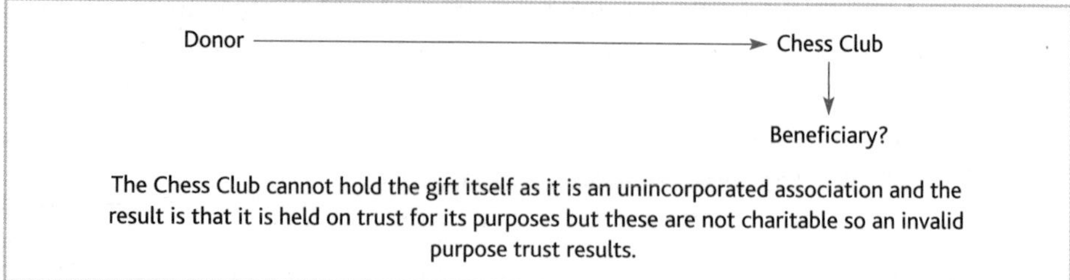

Figure 15.1 Gifts to unincorporated associations

a gift cannot be made to it. Thus the position is different from where a gift is made to a corporation (e.g. a company): here the gift is made to the body itself. But as an unincorporated association the gift must be held for its purposes. If those purposes are charitable then there is no problem but what if they are not?

Suppose that a gift of £100 is left by will to the Hanbury Chess Club. The club is not a corporation as, although it could be, the formalities would make this not worthwhile, and so the gift cannot be to the club itself and it is not charitable. This will be so even when the Charities Bill 2005 is in force, as it will be recalled that this only gives charitable status to amateur sporting organisations where the sport involves physical skill and exertion. Thus the gift is for non-charitable purposes.

If the gift is instead for the association's purposes there are two problems:

(a) Unless these purposes are charitable, the gift may be held to be for a non-charitable purpose trust as in *Leahy* v. *A-G for New South* (1959) (see above).
(b) The gift may contravene the inalienability rule if the capital comprised in it must be maintained for longer than the period.

The consequence is that what appears to be a straightforward everyday situation, the making of a gift to an unincorporated association, is fraught with legal difficulties. The only way to avoid the problems outlined above seems to be to hold that any gift is simply an outright one to the members, to be divided between them equally. Yet this is not what the donee usually intends. A gift to, for example, a local club, is meant to be immediately divided up by the members but to be used for the benefit of the club. Yet this requires some form of holding of the property which brings us back to the trust.

Possible solutions to the problem

Trust for the benefit of the members

The courts have sometimes been able to hold that a gift can be construed as a gift to the association's members and so a private trust is created. This was the approach in *Re Denley* (1969) (see above) and an earlier example is *Re Drummond* (1914) (see above). The reasoning is that as the gift is made to the association the members can claim it by winding up the association and dividing its assets among themselves and so they have a beneficial interest.

The trust will still be void, however, this time for infringing the rule against inalienability, if it is impracticable or impossible for the members to wind up the association. The gift then becomes one for future as well as present members. In *Carne* v. *Long* (1860) a testator left his house to the trustees of the Penzance Public Library to be for ever for the maintenance and support of the library. The court held that this was not a gift to the present members but instead to the library which was intended to be a perpetual institution and so the gift was void. In *Re Denley* (1969) the gift was expressly limited to the perpetuity period and in *Re Drummond* (1914) the inalienability point was not fully considered.

A more recent example of the inalienability problem is *Re Grant's Will Trusts* (1979) where a gift was made to the Chertsey Labour Party. In this case the members could not change the rules and divide the gift between themselves because the rules were subject to control by the National Executive Committee of the Labour Party. Thus they could not, even if they wished, divide the funds between themselves and accordingly the gift was for future members as well and was void for inalienability. This decision has been criticised by Matthews (1996) on the basis that in law the local party could, at a later date, have agreed to change their own rules and so allowed themselves to change rules without reference to the National Executive. In this way they could have gained access to the funds. Be that as it may, the Australian courts have come to the same conclusion as in *Bacon* v. *Pianta* (1966) where a legacy to 'the Communist Party of Australia for its sole use and benefit' was held void as a gift to both present and future members.

Gift to the members who will hold it on a contractual basis

In *Re Recher's Will Trust* (1972) a gift made to the London and Provincial Anti-Vivisection Society was held to be a beneficial gift to the members, not so as to entitle each of them to an immediate share but as an addition to the funds of the association subject to the contract between the members as set out in the rules. This approach was followed in *Re Lipinski's Will Trusts* (1976), where a testator bequeathed half of his residuary estate in trust to an association to be used solely in constructing or maintaining the association's buildings. This was held valid as a gift to the members subject to the contract between them as members even though the word 'solely' might have indicated that a trust was intended for the purpose specified.

The contract approach has the advantage over the trust approach in that the trust cases are open to attack as being inconsistent with *Leahy* v. *A-G for New South Wales* (1959). However, the contract approach, like the trust approach, will not validate a gift in circumstances like those in *Re Grant's Will Trusts* (1979), where the members do not control the association's property, because the members do not have complete control over the association's rules and so cannot end the association and divide the gift among themselves. It should be noted that the application of either the trust approach or the contract approach can have the same result and this was recognised by Oliver J in *Re Lipinski* (1976), who held that the gift would also have been valid on the trust approach.

Where the body is not an unincorporated association neither the trust nor the contract solution is appropriate (see *Conservative and Unionist Central Office*

v. *Burrell*). In this case the Conservative Party had no rules which enabled the members to gain control and so they could not divide the gift among themselves. The court held that the basis of the gift was that of mandate. A contributor gives funds to an official of the body, in this case the treasurer of the Conservative Party with a mandate to use them in a certain way. An agency relationship thus arises and, apart from the fiduciary relationship inherent in this, there is no question of any trust.

A '*Quistclose* trust?'

It has been argued that a possible solution to the problems outlined above lies in adopting the model utilised in *Barclays Bank* v. *Quistclose Investments Ltd* (1970). It will be recalled (see Chapters 4 and 10) that the trust arose on payment of money to be used for a specific purpose. When that purpose could not be carried out a resulting trust arose under which the property was held for the lender. The point here, however, is that until that time there was a trust for a purpose and Chambers (1997a) points out that the 'presence of an identifiable class of intended payees is irrelevant to the validity of the *Quistclose* trust'.

Disposal of surplus funds of unincorporated associations

We are not concerned now with whether a gift to an unincorporated association is valid but with what happens to the gift when the association ends and some funds remain. If the funds are for charitable purpose there is no problem: they can be applied *cy-près* and the construction in *Re Finger's Will Trust* (1972) may be used (see Chapter 14). If the purpose is not charitable then another solution must be found.

The 'Gillingham solution'

Re Gillingham Bus Disaster Fund (1958), although not concerned itself with an unincorporated association, provides a useful starting point. A surplus remained from a fund established in memory of Royal Marines cadets killed and injured in an accident. The purpose of the fund was to defray funeral expenses, care for the injured and then to be used for such worthy causes as the trustees might determine. About £9,000 was collected, partly in identifiable sums from individuals but mainly from street collections and other non-identifiable sources. The fund was held not to be charitable because funeral expenses and care of the boys did not come within relief of poverty. The solution therefore was to hold that the money was to be held on a resulting trust for the donors because, as Harman J said, 'the donor did not part with his money out and out absolutely' but only to the extent that his wishes as declared by the trust could be carried into effect. Thus when 'this has been done any surplus still belongs to him'. In fact it proved impossible to trace many of the subscribers, who often did not leave a record of their names, and so the money was paid into court. Finally, in 1995, 44 years after the disaster and after a local campaign, the money was allowed to be used for a memorial to the victims. One cannot escape the conclusion that this is a case which does the law no credit.

The '*West Sussex Constabulary* solution'

In *Re West Sussex Constabulary's Benevolent Fund Trusts* (1971) a fund had been established to provide benefits to widows and dependants of deceased members. The income came from members' subscriptions, proceeds of entertainments, sweepstakes, raffles, collecting boxes and various donations and legacies. When the constabulary was amalgamated with other police forces the question of the distribution of the fund arose.

(a) *The members' subscriptions*. The court held that the surviving members had no claim to those based on a resulting trust. They had received all that they had contracted for either because their widows and dependants had received benefits or because they had no widows or dependants. The members had no right themselves to the fund because it was not established for their benefit. Accordingly, this part of the fund went to the Crown as ***bona vacantia***, with the possibility of a successful claim by the members based on frustration of contract or total failure of consideration being met by the Crown giving an indemnity to the trustees.
(b) *Identifiable donations and legacies*. These were to be held on a resulting trust for the donors.
(c) *Proceeds of entertainments, raffles, sweepstakes and collecting boxes*. These were to go to the Crown as *bona vacantia*. Contributors must be taken to have parted with their money out and out. The relationship was one of contract not trust: those who paid for the entertainment, etc. had had their entertainment and so no longer had any claim to the money. Accordingly, the resulting trust solution in *Re Gillingham* (1958) was rejected.

Although this decision was a welcome advance on that in *Re Gillingham*, point (c) above has been criticised by Chambers (1997b) on the basis that Goff J 'did not address the question of who owned the fund prior to dissolution or how it became ownerless afterwards'. On Chambers' argument, the payments, having been made either for valuable consideration or as gifts, should have become the beneficial property of the recipients and so held on a resulting trust for them.

The '*Bucks Constabulary* solution'

The facts in *Re Bucks Constabulary Widows' and Orphans' Fund Friendly Society (No. 2)* (1979) were similar to those in *Re West Sussex* (1971): the fund was established to provide benefits for widows and dependants of deceased members and the fund was wound up on the amalgamation of the force with other forces. Here the court decided that the fund belonged to the members and the court did not follow that part of the decision in *Re West Sussex* (1971). It was held that the funds had belonged to the surviving members all the time because they could at any time have altered the rules and obtained the funds. The fact that the fund was not established for the benefit of the members did not alter the fact that the members controlled it. (There were no other contributions in this case and so the other parts of the *West Sussex* decision were not considered.)

Method of distribution among members

In *Re Hobourn Aero Components Ltd's Air Raid Distress Fund* (1946) it was held that assets should be distributed among both present and past members in shares proportionate to their contributions. However, inclusion of past members indicates a resulting trust approach. The contractual approach, as in *Re Bucks Constabulary Fund*, is more likely to be followed under which only present members benefit. The basis of distribution will normally be on a *per capita* basis in equal shares as in *Re Bucks* (1979), rather than in proportion to contributions made, unless the rules provide otherwise. In *Re Sick and Funeral Society of St John's Sunday School, Golcar* (1973), where there were two classes of members, adults and children, distribution was on a *per capita* basis, but the children received only a half share.

Surplus funds of pension fund trusts

The rules governing surplus funds of unincorporated associations have also been applied to surpluses of pension fund trusts. (*Davis* v. *Richards and Wallington Industries* (1991).)

When does an unincorporated association end?

In the *West Sussex* (1971) and *Bucks Constabulary* (1979) cases there was no doubt about the date when the association ceased to exist but matters may not always be so straightforward. In *Re GKN Bolts and Nuts Ltd and Social Club* (1982) the club had been in financial difficulties for some time and during 1975 membership cards ceased to be issued, the steward was dismissed and the stock of drinks was sold. On 18 December 1975 the club resolved to sell its sports ground but this was not sold until August 1978. The court held that although inactivity was not enough to dissolve an association, it might be that the inactivity was such that the only reasonable inference was that here the club had ceased to exist. On the facts this took place on 18 December 1975.

The effect of s. 53(1)(c) of the LPA 1925

It has been urged that the effect of s. 53(1)(c) has been overlooked in the cases above where it has been held that the members gain some interest in the property, as in *Re Bucks Constabulary*. If they do have an interest then it must be an equitable one and so, if at any time they resign or are expelled and their interest passes to other members, then there is a disposition of an equitable interest and so under s. 53(1)(c) this must be in writing. Yet there is no evidence that the courts have ever considered this point. (See Chapter 5 for details of s. 53(1)(c).)

The future for non-charitable purpose trusts

The present position is widely considered to be unsatisfactory but the solution is far from clear. There are the following possible ways forward:

(a) To hold that these trusts could take effect as mere powers. This would have the advantage that the enforceability point did not matter: a power is discretionary anyway and does not have to be carried out. (See Chapter 5.) Although this avenue was closed by *IRC* v. *Broadway Cottages Trust* (1955), which held that an invalid purpose trust cannot take effect as a power, such a solution has been adopted in other jurisdictions, for example by s. 16 of the Ontario Perpetuities Act 1966 and the American Restatement of the Law of Trusts, Second (1959) endorses it.

(b) That there should be an 'interested adversary principle'. Given that the initial problem is that these trusts have no beneficiary who can enforce them, it has been suggested that this should be an alternative instead to the 'beneficiary principle' and under it persons or institutions might be identified as being watchdogs to act in enforcing the trust (see Ford 1985). Legislation would probably be needed for this and one possibility is that the Attorney-General might undertake this role. This idea is similar to that of an 'enforcer', an office that exists in many trusts set up in Jersey, the Isle of Man and the Cayman Islands. Here legislation has been passed in order to make trusts for non-charitable purposes attractive for business purposes such as estate planning and it is suggested that there is no reason why the same should not apply in the United Kingdom. The only other express requirement would be that the trust was limited to the perpetuity period, but a particular period could be stated for this type of trust. (See Hayton (2005) for an illuminating discussion of this whole topic.)

FURTHER READING

Ford (1985) 'Dispositions for Purposes' in Finn (ed.) *Essays in Equity*, Sydney: The Law Book Company. Australian perspective makes this especially useful.

Hayton (2001) 'Developing the obligation characteristic of the Trust', 96 LQR 117. Considers how this area can be developed in a more satisfactory way.

Matthews (1996) 'The New Trust: Obligations without Rights?' in Oakley (ed.) *Trends in Contemporary Trust Law*, Oxford: Oxford University Press. Another attempt at charting a way forward.

Maudsley (1979) *The Modern Law of Perpetuities*, London: Butterworths. Not easy going, but invaluable.

CHAPTER SUMMARY

- Problems with non-charitable purpose trusts – beneficiary principle.
- Trusts for animals and monuments.
- Effect of the inalienability rules.
- *Re Denley* type of trust.

- Gifts to unincorporated associations.
- Trusts for the benefit of the members.
- Gift to the members who will hold it on a contractual basis.
- A *Quistclose* trust?
- Distribution of surplus funds of unincorporated associations.

QUESTION

Matilda died in 2002 and by her will she left £50,000 to the 'Select Christians', which was an unincorporated association consisting of a small number of people who lived a communal life and avoided contact with outsiders as much as possible. The association was wound up in 2001 but three of its members are continuing to live according to its precepts. Advise Jack, Matilda's executor, on what should be done with the £50,000.

How, if at all, would your answer differ if the Select Christians had been a corporation which at the date of Matilda's death had amalgamated with the 'Exclusive Christians', a body whose members also lived a communal life but who believed in mixing with outsiders?

> *Note 15.1: You will find suggested points for inclusion in this answer in Appendix 2.*

Part Four

TRUSTEESHIP AND BREACH OF TRUST

Until now, the focus of this book has been on the trust itself. Now it changes and looks at the administration of the trust by the trustees and liability if there is a breach of trust. It is as well to remember that in practice this is often the most important area of the law: most expressly created trusts are valid and so the issues revolve around the way in which the trust is carried out. Note that there is a link in this part with constructive trusts (dealt with in Chapter 11) as many of the cases where a constructive trust has been imposed have concerned breach by trustees of their fiduciary duties.

16 Trusteeship: appointment, retirement, removal and control. Fiduciary nature of trusteeship

INTRODUCTION

This chapter deals with the detailed statutory provisions on the appointment, removal and retirement of trustees and then goes on to look at the broader issue of the actual nature of trusteeship.

> *Note: There are special provisions dealing with Charity Trustees which are dealt with in Chapter 14.*

APPOINTMENT OF TRUSTEES

Who can be a trustee

Anyone who can hold the legal title to property can be a trustee of that property with the exception of minors who cannot be trustees, whether of realty or personalty (s. 20 LPA 1925). However, this only applies to express trusts: a minor can be a trustee under an implied, resulting or constructive trust. (See e.g. *Re Vinogradoff* (1935), Chapter 10.)

Special types of trustees

Public Trustee

The office of Public Trustee was created by the Public Trustee Act 1906 although it is no longer an entity on its own but is a separate agency within the Department for Constitutional Affairs. He can be used where there is no other person who is willing to act as a trustee. Another role is that he holds the property of a person who had died intestate pending the grant of letters of administration as, unlike the position where executors are appointed by will, administrators have no authority until appointed by the court (Law of Property (Miscellaneous Provisions) Act 1994, s. 14). The Public Trustee and Administration of Funds Act 1986 conferred on him all the functions with respect to the property and affairs of a mental patient which were conferred by the Mental Health Act 1983 on the judge of the Court of Protection, and this became his main work until this function was removed in 2001. His office is now combined with that of the Official Solicitor and there must be doubt as to his eventual survival. The Public Trustee can act alone or jointly with others or as a custodian trustee or a judicial trustee (see below). He has the same powers and duties as a private trustee but the State is responsible for any loss caused to the trust estate by his breach of duty (s. 7 Public Trustee Act 1906). He may decline to accept a trust except that he cannot do so only because the trust property is small. Particular limitations on his powers are that he cannot accept trusts exclusively for religious or charitable purposes (s. 2(5) Public Trustee Act 1906) and he can only accept English trusts (*Re Hewitt's Settlement* (1915)).

Judicial trustee

A judicial trustee is a person or corporation appointed by the court under the Judicial Trustee Act 1896. In *Re Ridsdell* (1947) Jenkins J said that the object is to provide 'a middle course in cases where the administration of the estate by the ordinary trustees had broken down and it was not desired to put the estate to the expense of a full administration' (by the court). They are therefore appointed where an excessively muddled or complex situation needs sorting out or where there has been gross mismanagement of the trust. An application to appoint a judicial trustee can be made by a settlor, or intending settlor, but is more likely to be made by or on behalf of a trustee or beneficiary. A judicial trustee is an officer of the court and the court may give him directions and also fix the level of remuneration but the court must take care not to supervise him so closely that in effect the court is administering the trust. The office of judicial trustee is not often used in practice.

Custodian trustees

A custodian trustee holds the legal title to the trust property but the management of the trust is in the hands of other trustees known as managing trustees. The advantage is that as managing trustees do not hold the legal title there is no need, when new managing trustees are appointed, to vest the legal title in them. The custodian trustee meanwhile must be a corporation and as such will, in most cases, never need to be replaced. One example of the use of custodian trustees is where local authorities act as custodian trustees under charitable trusts, although they are not allowed so to act if the charity is for the relief of poverty. Another frequent use of custodian trustees is where a parish council (or community council in Wales) holds the village hall as a custodian trustee and managing trustees are appointed from the local community to actually run the hall and deal with repairs and other matters. They are also often used in pension schemes. The office of custodian trustee was created by the Public Trustee Act 1906, which lays down detailed provisions in s. 4(2) on the relationship between custodian and managing trustee.

Trust corporations

A trust corporation is defined by s. 68(18) of the Trustee Act 1925 as either the Public Trustee, or a corporation appointed by the court in a particular case to be a trustee or a corporation entitled by rules made under the Public Trustee Act 1906 to be a custodian trustee. Executor and trustee companies of banks provide the major instance of the use of trust corporations and the rules at present allow most UK and EC registered companies to act as trust corporations. However, trust corporations are not custodian trustees. They have the following advantages over individual trustees:

(a) They can provide greater stability and expertise.
(b) They can act alone in cases where two or more individual trustees are required to act, e.g. in giving a valid receipt for capital money arising from a sale of land (s. 14(2) Trustee Act 1925 and s. 27(2) of the LPA 1925). The use of a trust corporation thus enables beneficial interest under a trust to be overreached and the property transferred to a purchaser free from it.

Under s. 28 of the Trustee Act 2000 a trust corporation can now charge for its services (see below), although it is still common practice for an express clause to be inserted in the trust instrument giving authority to charge.

Appointment of trustees

The settlor or testator who creates the trust usually appoints the first trustees. New trustees can be appointed under an express power given in the trust instrument. This is unusual in practice. New trustees are normally appointed by using the provisions of s. 36(1) of the Trustee Act 1925 (TA 1925), which are considered adequate. This provides that a new trustee can be appointed in place of an existing trustee who either:

(i) Is dead. This includes, by s. 36(8), a person nominated as trustee in the will but who dies before the testator.
(ii) Remains outside the United Kingdom for a continuous period exceeding 12 months. In *Re Walker* (1901) the trustee had been absent for more than 12 months but during this time he had visited London for a week. Thus the period was not continuous and s. 36 did not apply.
(iii) Desires to be discharged from either all or part of the trusts or powers. It should be noted that the words 'part of' allow a trustee to be discharged from part only of the trust.
(iv) Refuses to act. This also includes a trustee who disclaims. A disclaimer should preferably (but not necessarily) be by deed but can be implied e.g. by inaction. The fact that the trustee has meddled with the estate will be taken as an acceptance.
(v) Is unfit to act e.g. because he is bankrupt (*Re Roche* (1842)).
(vi) Is incapable of acting because of e.g. mental disorder (*Re East* (1873)) or infirmity caused by old age (*Re Lemman's Trusts* (1833)).
(vii) Is an infant. This can only apply to implied, resulting or constructive trusts because an infant cannot be a trustee of an express trust (see above).
(viii) Has been removed under a power in the trust instrument (see below).

The appointment of new trustees under s. 36 must be in writing and is normally made by deed because of the vesting provisions in s. 40 of the TA 1925 (see below). In *Adam & Co* v. *Goddard* (2000) it was held that two retiring trustees cannot be replaced by one, unless that one is a trust corporation.

The appointment may be made by either of the following, who can appoint themselves:

(a) The persons nominated in the trust instrument to do so but if there is no person able and willing then:
(b) The surviving or continuing trustee(s). The word 'continuing' includes not only a trustee who is to continue alongside the new trustees, but also a refusing or retiring trustee (s. 36(8) TA 1925) but not one removed against his will.
If there is no one in this category then:
(c) The personal representative of the last surviving or continuing trustee including the personal representative of a sole trustee. If, however, all the trustees of a will predecease the testator then the personal representatives of the last to die do not come within this provision (*Re Smirthwaite's Trusts* (1871)) and so the appointment must be made by:
(d) The court. Section 41(1) of the TA 1925 provides that the court may appoint new trustee(s) either in substitution for or in addition to any existing trustee(s) or where there is no trustee. This power can be exercised where it is expedient to appoint a new trustee and it is 'inexpedient, difficult or impracticable' to do so without the assistance of the court. Section 41 specifically provides that this power can be exercised to appoint a new trustee where the existing one is either:
    (i) incapable because of mental disorder of acting as trustee;
    (ii) bankrupt;
    (iii) a corporation which is in liquidation or has been dissolved.

In addition the court has exercised the power in, e.g. *Re Smirthwaithe* (see (c) above), where a sole trustee was aged 85, deaf and failing in mind (*Re Phelps' Settlement Trusts* (1885)). The court, when appointing under s. 41, can remove an existing trustee (as in *Re Henderson* (1940)) provided that a new trustee is appointed in his place.

The application under s. 41 can be made by a trustee or beneficiary and it should be made to the High Court unless the estate or trust funds do not exceed £30,000 when it should be made to the county court. Section 41 should not be used where trustees can be appointed under s. 36 (above).

In *Re Tempest* (1866) Turner LJ said that in making an appointment the court should have regard to:

(i) any ascertainable wishes of the settlor;
(ii) the interests of all the beneficiaries and not just some of them;
(iii) the promotion of the carrying out of the trust.

(e) By the beneficiaries. Section 19 of the Trusts of Land and Appointment of Trustees Act 1996, which here applies to trusts of both land and personalty, provides that if the beneficiaries are all of full age and capacity and absolutely entitled and there is no person with an express power to appoint, then they can direct the trustee(s) in writing to retire and can direct the trustees to appoint particular persons as trustees. It is believed that this provision is often excluded in practice but, if it is exercised, then it is of much greater width than that in s. 36 of the Trustee Act 1925 (above) as there are no set limits to when the beneficiaries can exercise this power.

Protection of purchasers

Section 38 of the TA (1925) provides that a statement contained in any instrument by which a trustee is appointed in connection with land to the effect that a trustee has remained out of the United Kingdom for more than 12 months or refuses, is unfit or is incapable of acting or that he is not entitled to a beneficial interest in the trust property in possession shall, in favour of a purchaser of the legal estate, be conclusive evidence of the matter. Thus where a trustee has been removed under those grounds in s. 36(1) of the TA 1925 a purchaser need not enquire into the circumstances. Where the trustee has died a purchaser ought to see the death certificate.

Appointment of additional trustees

Section 36(6) of the TA 1925 gives a power to appoint additional trustees to:

(a) Any persons given the power to do so by the trust instrument or, if there is none, or none able and willing to do so, then the trustees.
(b) There is no obligation to appoint extra trustees and no appointment can be made if there are already four or more trustees. The appointer cannot appoint himself.

Number of trustees

Any number of trustees of personalty may be appointed but a single trustee is undesirable because decisions of trustees must be unanimous (see below). Between two to four is the best number. Section 34(2) of the TA 1925 limits the number of trustees of a trust of land to four. Although there can be a sole trustee of land s. 14(2) of the TA 1925 does not allow him to give a valid receipt for the proceeds of sale or other capital money arising under the Settled Land Act 1925 or under a disposition of land held on a trust of land. Thus in practice at least two trustees (or a trust corporation) are needed.

Vesting of the trust property

Whichever way a trustee is appointed the trust property must be vested in him. Section 40 of the TA 1925 provides that if the appointment of the trustee has been made by deed then the vesting may be made by a vesting declaration and even if there is no such declaration the deed, if made after the commencement of the Act, will operate as if it contained one.

This convenient provision does not apply where property is held by personal representatives rather than trustees nor does it apply to:

(a) Stocks and shares.
(b) Land held on a mortgage by trustees as security for a loan of trust money.
(c) Leases containing a condition prohibiting dispositions without consent unless the consent has already been obtained. In these cases the property will have to be specifically transferred. Note that s. 40 does not apply to the initial vesting of the property in trustees. Here the requisite formalities must be observed for all the property (see Chapter 6).

RETIREMENT OF TRUSTEES

A trustee may retire either:

(a) Under a power given in the trust instrument.
(b) Under s. 36(1) of the TA 1925 where 'he desires to be discharged'. Here the retiring trustee will have to be replaced.
(c) Under s. 39 of the TA 1925 which allows a trustee to retire if there will be, after his retirement, at least two individuals or a trust corporation to act and the retiring trustee executes a deed declaring that he wishes to retire and the remaining trustees and any other person empowered to appoint new trustees consent. If s. 39 is used no new trustee need be appointed in place of the retiring trustee. A further difference is that a trustee retiring under the provision of s. 36 can retire from only part of the trusts but this is not so under s. 39.
(d) Under an order of the court. This can be where the court exercises its powers under s. 41 TA 1925 (see above) and in addition the court has an inherent jurisdiction to retire a trustee.

REMOVAL OF TRUSTEES

A trustee can be removed against his will where:

(a) The power in s. 36(1) TA 1925 is exercised where the trustee has remained out of the United Kingdom for more than 12 months or refuses or is incapable or is unfit to act.
(b) The court acts under s. 41 TA 1925.
(c) Under an express power of removal contained in the trust instrument, although this is rare.
(d) Under the court's inherent jurisdiction. In *Re Wrightson* (1908) Warrington J observed that the court must find 'something which induces the court to think either that the trust property will not be safe or that the trust will not be properly executed in the interests of the beneficiaries'. In *Clarke* v. *Heathfield* (1985) trustees of the funds of the National Union of Mineworkers were removed because they had refused to repatriate union funds which they had sent abroad to frustrate a sequestration order. In so doing they were in contempt of court and as such endangering union funds.

DUTIES AND POWERS OF TRUSTEES

General principles: duties and discretions of trustees

A trustee must carry out a duty, whereas she can decide whether or not to exercise a power. (The term sometimes used here is a 'discretion' but it is suggested that 'power' is a better description.) Thus the exercise of a power is discretionary. However, the carrying out of a duty, although by itself mandatory, may involve trustees in the exercise of a discretion, e.g. trustees may be under a duty to distribute income but if it is a discretionary trust they will have a discretion in deciding who is to receive it and the amount that each will receive. The point is that the discretion must be exercised. On the other hand, decisions by trustees on the payment of sums by way of maintenance and advancement to beneficiaries are powers and so the trustees are not obliged to exercise them at all.

Exercise of trustees' discretion

General principles

The law here is not entirely clear and is hardly satisfactory. The basic principles are that:

(i) The courts will not compel trustees to exercise a discretion. In *Tempest* v. *Lord Camoys* (1882) trustees were given a discretion to buy and sell land. One trustee wished to buy land but his co-trustee did not agree and the court refused to order him to agree to the purchase.

(ii) The courts will not compel trustees to give their reasons for exercising or not exercising a discretion. In *Re Beloved Wilkes Charity* (1851) trustees had a duty to select a boy to be educated for Holy Orders in the Church of England. They were obliged to give preference to suitable boys from certain parishes but they selected a boy from another parish, apparently after the boy's brother, a minister, had approached the trust on his behalf. The trustees refused to give any reason for their decision and the court would not compel them to.

If the trustees do give reasons for their decision then the court can investigate them but the grounds on which the courts can intervene are not clear. Can they intervene only if the trustees have made a mistake of law or acted in bad faith or can the courts act when the trustees have reached a conclusion which does not support the evidence? Truro LC in the *Beloved Wilkes* case spoke in wide terms which, if applied literally, could increase the powers of the court to act in these cases. He observed that, if the trustees do give a reason for their decision which does not justify their conclusion, then the court could correct it if trustees have acted by mistake or error. This would allow the courts to investigate in cases where the trustees have acted in good faith but their conclusion is not supported by the evidence. This statement was not taken up in later cases, however. In *Gisborne* v. *Gisborne* (1877) Cairns LC said that the court could intervene if there was '*mala fides*' (bad faith) on the part of the trustees and in *Tempest* v. *Lord Camoys* (1882) the phrase used by Jessel MR was that the court will prevent the trustees from 'exercising it' (the power) improperly. In *Dundee General Hospitals Board of Management* v. *Walker* (1952) there is a tenuous echo of principles of administrative law. Lord Normand observed that 'the principles on which the courts must proceed are the same whether the trustees' reasons for their decisions are disclosed or not'. Lord Reid said that if 'the trustees considered the wrong question, or that, although they purported to consider the right question, they did not really apply their minds to it or perversely shut their eyes to the facts or that they did not act honestly or in good faith, then there was no true decision and the court will intervene'. The implications of this are uncertain: does it require, for instance, the court to compel the giving of reasons? However, these remarks are of persuasive authority only, as their Lordships did not finally decide what test was appropriate. In *Scott* v. *National Trust* (1988) the words of Lord Reid were adopted by Robert Walker J in a case concerning charity law but it may be that the language of judicial review is less appropriate to small family trusts. On the other hand, why should the beneficiaries of these trusts have to suffer from bad decisions that cannot be remedied? If a reason is not given, this jurisdiction cannot apparently be exercised and so the right of beneficiaries to require information is obviously a counterpart of the exercise of the courts of a power to control discretions. The most recent decision is in the *Abacus* (2003) case (below), where the court held that it could interfere with the discretion of a trustee if it is clear that they have failed to take all relevant considerations into account and that, if they had, they would have acted differently. This is a welcome clarification of the law.

(iii) The trustees are not, in general, obliged to consult the beneficiaries, nor are they bound to do what the beneficiaries tell them to do. Indeed, blindly following the beneficiaries' directions could be a breach of trust. However, where there is a trust of land then the Trusts of Land and Trustees Act 1996 applies. Section 11(1) obliges the trustees to consult adult beneficiaries with an interest in possession and, so far as is consistent with the general interest of the trust, give effect to their wishes or, in cases of dispute, the wishes of the majority, according to the value of their combined interests. In practice this requirement is often excluded as it is felt to be potentially burdensome.

(iv) The trustees should not take directions from the settlor as to how to exercise their functions. The settlor has his/her opportunity to set out the terms of the trust when drawing up the trust instrument and, after that, should let go. The consequence of the trustees neglecting to observe this rule was seen in *Turner* v. *Turner* (below).

Particular instances where the courts have intervened

These instances are useful in themselves as a guide although they need to be read subject to the discussion above on the general principles. It must be admitted that these cases do not always fit easily with some of the statements of the judges outlined above, which merely reinforces the point that this area is badly in need of a coherent set of principles.

The courts have held trustees to be in breach of trust where a discretion is exercised:

(i) On irrelevant considerations. In *Klug* v. *Klug* (1918) one trustee, the beneficiary's mother, refused to approve the exercise of a power of advancement because she was annoyed by the daughter having married without her consent. (See also *Martin* v. *City of Edinburgh DC* (1989) and *Icarus Ltd* v. *Driscoll* (1990).)
(ii) For an improper purpose. In *Re Pauling's Settlement Trust* (1964) the trustees made advancements to children but knew that the money would be used to benefit their parents by, for instance, reducing their mother's bank overdraft. The trustees were held liable. This principle would also obviously apply where trustees act dishonestly by e.g. exercising a discretion so as to benefit themselves.
(iii) The discretion is not exercised at all. In *Turner* v. *Turner* (1983) the trustees, who had no knowledge of trust matters, signed deeds of appointment on the orders of the settlor who said in evidence that he still regarded himself as 'captain of the ship' and who had established the trust for tax purposes whilst retaining *de facto* control. These appointments were set aside. This ground is also a possible explanation of *Klug* v. *Klug* (above).
(iv) Where the trustees acted on incorrect information. In *Abacus Trust Co (Isle of Man)* v. *Barr* (2003) the settlor wished to create discretionary trusts in respect of 40 per cent of the trust fund but the trustees were incorrectly told that the figure was 60 per cent. The resulting appointment of 60 per cent was held voidable.
(v) In exceptional cases the courts can take over, and exercise, a fiduciary discretion as in *Mettoy Pension Trustees* v. *Evans* (1991).

Duty of the trustees to account and give information

A trustee must keep accounts and provide them, on request, to beneficiaries. In addition a beneficiary is entitled, in the absence of special reasons, to production and inspection of all trust documents in the possession of the trustee. In *O'Rourke* v. *Darbyshire* (1920) Lord Wrenbury said that 'the beneficiary is entitled to see all the documents because they are trust documents and he is a beneficiary. They are in a sense his own'.

There are, however, two problems: what precisely are trust documents and, if they disclose the reasons for the trustees' decisions, is this a reason for not disclosing them?

In *Re Londonderry's Settlement* (1965) a beneficiary under a discretionary trust was dissatisfied with the sum which the trustees intended to give her. She wanted to see various types of documents including agenda of trustees' meetings, minutes of meetings and documents prepared for them, and correspondence. The court held that the trustees were not bound to disclose these but the case unfortunately did not lay down any clear principles. It seemed to be held that some of these were not trust documents but, if they were trust documents, then they were protected from disclosure by the special reason that to do so would disclose trustees' reasons for their decisions. Disclosure of reasons might 'cause infinite trouble in the family'. However if a *prima facie* case of bad faith was made, then the court said, 'that is an entirely different matter'. Yet seeing the documents how can such a *prima facie* case be established? The only way seems to be to begin litigation so that an order for disclosure of the documents can be made or a witness can be questioned. Yet it is obviously unsatisfactory to have to resort to this.

Fortunately, the trend since *Re Londonderry* has been towards a greater degree of openness in releasing trust documents to the inspection of the beneficiaries. In *Re Murphy's Settlements* (1998) one of the beneficiaries under a discretionary trust was allowed an order compelling the disclosure of the names and addresses of the trustees. This modest request was allowed on the basis, as stated by Neuberger J, that as a discretionary object of the trust she was entitled to information as to the nature and value of the trust property, the trust income and how the trustees have been distributing it. This at least provides a starting point as to what information a beneficiary is entitled to.

A different issue arose in the Australian case of *Hartigan Nominees Pty Ltd* v. *Rydge* (1992), where disclosure of a letter of wishes was refused. The court also found that agenda of trustees meetings and their correspondence did not amount to trust documents. On a broader note, the general approach in this case to disclosure of trust documents commended itself to the Privy Council in *Schmidt* (below).

In *Schmidt* v. *Rosewood Trust Ltd* (2003) the Privy Council considered the whole issue of disclosure of trust documents and it was held that no distinction should be drawn between types of trusts in deciding if there was a right to disclosure. The right was not a proprietary one and so did not depend on whether a beneficiary had a proprietary interest in the trust property; on this basis objects of a power also had the right to seek disclosure. Instead the question was whether the court should make an order in the exercise of its supervisory jurisdiction over trusts. As Lord Walker put it: '(the) correct approach is to regard the right to seek disclosure of trust documents as one aspect of the court's inherent jurisdiction to supervise and, if necessary to intervene in, the administration of trusts'. The court has a discretion in the exercise of this jurisdiction to order disclosure and Lord Walker held that there were three areas on which the court will need to form a discretionary judgment: should a discretionary object of a trust be granted relief at all; what classes of documents should be disclosed, either completely or in a 'redacted' (i.e. edited) form and what safeguards should be imposed by the court, one example being the possibility of professional inspection. Furthermore, it was emphasised that, following *Re Cowan* (1886), the relief given will reflect the strength of a particular applicant's case. Here the applicant was not a nominated beneficiary of the trusts. (See also Davies (2003), where this litigation is viewed in a wider setting of 'the integrity of trusteeship', see below.)

The decision in *Schmidt* was applied by the Jersey Court of Appeal in *Boere* v. *Mourant & Co* (2004), where one beneficiary (X) was ordered to list all documents in his possession in connection with a claim by another beneficiary (Y) relating to the administration of the trust. The fact that the documents had been prepared in relation to another trust of which X was the settlor was not the point: the court held that the exercise of its jurisdiction merely required that the documents sought were relevant and in the possession and control of the person against whom the order was sought.

Trustees must be unanimous

The decision of trustees of a **private trust**, whether acting under a duty or a power, must be unanimous unless the trust instrument allows decisions to be by a majority. Trustees of charitable trusts may, however, be taken by a majority vote (*Re Whiteley* (1910)).

FIDUCIARY NATURE OF TRUSTEESHIP

General principles

An essential feature of the fiduciary position of the trustee is that he 'is not, unless otherwise expressly provided, entitled to make a profit; he is not allowed to put himself in a position where his interest and his duty conflict' (Lord Herschell in *Bray* v. *Ford* (1896)). Thus a trustee who makes unauthorised profits can be held to be a constructive trustee of them and this topic is dealt with fully in Chapter 11. Although Lord Herschell's words are considered one of the absolute bedrocks of equity, they have not escaped comment. They have been called 'rather a counsel of prudence than a rule of equity' *Re Jordan* (Jordan 1881 and see Koh (2003) to whom I am indebted for this reference). In *Movitex Ltd* v. *Bulfield* (1988) Vinelott J observed that 'I do not think that it is strictly accurate to say that a director owes a fiduciary *duty* to the company not to put himself in a position where his duty to the company may conflict with his personal interest or with his duty to another'. Although this decision involved company directors, the point is clearly of general application: in modern life, there are many situations where a trustee may be in a position where he/she has a personal interest. Suppose that a person is trustee of a small charity which provides facilities for disabled children and that that trustee is herself the parent of a disabled child. It may well be to the advantage of the trust to have a person with personal knowledge of the needs of the beneficiaries but there could clearly be a conflict between her duty as a trustee and her interest as a parent. The point is that the trustee must not allow that to happen. Thus Lord Herschell's words should perhaps be rephrased to say that where there is a conflict between personal interests and duty as a trustee then the duty is not to take advantage of that conflict and to consider only the interests of the trust.

Furthermore, it is also important to empathise what Davies (2003) has called the 'The Integrity of Trusteeship'. On many occasions a trustee may not have access to the trust funds and so the question of making a personal profit does not arise. What is, however, vital, is that trustees should make up their own minds on the matters which they are required to deal with and not be unduly swayed by, in particular, the wishes or indeed any instructions of the settlor. It is arguable that the concentration by equity on the issue of avoiding making a profit has obscured the need to also consider the trustee as a decision maker.

Payment of trustees

The fundamental rule is that a trustee is not entitled to payment although in practice payment is often authorised by the trust instrument and the Judicial Trustee, the Public Trustee and custodian trustees are by statute authorised to charge fees.

Section 29 of the Trustee Act 2000 provides that a trust corporation is entitled to reasonable remuneration for services provided to the trust and professional trustees are also entitled to remuneration provided that all the other trustees have agreed in writing to this. In practice, remuneration clauses are still included in trusts as they were before the Trustee Act came into force on the basis that they make the position clear to the other trustees and beneficiaries. Section 28 widens the power to pay expenses by providing that where there is an express clause in the trust instrument authorising payment of expenses and the trustee is either a trust corporation or is acting as a professional trustee, then payment may be made even though the services could have been provided by a lay trustee. This could cover, for example, a situation where a firm of solicitors, acting as professional trustees, was asked to arrange the funeral of a beneficiary under the trust.

In addition the court has an inherent jurisdiction to authorise payment and in *Re Duke of Norfolk's Settlement Trusts* (1982) the court held that this jurisdiction extended to increasing the level of payment beyond what had been authorised by the settlor, if this was beneficial to the trust, by ensuring that it was properly administered. Here a corporate trustee's work had become exceptionally burdensome and the level of fees sought was in itself low.

Payment for litigious work

A trustee is entitled to his costs when properly bringing or defending an action on behalf of the trust. If in doubt about whether to bring proceedings a trustee should seek directions from the court under s. 57 of the Trustee Act 1925. If he does not and the proceedings are unsuccessful then the trustee, to claim his costs, must show that they were properly incurred. Any advice given by counsel here will be an important factor. In *Holding and Management Ltd* v. *Property Holding and Investment Trust plc* (1988) the trustee was a maintenance trustee appointed by a landlord of a block of flats. The trustee had proposed a scheme of work to which the tenants and the landlord had objected and legal proceedings resulting from this were eventually settled on terms which admitted that the tenants' case was correct. The court held that the trustee was not entitled to his costs from the trust fund because, the tenants were, in effect, the beneficiaries, and the trustee was acting in a way which was hostile to their interests. Section 15 of the Trustee Act allows a trustee to make reasonable compromises as an alternative to litigation by e.g. accepting compositions of debts and allowing extra time for payment of debts.

Payment for work done by solicitor-trustees is subject to the rule in *Craddock* v. *Piper* (1850). This allows him to charge costs if he has acted for a co-trustee as well as himself in litigation relating to the trust and the costs of acting for both of them do not exceed the costs which would have been incurred if he had been acting only for the co-trustee. It is illogical that this rule does not apply to non-litigious work.

It should be noted that there is a strict duty on trustees to, where necessary, engage in litigation to protect the trust assets (see Chapter 17 and especially *Re Brogden* (1888)).

Purchase of the trust property

A trustee must not purchase trust property because to do so can conflict with his duty as a trustee. The honesty of the trustee is irrelevant: the rule is based on the trustee's status as a trustee. Such a purchase is voidable at the option of a beneficiary. In *Kane* v. *Radley-Kane* (1999) a widow, who was the sole personal representative of the estate of her husband, who had died intestate, appropriated to herself unquoted shares valued at £50,000 in satisfaction of her statutory legacy. It was held that as she did not have the consent of her stepsons nor the approval of the court this appropriation was equivalent to a purchase by her of trust property and so she held the shares on trust for the estate. A trustee can, however, purchase if the court allows it, or the beneficiaries, all being ***sui iuris***, agree, or the trust instrument permits it. An exceptional case is *Holder* v. *Holder* (1968) where an executor had tried to renounce his executorship but the renunciation was invalid as he had done some minor acts in the administration of the estate. Although he took no further part in administration he did buy land at an auction which had belonged to the estate and the court refused to set the purchase aside. This case was distinguished in *Re Thompson's Settlement* (1986) and must be considered doubtful authority.

Trustees in competition with the trust

A trustee must not carry on a business in competition with the trust. In *Re Thompson* (1934) the executors of a will carried on the testator's business of a yacht broker and one executor wished to set up a competing business. He was restrained by injunction from doing so.

EXEMPTION CLAUSES AND TRUSTEES

The use of exemption clauses has become common in trusts, especially where the trustees are professional trustees. The Trustee Act 2000 does not restrict the scope of these, nor does it lay down any conditions on their use. However, it does provide (Sch. 1. para. 7) that the statutory duty of care (see Chapter 17) is inapplicable 'if and so far as it appears from the trust instrument that the duty is not meant to apply'. Thus it is possible to restrict the scope of the statutory duty.

Trustees have a fundamental fiduciary duty to act in good faith and Hayton (1996) convincingly argues that this cannot be excluded as 'that would empty the area of obligation so as to leave no room for any obligation'. Quite simply, the trustee would have complete immunity from liability if this basic duty were excluded. If this argument is right than it would not be possible to exclude the liability of the trustee if he/she acted fraudulently or dishonestly. This seems obviously right. For instance, it would be nonsense if a trustee could act dishonestly by misappropriating trust property by taking it for his own benefit and then sheltering behind an exemption clause.

The leading case on these clauses is *Armitage* v. *Nurse* (1998) where the clause provided that the trustees would not be liable for loss or damage unless caused by their own actual fraud. The Court of Appeal upheld this clause on the basis that it protected the trustees so long as they did not act dishonestly. It would, however, protect them if they were negligent. This case concerned a family trust but in *Walker* v. *Stones* (2001) a solicitor sought to rely on a clause which covered defaults except dishonesty in a case where he had committed a deliberate breach of trust. The court held that it could not be relied on as no reasonable solicitor in the position of the solicitor at the time could have thought that it was for the benefit of the beneficiaries. One unresolved issue is whether there is any distinction between negligence and gross negligence and that exemption clauses can only protect in cases of negligence. Millett LJ in *Armitage* v. *Nurse* saw only a difference of degree between the two and so would allow exemption clauses for even gross negligence.

Hayton (1996) suggests that a clause could be allowed which provided that the trustees could do anything or omit to do anything that would otherwise amount to a breach of trust if they ***bona fide*** consider such action to be in the best interests of the beneficiaries as whole. This would cover unforeseen eventualities. The Law Commission is looking at this area and has issued a Consultation Paper in 1999. Legislation may be the eventual solution.

FURTHER READING

Davies (2003) 'The integrity of trusteeship', 119 LQR 1. This stresses trustees' qualities of integrity and independence.

Hayton (1996) 'The Irreducible Content of Core Trusteeship' in Oakley (ed.) *Trends in Contemporary Trust Law*, Oxford: Oxford University Press. Looks at trusteeship in a modern context.

Koh (2003) 'Once a director, always a fiduciary?' 62 CLJ 403. Examines the extent of the fiduciary duties of directors and challenges some accepted thinking.

Law Reform Committee, 'Powers and Duties of Trustees', 23rd Report on Powers and Duties of Trustees. This led ultimately to the Trustee Act 2000.

Willoughby (1999) *Misplaced Trust*, 2nd edn, Saffron Waldon: Gostick Hall Publications. A stimulating and very clear and entertaining guide to modern cases involving trustees. This compact book deserves to be better known as it gives a real insight into trusteeship today.

CHAPTER SUMMARY

- Special types of trustees.
- Appointment, removal and retirement of trustees.
- Duties and powers.
- Control of trustees.
- Duty of trustees to account and to give information.
- Fiduciary nature of trusteeship.
- Payment of trustees.
- Trustees in competition with the trust.
- Exemption clauses and trustees.

QUESTION

Do you consider that the law on the control by the courts of the decisions of trustees is satisfactory?

> ***Note 16.1:** You will find suggested points for inclusion in this answer in Appendix 2.*

17 Duties of trustees

INTRODUCTION

Trustees have some matters which they must carry out and these are their duties. The next chapter looks at matters which trustees need not carry out but have a discretion whether or not to do so. The other point to note is the interplay between the express statutory provisions governing trustees and the rules laid down in the trust instrument. Which has precedence in a particular situation?

DUTIES ON BECOMING A TRUSTEE

> *Note 17.1: When reading this chapter look at the specimen trust deed in the Appendix to Chapter 18: clause 3 sets out investment powers and you should check this clause in the light of the statutory provisions set out below.*

Trustees must, on becoming a trustee:

(a) See that they have been properly appointed and enquire into the terms of the trust and the state of the trust property (*Harvey* v. *Olliver* (1887)).

(b) Satisfy themselves that neither their predecessors nor the continuing trustees have committed a breach of trust. To enable them to do this the continuing trustees must provide them with all necessary information (*Tiger* v. *Barclays Bank* (1952)).

(c) Ensure that the trust fund is properly invested in accordance with the trust deed and the Trustee Act 2000 (see below).

(d) See that all securities and chattels are in proper custody (*Re Miller's Deed Trusts* (1978)).

(e) Safeguard the trust assets by, where necessary, insisting on the transfer to them of trust property held by others and on the payment of debts owed to the trust. In *Re Brogden* (1888) a covenant had been entered into to pay £10,000 to trustees of the covenantor's daughter's marriage settlement but, after the covenantor's death, although the trustees asked many times for payment they did not sue for the money. This was because the covenantor's estate was now the basis of a partnership between his sons and they feared disturbances in the family and a crisis which might upset the firm. The firm eventually became insolvent and the trustees were held liable for not initially demanding (rather than merely asking) for payment and when it was not made, failing to sue. The court held that the only excuse a trustee has for not taking action to enforce payment is a reasonable belief on his part that to do so would be fruitless. In *Buttle* v. *Saunders* (1950) it was held that trustees commit a breach of trust when, having made an oral, but not legally binding, agreement to sell, they refuse to consider another offer at a higher price, a course of conduct described by Megarry V-C in *Cowan* v. *Scargill* (1984) as acting dishonourably but not illegally. A slightly less stringent view of trustees' duties had been taken in *Ward* v. *Ward* (1843), where it was held that a trustee acted reasonably in not suing a debtor who was also a beneficiary to the trust because such proceedings would not only have ruined the beneficiary but made life difficult for his children, who were also beneficiaries. On the other hand, a trustee must not engage in speculative litigation and will not be entitled to the costs of it (*Re Beddoe* (1893)). Their proper course in cases of doubt is to apply to the court for directions under s. 57 of the Trustee Act 1925. It is suggested by Pettit (2005) that where trustees exercise their power under s. 15 of the Trustee Act 1925 to compound liabilities and so settle a claim then they will not be liable provided that they have complied with the statutory duty of care in the Trustee Act 2000 (see below).

Trustees must not regard their duties on becoming a trustee as having been performed once and for all. Their duties in connection with investments, ensuring that securities and chattels are in proper custody and safeguarding the trust property are continuing ones.

STATUTORY DUTY OF CARE OF TRUSTEES UNDER THE TRUSTEE ACT 2000

The **statutory duty of care** under the Act is set out in s. 1. This replaces the duty laid down in *Speight* v. *Gaunt* (1883), which provided that a trustee should, when administering the trust, act as an ordinary prudent businessman would in managing his own affairs. The problem was that this did not distinguish between the paid, professional trustee and the lay trustee. The courts had, before the passage of the Trustee Act 2000, established that professional trustees did owe a higher standard (see e.g. Harman J in *Re Waterman's Will Trusts* (1952)) but the Act now makes the position clear.

Section 1 provides that a trustee must exercise such care and skill as is reasonable in the circumstances having regard in particular to:

(a) Any special knowledge or experience which he has or holds himself out as having.
(b) If he acts in the course of a business or profession, to any special knowledge or experience that it is reasonable to expect of a person acting in the course of that business or profession.

The trust instrument may exclude this duty although some duty would need to be stated instead. The Act is silent on the question of clauses exempting trustees from liability, which are still governed by the general law (see Chapter 16).

The duty applies to the following functions of trustees:

(a) Investment.
(b) Acquisition of land.
(c) Appointment of agents, nominees and custodians.
(d) Insurance.
(e) Compounding liabilities.
(f) Powers relating to reversionary interests, valuations and audit.

It does not apply to powers of maintenance and advancement which are different in that they are mainly concerned with actual dispositions if money. These are dealt in Chapter 18.

DUTY TO INVEST

Note 17.2: Look at the investment clause in the specimen trust deed in the Appendix to Chapter 18.

Statutory investment powers under the Trustee Act 2000

Trustees have a **duty** to invest and a failure to do so within a reasonable time will be a breach of trust (Trustee Act 2000, Sch. 1 para. 1). However, it is common to speak of **powers** of trustees to invest. This really means the powers which trustees have to carry out their duty. The **statutory investment powers** have been radically altered by the Trustee Act 2000, which has swept away the restrictions in the old law contained in the Trustee Investments Act 1961, which is now almost entirely repealed. It should, however, be noted that these powers are default powers in that they apply in the absence of any contrary provisions in the trust instrument. This may accordingly modify these powers. One example could be the introduction of a duty to invest according to ethical principles – see below.

Section 3 of the new Act provides that a trustee may make any investment that he could make if he was absolutely entitled under the trust. This reflects the clause commonly used in trusts before the Act, which provided that the trustee could invest as if he/she was the sole beneficial owner and thus the law is brought into line with what was current practice. The new provision may be restricted in the trust instrument by the settlor, e.g. investments which the settlor does not consider ethical may be excluded. The effect is that in future trusts may cut down the width of statutory powers, the exact opposite of the previous position. It should be pointed out, however, that the phrase 'as if he were absolutely entitled to the assets of the trust' can, if taken at face value, give a misleading impression. The legal effect is that no type of investment is now unauthorised, so that, for example, trustees can now invest in overseas companies. Whether they should do so is a different matter, as they must remember that they are not investing their own money but, in equity, that of the beneficiaries. Moreover, they may need to consider the different types of beneficiaries and their different needs. For example, they may need to balance the need of some beneficiaries for income against that of others for capital growth. (See also below under the duty to maintain evenhandedness between the beneficiaries.)

Section 3 does not extend to certain trusts, e.g. pension funds, to which a special statutory regime applies.

When trustees are investing they must have regard to the **standard investment criteria** in s. 4. These are in addition to the statutory duty laid down by s. 1 above. The criteria are:

(a) The suitability to the trust of particular investments.
(b) The need for diversification of investments, so far as this is appropriate.

These criteria reflect the portfolio theory of investments whereby investments must not be considered in isolation but looked at in the context of the portfolio as a whole and an overall investment strategy.

Section 5 provides that trustees must obtain and consider advice about the way in which the power on investment should be exercised having regard to the standard investment criteria. 'Proper advice' should also be obtained when reviewing investments. Proper advice is defined as the advice of a person reasonably believed by the trustees to be qualified to give it by reason of their ability in and practical experience of financial matters relating to the proposed investment. Advice need not be written. Trustees need not obtain advice if they reasonably conclude that in the circumstances it is unnecessary or inappropriate to do so. In the end, however, investment decisions are those of the trustees and not the advisors although they can be delegated (see s. 11 of the Act in Chapter 18).

Duty to invest – general equitable principles

(a) *Before investing*. The trustees can place the money at a current or deposit account at a bank before making investments but any investments must be made within a reasonable time otherwise the trustees can be charged with interest, the rate being at the court's discretion (*Holgate* v. *Haworth* (1853)). It follows that even money held in a bank deposit account producing interest is not classified as an investment.
(b) *General principles*. The decisions in these cases must now be read subject to both the statutory duty of care in s. 1 of the Trustee Act 2000 and the standard investment criteria in s. 4. With this in mind, they are still a useful guide. In *Learoyd* v. *Whiteley* (1887) Lord Watson said that a trustee must 'avoid all . . . investments which are attended with hazard' and thus the standard is higher, as he observed, than the standard expected of a prudent man of business when dealing with his own money. However, the emphasis on avoiding hazardous investments is balanced today by the need to ensure that the capital value of the fund, at a time of inflation, appreciates in

value. In *Steel* v. *Wellcome Custodian Trustees Ltd* (1988) Hoffmann J observed that to insist on a certain proportion of the fund being retained in safe investments could result 'in tension with a trustee's obligation to behave with the prudence of an ordinary man of business'. Such a prudent man will no longer confine himself to investments such as Government stocks but will wish to invest in equities (shares and companies), unit trusts and similar investments. In *Nestlé* v. *National Westminster Bank plc* (1994) it was alleged that the bank was in breach of its duty as a trustee by failing to review investments regularly and that it misunderstood an investment clause with the result that it had invested only in bank and insurance shares rather than a wider spread of equities. The result was that the value of the investment stood at £269,000 when, it was alleged, it should have been at about £l million. The court, while deprecating the conduct of the bank, held that any breaches of trust could not be proved to have caused losses. It applied 'the undemanding standard of prudence' and also emphasised that the importance of preserving a trust fund would always outweigh success in its advancement. It may well be that the outcome of this case would be different had the standard investment criteria under s. 4 of the Trustee Act 2000 applied. However, in all cases where it is alleged that trustees have failed to increase the value of the fund as they should, the problem will be actually proving that, had they made certain investment decisions, the value of the fund would necessarily have increased.

(c) *Should trustees be influenced by ethical and other considerations when investing?* In *Cowan* v. *Scargill* (1984) the defendant and others were trustees of the Mineworkers Pension Scheme. They objected to an investment plan unless it provided for withdrawal from overseas investments and that there should be no investment in energies in competition with coal. Megarry V-C held that trustees, when considering investments, must put aside their own views and consider the best interests of present and future beneficiaries. Best interests usually mean best financial interests. Thus, for example, merely because a trustee is opposed to investment in a certain country on moral or political grounds it is no reason for not investing there. However, benefit does not always mean financial benefit, e.g. if all the beneficiaries condemned 'all forms of alcohol, tobacco and popular entertainment' it might not be for their benefit to invest in these although this might be financially advantageous. This decision has been criticised for taking too narrow a view of the duties of trustees.

In *Harries* v. *Church Commissioners for England* (1993) the Bishop of Oxford questioned the Commissioners' investment statement alleging that they attached overriding importance to financial considerations, which was wrong, and that they should have in mind the underlying purpose for which they held their assets which was promotion of the Christian faith through the Church of England. The court disagreed and held that the Commissioners' strategy was legally correct. The general rule was that trustees must obtain the maximum return. In fact the Commissioners did not invest in companies whose main business was armaments, gambling, alcohol, tobacco and newspapers and this was justified because there were conflicting views about the morality of these and there were alternative investments. It would, however, be wrong to take non-financial considerations into account which might put investment profits in jeopardy. Thus it seems that the Commissioners cannot, for instance, sell land to a developer at an undervalue to provide low cost housing for needy families. This seems strange because the Church often funds for hostels for the homeless and no one questions the legality of this. In *Martin* v. *City of Edinburgh DC* (1989) the council was held to be in breach of trust by withdrawing all investments from South Africa because it had not expressly considered whether this was in the best interests of the beneficiaries nor had it sought professional advice on this issue. The best way forward here is for the settlor to expressly provide in the trust instrument that the trustees can adopt an ethical investment strategy. It may also be that a court, when considering a case such as *Harries* (above), would emphasise the standard investment criteria that the investment must be suitable to the trust. Certain types of investments might not, for example, be held suitable to a trust for a particular religion.

(d) *Duties of trustees who hold a controlling interest in a company*. Trustees who hold such an interest have a higher duty than in other cases because, by virtue of their interest, they may be able to control the activities of the company and so may be liable for breach of trust if, through their failure to exert themselves, the company gets into financial difficulties and the trust suffers a loss. In *Re Lucking's Will Trusts* (1967) Cross J suggested that trustees in this situation should ensure that they have the same information about the progress of the company's affairs as the directors have and the trustees should act on that information appropriately. Here, one of the trustees was on the board of the company but had failed to supervise the activities of the managing director, who was an old friend of his, and as a result the managing director appropriated about £15,000 of company funds which could not be recovered from him when he went bankrupt. The trustee was held liable for his failure to exercise adequate supervision.

In *Bartlett* v. *Barclays Bank Trust Co Ltd* (1980) the bank was trustee of the Bartlett Trust, which held almost all the shares in a family property company. The directors embarked on speculative property developments, one of which was a disaster and the bank was held liable. Their duty was to act as trustee in the same way that an ordinary prudent man would act in relation to his own affairs and so here they should have insisted on full information about what was going on and not been content with the information given to them as shareholders. However the court held that a trustee who is a controlling shareholder need not insist on being represented on the board of directors although Cross J in *Re Lucking* (1967) had said that he should. Brightman J in this case said that this was only one possible way of ensuring that the trustee was fully informed.

It remains to be seen what, if any, effect the statutory duty of case will have on the above position.

Applications to the court for wider investment powers than those in the trust instrument

Section 3 of the Trustee Act 2000 (above) now gives trustees very wide powers where no type of investment is prohibited to them. However, it operates as a default power so that the trust instrument may provide for much narrower investment powers. In such situations the principles established in cases decided under the old law, when the Trustee Investments Act 1961 greatly restricted the powers of trustees, may still be relevant.

(a) *Types of application.* Trustees may apply under the Variation of Trusts Act 1958 (see Chapter 19) for wider investment powers generally or under s. 57 of the Trustee Act 1925 for authority for a particular investment. In *Anker-Petersen* v. *Anker-Petersen* (2001) it was held that where the application does not involve a change in the beneficial interests then it is more convenient to proceed under s. 57.

(b) *Principles applied by the court.* In *Re Kolb's Will Trusts* (1962) it was held that the recently widened powers to invest contained in the Trustee Investments Act (TIA) 1961 should *prima facie* be sufficient and should only be widened if a special case was made out for doing so. In *Mason* v. *Farbrother* (1983) a scheme to widen the investment powers of trustees of the employees of the Co-operative Society's pension fund beyond those contained in the TIA was approved. The special circumstances here were the extent of inflation since 1961, the fact that the fund was large (valued at £127 million) and, as a pension fund, it had 'something of a public element in it'. In *Trustees of the British Museum* v. *A-G* (1984) Megarry V-C went further and held that the principle in *Re Kolb* should not be followed since conditions, especially the extent of inflation, had changed so greatly in the last 20 years. He held that each application should be considered on its merits and identified the following factors as being relevant: the standing of the trustees; the width and efficacy of provisions for advice and control; the size of the fund and the objects of the trust. Here the trustees were eminent, they had access to skilled advice, the fund was large (between £5 million and £6 million) and as one of the objects of the fund was to acquire works of art there was a need for capital appreciation to finance this. Accordingly the trustees were allowed wider powers, including a power to invest abroad. The approach in this case was followed in *Steel* v. *Wellcome Custodian Trustees* (1988). The trustees of the Wellcome Trust, a group of charitable trusts with a combined value of £3,200 million sought to invest as beneficial owners. The court granted the application taking into account the size of the fund, the eminence of the trustees, and the provisions in the proposed scheme requiring advice. (This case also involved delegation of trustees' powers – see Chapter 18.)

Measure of liability of trustees for breach of their duty to invest trust funds properly

The general principle is that trustees are liable for the loss caused to the trust estate. This principle is subject to the following detailed rule:

(a) Profits made on the sale of unauthorised investments belong to the trust. If they are sold at a loss then the trustees must make good the loss to the trust estate. The beneficiaries may, if they are *sui iuris*, accept an improper investment (*Re Patten and Edmonton Union Poor Guardians* (1883)).
(b) Where trustees improperly retain unauthorised investments they are liable for the difference between the present value (or selling price) and the price which it would have fetched had it been sold when the trustees first became under a duty to sell (*Fry* v. *Fry* (1859)).
(c) Where trustees decide to retain authorised investments they will normally be protected from liability if they sought advice.
(d) Where trustees improperly sell authorised investments in order to e.g. invest in unauthorised ones then they can be required to either account for the proceeds of sale or replace the investment. In *Re Bell's Indenture* (1980) it was held that the value should be ascertained as at the date of judgment.
(e) If trustees ought, as is usual, to have invested in a range of investments, but failed to do so, their liability is to make good the difference between any interest actually received and the rate fixed by the court. If the trustees ought to have invested in one particular security but failed to do so they can be made to purchase as much of that security as they could have purchased had they done so at the proper time.
(f) Any gains made in one unauthorised transaction cannot be set off against losses made in another transaction so as to reduce the trustees' liability (*Dimes* v. *Scott* (1828)). This rule does not apply where the gain and loss were part of the same transaction and in *Bartlett* v. *Barclays Bank Trust Co Ltd* (1980) (see above) it was held that a gain could be set off against a loss arising from the same course of conduct, in this case a policy of speculative investment, even though they were not part of the same transaction.
(g) Calculation of interest. Trustees are liable to pay interest on trust funds wrongly invested, calculated as from the date of the misapplication. In *Bartlett* v. *Barclays Bank* the court fixed the rate as the court's short-term investment account rate.

DUTY OF THE TRUSTEE TO DISTRIBUTE THE TRUST PROPERTY TO THOSE ENTITLED

(a) A trustee must pay the beneficiaries the sums to which they are entitled. In *Eaves* v. *Hickson* (1861) trustees were held liable to the beneficiaries when they paid the wrong persons because of acting on the basis of a forged marriage certificate. A trustee who has paid the wrong person when acting under a mistake of fact, as in the above case, may recover it in quasi-contract but the trustee cannot recover it if the mistake was one of law (*Re Diplock* (1948)). However, a trustee who makes an error in distributing the fund may apply under s. 61 of the Trustee Act 1925 to be excused from liability (see Chapter 20).
(b) Doubtful claims. Where a trustee is doubtful as to who is entitled to trust property he should apply to the court for directions and will then be

protected if he complies with them. If beneficiaries cannot be traced the money can be paid into court or the court may authorise the trustees to distribute the trust fund as if the untraced beneficiaries were dead (*Re Benjamin* (1902) (*Benjamin* order). This will protect the trustees but if those entitled come forward within the limitation period (see Chapter 19) they may proceed either against the property or those wrongly paid. In *Re Green's Will Trusts* (1985) the testatrix had left her property to her son but also provided that it should go to charity instead if he did not claim it by 2020. The son had disappeared on a bombing mission in 1943 and everyone except his mother was convinced that he was dead. A *Benjamin* order was made.

Section 27 of the Trustee Act 1925 deals with the possibility of outstanding debts owed by the trust and also claims by beneficiaries of whom the trustees are unaware. If the trustees comply with the rules here on advertising for claims they will be safe in distributing the funds to those creditors, and satisfying the claims of those beneficiaries, of whom they have notice. A creditor or beneficiary who comes forward later may, however, be able to follow the trust property into the hands of beneficiaries who have received it. The effect of s. 27 is thus to protect the trustees from claims and not to prevent the beneficiaries from obtaining the property by other means. The trustees must advertise in the London Gazette and, where land is involved, any newspaper circulating in the district where the land is situated. Additionally, such other notices must be made as would be directed by a court on an action for administration of an estate. The notices must require claimants to send particulars of their claims to the trustees within a period of not less than two months fixed in the notice.

DUTY TO ACT IMPARTIALLY BETWEEN THE BENEFICIARIES (DUTY OF EVENHANDEDNESS)

Note 17.3: The rules explained below are likely to be reformed and it is hoped that this will be in the near future. Details of the proposed reforms are set out at the end of the discussion.

(a) *General principle.* Trustees must not favour one beneficiary rather than another. In *Lloyds Bank* v. *Duker* (1987) a beneficiary, Duker, was entitled under a will to 46/80th of the residuary estate, and claimed 574 out of 999 shares which formed part of the estate. The court held that it would be unfair on the other beneficiaries if he received this because he would then have a majority shareholding in the company which would be worth more per share than the other shareholdings. Instead, all the shares were directed to be sold and the proceeds were divided between the beneficiaries in the proportion set out in the will. Thus Duker would receive 46/80th of the proceeds.

(b) *Rule in* Howe *v.* Earl of Dartmouth *(1802).* The object of this to maintain equality between the tenants and those entitled in remainder (remaindermen).

The reasoning underlying the rule is that life tenants are more interested in income but remaindermen are interested in the preservation and possible appreciation of capital. The rule states that there is a duty to convert such parts of the property as are of a wasting (i.e. short-lived such as animals) or hazardous (i.e. possibly investments which are in breach of the investment provisions of the Trustee Act 2000 – see above) character into property of a permanent or income-bearing character. Until the law on investments changed with the coming into force of s. 3 of the Trustee Act 2000 it was said that the rule considered unauthorised investments as wasting and hazardous. Now that there are no investments which are specifically unauthorised the true rule can once more be seen to be that the trustees must convert investments which are of a wasting or perishable nature to those which are of a permanent character. (See Wigram V-C in *Hinves* v. *Hinves* (1844).) Therefore, the effect will be that the life tenant still receive income but the capital will be protected. In fact, the rule in *Howe* v. *Dartmouth* is often excluded, as it does not always reflect what the beneficiaries wish. In 1802 inflation and its effects were not so well known and it is realised that the idea of simply preserving the capital value of property will in fact, cause its real value to fall. Thus the remainderman may well wish the property to be invested so that its real value will keep pace with inflation. The Law Reform Committee in 1982 recommended that the rule should be replaced by one which obliged the trustees to hold a fair balance between all the beneficiaries, particularly those entitled to income and those entitled to capital.

In any event, it does not apply in the following cases:

(i) where there is a contrary provision in the will;

(ii) to personal property;

(iii) to freehold land and to leaseholds held for a term exceeding 60 years. These are authorised investments (there is doubt about whether the rule applies to shorter leaseholds (see *Re Brooker* (1926)) although it probably does);

(iv) to specific (as opposed to residuary) bequests.

(c) *Duty to apportion*. The trustees may not be able to convert the property in accordance with the rule in *Howe* v. *Earl of Dartmouth* immediately. What rights do the life tenant and the remaindermen have to the income meanwhile? In practice there is often a clear intention that the life tenant should receive the income, but if not, then the following rules apply to decide how the income should be apportioned. It should be noted that these rules have also lost some force, as s. 3 of the Trustee Act 2000 has removed the previous sharp distinction between authorised and unauthorised investments and the notion of an unauthorised investment will now depend on whether the provisions of the Trustee Act on investments have been complied with.

(i) *Authorised investments*. The tenant for life is entitled to all the income from these.

(ii) *Unauthorised investments*. Pending sale of unauthorised investments other than leaseholds there is an apportionment so that the life tenant receives an income representing the current yield on authorised investments and any excess is added to capital. Trustees in determining what the current yield should be could follow the precedent in *Bartlett* v. *Barclays Bank Trust Co Ltd* (1980) (see above) and pay the same rate as is paid on the court short-term investment account. The old rule was to pay 4 per cent but, although interest rates are currently low, trustees in doubt as to the correct rate would be advised to apply to the court for directions under s. 57 of the Trustee Act 1925. If there is insufficient income to pay the interest any shortfall can be made up out of future income or from capital.

The time at which capital should be valued in order to calculate the income depends on whether there is a power to postpone sale. If there is, then the date of valuation is the date of the testator's death (*Brown* v. *Gellatly* (1867)). If there is not, then trustees should convert within the executor's year and the proceeds of sale of investments sold during that year are taken as their value (*Re Fawcett* (1940)). If any investments are not sold during that time they are valued at the end of the executor's year (*Dimes* v. *Scott* (1828)).

(iii) *Leaseholds*. There is probably no duty to apportion those leaseholds covered by the rule and so the life tenant is entitled to the whole of the income.

(iv) *Reversionary interests*. A reversionary interest produces no actual income and so, when it is sold, some of the proceeds of sale should be paid to the life tenant in compensation. The rule in *Re Earl of Chesterfield's Trusts* (1883) provides that if, e.g. the property is sold for £1,000 then the capital sum, to which the remainderman is entitled, is the amount which, had it been invested at 4 per cent compound interest, would have produced £1,000. The life tenant receives the rest. The effect is that part of the proceeds go as income to the life tenant and part to the remainderman as an addition to capital.

(v) *Payment of debts*. The rule in *Allhusen* v. *Whittell* (1867) attempts to deal with the problem that, before the debts of the estate are paid, the life tenant is being paid income from the assets which, pending payment, include those debts. Accordingly, the rule provides a method, based on 4 per cent per annum interest, of apportioning liability for making these payments between capital and income. In practice the rules in *Re Earl of Chesterfield's Trusts* (1883) and *Allhusen* v. *Whittell* (1867) are so complicated to apply, and are on what is at times an artificially low rate of interest, that they are often excluded.

Proposals for reform

The Law Commission has recently recommended (Law Commission 2004) that all the above rules dealing with apportionment (*Howe* v. *Lord Dartmouth, Re Earl of Chesterfield's Trusts* and *Allhusen* v. *Whittel*) should be replaced by a statutory power of allocation where trustees will be able to allocate receipts and expenses between capital and income in accordance with their fundamental duty to maintain the balance between capital and income. This power will apply to private trusts where there is a life tenancy and an interest in remainder and also to discretionary trusts where there is a distinction between interests in income and capital.

FURTHER READING

Clements, (2004) 'Bringing trusts law into the twenty-first century', 2 Web JCLI. Excellent and practical.

Law Commission Consultation Paper 146 (1999), Trustees' powers and duties.

Law Commission Consultation Paper 175 (2004), Capital and income in trusts: classification and apportionment.

CHAPTER SUMMARY

- Duties on becoming a trustee.
- Statutory duty of care.
- Investment: statutory provisions and general equitable principles.
- Applications for wider investment powers.
- Measure of liability of trustees.
- Duty to pay those beneficiaries entitled.
- Evenhandedness.

QUESTION

Peter and Lucy have recently been appointed trustees of the Hanbury Trust, a family trust. The beneficiaries are Mary (24) and Christopher (22), each of whom is entitled to half the fund at the age of 25. The value of the fund at present is £110,000. Mary wants the trustees to invest in the shares of companies having strong links with Europe as she is an ardent enthusiast for greater European integration. There are no special investment powers in the trust instrument. Christopher is opposed to this.

Advise Peter and Lucy on:

(a) Whether they should invest the money as Mary wishes.
(b) Their general investment strategy.

Note 17.4: You will find suggested points for inclusion in this answer in Appendix 2.

18 Powers of trustees

INTRODUCTION

This chapter is concerned with powers and so it is vital to reiterate the points made in Chapter 16: powers are discretionary and so the trustees need not exercise them. If they give reasons for the exercise of their discretion to exercise or not to exercise them, then the court can investigate these but it will not compel the giving of reasons.

> *Note 18.1: When reading this chapter look at the specimen trust deed in the Appendix at the end: clause 4 contains powers of maintenance and advancement (see below) and you should check the extent to which this clause alters/extends the statutory powers set out below.*

POWER TO PURCHASE LAND

Section 8 of the Trustee Act 2000 provides that a trustee may, subject to any restriction in the trust instrument, purchase land in the United Kingdom:

(a) As an investment.
(b) For occupation by a beneficiary.
(c) For any other reason.

Thus the old restrictions are gone and the only point is that the statutory duty of care applies. This extended power originally appeared in the Trusts of Land and Appointment of Trustees Act 1996 but it only applied to trusts of land. Now it applies to all trusts. The statutory duty of care applies to this power, unlike the powers of maintenance and advancement.

POWERS OF MAINTENANCE AND ADVANCEMENT

Introduction

The way in which powers of maintenance and advancement work is illustrated by Example 18.1.

Example 18.1

X is entitled under the provision of a trust to receive £10,000 at the age of 21. He is now 17 and is a promising cricketer. He needs some money to pay for a special coaching course. Can the trustees pay him any part of his entitlement in advance to enable him to do so?

The trustees may have some choices here:

(a) To pay X some of the income from the £10,000 capital. This is a power of maintenance.
(b) Actually to pay X some of the £10,000 capital in advance. This is a power of advancement.

Relationship between statutory powers and powers contained in the trust instrument

The statutory powers, in ss. 31 and 32 of the Trustee Act 1925, are additional to any powers contained in the trust instrument and are also subject to the general provision in s. 69(2) of the Trustee Act (1925) that the statutory powers conferred on trustees only apply in the absence of a contrary intention. Therefore, they are another example (investment powers under s. 3 of the Trustee Act 2000 – see Chapter 17 – are another) of default powers in that they apply only in default of the trust instrument providing otherwise. Thus the trust instrument may restrict or even completely take away trustees' powers of maintenance and advancement (see e.g. *Re McGeorge* (1963) below). It is, in fact, common to increase the powers of advancement so that 100 per cent of the capital may be advanced and so displace the statutory maximum of 50 per cent.

Power of maintenance

This is a power to pay income for the maintenance, education or benefit of an infant beneficiary. Trustees may pay the income to the infant (minor's) parent or guardian, if any, or otherwise apply the money (s. 31(1)(i) Trustee Act 1925). Thus the money could be paid direct to a school for school fees.

Section 31(3) provides that maintenance only can be paid when a person is entitled to the income. A life tenant will normally be entitled to income and so his existence will mean that the power of maintenance cannot be exercised in favour of those entitled in remainder. The same will apply if there is any other prior interest.

If there is no prior interest then the minor will be entitled to income if he has either:

(a) A vested interest, i.e. a present interest or a future interest where possession is postponed to a future date (to X on the death of Y); on the termination of a prior life interest (to X for life, remainder to Y) although it may be in the second example that Y is not entitled to income anyway.

(b) A contingent interest which carries the intermediate income. Therefore, if the gift is Blackacre to X at 25, this is a contingent gift and so one needs to determine whether X is entitled to the intermediate income in order to determine his entitlement to maintenance.

When does a gift carry the intermediate income?

A contingent residuary bequest of personalty (including leaseholds) carries the intermediate income and so does a specific bequest of personalty, a devise of realty, and a residuary devise of freehold land (s. 175 LPA 1925). However, a contingent pecuniary legacy (e.g. to X at 25) does not carry the intermediate income unless either:

(a) The legacy was given by the father of the minor or some person ***in loco parentis*** to him, provided that no other fund is set aside for the maintenance of the legatee (*Re West* (1913)) and the contingency is the attainment of the legatee's majority (*Re Jones* (1932)).
(b) The testator shows an intention to maintain the legatee (*Re Churchill* (1909)).
(c) The testator sets the legacy aside so as to be available for the legatee as soon as the contingency arises (*Re Medlock* (1886)).

Thus in the above example, Blackacre to X at 25, X is entitled to the intermediate income because there is a contingent specific devise of realty. The rules on whether a gift carries the intermediate income are illustrated by the following example.

Example 18.2

Alfred by will leaves £100,000 to his grandson, Ethelbert, provided that he attains the age of 25. Before considering if any of the income from this money should be paid to Ethelbert before he reaches the age of 25, it is necessary to ask if the trustees have a power to pay it. Assuming that they do, the next point is that this is a pecuniary legacy (i.e. it is a legacy of money) and it is contingent on Ethelbert reaching the age of 25. If the situations in (a) (b) and (c) above are examined it will be seen that none of them applies. Had Alfred been Ethelbert's father then (a) would have applied provided that no other provision had been made for Ethelbert in Alfred's will.

If Albert's will had simply left £100,000 to Ethelbert without specifying the age at which he was to receive it (i.e. no contingency) this would take the gift right out of this area as it would no longer be a contingent pecuniary legacy. Thus although Ethelbert is not entitled to the capital until 18 (at which date he can give a valid receipt), the power of maintenance is not excluded and may, at the discretion of the trustees, be exercised in his favour.

Exercising the power of maintenance

Trustees are not obliged to exercise their power, but, in common with all their other powers, they must apply their minds to the question of whether or not to do so (*Wilson* v. *Turner* (1883) and Chapter 16).

Section 31(1)(ii) provides that in deciding whether to pay maintenance the trustees must have regard to the age of the infant, any other income which is available for his maintenance, his requirements and all other relevant circumstances. If they know that other income is available for his maintenance then only a proportionate part of the fund should be paid over unless the court otherwise directs.

Section 31(2) provides that income not paid for maintenance shall be accumulated by investment during the minority of the person contingently entitled. Any accumulations which are not paid over later for maintenance will be added to capital. Once the minor is entitled to the capital he will, unless there is a contrary intention, also be entitled to the accumulations.

Position where the minor reaches the age of majority

The statutory power to pay maintenance ceases at the age of 18 and the adult is entitled to the income unless there is a contrary intention, as where there was a direction to accumulate, as in *Re Turner's Will Trusts* (1937), where a beneficiary was entitled to capital at the age of 28 with a direction to accumulate until then (see also *Re McGeorge* (1963)).

Thus in the above example, when Ethelbert reaches 18 the trustees must pay him maintenance as the discretionary power has gone, even though he is not entitled to the capital sum of £100,000 until 25.

Note: This area has not attracted the attention of academic writers in the same way as others have, but a most useful article is by Ker (1953).

Power of advancement

This is a power to pay over part of the capital to the beneficiary, before he is entitled to the whole sum for his advancement or benefit.

The statutory power is contained in s. 32 of the Trustee Act (1925) although, as with the power of maintenance, it can be excluded by evidence of a contrary intention. In *Re Evans's Settlement* (1967) a provision in the trust instrument allowing trustees to advance up to £5,000 was held to exclude the statutory provisions. In *IRC* v. *Bernstein* (1961) a direction to accumulate income during the settlor's lifetime likewise excluded the statutory provisions. In *CD (a minor)* v. *O* (2004) an application under the Variation of Trusts Act was used to increase the amount which could be advanced from the statutory 50 per cent to the whole sum (see also Chapter 19).

Section 32 allows trustees to make advancements out of capital provided that:

(a) The total sum which is paid does not exceed half of the beneficiary's share. In *The Marquess of Abergavenny* v. *Ram* (1981) it was held that this means that, once this sum has been paid, no further advancement can be made even though the value of the capital subsequently appreciates, e.g. X is entitled to a trust fund at the age of 25. He asks for an advancement of half, and as at that time the fund stands at £50,000, he is paid £25,000. The fund later increases in value to £100,000 but no further payments can be made to X. If, however, X had been paid only £20,000 instead of £25,000 then further advances could be made based on increased capital value. In *CD (a minor)* v. *O* (2004) an application under the Variation of Trusts Act 1958 was used to increase the amount which could be advanced from the statutory 50 per cent to the whole sum (see also Chapter 19).

(b) If a beneficiary has a prior interest he must be of full age and consent in writing to the advancement. This is because if an advancement is made then the capital sum available to earn income for a life tenant is reduced.

A beneficiary to whom an advancement is made must bring the amount of the advancement into account when the fund is distributed (s. 32(1)(b)) otherwise he would be paid twice.

The trust property out of which an advancement can be made consists of money or securities, or land held on a trust of land.

Principles on which an advancement should be made

(a) *General principles*. Section 32 refers to 'advancement or benefit'. Advancement has been held to refer to establishing the beneficiary in life through e.g. buying or furnishing a house (*Perry* v. *Perry*). However, the word 'benefit' seems to give a wider meaning to the term. Thus in *Re Kershaw's Trusts* (1868) an advancement to the beneficiary's husband to enable him to set up a business in England and so prevent the family from separating was held valid. A remarkable example is *Re Clore's Settlement Trusts* (1966), where the beneficiary was entitled to a considerable interest in a trust fund and felt under an obligation to make payments to charity. An advancement to him to do this was held valid because otherwise he would have to make the charitable payments out of his taxed income. In *Pilkington* v. *IRC* (1964) saving of estate duty (now Inheritance Tax) was held to be a benefit. The court said that there was no need to show that the benefit related to the beneficiary's personal needs.

(b) *Benefit to others*. In *Pilkington* v. *IRC* (1964) it was held that the fact that others might benefit incidentally, in this case any children whom the beneficiary, then aged two, might have, did not prevent an advancement being made.

(c) *Setting up a new trust*. In *Pilkington* v. *IRC* (1964) the use of s. 32 of the Trustee Act 1925 to set up a new trust was held lawful, even though the new trust might have (as in this case) powers not contained in the original trust instrument. The motive for this is tax saving.

(d) *Payment of a beneficiary's debts*. In *Lowther* v. *Bentinck* (1874) payment of a beneficiary's debts was held not to be a proper use of the power of advancement although it is submitted that it might be if the payments were made direct to his creditors and, as a result, the beneficiary was enabled to 'wipe the slate clean' and begin life afresh.

(e) *Payments in bad faith*. In *Molyneux* v. *Fletcher* (1898) an advancement to a beneficiary to enable her to pay a debt her father owed to one of the trustees was held to be improper.

(f) *Supervision by the trustees.* In *Re Paulin's Settlement Trusts* (1964) a series of advancements were made, nominally to the child beneficiaries, but in reality to benefit their parents. Thus a house was bought for their father and a debt incurred by their mother was paid off. The court held that where trustees prescribe a particular purpose for which the money is to be used they cannot leave the beneficiary entirely free to spend it for that purpose or in any other way that he chooses.

POWER OF DELEGATION

The basic equitable rule

Equity always considered trusteeship to be a personal matter: a trustee was chosen because of his particular qualities and so he should not be allowed to delegate his duties and powers to another. This has long been relaxed to the extent that trustees can employ agents, such as solicitors and stockbrokers, to carry out specialised tasks and as long ago as 1754 in *Re Parsons, ex parte Belchier* Hardwicke LC recognised that agents could be employed for these types of purposes. The position was governed by s. 23(1) of the Trustee Act 1925 until the coming into force of the Trustee Act 2000, which has clarified the law.

There are two issues: what can be delegated and, if delegation has taken place, to what extent is the trustee liable for the acts of the agent?

What can be delegated?

Section 11(2) of the 2000 Act provides that, in the case of trusts other than charitable trusts, trusts of pension funds and authorised unit trusts all functions can be delegated except:

(a) Functions relating to whether and how the trust assets should be distributed e.g. power to decide which beneficiaries should benefit on a particular occasion.
(b) Power to decide whether any fees or payments should be made from income or capital.
(c) Power to appoint new trustees.
(d) Power to delegate functions. However, it is possible for the trustees themselves to decide to sub-delegate if this is reasonably necessary.

The effect is that the trustees cannot, for example, delegate their powers of distribution among the beneficiaries under a discretionary trust but they can delegate what may be called administrative powers such as that of deciding on investments.

In the case of charitable trusts s. 11(3) of the Trustee Act 2000 allows the delegation of administrative acts such as investment and the actual carrying out of a decision taken by the trustees.

In addition, s. 1 of the Trustee Delegation Act 1999 allows delegation by trustees of land who are also co-owners under which a trustee may, by a power of attorney, delegate all functions relating to the land or income arising from it or the proceeds of sale. Thus a co-owner of land may provide for the disposition of the land by two trustees (the donee and the other co-trustee) if he/she becomes incapable and so overreaching under the provisions of s. 27 of the Trustee Act 1925 can take place. A further power authorising delegation is found in s. 25 of the Trustee Act 1925 allowing the delegation by a trustee, acting under a power of attorney, of all his functions for a period of up to 12 months. This will be useful where, for example, he will be absent abroad.

In the case of trusts of land s. 9 of the Trusts of Land and Appointment of Trustees Act 1996 allows trustees to delegate any or all of their functions as trustees of the land to one or more beneficiaries who are of full age and beneficially entitled to an interest in possession. Such delegates will be in the same position as trustees when they actually exercise their functions but will not be trustees for any other purpose. They cannot, for example, give a valid receipt for capital money arising on a sale.

LIABILITY FOR THE AGENT'S ACTS

There are two situations:

(a) *The actual exercise of the power of delegation.* Here the statutory duty of care in the Trustee Act 2000 applies and so the test is whether the trustee has exercised such care and skill as is reasonable in the circumstances (s. 1). The standard varies according to whether the trustee is a professional or a lay trustee (see Chapter 17). Thus the duty applies when actually appointing the agent, deciding on the terms on which the function is delegated and when keeping the delegation to the agent under review.

(b) *Liability for the defaults of the agent.* Section 23 of the Trustee Act 2000 provides that a trustee is not liable for the acts or defaults of the agent unless he has failed to observe the standard of care when appointing the agent or keeping the arrangement under review. When the agent is allowed to appoint a substitute, the trustee is only liable for the acts of that substitute if he failed to observe the standard of care in agreeing to the term permitting a substitute or in reviewing it. However, when an agent is appointed as a donee of a power of attorney then s. 25(5) of the Trustee Act 1925 provides that the trustee is always liable for the acts of the donee of the power.

OTHER POWERS OF TRUSTEES

Power to sell

Section 12 of the Trustee Act 1925 allows the trustees to sell any trust property but they must obtain the best price for the beneficiaries. Section 14(1) of the Trustee Act 1925 provides that trustees, having sold property, can give a valid receipt to the purchaser for the purchase money. Thus a purchaser is not obliged to enquire whether the trustees have actually applied the money in accordance with the terms of the trust.

Power to insure

Section 19 of the Trustee Act 2000 gives trustees power to insure trust property against loss or damage by any event and to pay the premiums out of income or capital. Where property is held on a bare trust (see Chapter 4) then the power is subject to any directions which may be given by the beneficiaries. The statutory duty of care applies to the exercise of this power.

Power to compound liabilities

Trustees have, under s. 15 of the Trustee Act 1925, wide powers to settle claims made against the trust estate by compromises. They may, for example, abandon a claim, compromise it or submit it to arbitration. This power is also discussed in Chapter 17 in connection with the duties of trustees when accepting office.

FURTHER READING

Ker (1953) 117 Conv. (N.S.) 273. Still useful on powers of maintenance and advancement.

See also Further Reading for Chapter 17.

CHAPTER SUMMARY

Powers of:

- Maintenance.
- Advancement.
- Delegation.
- Sale.
- Insurance.
- Compound liabilities.

QUESTION

Ted and Susan are trustees of a fund currently valued at £50,000 set up by Keith for such of his children as attain the age of 21. He has two children Andrew, 20 and Fiona, 17.

(a) Andrew has asked the trustees for £5,000 to put down a deposit on a house which he wishes to buy. He intends to live there with his girlfriend, Debbie, and to use the house as a base for his interior decorating business.

(b) Fiona is a promising musician and wishes her fees at a summer school for promising musicians to be paid for the next five years. The annual fees are currently £1,000.

> *Note 18.2: You will find suggested points for inclusion in these answers in Appendix 2.*

APPENDIX

Trust created by will

This is an example of a trust created by will. The testator has a son who is under 18 and wishes to leave the son all of his property. However, as land cannot be owned by someone under 18, and as in any case it would be undesirable to leave money to someone very young, the testator has set up a trust in his will under which the executors are both executors and trustees. As executors they must gather any debts due to the deceased and otherwise distribute the estate, but in this case they also have a continuing role of acting as trustees for the son until he comes of age.

> *Note 18.3:*
> *(a) Clause 3 gives the trustees their power of investment. In fact, this wide power of investment is now given to trustees anyway by s. 3 of the Trustee Act 2000 (see Chapter 17) but it is still common to include it so that the position is clear to everyone.*
> *(b) Clause 4 deals with the trustees' powers to pay sums by way of maintenance and advancement (see Chapter 18) and, as is common, it has widened the power of advancement so that up to 100 per cent of the capital can be advanced.*

TRUST CREATED BY WILL

I (name) of (address) HEREBY REVOKE all wills and testamentary dispositions heretofore made by me AND DECLARE this to be my last Will ________________

1. I APPOINT (name) and (name) (hereinafter called 'my trustees') to be executors and trustees of this my Will

2. I GIVE all my real and personal estate not otherwise disposed of (subject to payment of my funeral and testamentary expenses debts and legacies and all duties payable on or by reason of my death in respect of my estate or any part thereof or any legacy hereby given or any gift made by me during my lifetime or the property comprised in any such gift) and all the property over which I shall at my death have any general or special power of disposition unto my son (name) of (address) as aforesaid absolutely on attaining the age of 21 years. ________

____

3. ANY MONEYS requiring investment hereunder may be laid out in or upon the acquisition or security of any property of whatsoever nature and wheresoever situate including (but without prejudice to the generality of the foregoing words) insurance policies on the life of any beneficiary or any other person and any house or flat as a residence for any beneficiary to the intent that my Trustees shall have the same full and unrestricted power of investing in all respects as if they were absolutely entitled thereto beneficially and subject to no restriction with regard to advice or otherwise in relation to investment ____________________

4. IN ADDITION to all other powers conferred by law my Trustees may at any time and from time to time raise the whole or any part of the vested contingent expectant or presumptive share or shares of any beneficiary hereunder and pay the same to or apply the same for the advancement maintenance education or otherwise howsoever for the benefit of any such beneficiary ________________

AS WITNESS my hand this _____ day of _____ Two thousand and _____

SIGNED by the above-named)
Testator in our presence and)
then by us in his.)

Witness signature	Witness signature ....
Name	Name ....
Address	Address ....
....	....
....	....
Occupation	Occupation ....

19 Variation of trusts

INTRODUCTION

A trustee must carry out the trust according to the terms laid out in the trust instrument. A failure to do so will render him/her liable to an action for breach of trust. It may be, though, that the trustees wish to vary the terms of the trust so as, for example, to give themselves wider powers of investment or to effect tax saving. However, the instrument reflects the wishes of the settlor and so the courts, in the absence of express statutory authority, will only rarely consent to a variation of it. Accordingly, this topic reflects what is often a tension between the wishes of the settlor, as expressed in the trust instrument, those of the beneficiaries (or some of them), and possibly the wishes of the trustees and the present wishes of the settlor, who may have changed her mind.

The circumstances where a variation in the trust may be sought is illustrated by Example 19.1.

Example 19.1

John (23), Eileen (21) and Mary (16) are beneficiaries under which they are each to receive a one-third share of a capital fund provided that they qualify as barristers. They wish this restriction to be removed so that they each receive their share absolutely at the age of 25. The trustees support the application and so does Egbert, who would be entitled to the capital if none of the beneficiaries qualified as barristers.

John and Eileen are both over 21 and of sound mind (the Latin term for this is *in sui juris* as we shall see) and so can apply and give consent themselves. Mary, however, as she is only 16 cannot do so although she is in favour. How can her consent be obtained? This is the issue which emerges in many cases in this chapter. Keep this example in mind as you read through the chapter.

VARIATION OF TRUSTS BY THE TRUSTEES

The trustees may be given express power by the trust instrument to vary the terms of the trust, e.g. dealing with management and administration.

In addition, the rule in *Saunders* v. *Vautier* (1841) can be viewed as an indirect way of varying the terms of a trust. This allows a beneficiary who is:

(a) *sui juris*, of full age (i.e. over 18) and of sound mind; and
(b) is entitled to the whole equitable interest.

to require the trustees to transfer the property to him, or to such other person(s) as he may direct, and so terminate the trust. *Saunders* v. *Vautier* itself concerned a beneficiary under a trust, the terms of which required the trustees to accumulate dividends received on stock until the beneficiary attained the age of 25 and then to transfer the capital and accumulated dividends to him. It was held that he could claim the fund at the age of 21.

Examples of where the rule applies:

(a) Where there are two or more beneficiaries who are *sui juris* and presently entitled (*Stokes* v. *Cheek* (1860)).
(b) Where there are two or more beneficiaries who are *sui juris* and entitled in succession, e.g. if X leaves property to Y for life and then to W and Z in equal shares, then Y, W and Z may, having agreed between themselves on how the property should be divided, require the trustees to act in *accordance* with their directions (*Haynes* v. *Haynes* (1861)).
(c) One beneficiary who is *sui juris* and who has an absolutely vested interest in a share of the trust fund is entitled to have transferred to him a share of every asset of the trust fund which can easily be divided such as cash, money in a bank account and shares, but not land (see Walton J in *Stephenson* v. *Barclays Bank Trust Co Ltd* (1975)). An instance of the application of the rule here is *Lloyds Bank* v. *Duker* (1987) (see Chapter 17), which involved shares in a private company although Walton J in *Stephenson* v. *Barclays Bank* held that the rule would not always apply to these types of shares.
(d) Where all the beneficiaries, being *sui juris,* are entitled under a discretionary trust where the trustees' discretion applies to the amount of the shares rather than who is to benefit. In *Re Smith* (1928) a fund was held to pay, at the trustee's discretion, the whole or any part of the income or capital for the benefit of a lady and any surplus income was to be accumulated. At her death this, together with the remaining capital, was to pass to her children in equal shares. It was held that the rule applied and accordingly a company, to whom all the beneficiaries' interests had been mortgaged, could require the trustees to pay the whole of the income to them.

Examples of where the rule does not apply:

(a) Where the trustees have a discretion as to whether a person is to receive anything at all 'for the whole fund has not been given to him but only so much as the trustees think fit to let him have' (Romer J in *Re Smith*). Thus it is possible that the rule does not apply to discretionary trusts held valid under the individual ascertainability test in *McPhail* v. *Doulton* (1971).
(b) Where some beneficiaries are unidentified, unborn or under age. Thus as Lord Maugham put it in *Berry* v. *Green* (1938): 'the rule has no operation unless the

persons who have any present or contingent interest in the property are *sui juris* and consent'.

(c) To enable the beneficiaries to control the trust while it remains in being as in *Re Brockbank* (1948). Here the court refused to compel one of two trustees of a will, who had the power to appoint new trustees, to agree to the appointment of a new trustee whose appointment was being demanded by the other trustee and all the beneficiaries, all being *sui juris* and absolutely entitled. Similarly it will not allow the beneficiaries to direct the trustees to make particular investments (Walton J in *Stephenson* v. *Barclays Bank* (1975)). Their proper course here is to end the trust under the rule in which case they can, if they wish, establish a new trust.

VARIATION OF TRUSTS BY THE COURT

Miscellaneous powers

Under the inherent jurisdiction of the court

The court has power in cases of emergency to allow the trustees to take action not authorised by the trust instrument, but the jurisdiction seems to be confined to three types of cases:

(i) *Salvage*, i.e. where there is an absolute necessity to incur expenditure, such as mortgaging an infant's property, or to prevent buildings falling down. This is probably the explanation of *Frith* v. *Cameron* (1871), where the court sanctioned the rebuilding of a mansion house where the foundations of the previous house were giving way, as otherwise the estate would not have had a mansion house, but it also shows how the courts have sometimes strained the word 'salvage' beyond its strict meaning. A more straightforward case is *Hibbert* v. *Cooke* (1824), where the testator had begun a house but had not completed it. The court allowed completion out of the trust funds as an act of salvage. Rigby LJ vividly pointed out that 'there was a carcass which would have gone to ruin unless completed'. A case where the court declined jurisdiction was *Re Montagu* (1896), where permission was sought to raise a mortgage on trust property in order to rebuild houses on an estate which were in bad repair. The court held that this was not strictly necessary as an act of salvage. (Note that now under ss. 3(3) and 4 of the TA 2002 trustees have a general power to take mortgages.)

(ii) *Emergency*. Here the jurisdiction is slightly wider and allows the court to vary the terms of a trust to deal with an emergency unforeseen by the settlor. It was used in *Re New* (1901)) to allow the reconstruction of the capital of a company, although in *Re Tollemache* (1903) this was said to be the 'high water mark' of jurisdiction under this head.

(iii) General powers of the court to approve compromises. In *Chapman* v. *Chapman* (1954) it was held that the court can sanction a compromise but only where the rights of the beneficiaries are in dispute. Lord Simonds expressly denied that the courts had any power to use their jurisdiction to approve compromises where there is no real dispute and the reason for seeking the aid of the court is, as he put it, 'to rearrange the beneficial interests under the trust instrument'. The major reason for this was that, according to Lord Simonds, it would be a strange way for court of conscience to execute a trust if it had to override 'the wishes of a living and expostulating settlor'. (It could, however, be remarked that, if fidelity to the settlor's wishes was to be the criterion then the court in *Chapman* should have sanctioned the variation as the settlor was in favour of it!) One example of compromise jurisdiction did arise in the litigation following the thalidomide case (see *Allen* v. *Distillers Co (Biochemicals) Ltd* (1974) – below). However, this is in reality not a variation because the court is simply clarifying rights that were doubtful before. The effect of the decision in *Chapman* was to deny the courts power to use their compromise jurisdiction to to vary trusts, and it is arguable that it actually reduced their powers as there had been a practice whereby the courts sanctioned a compromise, often to save tax, without there being a genuine dispute at all. In the long run the decision in *Chapman* was beneficial as it was clear that this whole area cried out for statutory intervention, as had been pointed out by Lindley LJ in *Re Montagu* (1896): 'it is very desirable that the Courts should have jurisdiction to deal with such a case; but Parliament has never gone so far as to give it that jurisdiction'. In addition we have seen above in the salvage and emergency cases how the courts at times strained these terms in order to give approval to variations. Thus, following *Chapman*, this whole area was referred to the Law Reform Committee. Its report led to the passing of the Variation of Trusts Act (1958) (below).

Under s. 57(1) of the Trustee Act 1925

This allows the court, on the application of the trustees, to confer on the trustees power in the management or administration of the trust to dispose of the trust property by e.g. sale or lease, or to engage in any transaction such as purchase or investment, in any case where this is expedient but there is no power in the trust instrument to do so.

Note 19.1:

- *The basis of the jurisdiction is expediency, not emergency as in (a) (ii) above, and therefore this jurisdiction is wider.*
- *It applies only to matters arising in the management or administration of the trust and so cannot be used to vary beneficial interests.*
- *This power is important in practice and was often used, e.g. to apply for sanction of a wider investment clause as in* Mason *v.* Farbrother *(1983) (see Chapter 17). As an alternative, applications to widen investment powers could be made under the Variation of Trusts Act 1958 as in* Trustees of the British Museum *v.* A-G *(1984) (see Chapter 17). The extension of investment powers of trustees by s. 3 of the Trustee Act 2000 has meant that this particular type of application will probably be made less often. (See also Chapter 17.)*
- *There is no requirement that the beneficiaries must consent to the application.*

Under s. 53 of the Trustee Act 1925

This gives the court power, where a minor is beneficially entitled to property, to make an order appointing a person to dispose of such property with a view to the application of it for the maintenance, education or benefit of the minor. In *Re Meux's Will Trusts* (1958) an arrangement involving the sale of some of a minor's property to reduce estate duty was approved. In all cases any proceeds of sale should be resettled on trust, as happened in *Re Meux*, rather than simply paid outright to the minor. It appears that this power is little used in practice.

Under s. 64(1) of the Settled Land Act 1925

This allows the court to authorise the tenant for life to make any transaction 'affecting or concerning the settled land . . . which in the opinion of the court would be for the benefit of the settled land, or any part thereof, or the persons interested in the settlement'.

This is to some extent the counterpart of s. 57(1) of the Trustee Act 1925 in relation to settlements but it goes wider in allowing not just arrangements concerned with management or administration but alteration (see *Re Downshire Settled Estates* (1953)). Section 64(1) can be, and often is, used to vary beneficial interests to avoid tax liability. In *Hambro* v. *Duke of Marlborough* (1994) an application under s. 64(1) was made by the Duke and the trustees on the basis that the Marquess of Blandford, who was tenant in tail of the remainder, was not sufficiently businesslike and responsible to be able to manage the Blenheim estate. The court agreed and approved a scheme whereby the estate would be held under new trusts under which, on the death of the Duke, the Marquess would have an interest only under a protective trust. (See Chapter 11 for protective trusts.) The fact that the Marquess, as a beneficiary, not only did not consent but opposed the application, was not a bar to its making.

Under s. 24 of the Matrimonial Causes Act 1973

This gives power to the court in granting a decree of divorce, nullity or judicial separation or at any time thereafter to vary ante- or post-nuptial settlements or to extinguish or reduce the interest of either spouse under such a settlement. This topic belongs more to family law than trusts.

Under s. 96(1)(d) of the Mental Health Act 1983

This allows the Court of Protection not only to make a settlement of the patient's property but, having done so, to vary it as the judge thinks fit.

Under the Variation of Trusts Act (VTA) 1958

If the particular situations dealt with above are excluded, then, as a general principle, the courts had little power actually to vary beneficial interests under trusts. Section 1(1) of the VTA, however, gives the court power, on behalf of certain classes of persons, to approve any arrangement 'varying or revoking any of the trusts' which allows variations in beneficial interests to be sanctioned. In addition, s. 11(c) also allows the court, on behalf of the same classes of persons,

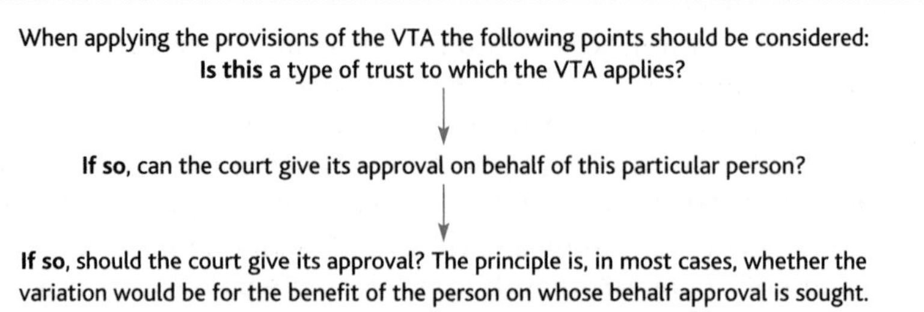

When applying the provisions of the VTA the following points should be considered:
Is this a type of trust to which the VTA applies?
If so, can the court give its approval on behalf of this particular person?
If so, should the court give its approval? The principle is, in most cases, whether the variation would be for the benefit of the person on whose behalf approval is sought.

Figure 19.1 Scheme of the Variation of Trusts Act 1958

to enlarge the trustees' powers of management or administration. The principle behind the way in which the courts operate under the VTA was explained by Lord Reid in *Re Holmden's Settlement Trust* (1966): 'the court does not itself amend or vary the trusts of the original settlement. . . . Each beneficiary is bound because he has consented to the variation. . . . The court merely acted on behalf of or as representing those beneficiaries who were not in a position to give their consent or approval'.

Trusts to which the Act applies

Section 1(1) of the Act states that it applies to trusts arising under 'any will, settlement or other disposition' but this wide language was not held in *Allen* v. *Distillers Co (Biochemicals) Ltd* (1974) to cover the payment out to trustees of money paid into court in settlement of an action brought by minors who had been victims of the thalidomide drug. As the money paid was as damages and belonged absolutely to the minors, the court held that the variation sought, which was the postponement of the minors' entitlement beyond the age of majority, would create a new trust, not vary an existing one. However, it found that the terms of the settlement of the action, to which all the beneficiaries had consented, were wide enough to allow the court to authorise such a postponement.

Classes of persons on whose behalf the court may give approval

It must be emphasised that the Act only allows the court to give approval in the following cases, and if a person is not within these cases then their approval will be necessary to the proposed variation (*Re Suffert's Settlement* (1961) (below)), unless the matter falls within the other exceptions above. This can cause problems where the whereabouts of a beneficiary is unknown. The classes are set out in s. 1(1) of the Act and are:

(a) Section 1(1)(a) infants and persons who by means of (mental) incapacity are incapable of assenting.
(b) Section 1(1)(b), which provides that the court can give approval on behalf of persons, whether ascertained or not, who may become entitled, directly or indirectly, to an interest at a future date or on the happening of a future event, if they answer a specified description or are a member of a specified class. *However, these persons are not included if the future date or event had happened at*

the date of the application to the court. The meaning of the first sentence is clear: these are persons who have only an expectation of succeeding, as indicated by the word 'may', such as a potential future spouse (see *Re Clitheroe's Settlement Trust* (1959)), and whose consent is not therefore needed. On the other hand, those who have a contingent interest are not included and must give their consent. Thus in *Knocker* v. *Youle* (1986) on the facts it was difficult for cousins who had a remote contingent interest to give their consent as there were many of them and not all were easy to locate. However, as the VTA did not apply, their consent was needed.

The second sentence (in italics above) has caused difficulties: its effect is that if e.g. there is a gift to the next-of-kin of X, who is alive, then X is treated as being dead at the date of the application to the court and so the next-of-kin are ascertainable. Thus one effect of s. 1(1)(b) is that the next of kin must consent to an order for variation. Thus in *Re Suffert's Settlement* (1961) the refusal of two cousins, the cousins being the next-of-kin, to consent to an order prevented it from being made.

(c) Section 1(1)(c) persons unborn.
(d) Section 1(1)(d) persons with a discretionary interest under a protective trust, e.g. if property is left to X for life under a protective trust the court can approve an application on behalf of X's wife. An application on behalf of X's children, if minors, could be made under (a) above. This can include those with a contingent interest as in *Re Steed's Will Trusts* (1960) (below), where the court's approval was required on behalf of any future spouse whom the beneficiary might marry.

Making the application

The application should be made by a beneficiary, usually the person who is presently receiving the income, such as the life tenant. The trustees may apply if no one else will and if they are satisfied that the proposals are beneficial to the persons interested and have a good chance of being approved by the court (Russell J in *Re Druce's Settlement Trust* (1953)). The settlor, if alive, should be a defendant.

Principles governing the exercise of the court's jurisdiction

Section 1(1) of the Act provides that the court cannot approve an arrangement on behalf of persons in categories (a), (b) and (c) (see above) unless satisfied that the arrangement is for their benefit. Thus the court must, as it were, stand proxy for that person and, putting itself in their shoes, ask if they would have wished the particular variation to be made. This requirement does not apply to persons in category (d) but even so the court must not simply ignore their interests. Wilberforce J in *Re Burney's Settlement Trusts* (1961) said that the court must exercise its discretion to approve judicially and it is for the applicant to show that there is a need to interfere with the protective trusts.

Meaning of the term 'benefit'

It must be emphasised that, although the cases about to be discussed deal mainly with difficult assessments of competing benefits, most applications under the Act have been straightforward. The term 'benefit' is not defined by the VTA but under s. 1(1) it is provided that 'the court *may as it thinks fit*' (my italics) approve a variation which is, except in case (d) is for the benefit of the beneficiaries. Thus the courts have a considerable discretion but in practice most cases have concerned financial benefit such as tax saving although, as we shall see, other types of benefit have also been enough for an application to succeed. A recent example of a financial benefit other then tax saving is *CD (a minor)* v. *O* (2004), where the court agreed to vary a trust fund for the education of a minor so that she could receive an advancement of the whole sum rather than just half, which is the statutory maximum under s. 32 of the TA 1925 (see also Chapter 18). The court sometimes requires an insurance policy to be taken out to cover risks, as in *Re Robinson's Settlement Trust* (1976) (see below). In *Goulding* v. *James* (1997) the court approved the statement of Ungoed-Thomas J in *Re Van Gruisen's Will Trusts* (1964) that where there is financial benefit approval will not necessarily follow. A 'practical and business like consideration' of the arrangement is needed, looking at the total advantages which each party obtains, including their bargaining strength.

(a) *Financial benefit.* This often means a benefit in the form of tax-saving. In *Re Weston's Settlement Trust* (1969) Denning MR observed that 'nearly every variation that has come before this court has tax-avoidance for its principal object'. One example is a division of property between a life tenant and a remainderman which can mean a saving in inheritance tax (IHT).
(b) *Moral and social benefit.* In *Re Holt's Settlement* (1969) Megarry J approved a variation which postponed the absolute vesting of interests from the age of 21 to 30 and concurred with the life tenant's argument that it was 'most important that young people should be reasonably advanced in a career and settled in life before they were in receipt of an income sufficient to make them independent of the need to work'. There were, in fact, financial advantages in the variation such as savings in estate duty (the predecessor of IHT). A similar decision was reached *Re T's Settlement Trust* (1964), where the interest of an irresponsible and immature minor, which would have been vested in a few months, was varied so that the capital was held on protective trusts until she reached a later age.

In *Re Weston's Settlement Trust* (1969) Lord Denning's ground for refusing consent to a variation was based on considerations other than financial. The court refused to sanction a removal of trusts from England to Jersey because, in Lord Denning's view, the tax advantages of a move were outweighed by the educational and social advantages to the children, who were beneficiaries, of being brought up in England and the court was concerned by the danger of the children's lives being organised purely round tax saving considerations. (The reasoning behind this decision is considered further below.) However, in many other cases the court has approved an arrangement which exported a trust to another country (e.g. *Re Seale's Marriage Settlement* (1961)). It is probable that the court in *Weston* was influenced by the doubt as to whether the settlor and the children, who were the beneficiaries, were going to settle permanently in Jersey, whereas in *Re Seale* the beneficiaries were permanently resident abroad.

In *Re CL* (1969) the court probably went as far as is possible in disregarding financial benefits in favour of other benefits. A scheme was approved under which an elderly mental patient made in effect a gift of her life interest to her adopted daughter. The patient did not need the interest, as she was well cared for anyway and it was likely that this arrangement, which saved tax, was what she would have made herself. The benefit to her was, in essence, a moral one.

(c) *Benefit through avoidance of family trouble.* A good example is *Re Remnant's Settlement Trusts* (1970), where the court approved the deletion of a clause under which children who became Roman Catholics or who married Roman Catholics forfeited their interests. Some children were Roman Catholics but others were Protestants and the latter would clearly benefit if the clause remained. Nevertheless, the court, in approving its deletion, said that the clause could cause family dissension as well as possibly hindering the selection of a spouse.

Taking of risks

In *Re Robinson's Settlement Trust* (1976) Templeman J said that the test was whether an adult beneficiary would have taken the risk. One should take a broad view, but not a 'galloping gambling view'. Here, a variation would be beneficial to a child beneficiary if her mother (now aged 55) lived for a reasonable period of time. If the mother died immediately the variation would not be beneficial. The court approved the variation subject to a policy of insurance being taken out to protect the infant's interest.

Intentions of the settlor

It is probable that where an arrangement is considered clearly beneficial it will be sanctioned, even though such a variation is not in accordance with the settlor's intentions. In any event, as mentioned above, the settlor, if alive, should be a defendant to the application.

In *Re Steed's Will Trusts* (1960) Evershed MR emphasised that the intentions of the settlor must be considered. Here a testator had left his property to his housekeeper on protective trusts to prevent her from 'being sponged upon by one of her brothers'. The court refused to sanction the removal of the protective element, which would mean that she would be absolutely entitled to the trust property, because this would undermine the testator's intention that she should not be exposed to risk. The decision is thus an interesting example of where the wishes of the settlor prevailed over the clearly expressed wishes of the beneficiary. However, in *Re Remnant* (1970) (above) the fact that the deletion of the forfeiture clause would defeat the settlor's intention, although considered to be an important point, did not prevent its deletion. In *Goulding* v. *James* (1997) property was left to the testatrix's daughter for life with remainder to her grandson, then aged 32, contingent on his reaching the age of 40. This was because she felt that he had not yet settled down. If he did not reach 40, or if he predeceased his mother, then his share would go to the testatrix's great-grandchildren. The court approved a proposal that 90 per cent of the capital would go immediately to the daughter and grandson equally and the other 10 per cent would be put into trust for the great-grandchildren. It was held that the benefit to the great-grandchildren would increase, as they received an actual share rather than just an expectancy, and this outweighed the fact that the change was clearly contrary to the wishes of the settlor.

The attitude of the courts: some thoughts

Lord Simonds' approach in *Chapman* v. *Chapman* (1954) at least had the merit of consistency in that it insisted that the words of the trust instrument had priority over any other values whether expressed by the beneficiaries, the trustees, the court or even those of the settlor at the time of the application. Once away from this firm, if too restrictive principle, it then becomes difficult to see precisely where the courts are to start in acting under the VTA.

The relevant words of the VTA are that, if the court considers that there is benefit, then the words in the VTA (s. 1(1)) 'as it thinks fit' give it a considerable discretion in deciding if to grant approval. What conclusions can be drawn from the cases on how this discretion has been exercised?

It is of course wrong for the judges to impose their own value judgments onto the application, although Denning MR came close to doing so in *Re Weston* when, in refusing the application to move trusts from England to Jersey, he observed that 'There are many things in life more worthwhile than money. One of these things is to be brought up in this our England, which is still "the envy of less happier lands"'. Too much can be made of this, however, as the reason for the decision as the *ratio* was, in effect, that tax saving is not necessarily a sufficient benefit for the court to give its approval. However, this has been precisely the reason for so many successful applications and if *Re Weston* rests on not exposing the children to a completely materialistic lifestyle by shunting them around the world to save tax, then is this what the courts should be about or is it just paternalism gone too far? A similar point can be made about the decision in *Re Holt*: character building is an excellent thing but once the courts make moral judgments of this kind where will it stop?

Another difficulty is that the judges may move away from the essential question: is this a benefit which the person on whose behalf consent is sought would have wanted? *Re CL* (above) is a good example of the court trying to grapple with this issue. Yet again, can the decision in *Re Remnant* be supported on the proxy principle? The problem is that the VTA says nothing about the precise issue in that case: where a proposed variation is beneficial for some but not all beneficiaries.

Limit to the court's power

The court has power under the Act to vary trusts but not to resettle trust property. In *Re Ball's Settlement* (1968) Megarry J said that the test for deciding whether the changes sought did amount to a variation was whether the whole substratum of the trust was changed. However, it is difficult to find evidence from the cases that this distinction has caused any problems for the court and, and as we have seen, in many cases the variation was substantial.

When is the variation actually made?

Does the order made by the court actually bring the variation into effect or does it merely consent to the beneficiaries doing so? If the court makes the order then there is no disposition of equitable interests within the meaning of s. 53(1)(c) of the LPA 1925 (see Chapter 6) and so there is no need for the consent of the beneficiaries in writing. However, in *IRC* v. *Holmden* (1968) Lord Reid said that the variation was made by the beneficiaries. However, beneficiaries normally give consent orally through counsel and so if Lord Reid is correct s. 53(1)(c) is not complied with. In *Re Holt's ST* Megarry J felt that the VTA could be construed so that it was the court which made the variation. Even if it was made by the beneficiaries, he felt that if there was consideration for the variation and thus a contract then this contract would be capable of specific performance and so the consenting adult beneficiaries would hold their original interests on a constructive trust in favour of those who would benefit. As s. 53(2) of the LPA exempts constructive trusts from the requirements of s. 53(1)(c), writing is not needed. (It will be recalled that this argument was put forward in *Oughtred* v. *IRC* (1960) – see Chapter 5.) The point remains undecided.

FURTHER READING

Harris (1975) *Variation of Trusts*, London: Sweet & Maxwell. This is an excellent general survey of this area.

CHAPTER SUMMARY

- Variation of trusts by the trustees.
- Rule in *Saunders* v. *Vautier.*
- Variation by the court under general powers: miscellaneous and statutory.
- Problems caused by the decision in *Chapman* v. *Chapman.*
- Variation by the court under the Variation of Trusts Act 1958.
- Persons on whose behalf the court can consent.
- Meaning of the term 'benefit'.
- Significance of the intentions of the settlor.

QUESTION

To what extent do you consider that the courts, when considering applications to vary the beneficial interests under trusts, give adequate weight to the wishes of the settlor and the interests of competing beneficiaries?

> ***Note 19.2:*** *You will find suggested points for inclusion in this answer in Appendix 2.*

20 Breach of trust

INTRODUCTION

Trustees are in breach of trust if they fail to observe the duties laid on them by equity and by the trust instrument. Various examples of breaches of trust can be found in the previous chapters, e.g. purchasing trust property without authority, investing in unauthorised investments.

REMEDIES OF THE BENEFICIARY: A SUMMARY

Actions *in rem* and actions *in personam*

The various remedies which we are about to consider may seem complex but this is because they are designed to cover different situations. These examples illustrate this.

Example 20.1

A trustee has, of course, a duty to invest the trust property and in this case a trustee of £5 million, without taking advice, invests all of it in a small company on the advice of an inexperienced financial advisor who predicts that the company will do well. In fact all of the money is lost when it goes into liquidation. The beneficiaries are, of course, entitled to a remedy but the position is not straightforward as they may not be entitled to all of the money back. It may be that there was a reason for investing some of the money in that company but not all of it, or it may be that, on the facts, there was no liability at all as the advice was not negligent. Whatever the outcome, the point is that the remedy is for money compensation and is against the trustee personally (*in personam*).

Example 20.2

A trustee of money in a bank account in the name of the trust wrongfully withdraws that money and puts it in his own bank account. The beneficiaries have a straightforward remedy: the return of the money. This is remedy *in rem*, i.e. against the thing itself, here the restitution of the money.

Therefore an action *in personam* may be brought against the trustee for damages for breach of trust, but an action *in rem* may be brought to recover the trust property. The effect of this action is that a beneficiary can, as we shall see, sometimes trace trust property into the hands of a transferee and recover it, but not where it is in the hands of a *bona fide* purchaser of the legal estate for value without notice of the beneficiary's equitable right. The right to bring an action *in rem* is important where the trustee or transferee is insolvent because the beneficiary can claim the property in preference to other creditors.

REMEDIES FOR BREACH OF TRUST: A SUMMARY

(a) Compensation for breach of trust, as in Example 20.1.
(b) Restitution of unauthorised profits.
(c) Liability to account as a constructive trustee where there is a right to trace trust property into that person's hands, as in Example 20.2.
(d) Personal liability as a constructive trustee to make restitution of trust property.
(e) Liability of a person who has assisted in breach of trust.
(f) An injunction to restrain a breach of trust.

All of these, with the exception of injunctions, which were considered in Chapter 2, will be looked at now.

Compensation for breach of trust

The principles governing the assessment of compensation are illustrated by the following examples.

Example 20.3

X, a trustee has parted with trust property to the value of £10,000 in breach of trust. Here the issue is whether compensation should be paid on the same basic principles as at common law, i.e. X should be liable for loss to the trust which was reasonably foreseeable, or whether X should simply be liable to make restitution of the property. This is considered below.

Example 20.4

Y, a trustee has been guilty of negligence in the administration of the trust by failing to review investments at proper intervals. In this case the rules on liability must obviously be the same as for negligence at common law with, in particular, a requirement of forseeability.

The leading case is *Target Holdings Ltd* v. *Redferns* (1995). The claimant, a finance company, lent £1.7 million to a company, Crowngate Developments, on the security of two properties which were in fact being purchased for only £775,000 but appeared to be purchased for £2 million. In short, there was mortgage fraud. Redferns acted for both parties and they received the mortgage advance on trust for the claimant to release it to Crowngate when the transfers of the properties were executed. However, in breach of trust they released it early, on the day before contracts were exchanged. Crowngate subsequently went into liquidation, and the claimant sold the properties for only £500,000. They claimed against Redferns for their loss on the transaction but failed. The House of Lords held that the principle in assessing compensation for breach of trust in commercial dealings such as this, bearing in mind that the solicitor was only a bare trustee, is that a trustee is only liable for losses caused by the breach and not for losses which would have occurred in any event. Thus, here although the solicitors, the trustees, had acted in breach of trust by releasing the funds early the claimants did obtain the mortgage securities which it would have obtained anyway. The early release of the funds did not decide if the mortgage would go through, and it was this which had caused the loss. On the other hand, Lord Browne-Wilkinson felt that in traditional family trusts beneficiaries are entitled to a restoration of the fund.

There is, however, a view that this decision overlooks the need for the trustee to account to the beneficiary for property which has been misapplied and until then the trustee cannot be discharged. (See e.g. Millett (1998).) However, as he points out, in *Target* the trustee could be said to have restored the trust property (i.e. the money held by Redferns) but in a different form (i.e. in the form of the charge which was later executed). It is interesting that the High Court in Australia has applied this principle in *Youyang Pty Ltd* v. *Minter Ellison Morris Fletcher* (2003) (see Ellliott and Edelman (2003)).

This decision in *Target* was applied in *Swindle* v. *Harrison* (1997). A firm of solicitors made a bridging loan to a client to enable a purchase of a house, which was to be used as a hotel, to go through. Later the hotel business failed and the client claimed that, as the solicitors were in breach of duty by failing to disclose that they would be receiving commission on the loan, they were liable for all the loss which she had suffered through completing the purchase. The Court of Appeal rejected this on the ground that she would have gone through with the purchase anyway. Evans LJ did, however, hold that had the breach of trust been fraudulent there would have been liability for all loss, even that not caused by the breach. A distinction was therefore drawn between the extent of liability for fraudulent and non-fraudulent breach of trust which one hopes will not lead to fine distinctions in the future.

Restitution of unauthorised profits

The vital word here is restitution. This term has caused difficulty in the past due to its being used in connection with compensation, as indeed occurred in *Target Holdings* (above). As Birks (1985) has observed, restitution is concerned with 'gains to be given up, not losses to be made good'. Thus restitution should be confined to the type of situation with which we are now dealing.

The essence of restitution is that, unlike compensation, which is personal, it is a proprietary remedy against, in this context, trust profits in the hands of a trustee. As it is proprietary, it will rank before the claims of creditors if the trustee is insolvent, whereas a personal claim for compensation will rank alongside personal claims of creditors.

A restitutionary claim will be appropriate when the trustee is in breach of a fiduciary duty as distinct from one of the specific duties under the trust, such as a duty to invest. Whereas a compensatory remedy is appropriate when there is a breach of a specific duty, breach of a fiduciary duty brings with it a duty to restore unauthorised profits to the trust. As we saw in Chapter 11, fiduciaries owe a duty not to profit from their position as fiduciaries and, if they do so, they will hold the profits on a constructive trust to restore them.

It may not be easy to decide whether a compensatory or restitutionary remedy is appropriate and, indeed the two may overlap. Here the claimant must elect between the two. In *Tang Man Sit* v. *Capacious Investments Ltd* (1996) a joint venture for the development of land allowed the defendant to provide the land and the claimants to provide the funding. It was agreed that the defendant would assign the title to 16 of the houses to the claimants. In breach of trust, the defendant did not perform their part of the bargain. It was held that the claimants could either:

(i) claim the profits (i.e. restitutionary) which the defendant made when he let the houses out himself, or
(ii) claim compensation for the rent which they could have received had the houses been assigned to them and they had the opportunity to let them.

Liability as a constructive trustee where there is a right to trace trust property into that person's hands

The term tracing, as with restitution, is often misunderstood. It is not a remedy as such but a right to trace (i.e. follow) trust property into the hands of a person who then becomes a constructive trustee of it. Thus, tracing leads to a proprietary remedy and it is the imposition of a trust which gives rise to the remedy as this gives rise to the equitable right. Tracing is therefore more of a process and the basic idea is illustrated by the following example.

Example 20.5

Maria is treasurer of the Hanbury Begonia Society. She is allowed to sign cheques on behalf of the society and she wrongly pays £1,000 of the society's money into her own bank account and uses another £5,000 to buy herself a new suite of furniture.

The fraud is discovered and Maria is imprisoned. However, the members want their funds back. Tracing is the process by which they follow their money both into the bank account and into the property which was bought with trust funds.

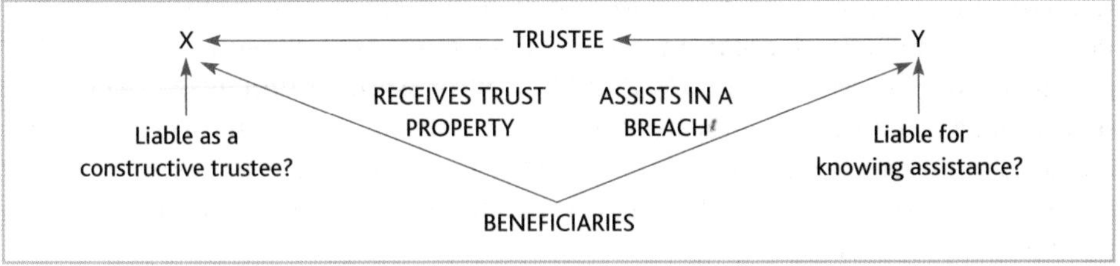

Figure 20.1 Liability of trustees

The details of how tracing is accomplished are set out later in this chapter but here it is important to establish the persons against whom there is a right to trace. These are anyone except a *bona fide* purchaser of the trust property for value without notice that it was trust property. The term 'notice' means either actual knowledge that it was trust property (actual notice) or constructive notice (knowledge which an honest and reasonable person in their position would have had – see *Kingsnorth Trust Ltd* v. *Tizard* (1986) in Chapter 4).

Where a person is a volunteer (i.e. they have not provided consideration (value) for the property) then they will be liable to return it to the beneficiaries even though they had no notice that it was transferred to them in breach of trust. There is doubt whether it is right to label volunteers constructive trustees pending the return of the property as liability as a constructive trustee is fault based. Whatever the label, there is no doubt that, pending its return, they hold the property subject to the equitable interests of the beneficiaries.

Personal liability as a constructive trustee to make restitution of trust property

This remedy, which is often known as liability for 'dishonest receipt of trust property', will be the appropriate one, rather then the remedy, where the recipient no longer has the trust property, or it has depreciated in value, or the recipient has made a profit from the use of that property. Here liability is based on fault, although the principles are different from those and are considered below.

It should be noted that Millett J (1991), considers that to label a person in these circumstances a constructive trustee is 'profoundly mistaken'. He considers that whether or not 'a recipient has retained or parted with the property his liability remains the same, i.e. the receipt of trust property to which he is not entitled' and he views this liability as arising under a resulting, rather than a constructive, trust.

The courts have found difficulty in establishing an all-embracing principle for determining when a stranger who has received trust property can be liable. In *Baden Delvaux and Lecuit* v. *Société Générale* (1987) Peter Gibson J proposed five categories which stretched to 'knowledge of circumstances which would put an honest and reasonable man on enquiry'. This gets close to the test for constructive notice in land law. There has, in more recent years, been a move away from this. Edmund Davies LJ in *Carl Zeiss Stiftung* v. *Herbert Smith & Co (No. 2)* (1969), referred to the need for a 'want of probity', a phrase also used by Megarry V-C in *Re Montagu* (1896). In *Royal Brunei Airlines* v. *Tan* (1995) the Privy Council held that the liability of the third party depended on dishonesty although this was a dishonest assistance case. However, Lord Millett in *Twinsectra* v. *Yardley* (2002) strongly dissented from this view and held that 'liability for knowing receipt is receipt based. It does not depend on fault'. The action was, he held, restitutionary, in line with his views expressed earlier (see above). The majority held, however, that fault was required but the issue is precisely what degree of fault. The present law is probably best summed up by the decision in *Bank of Credit and Commerce International (Overseas) Ltd* v. *Akindele* (2000), where Nourse LJ held that dishonesty was not required and there should be a single test of knowledge: did 'the recipient's state of knowledge . . . make it unconscionable for him to retain the benefit of the receipt?'

Liability of a person who has assisted in a breach of trust

Here there is no acquisition of trust property and so it is incorrect to speak of such a person as a constructive trustee. The remedy is a personal one against the wrongdoer and is called liability for 'dishonest assistance' in a breach of trust.

Once again the issue is the degree of knowledge required. In *Royal Brunei Airlnes* v. *Tan* (1995) Lord Nicholls held that the accessory's liability should depend on whether he had been dishonest and he disliked the idea that liability could depend on unconscionability, a term which, he felt, meant little to anyone but equity lawyers. In *Twinsectra Ltd* v. *Yardley* (2002) the House of Lords held that a person will not be dishonest unless it is established that his conduct had been dishonest by the ordinary standards of reasonable and honest people and that he realised that by those standards his conduct was dishonest. This test may prove difficult to apply in practice and there may be something to be said for Millett J's observation in *Agip (Africa) Ltd* v. *Jackson* (1992) that the distinction between honesty and dishonesty is 'essentially a jury question'.

A final point is that in *Metall und Rohstoff AG* v. *Donaldson Lufkin & Jenrette Inc* (1989) it was held that no action lay in tort for procuring a breach of trust. Gatehouse J held that as a person who procures a breach of trust himself becomes liable as a constructive trustee, a beneficiary does not need the extra protection of an action in tort.

Position where land is sold in breach of trust

The position where land is sold in breach of trust is complex and detailed consideration really belongs to land law. The following is a brief summary. If there are two or more trustees or a trust corporation and the purchaser pays the purchase money to them then, by s. 27 of the LPA 1925, the beneficiaries' interests under the trust would be overreached and the purchaser would take free of them even if they had notice of them. The beneficiaries would be able to trace the proceeds of sale against the trustees and claim those, but would not have any claim on the land (see also *City of London Building Society* v. *Flegg* (1988)). If a single trustee disposes of unregistered land in breach of trust, then whether or not a purchaser is bound will depend on if he had actual, constructive or imputed notice of the beneficiaries' interests, provided that he is also *bona fide* and has given value. If title to the land is registered, then the beneficiaries' interests may be binding on a purchaser if they are overriding interests e.g. if the beneficiaries are in actual occupation *of* the land (see *Williams and Glyn's Bank Ltd* v. *Boland* (1981)) and the Land Registration Act 2000, especially Schedule 3, para. 2).

Unjust enrichment

Although not strictly part of equity, the topic of unjust enrichment needs a mention here. It has appeared in Commonwealth cases on the family home (see Chapter 12), and it now forms a distinct part of the law whereby a defendant who is unjustly enriched at the expense of the claimant can claim redress on the basis of unjust enrichment. One example is where a person receives money paid to her on the basis of a mistake of fact. Here there may be a claim to restore it. The link with equity, if any, arises when it sought to establish a proprietary right to the money. Suppose that the recipient is bankrupt? Can the money be claimed by the person who provided it in preference to the recipient's creditors? The answer is yes if there is a fiduciary relationship between the giver and the receiver, but probably not otherwise. There is a need for clear principles to be worked out here. The whole topic is dealt with by Birks (2005).

Trustee *de son tort*

This is sometimes considered a separate category of liability (see A.L. Smith LJ in *Mara* v. *Browne* (1896)). The unauthorised assumption of trusteeship is not by itself a ground of liability but if the person continues to act as a trustee he will be liable in the same way as any other trustee and so here discussion of the extent of his knowledge as a separate issue will be irrelevant.

TRACING

Remember that, as was explained earlier, the term tracing, as with restitution, is often misunderstood. It is not a remedy as such but a right to trace (i.e. follow) trust property into the hands of a person who then becomes a constructive trustee of it.

Tracing at common law

The right of recovery of a specific chattel was recognised by s. 78 of the Common Law Procedure Act 1854. What if the chattel had been sold? Could the proceeds of sale be recovered? In *Taylor* v. *Plumer* (1815) Lord Ellenborough held that if the money could be identified as the proceeds of sale, then it could be traced and recovered. In that case, money handed over to a stockbroker to buy exchequer bonds had instead been used to buy investments and bullion with which the stockbroker intended to abscond. Tracing was allowed. However, the common law right is limited in the following ways:

(a) It probably does not allow tracing where the money representing the proceeds of sale has been mixed with other money. (See *Agip (Africa) Ltd* v. *Jackson* (1989).)
(b) It does not allow a beneficiary under a trust to trace as no one with an equitable interest can trace at common law. Even so, the beneficiary can compel the trustee, under the principle in *Re Brogden* (1888) (see Chapter 16), to take any necessary steps to recover a trust asset.

Tracing in equity

The limitations on tracing at common law and especially the impossibility of tracing into a mixed fund, mean that the equitable right is far more important. However, as explained above, the equitable right to trace ends when the property comes into the hands of a *bona fide* purchaser for value without notice of the plaintiff's rights. The following are the requirements for tracing in equity.

(a) Fiduciary relationship. Clearly a beneficiary under an existing trust can trace but the courts have extended the concept of a fiduciary relationship further than this. In *Elders Pastoral Ltd* v. *Bank of New Zealand* (1990) the court held that a fiduciary relationship was not necessary and unconscionability was the key requirement. In practice the requirement of a fiduciary relationship is easily satisfied in cases of commercial fraud because whenever an employee of a company wrongfully takes property they will be in breach of a fiduciary duty.

    In *Aluminium Industrie Vaassen BV* v. *Romalpa Aluminium Ltd* (1976) it was held that the incorporation of a reservation of title clause in a contract for the sale of goods, providing that the goods should remain the property of the seller until the purchase price has been paid, enabled the seller to trace the proceeds of sale of those goods and recover this money in priority to the buyer's other creditors when the buyer became insolvent. The reservation of title clause meant that when the buyer resold the goods he did so as the seller's agent and this created a fiduciary relationship.

    In *Re Diplock* (1948) the defendant by will gave the residue of his property on trust for charitable benevolent objects. This was held not to be charitable in *Chichester Diocesan Fund* v. *Simpson* (1944) (see Chapter 13) but the executors previously thought that it was and so had distributed money to various charities. The next-of-kin were allowed to trace the money into the hands of the charities. The court held that provided there is an initial fiduciary relationship the beneficial owner of an equitable interest in property can trace it into the hands of anyone except a *bona fide* purchaser for value without notice. Here the initial fiduciary relationship was between the next-of-kin and the executors. One case where there is no fiduciary relationship and thus no right to trace is where money is stolen by a thief. The requirement of a fiduciary relationship was described by Millett J (extra-judicially in 1991) as 'difficult to understand and impossible to defend' and he also suggested that in this situation the thief could be liable on a resulting trust. In *Foskett* v. *McKeown* (2000) Lord Millett (as he had then become) returned to this theme by observing that there was no logical justification for insisting on this requirement and that, in addition, there should be the same rules for tracing both in common law and in equity.

(b) Equitable proprietary interest. A beneficiary under a trust clearly has such an interest and, as with fiduciary relationships, this concept too has been extended as in the above cases. It is not clear whether a legal, as distinct from an equitable owner, can trace in equity. In principle there seems no reason why not and in the *Romalpa* case (above) tracing by a legal owner was accepted although without any argument on the point.

(c) Tracing would not be inequitable. In *Re Diplock* money had been spent on alterations to buildings and the erection of new buildings. It was held that it would be inequitable to allow tracing here with the result that a charge on the land would be imposed and an innocent volunteer might have to sell his own land.

(d) The property must be in a traceable form. If the trustee has sold trust property and still has the proceeds of sale then the beneficiary can take them if they are identifiable. If the trustee has used the proceeds to buy other property then the beneficiary can follow this and either take the property bought or have a charge on it for the amount of trust money used to buy it (Jessel MR in *Re Hallett's Estate* (1880)). If, however, the money has been spent, e.g. on a holiday, then it is no longer identifiable and equity can give no remedy. In *Re Diplock* money which had been used to discharge a charity's debts was not traceable because the repayment had extinguished the debt.

Mixed funds

The issue of identification arises most often where the trustee has mixed trust money with other money. The rules here are:

(a) Position between trustee and beneficiary. Beneficiaries have a first charge over the mixed fund or any property bought with it. It is for the trustee to show that a particular part of the trust fund is his own.

(b) Position as between two or more trusts or a trust and an innocent volunteer. Where a trustee has mixed funds belonging to two or more trusts, or has transferred funds to an innocent volunteer, then the trusts, or the trust and the volunteer, share in ***pari passu*** (in proportion to the amount contributed by each) in both the mixed funds and property bought with them.

(c) Bank accounts. Mixing is most likely to take place in bank accounts and the following rules apply:

    (i) Position between a trustee and a beneficiary. In *Re Hallett's Estate* (1880) the rule was established that when making withdrawals from an account a trustee is presumed to spend his own money first. Once the amount in the account falls below the amount of trust funds then it is assumed that part of the trust funds must have been spent. Any later payments in are not treated as repayments of the trust money unless the trustee has shown an intention to do this (*Roscoe* v. *Winder* (1915)).

Example 20.6 illustrates the process of tracing.

Example 20.6

A trustee (X) puts £10,000 of trust money and £3,000 of his own money into the trust account. He takes out £11,000 and spends it. £3,000 of this is presumed to be his own money, but the remainder must be trust money. Therefore there is now £2,000 of trust money left. He then puts £3,000 into the account. This is presumed to be his own money unless X shows an intention to repay the trust money. If he does not then although the beneficiaries can claim the £2,000 in the account they will have to take their place along with X's other creditors in a claim for the balance.

In *Re Oatway* (1903) it was held that if a trustee mixes his own and trust money in an account and then takes all the money and spends it on identifiable property the beneficiaries have a first charge on this property for the recovery of the trust money. If the rule in *Re Hallett* applied to this situation the trustee, being presumed to have spent his own money first, would be treated as owner of the property as it was bought with his own money. Thus *Re Oatway* (1903) establishes a different principle here.

In *Foskett* v. *McKeown* (2002) Lord Millett has clarified the position as against the defaulting trustee. He held that where trust money is mixed with the trustee's own money then the beneficiary is 'entitled to locate his contribution in any part of the mixture' and to subordinate the claims of the defaulting trustee and their successors to those of the beneficiary.

Suppose that the property bought has increased in value. Is the charge limited to the amount of trust money spent on the purchase? In *Re Hallett* Jessel MR indicated that this was so but in *Re Tilley's Will Trust* (1967) it was said, *obiter*, that beneficiaries would be entitled to any profit to the extent that it resulted from the use of trust money. Any other rule would allow a dishonest trustee to profit from his breach of trust. It has now been confirmed by the House of Lords in *Foskett* v. *McKeown* (2000) that where the trust fund has increased in value then the beneficiary may claim either: (a) a share in the fund in proportion to which the original trust fund bore to the mixed fund at the date when it was mixed; or (b) they may have a lien on the fund to secure a personal claim against the fund for the return of the money (per Lord Millett).

Thus any increase in value can be claimed under option (a) but if the fund has decreased in value, then the beneficiaries can have a lien under option (b) for the amount that they are owed. In *Foskett*, trust money was wrongly used to pay for two life insurance premiums which were paid just before the death of the trustee. The amount wrongly paid in was just over £20,000 and the value of the policy was just over £1 million. The beneficiaries were entitled to 40 per cent of this, which was the amount which their trust fund bore to the total fund.

(ii) Position where mixed funds in an account represent the funds of two or more trusts or the funds of a trust and an innocent volunteer. We are concerned here with two types of competing claim: (a) between two or more persons with a right to trace; (b) between a person with a right to trace and an innocent volunteer. The rule in *Clayton's Case* (1816) provides that in the case of an active continuing bank account the trustee is regarded as having taken out of the fund whatever had been first put in: 'first in, first out'.

The position where funds are mixed is illustrated by Example 20.7.

Example 20.7

X, a trustee, puts £1,000 of trust A money into a bank account on 1 June and £500 of trust B money into the same account on 2 June. There is now a total of £1,500 trust money in the account. X then takes out £1,200, and, in breach of trust, spends this. As the trust A money was put in first he is presumed to have taken all of this out together with £200 of trust B money. The remaining £300 belongs to trust B.

In *Barlow Clowes International* v. *Vaughan* (1992) the rule in *Clayton's Case* (1816) was not applied to claims by investors to share in the assets of a company which had managed investment plans for them. The investments were in a collective scheme by which investors' money was mixed together and invested in a common fund and it was held to be wrong that those who invested first could expect least. In fact, the date when investments were actually received often depended on agents combining the investments of a number of clients and forwarding a lump sum to the company. The court held that the rule in *Clayton's Case* is only one of convenience and would therefore be displaced here and instead investors would share rateably in the company's assets in proportion to the amounts due to them. In the recent case *of Russell-Cooke Trust Co* v. *Prentis* (2002) many hundreds of investors paid money to a firm of solicitors run by Prentis to be invested in short-term high interest mortgages. The Law Society intervened and Prentis was struck off. How were the funds remaining in the client account of Prentis to be distributed? Here there was the extra problem which did not apply in the *Barlow Clowes* case (above) that how much of each investor's money had been used in particular investments was unknown. Thus it was held inappropriate to apply *Clayton's Case* and instead the mortgage investments were held rateably for each investor according to the proportion to which they had contributed capital.

PERSONAL ACTION AGAINST RECIPIENTS OF TRUST PROPERTY (ACTION *IN PERSONAM*)

A personal action may be brought in equity against recipients of trust property for repayment for the sum owing but, surprisingly, no interest can be claimed. Thus in *Re Diplock* (1948) a personal action against the charities succeeded. The personal representative can base the claim on a mistake of fact or law. There are the following limitations on this type of action:

(a) It cannot be brought against a bona fide purchaser of the legal estate without notice.
(b) It is limited to claims arising out of the administration of estates as in *Re Diplock*.
(c) The claim is limited to the amount which cannot be recovered from the personal representative because e.g. he is insolvent or is protected by s. 27 of the Trustee Act 1925 or has acted under a *Benjamin* or other court order. (See Chapter 17.)

PERSONAL LIABILITY OF TRUSTEES

A trustee is liable for breaches of trust committed by him, but is not vicariously liable for breaches committed by other trustees. Thus in *Re Lucking* (1967) (see Chapter 16) the fact that one trustee was liable for failing to supervise the managing director of the company did not mean that his co-trustee was liable. However, a trustee can be personally liable if he stands by while his co-trustee commits a breach of trust, or if he leaves funds under the control of a co-trustee without making proper enquiry as to what he is doing with them (*Bahin* v. *Hughes* (1886)).

Liability for breaches before and after appointment

A trustee is not liable for breaches committed before his appointment. However, if there is evidence that breaches have been committed, then a new trustee can be liable if he/she fails to take steps against those responsible. A trustee remains liable after retirement for breaches committed by him during his time as trustee. However, it is possible for the trustee, when he retires, to be released from liability by either the trustees or by all the beneficiaries, so long as they are of full age and capacity and in possession of all the material facts.

A trustee will not be liable for breaches committed after his retirement unless he retired in order assist in a breach of trust taking place (*Head* v. *Gould* (1898)).

Liability between trustees

The general principle is that one trustee is not liable for the acts of another trustee (*Townley* v. *Sherborne* (1633)). However, although all are individually liable for their own actual breaches, when it comes to paying compensation for breaches to the beneficiaries, they are jointly and severally liable and the fundamental equitable rule is that no regard is taken of fault. Therefore, a trustee who was actively involved in the breach and a completely passive trustee are equally liable. Accordingly, a beneficiary can sue one or some or all of them and recover the entire loss from those trustees against whom he brings the action. (See *Bahin* v. *Hughes* (1886)). An innocent trustee who has paid compensation for the breach of a fraudulent trustee can then claim a contribution against the fraudulent trustee for the compensation that he has paid.

This rule is modified by the Civil Liability (Contribution) Act 1978, which provides that the amount recoverable from any defendant shall be such as may be found by the court just and equitable, having regard to the extent of that person's responsibility for the damage in question. It is probable that the old equitable rule that a fraudulent trustee is solely liable and cannot claim any contribution from his fellow trustees (*Bahin* v. *Hughes* (1886)) has survived the Act.

The Act does not, however, apply to cases where one trustee is liable to indemnify his fellow trustees and this applies in the following cases:

(a) A trustee who is also a beneficiary must indemnify his co-trustee to the extent of his beneficial interest (*Chillingworth* v. *Chambers* (1896)). After that property has been used to meet the claim, liability can be shared according to the Act.
(b) Where one trustee is a solicitor and the breach was committed solely as a result of his advice, then he must indemnify his co-trustee against any damages which they have had to pay as a result of the breach of trust (*Re Partington* (1887)).
(c) Where the trustee has obtained trust property and used it for his own fraudulent purposes (*Bahin* v. *Hughes*).

Liability for losses on improper investments

This is dealt with in Chapter 17.

Criminal liability of trustees

A breach of trust is not a crime at common law precisely because the common law regarded the trustee as the owner of the trust property. However, statute law first made breach of trust a crime in 1857 and the law is now contained in the Theft Act 1968. Section 1 of this Act defines theft as the dishonest appropriation of property belonging to another with the intention of permanently depriving the other of it, and under s. 5(2), any person with a right to enforce the trust (e.g. a beneficiary) is regarded as a person to whom the trust property belongs. Thus in this slightly roundabout way where trustees take trust property and treat it as their own this is theft from the beneficiaries.

Protection of trustees

(a) Section 61 of the Trustee Act 1925 provides that the court may relieve a trustee from liability if he has acted honestly and reasonably and ought fairly to be excused both for the breach and for omitting to obtain the directions of the court.

Thus a trustee must show not only that he acted honestly, but also that he acted reasonably. The standard here has been held to be that of the 'prudent man of business' but it seems logical now to apply the statutory duty of care in s. 1 of the Trustee Act 2000 and other criteria, such as the standard investment criteria in s. 4. What s. 61 is not, in the words of Evershed MR in *Marsden* v. *Regan* (1954), is a 'passport to relief'. In *Bartlett* v. *Barclays Bank Trusts Co Ltd* (1980) (see Chapter 16), the bank was held not to have acted reasonably in failing to obtain proper information about the activities of the company, although the bank had acted honestly. The words beginning 'ought fairly to be excused' seem to add little, or nothing. A recent example of the use of s. 61 is *Re Evans* (1999). A father died intestate leaving a son and daughter, who would each be entitled to a 50 per cent share of his estate. The daughter was appointed administratrix, having been estranged from the brother for 30 years. She advertised for him to come forward, but with no result, and was then advised that, rather than obtaining a *Benjamin* order, she should take out an insurance policy to cover herself if the brother reappeared. She then transferred all the assets to herself. It turned out that the insurance policy was inadequate, as it did not take account of interest which was due to the brother from the date when he should have received his share. The brother then finally reappeared and it was held that the daughter was covered by s. 61 so that, despite the inadequate policy of insurance, she was not liable to compensate her brother to the full extent of his entitlement, but only to the extent that she still had estate property in her hands.

(b) Where a beneficiary participates in, or consents to, a breach of trust. The court can impound the beneficiary's interest, so that it is available to replace any loss to the trust and the trustees are therefore given an indemnity to this extent from actions by beneficiaries in respect of the breach. The following conditions must be satisfied:
   (i) The beneficiary had full knowledge of all relevant facts. In *Re Somerset* (1894), trustees had wrongly invested trust funds on a mortgage of particular property at the instigation of a beneficiary, but the beneficiary had left it to them to decide how much to lend. The court refused to impound the beneficiary's interest.
   (ii) The beneficiary was of full age and sound mind.
   (iii) The beneficiary freely consented to the breach of trust. Thus in *Re Pauling* (1964) it was held that consent by a beneficiary to advances of capital which she knew would be used to benefit her parents was not free consent because the presumption of undue influence by a parent over a child continues to exist, as in this case, for a period after the child attains its majority.
   (iv) The beneficiary must have intended to derive a personal benefit from the breach, even though he may not have actually received one.

(c) Power under s. 62 of the Trustee Act 1925 to impound a beneficiary's interest. This also allows the court to impound a beneficiary's interest where he has instigated or requested the breach of trust or has consented in writing to it. The principles on which the court exercises its jurisdiction here are similar to those under its inherent equitable jurisdiction (b) (above). Thus *Re Somerset* (1894) involved the predecessor of s. 62. The main difference is that, for s. 62 to apply, there is no requirement that the beneficiary should have intended to obtain a benefit. In addition, s. 62 only applies to a written consent to a breach, whereas the equitable power to impound can be exercised even if the consent was oral.

The way in which the above rules work is illustrated by Example 20.8.

Example 20.8

Jane is a trustee. There are three beneficiaries: Sarah, aged 17, Michael, aged 25 and Denis, aged 30. Denis persuades Jane to invest all the trust property in a speculative property venture and Sarah agrees to this. The venture turns out to be a complete failure and all the trust property is lost. Quite clearly Denis cannot sue Jane, as the idea was his and she merely acted on it. Can Michael and Sarah sue? Yes. Although Sarah consented, she was not of full age (see (b) above). Michael did not consent, so he obviously can. If they succeed, and this will depend on whether the investment was in breach of the standard investment criteria in the Trustee Act 2000, then Michael's beneficial interest under the trust can be taken to satisfy their claims.

Limitation of actions against trustees

Under the Limitation Act 1980

Section 21(3) lays down a general rule that a beneficiary has six years from the date when the breach was committed to bring the action, i.e. in which to issue the claim or other originating process. This applies to actions for breach of trust in relation to trust property. Time limits for claims based on breach of fiduciary duty based on conflict of interest are considered below. There are the following special rules:

(i) Time does not begin to run against those beneficiaries who were under a disability at the date of the breach until their disability ends (s. 28).

(ii) A right of action in respect of future interests is not treated as having accrued until the interest falls into possession: only then does time begin to run (s. 21(3)).

(iii) No limitation period applies where the action is in respect of any fraud to which the trustee was a party, or privy, or where the action is to recover from the trustee either trust property which is still in his possession, or the proceeds of a sale of it (s. 21(1)). Nor is there any limitation period if the action is against defendants who claim through a fraudulent trustee, unless they are bona fide purchasers for value without notice (*Re Dixon* (1900)).

(iv) No limitation period applies to an action *in rem* (for a proprietary remedy – see below) against those who have received trust property, other than purchasers in good faith and without notice. Where a right of action has been concealed by fraud or where the action is for relief from the consequence of a mistake, then time does not begin to run until the plaintiff has discovered the fraud, concealment or mistake or ought with reasonable diligence to have done so (s. 32). In this case, the actual breach of trust will not have been fraudulent, as if it was there would have been no period of limitation. It is the concealment of the breach which is fraudulent. In *Eddis* v. *Chichester Constable* (1969), the life tenant sold a painting, in breach of trust, in 1950, but the trustees did not discover this until 1963. It was held that the life tenant had concealed the fraud by saying nothing about the sale and so the limitation period did not begin to run until 1963. However, a stricter test was proposed in *Paragon Finance* v. *D.B. Thakerar & Co* (1999), where the Court of Appeal held that the burden of proof is on the claimant (i.e. the person claiming a breach of trust) to prove that he/she could not have discovered the fraud without exceptional measures, which it would not have been reasonable for him to take.

(v) An action in respect of any claim to the estate of a deceased person must be brought within 12 years (s. 22). If the personal representatives are also trustees, this 12-year period probably still applies. The provision is subject to the exceptions in (v) above.

(vi) *Where the claim is for the remedy of account.* Section 23 provides that an action for an account 'shall not be brought after the expiration of any time limit under this Act which is applicable to the claim which is the basis of the duty to account'. This means that if the right to an account flows from a particular cause of action, then the time limit for bringing the claim for an account is the same as that for the particular cause of action. In *Coulthard* v. *Disco Mix Club Ltd* (2000) it was held that where an action for an account arose out of a contractual relationship which had a fiduciary element to it then the limitation period was the ordinary contractual one.

(vii) In *A-G* v. *Cocke* (1988) it was held that the six-year limitation period did not apply to actions for an account brought by the Attorney-General against a charitable trust. One reason was that as such a trust has no beneficiaries in the way that a private trust has, s. 21(3) of the Limitation Act cannot, on its wording, apply.

Under the doctrine of laches

Where the Act does not apply, e.g. (iii) and (iv) above, a claim can still be barred by laches under which delay by a claimant in bringing a claim may prevent them from obtaining an equitable remedy. The court will look at any hardship caused to the claimant by the delay and decide whether, on balance, the interests of justice would still be served by granting relief.

FURTHER READING

Birks (1985) *An Introduction to the Law of Restitution*, 2nd edn, Oxford: Oxford University Press.

Birks (2005) *Unjust Enrichment*, 2nd edn, Oxford: Oxford University Press. Although this area is not as yet central to the equity it is a developing one.

Elliott and Edelman (2003) 'Target holdings considered in Australia', 119 LQR 545.

Conaglen (2003) 'Equitable compensation for breach of fiduciary dealing rules', 119 LQR 246. Interesting angle on compensation in equity.

Fox (1998) 'Constructive notice and knowing receipt: an economic analysis', 57 CLJ 391. Another slightly different perspective and a most useful one.

Gardner (1996) 'Knowing assistance and Knowing Receipt: Taking Stock', 112 LQR 56. Very useful survey.

Millett (1991) 'Tracing the proceeds of fraud', 107 LQR 76.

Millett (1998) 'Restitution and constructive trusts', 114 LQR 399.

Both of the above two articles are of central importance in this area. You should, having read the articles, also read Lord Millet's speech in *Twinsectra* v. *Yardley*.

CHAPTER SUMMARY

- Equitable damages.
- Proprietary remedies: liability for knowing receipt.
- Liability for knowing assistance.
- Compensation and restitution.
- Unjust enrichment.
- Personal liability of trustees.
- Limitation periods.

QUESTION

D'Arcy is a trustee of the Hanbury Cricket Club and is responsible for its funds. He withdraws £10,000 from the trust account and pays it into his own private bank account, which previously had £5,000 in it. He then withdraws £7,000 from this account and uses the money to purchase a yacht.

Advise the members on any remedies which they may have.

Note 20.1: *You will find suggested points for inclusion in this answer in Appendix 2.*

Part Five

THE FLAVOUR OF EQUITY

This part differs from the preceding ones in that it is more reflective. It looks back, either through the equitable maxims in Chapter 21 or at ideas of equity in Chapter 22, at equity as a whole and tries to capture some of the essence of equity. These chapters link with Chapter 1 which, at the start, looked at the nature and development of equity. Chapter 22 is deliberately more personal than the other chapters and, if you do not agree with the author then so much the better: this chapter will have set you thinking!

21 The equitable maxims

INTRODUCTION

Note 21.1: As this chapter consists only of the maxims of equity, a summary is not really appropriate.

The maxims of equity describe some of the main principles that guide equitable intervention but their importance should not be over stressed. They consist of brief, pithy phrases which remain easily in the mind but in fact judges today do not use them so often. Their historical importance is greater because they began to be formulated in the time of Lord Nottingham C (1673–82) and were one of the reasons why equity changed from being based on the general notion of conscience to a more formal and predictable system. In addition, when they are used, it is possible for different courts to come to different decisions on the same set of facts as the application of a maxim may point one way and the application of another equitable rule may point another. One of the best modern examples of this is *Tinsley* v. *Milligan* (1993), where the maxim 'he who comes into equity must come with clean hands' was applied by the Court of Appeal whilst the House of Lords applied the presumption that contributions to the purchase of property which is then placed in the name of another will lead to the presumption of a resulting trust.

Nevertheless there is still a value in studying them because they remind us that, despite all of the complex doctrines which it has developed, equity remains a system based on conscience and justice. In addition it is hoped that the reader will find this chapter a useful aide-mémoire to topics covered in this book.

THE EQUITABLE MAXIMS

The following are 13 principal maxims:

1. Equity will not suffer a wrong to be without a remedy

Example 21.1

Enabling a beneficiary under a trust to enforce it when the common law would allow the trustee, as legal owner, to ignore the beneficiary's rights (Chapter 4).

Example 21.2

Granting an equitable remedy, e.g. specific performance or injunction, where the common law remedy of damages would be inadequate (Chapter 2).

2. Equity follows the law

Example 21.3

Where a lease is equitable (as in *Walsh* v. *Lonsdale* (1882) (Chapter 1)) the obligations of the parties are the same as if it was legal.

However, equity will interfere with a person's legal rights if it would be unconscionable for him to insist on them, e.g. the legal right of a trustee to dispose of trust property (Chapter 20).

3. Where there is equal equity, the law shall prevail
4. Where the equities are equal, the first in time shall prevail

Example 21.4

If X has a prior equitable interest in land and Y later takes the legal estate in the land *bona fide* and without notice of X's interest then the equities are equal and Y's legal estate prevails. If, however, X and Y both have equitable interests then X's, as the first in time, will prevail.

5. He who seeks equity must do equity

Example 21.5

The doctrine of election (Chapter 3) is based on this principle: 'a person cannot accept and reject the same instrument' (Lord Redesdale in *Birmingham* v. *Kirwan* (1805)).

6. He who comes into equity must come with clean hands

Example 21.6

A tenant who has made an agreement for a lease (as in *Walsh* v. *Lonsdale* (1882) Chapter 1) cannot obtain specific performance of that agreement if he has broken the covenants contained in the lease (*Coatsworth* v. *Johnson* (1886)). In *Tinsley* v. *Milligan* (1993) (see Chapter 10) the Court of Appeal held that this maxim should not be rigidly applied where to do so would cause injustice but the whole area of law around this decision is an excellent illustration of this maxim.

7. Delay defeats equities

Example 21.7

The doctrine of laches, e.g. as applied to the claim for rescission in *Leaf* v. *International Galleries* (1950) (Chapter 2). However, the equitable doctrine of laches does not apply where the Limitation Act 1980 covers the situation, this being another example of the maxim 'equity follows the law'.

8. Equality is equity

Example 21.8

In *Jones* v. *Maynard* (1951) (see also Chapter 10) a husband and wife had a joint bank account into which both paid and drew. The court, after they were divorced, divided the balance in it equally between them.

9. Equity looks to the intent rather than the form

Example 21.9

Equity will hold that a trust has been created even though the word 'trust' has not been used provided that there was the intent to create a trust (see Chapter 5). The whole area of certainties, formalities and constitution is an excellent example of this maxim.

10. Equity looks on that as done which ought to be done

Example 21.10

In *Walsh* v. *Lonsdale* (1882) (see Chapter 1) a specifically enforceable contract for a lease was held to actually create an equitable lease.

11. Equity imputes an intention to fulfill an obligation

Example 21.11

The doctrines of performance and satisfaction (see Chapter 3).

12. Equity acts *in personam*

Example 21.12

The remedies of specific performance and injunction (see Chapters 1 and 2) as contrasted with the common law remedy of damages.

13. Equity will not assist a volunteer

Example 21.13

Where a trust is not constituted, equity will not, with certain exceptions, assist a beneficiary who has not provided consideration and so is a volunteer to enforce it. This underlies the law on constitution of trusts in Chapter 7.

QUESTION

'The maxims of equity are still useful today.'

Do you agree?

Note 21.2: You will find suggested points for inclusion in this answer in Appendix 2.

Note 21.3: Further Reading: The main textbooks deal with the maxims in detail.

22 The future of equity

INTRODUCTION

If it were possible to be transported in time to the beginning of the twenty-second century, what place might equity then occupy in the legal system? There are two possibilities:

(a) Equity as such might not occupy any place at all, as it will have merged with the common law. In effect, the fusion debate, which was discussed in Chapter 1, will have ended and it could be said that the Judicature Acts will have achieved their ultimate objective with a complete fusion of law and equity. This view is strongly put by Worthington (2003) in a stimulating study.
(b) Equity will continue to exist as a separate system, but with changes of emphasis. For example, there may be a greater role for the notion of unconscionability and the law of the administration of express trusts may be hived off from equitable jurisdiction.

There is a possible 'Third Way', in which trust law at least ceases to have an equitable base. This is argued by Honore (2003) who argues that equitable concepts, such as the equitable proprietary interest, are not essential to the trust. On a long historical view, it is possible to view the current debate about the future of equity as a reaction to differing judicial attitudes in both the common law and equity. It now seems clear that, compared with the later years of the last century, the period until roughly the end of the 1950s was one of stagnation in many areas of the law. We have seen in this book how, for example, the House of Lords, and particularly Lord Simonds, gave a very restrictive interpretation to the term 'public benefit' in charity cases (see Chapter 13 and especially *Gilmour* v. *Coats* (1949)). Another example of a decision which does not seem to have any flavour of equity about it is *Re Gillingham Bus Disaster Fund* (1958) (see Chapter 10). Yet the same is true of many areas of the common law. In the field of public law, look at the subservient attitude of the courts to the administration as shown in *Local Government Board* v. *Arlidge* (1915). In more recent times the common law has displayed much more inventiveness, an obvious example being the line of cases on judicial review beginning with *Ridge* v. *Baldwin* (1964). Another example, familiar to contract law students, is *Williams* v. *Roffey* (1991) on the need for consideration where a contractual promise is altered and the development of the duty of care in negligence is perhaps the best example of all of how judges are prepared to develop the common law in far more adventurous ways then before.

Many of these developments have been achieved through the increasing use by the common law of general principles and in particular that of reasonableness. In the circumstances, one could say that the common law has caught up with equity, in that it is no longer possible to contrast the two, with one (common law) being rule based and the other (equity) based on wider principles, especially in view of the lack of vigour in equity. This is not, however, the case, as this book has tried to make clear. There has been an astonishing renaissance of equity in many fields: trusts of the family home, estoppel, freezing and search orders, the *Quistclose* trust, the development of equitable compensation and the continuing vigour and development of the fiduciary principle are all examples. More particularly, equity has become involved in the regulation of commercial transactions to an extent which would have been undreamt of a century ago. If I may be allowed a personal comment, I well remember as a young lawyer being told by senior silks that in their days before the Second World War equity was not a compulsory subject for study as it was not then considered of great importance. The development of the constructive trust had, in their view, been the major factor in the renaissance of equity and few would disagree with this. In addition, there is the growing development of old principles by applying them in ways which, whilst still principled, are less rigid and are based on the notion of, for example, unconscionability. *Pennington* v. *Waine* (2002) and *Choithram (T) International SA* v. *Pagarani* (2001) (see Chapter 7) are noteable examples. Why cut off a system when it is still capable of such development?

MISTAKE IN CONTRACTS: CONTINUING RESILIENCE OF EQUITY?

On a more particular level, recent developments in the area of mistake provide an excellent example of the continuing desirability of two separate jurisdictions and this area may serve as a case study in the continuing relevance of equity. (On the other hand, others may argue that this topic shows the need for an integrated system!)

The decision in *Solle* v. *Butcher*

In *Solle* v. *Butcher* (1950) Denning LJ sought to develop an equitable jurisdiction to set aside contracts made on the basis of common mistake. The common law's jurisdiction in this area has always been limited, in particular by the decision of the House of Lords in *Bell* v. *Lever Bros Ltd* (1932), and there seems to be no right at common laws to set aside contracts on the ground of mistake of quality alone.

It was this gap which Denning LJ sought to plug. In *Solle* v. *Butcher* a lease of a flat for seven years fixed the rent at £250 p.a. Both parties mistakenly believed that the property was not subject to rent control but in fact it was and so the rent should have been only £140 p.a. However, had the landlord served the correct statutory notices the rent could have been £250 p.a. anyway. He did not do so as he mistakenly thought that there was no need to do this. Thus there was a mistake but not a fundamental one. The court gave the tenant the choice of either remaining in possession and paying the full rent of £250 p.a. or of surrendering the lease. It can be seen that this approach has the advantage of flexibility over the common law which could only have declared the contract void rather then in effect offering to set it aside on terms that a proper rent would be paid.

Recent developments: the decision in *The Great Peace* and afterwards

This approach of Denning LJ was felt by some not to rest on any line of authority (see Poole (2004)) and the doctrine that equity can set aside contracts for mistake was apparently extinguished by the House of Lords in *Great Peace Shipping Ltd* v. *Tsavliris (International) Ltd* (2002). The facts were that the ship 'Great Peace' was engaged for a minimum period of five days to deviate in its journey towards another ship which had been damaged. Both parties thought that the distance was about 35 miles when it was in fact about 410 miles. When the truth was discovered the salvage company what had engaged the 'Great Peace' cancelled the contract and sought an alternative vessel. The question was the simple one of whether the contract for the hire of the 'Great Peace' was void. If it was, then no fee at all was payable but the court held that it was not and so the hiring fee was due.

Whilst this decision may have achieved justice on its facts, the denial of a separate equitable jurisdiction to set aside contracts for mistake is controversial The Court of Appeal in *The Great Peace* found that *Solle* v. *Butcher* could not be reconciled with *Bell* v. *Lever*, to which it had to give way as *Bell* was decided by the House of Lords. Even so, Lord Phillips in *The Great Peace* saw some merit in *Solle* v. *Butcher* as he conceded that the equitable remedy of rescission (with the possibility of the court imposing terms) gave 'greater flexibility' to the law as compared to the common law which simply holds that a contract is void.

However, fears that this area of equitable jurisdiction has been consigned to history may be misplaced for in *Chwee Kin Keong* v. *Digilandmall.com Pte Ltd* (2005) the Singapore Court of Appeal held that the court had an equitable jurisdiction to rescind a contract for unilateral mistake. The case involved a sale on a website of laser printers for a price of S$66 when their real value was S$4,000, and there was the possibility of extra profits totalling S$6 million. Six persons accepted the offer, but there seemed to be doubt as to whether they knew that the price was wrong or if they just had constructive knowledge. The Singapore Court of Appeal held that the common law jurisdiction to hold contracts void for unilateral mistake only applied where the other party knew of the other's mistake. However, in equity the court had power to set a contract aside if the other party had constructive knowledge of the other's mistake and had also been guilty of some sharp practice or unconscionability. This was the case here; the court found the conduct of the offerees to have been 'predatory' (see Yeo (2005)). It was true that equity's jurisdiction to set contracts on the ground of unilateral mistake differs from that in common mistake but one cannot help but think that the effect of the decision in the *Great Peace* has been lessened.

The obvious moral from all this is that equity does have a continuing role to play. The decision in *Chwee Kin Keong* is based squarely on traditional equitable principles: constructive notice coupled with the need to prevent a party gaining by unconscionable conduct. Moreover, the respective jurisdictions of equity and common law dovetail into each other well: common law dealing with straightforward situations where knowledge of the other's mistake makes the contract void and equity dealing with the more subtle situation of taking advantage of the mistake when perhaps actual knowledge cannot be proved but there is constructive notice.

WHY SHOULD THERE BE A UNIFIED SYSTEM?

In the end, one can ask the simple question: what would be achieved if there was an end of the dual system of equity and common law and what would be lost? No doubt there is something to be said for rationalisation but an over concentration on tidiness in the law can obscure greater and higher virtues. Mason (1994), from an Australian perspective, saw a great contrast between equity and the common law: 'Its concern with standards of conscience, fairness, equality and its protection of relationships of trust and confidence, as well as its discretionary relief, stand in marked contrast to the more rigid formulae applied by the common law'. This may be putting the case somewhat too high but there is no doubt that equity's conscience based approach is a distinctive one and one which adds much to the strength of the law as whole. As Millett LJ put it (Millett 1998): 'The common law insists on honesty, diligence and the due performance of contractual obligations. But equity insists on nobler and subtler qualities: loyalty, fidelity, integrity, respect for confidentiality, and the disinterested discharge of obligations of trust and confidence'. He was speaking in the context of equity and commerce but his words can, it is submitted, be applied to all areas in which equity engages. There is nothing wrong with the distinct values inherent in the common law. What is wrong, however, in having alongside them those higher values inherent in a system based squarely on ethical standards?

SOME TASKS AHEAD

On the assumption that there is still work ahead for equity, it might be a good and practical way to end by suggesting some areas where equity might develop and where those developments may lead. Here then are some ideas:

(a) The idea of Lord Browne-Wilkinson in *Target Holdings Ltd* v. *Redferns* (1995) that equitable rules may differ according to whether the trust is a traditional family trust or one in the commercial sphere may have been taken further.
(b) The relationship between equitable proprietary remedies and unjust enrichment needs to be clarified so that there is one proprietary remedy which is available for both equitable and some common law claims.
(c) The courts will be faced with further problems in situations such as *Schmidt* v. *Rosewood Trust* (2003) (see Chapters 4 and 17), where a settlor wishes to retain control over the trust and the need to protect the integrity of the office of trustee will come to the forefront. This problem may be more acute with greater movement of capital between different countries with the result that trusts may be set up by settlors who may not be familiar with the nature of the office of trustee.
(d) The role of equity in commercial relationships also needs to be clarified along with the nature and extent of fiduciary duties. Useful thinking here is provided by Conaglen (2005).
(e) The law on beneficial interests in the family home will probably be put on a statutory basis but in the application of the statutory rules the courts will be faced by the same conflicting demands which perplex the courts today.
(f) Trusts for non-charitable purposes need to be recognised as valid, at least for some purposes.
(g) There may be other areas where trusts are require to be regulated by statute, as are trusts of pension funds today by the Pensions Act 1995.

FURTHER READING

Honore (2003) 'Trusts – The Inessentials' in Getzler (ed.) *Rationalising property, equity and trusts: essays in honour of Edward Burn*, London: Butterworths. Argues that the express trust is not an essential characteristic of equity.

Yeo (2005) 'The great peace; a distinct disturbance?', 121 LQR 393. Brings the case law on this topic up to date.

See also the further reading for Chapter 1, especially Worthington, *Equity*.

CHAPTER SUMMARY

- Views of the future of equity.
- Historical perspective.
- Mistake in contracts – a case study.
- Should there be a unified system?
- Some tasks ahead.

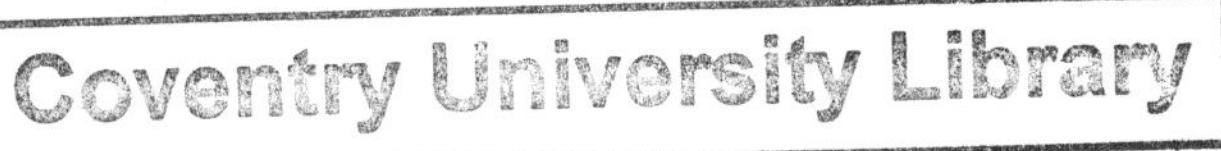

QUESTION

'Integration, pursued with determination and a keen eye for detailed and rigorous analysis, could readily deliver a coherent, sophisticated, and discriminating legal system, well equipped to met the needs of modern society' (Worthington, *Equity* (2003)).

Do you agree?

> ***Note 22.1:*** *You will find suggested points for inclusion in these answers in Appendix 2.*

Appendices

Appendix 1 Answering examination questions in Equity and Trusts

Examinations in this subject, like most other law examinations, consist of questions of the problem and essay type. With both types of question you must remember that although examiners are looking for an accurate knowledge of the area, they are also looking for the ability to analyse, and to be able to make critical judgements supported by clear reasoning. Above all, they are looking for a direct answer to the question. I have marked many examination scripts where candidates have written an enormous amount and have been surprised to find that they have obtained, at most, a bare pass. The reason is that they adopted a 'machine gun technique': they simply wrote down all they knew about the topic. For example, a question inviting a discussion on the merits of the 'new model constructive trust' should never be answered simply by a rehearsal of all the cases you know on the subject. Instead, when you open the examination paper, take a deep breath, try to keep calm and think just what each question really is about. Then answer it directly! Take the following sample question:

> 'There is no all embracing definition of a constructive trust. They represent the response by equity at different times to different needs'. Do you agree?

The worst answers will begin with a list of the circumstances in which equity has imposed a constructive trust, with much discussion about such areas as trusts of the home, equity not allowing a statute to be used as an engine of fraud etc. Although this material may be used in answering the question, you should not start with it but instead begin by addressing the precise point posed in the question: Is there an all embracing definition of a constructive trust? Look at the discussion at the beginning of Part Three of this book for some ideas to get you going and then, and only then, discuss particular examples of constructive trusts in the light of the general point: is there a unifying theory? The answer is that there probably is not, but you can argue to the contrary and original answers backed up by good research are always welcome!

Remember also the following points about each type of question.

The problem type

This type of question normally contains a number of issues. Take each point separately, state the relevant law, apply it and then move on to the next point. *Never* state all the points of law and only then begin to apply them. If you do, you will have little time for detailed analysis, which is what will obtain the marks.

When revising, pay particular attention to both the vital cases and the somewhat awkward ones. In secret and half-secret trusts, for example, *Re Keen* (1937) is an example of the former and *Re Stead* (1900) of the latter.

The essay type

These questions ask for a discussion of a particular issue and it is a good idea before the examination to think of areas which particularly lend themselves to such a question and try to sort out the general lines of an argument so that in the examination room you do not have to start thinking for the first time of what your views are on a certain topic. For example, the idea of the 'new model constructive trust' lends itself to an essay question. Try beforehand to think of the advantages and disadvantages of this and work out an argument.

As a general point, do remember that in many answers you will find it necessary to cross the boundaries of particular topics and an ability to do this is often the mark of a good student. For example, a problem question on secret trusts may also involve a certainties issue – was there certainty to create a trust all?

Appendix 2 Suggested points for inclusion in answers at the end of chapters

(Not to be looked at until you have completed the answers!)

Ch. 1

The question is really asking: the idea of unconscionability is the mainspring of equity: is it the idea which lies behind the intervention of equity? The answer to this is a mixed one: you should quote cases (especially recent ones) where unconscionability has been used (e.g. *Pennington* v. *Waine* (2002) – Chapter 7) but also point out that there are areas where it does not figure at all, e.g. the detailed rules on certainties – Chapter 5. (You may prefer to complete this question when you have studied further.)

Ch. 2

The idea of equitable remedies being discretionary is a familiar one but you need to look behind the cases and try to arrive at an estimate of what 'discretionary' actually means. Look at e.g. *Patel* v. *Ali* (1984) in Chapter 1.

Ch. 3

(a) Breach of confidence. Injunction. Search order?
(b) Possibility of an injunction? Application of *Irani* v. *Southampton and South West Hampshire Health Authority* (1985).

Ch. 4

This, on one level, is a straightforward question asking you to look at the uses to which trusts have been put and many examples are given in this chapter. However, when you have read further, and especially looked at the introduction to Part Three, you will see that there are broader issues to consider in addition to just a list of the practical uses of trusts. One example is the intervention of equity in disputes over the family home.

Ch. 5

(a) Consider certainty of intention and subject matter. Compare with *Re Golays'* (1965).
(b) Certainty of objects. Application of *McPhail* v. *Doulton* (1970).

Ch. 6

Look at the discussion at the start of this chapter and discuss precisely why formal requirements are needed. Discuss the requirements in s. 53(1)(b) separately from those in ss. 53(1)(c) as it is arguable that there is great need for formality in cases involving land as the actual transfer of land must be by deed (see Chapter 7). If you do feel that some formal requirements are needed when the beneficial interests are disposed of, then ask whether the present ones are too complex. Is there any good reason for exempting certain contracts from this requirement?

Ch. 7

Imperfect gifts: consider why. Therefore you need to consider whether there is a valid *donationes mortis causa.* Is the property in each gift capable of being the subject of a DMC? Apply the three conditions for a DMC to each part: contemplation of death, parting with control, and the gift must be conditional on death.

Ch. 8

(a) Secret trust. Requirements for validity – see Brightman J in *Ottaway* v. *Norman* (1972). Bequest to tenants in common, therefore application of *Re Stead* (1900). Subsequent communication to Josephine too late.
(b) Half-secret trust. Application of *Re Keen* (1937).

Ch. 9

Public policy is undoubtedly an unsatisfactory instrument here, as the courts have said, but should it be replaced and, if so, by what? Here again a good answer will go beyond a mere recital of cases and look at the underlying issues.

Ch. 10

Resulting trusts said to be based on intention, but how? Presence of intention or absence of it? Constructive trusts arise by operation of law yet in some cases intention plays a part, e.g. trusts of the home cases.

Ch. 11

The question does not ask for a description of when constructive trusts occur but of whether it is possible to find an all-embracing description of what they are and what they do. Begin with the points made at the beginning of the chapter on the nature of constructive trusts – probably not possible to find an all-embracing description of what they are – look e.g. at the need in some cases to find intention and in other cases intention is obviously absent. What do they do? Again difficult – are they remedial and, if so, in what sense? Look at the suggested answer on this topic below.

Ch. 12

Principles established in *Lloyds Bank* v. *Rosset* (1990). Was there direct evidence of common intention about ownership? If so, did Samantha act on it to her detriment? If not, did the acts of the parties indicate the existence of a common intention? If she is entitled to a share then on what principles will its size be decided? *Oxley* v. *Hiscock* (2004).

Ch. 13

(a) Valid as being for the advancement of education? Or is it a political trust?
(b) Possibly educational – *IRC* v. *McMullen* (1981) – but is there sufficient public benefit? See e.g. *Re Koettgen's Will Trusts* (1954) and *IRC* v. *Educational Grants Association Ltd* (1967).

Charities Bill could certainly affect (b). Doubt re (a).

Ch. 14

(a) Application of *Re Slevin* (1891): as the charity ceases to exist after the death of the testator it is a case of subsequent failure because the gift is effectively dedicated to charity. Thus *cy-près* application is automatic.
(b) Possible application of *Re Faraker* (1912): amalgamation of charities – are the purposes of the charity continuing in another form?
(c) As the body has never existed it appears from *Re Harwood* (1936) that a general charitable intention is assumed and so, as the gift has undoubtedly failed within the terms of s. 13 of the Charities Act, *cy-près* application will follow.

> **Note:** *You will gain no marks at all for a discussion of whether these gifts are charitable as you are told in the question that they are!*

Ch. 15

(a) Is the body charitable? Lack of public benefit (*Gilmour* v. *Coats* (1949))? If not charitable, the gift fails. If charitable then possible application of *Re Finger's Will Trust* (1972).
(b) Possible application of *Re Faraker* (1912). But are the purposes the same?

Ch. 16

This requires a discussion of the manner in which the courts control the decisions of trustees, e.g. extent to which they will intervene, can they require trustees to give reasons for their decisions, rights of the beneficiaries to require accounts and other information. You need to stress that the attitude of the courts is changing and refer to recent decisions.

Ch. 17

(a) Trustee Act 2000. Statutory duty of care (s. 1) and standard investment criteria (s. 4). Note purposes of the trust. *Cowan* v. *Scargill* (1984).
(b) General investment powers in the TA 2000 – consider the standard investment criteria in the light of the trust: Mary and Christopher will soon be entitled absolutely.

Ch. 18

Powers of trustees to pay maintenance and advancement. Appear to be no special powers in the trust instrument so the position is governed by ss. 31 and 32 of the Trustee Act 1925.

(a) Andrew is entitled to the income as he is over 18 – may also need an advance of capital – look at cases on this – is it for his benefit? Possibility of incidental benefit to girlfriend may not rule advancement out.
(b) Fiona – may be paid out of maintenance – but does the gift carry the intermediate income – see s. 175 LPA 1925. If so, look at criteria in s. 31 TA 1925. Trustees have a discretion and may be unwilling to commit themselves to five years' payments.

Ch. 19

This essay calls for a consideration of the cases where the courts have varied the beneficial interests under a trust. Note that you should not restrict your answer to cases under the Variation of Trusts Act but look at other cases e.g. *Hambro* v. *Duke of Marlborough* (1994). Select about five cases and look at the decision in the light of the quotation – do not just go through the VTA!

Ch. 20

Breach of trust. Tracing in equity. Fiduciary relationship. Application of *Re Hallett's Estate* (1880) and *Re Oatway* (1903).

Ch. 21

The way to write a good answer here is to select a few maxims and consider how they have been applied in the cases – e.g. the clean hands maxim can be studied through *Tinsley* v. *Milligan*. A close study of the judgments will show a divergence of views between the Court of Appeal and the House of Lords. Does this tell us that the maxim is still useful or that it is misleading? Concentrate on a few maxims and look at them in depth.

Ch. 22

This is not an easy question but can reward you with excellent marks if you really know the arguments. Worthington is not arguing for the end of equity but for integration with the common law. Look at the words 'rigorous analysis' and 'modern society'. Look at some areas of equity – remedies is a good one – and consider whether there is any need for two divergent systems. Concentrate on the 'rigorous analysis' point: integration will mean looking clearly at both systems. Consider opposing views. You may find the case study on equity and mistake useful.

In addition, I have set out a longer answer, in Appendix 3, to an essay question on constructive trusts which is a topic always found difficult by students.

Appendix 3 Hints on answering exam questions on particular topics

Students may find the following hints helpful in relation to these particular types of question:

1. Certainties

There may be a connection with the area of purpose trusts, e.g.: X leaves the following gifts:

(a) £5,000 to such employees of XYZ Co, ex-employees, their relatives and dependants as my executors shall in their absolute discretion select. A straightforward application of *McPhail* v. *Doulton* (1970) is needed.
(b) £5,000 for the maintenance of my cat D'Arcy. This would be an invalid purpose trust but for the exception in the case of animals *Re Dean* (1889).
(c) £5,000 to the Worcester Riding Club, an unincorporated association. This cannot be a gift to the association as it does not exist, and so it will be an invalid purpose trust unless the reasoning in *Re Denley* (1969) or perhaps *Re Recher's Will Trusts* (1972) can be applied.

2. Secret and half-secret trusts

Do make certain what type of trust this is and say so at the outset of your answer. The way to find this out is to look *first of all* at the will: does it disclose the existence of a trust or not?

3. Constitution of trusts

Watch out for where the examiner has set a question where the trust is partly constituted and partly not. Obviously a detailed discussion is only needed of the second part, e.g.: X transfers his cottage 'Westview' to Y and Z, to his trustees to hold upon trust for X's wife and children and covenants with Y and Z to transfer property, which he may acquire under the will of his Great Uncle Albert, to Y and Z to hold on the same trusts.

The cottage causes no problem: the trust is constituted. The trust of the other property is not constituted so the issues of marriage consideration, after acquired property, *Fletcher* v. *Fletcher* (1844) and action which can be taken by the trustees (*Re Pryce* (1917), *Re Kay* (1939), etc.) need to be discussed. Note that if either Y, Z or both is also stated to be the executor of X's will then *Re Ralli's Will Trusts* (1964), and perhaps *Strong* v. *Bird* (1874), will almost certainly come into the question.

4. Charitable trusts

Questions here are usually of two kinds:

(a) Is a trust charitable at all? Do remember to go through the three requirements:
   (i) Does the trust come within one of the four heads of charity? Or, when the Charities Bill 2005 is in force, the new heads of charity? *If so*
   (ii) Is it for the public benefit? (except, possibly, in the case of trusts for the relief of poverty) *If so*
   (iii) Is it exclusively charitable?

(b) Failure of charitable gifts and consequent application of the *cy-prés* rule. Often the question will state that the gift *is* charitable so that you must spend all of your time discussing the issue of failure. Please do not discuss the question of charitable status if you are told that the gift *is* charitable!

> *Note: A question on whether a trust is charitable may ask either:*
> *(a) is the trust a valid charitable trust? or*
> *(b) is it a valid trust?*

In the case of (b) it will be necessary to consider the position if the trust is not charitable. Is it a valid private trust? If it is for individuals and it is a discretionary trust which satisfies the *McPhail* v. *Doulton* (1970) test then it will be valid. If it is a fixed trust then each beneficiary will need to be known. If it is not a trust for individuals at all it will be invalid as a (non-charitable) purpose trust unless it comes within one of the exception trusts for animals or monuments or it is a *Re Denley* (1969) type of trust.

5. Trustee's duties and powers.

Look first to see if the situation deals with a duty or a power. Note the distinction between the two carefully.

6. Undue influence

Discuss *first* whether the situation is likely to fall within actual undue influence or whether undue influence can be presumed. Once you have done this, then discuss whether undue influence might have taken place.

7. Constructive trusts

Students often find essays on this topic difficult and so I have set out below a full suggested answer to such an essay question.

> 'A constructive trust is the formula through which the conscience of equity finds expression.'
>
> (Cardozo J in *Beatty* v. *Guggenheim Exploration Co* (1919))

The American approach is to treat constructive trusts as remedies. Thus Cardozo J continued in the above passage:

> '. . . when property has been acquired in such circumstances that the holder of the legal estate may not in good conscience retain the beneficial interest, equity converts him into a trustee.'

Constructive trusts, in American eyes, are to be used as a remedy to prevent unjust enrichment, although not all American judges would take such a wide view. English law, on the other hand, regards constructive trusts as substantive institutions which will only be imposed where there has been a breach of fiduciary duty. Thus English law, as a general rule, will only impose a constructive trusts when the conduct in issue comes within certain recognised situations, for instance, where a fiduciary has made a profit for himself as in *Keech* v. *Sandford* (1726) and *Boardman* v. *Phipps* (1967), and in cases involving company directors such as *Industrial Developments* v. *Cooley* (1972). Nevertheless, it is clear that in these cases a constructive trust was primarily being used as a remedy. In *Keech* v. *Sandford* the decision that the trustee held the lease on a constructive trust for the minor remedied the wrong done to the minor by the trustee obtaining a renewal of the lease in his own right.

Similarly, in *Boardman* v. *Phipps*, the decision that the defendants were liable to account to the trust for the profits which they had made through their fiduciary position remedied the defendant's breach of fiduciary duty. The difference, however, between English and American approaches is that in England the starting point is whether there has been a breach of fiduciary duty so that a constructive trust can be imposed and, if it is, a remedy may result. In America the remedy is the starting point: what is to be done to prevent unjust enrichment?

The difference can be seen in a series of English cases in the 1970s which did indeed impose a constructive trust on American principles, the so-called 'new model constructive trust'. In *Binions* v. *Evans* (1972) a constructive trust was imposed on a purchaser of a cottage in favour of the occupant because of an agreement between the vendor and the occupant that the occupant could reside in the cottage rent free for the rest of her life. Lord Denning protected her right to remain by holding that the occupant had a contractual licence to remain, and *then* holding that the purchasers had taken subject to that licence and, so as to protect that licence, holding that the purchaser held the cottage on a constructive trust with the occupant as beneficiary. The use of a constructive trust as a remedy here can be clearly seen by the fact that, instead of imposing a constructive trust, the court could have protected the occupant's right to remain by granting an injunction restraining the purchasers from evicting her, as indeed Lord Denning said could be done. It should be added that there is no dispute that the occupant here deserved to be protected: the purchasers had paid a low price for the cottage knowing of the agreement between the vendor and the occupant. What is controversial is the *way* in which Lord Denning protected her rights. The majority of the Court of Appeal held for the occupant on the basis that the agreement between the vendor and the occupant made the occupant a tenant for life and so the vendor held on an existing trust for her. The purchasers, on equitable notice principles, were bound by this trust. The fact that there was no written evidence of the trust did not matter because, as was held in the similar case of *Bannister* v. *Bannister* (1948), the trust is constructive, and so s. 53(1)(b) of the LPA 1925 does not apply. Lord Denning, however, held that the trust arose on the actual sale to the purchaser, a clear example of the remedial idea.

In recent years the concept of the new model (or remedial) constructive trust has, with the departure of Lord Denning, become out of favour, as seen in, e.g. *Grant* v. *Edwards* (1986) where disputes relating to ownership of the family home were decided on traditional principles. There was some sign that it might be in favour again with some remarks of Lord Browne-Wilkinson in *Westdeutsche Landesbank Girozentrale* v. *Islington LBC* (1996) but in *Re Polly Peck International plc* (1998) the Court of Appeal saw no room for the remedial constructive trust. In *Lipkin Gorman* v. *Karpnale Ltd* (1992) the House of Lords decided a claim which had been decided on constructive trust principles in the lower courts on the basis instead that a recipient of stolen money was obliged to restore an equivalent sum to the victim if he had not given full consideration for the money and was thus unjustly enriched. The basis of the action was one for money had and received, rather than an equitable one, but it may be that unjust enrichment will re-appear in a different guise.

In the end it may be wondered whether the use of American approaches or the English one makes much difference. Whichever view is taken, the only duty which the constructive trustee normally has is to hand over the trust property to those entitled. Whether these are the beneficiaries under the rule in *Saunders* v. *Vautier* (1841) or the trustees, this is obviously using the constructive trust as a remedy. On the other hand, property which is subject to a constructive trust is trust property, which gives the beneficiaries rights over the property itself and not just a personal action against the trustees. This suggests that constructive trusts are, to an extent, substantive institutions. What can certainly be said with truth is that this is a debate which is not likely to be finally settled.

Bibliography

Allen (1964) *Law in the Making*, 7th edn, Oxford: Oxford University Press.

Aristotle (1925) *Nicomacheaman Ethics*. Translation by Ross, Oxford: Oxford University Press.

Ashburner (1933) *Principles of Equity*, 2nd edn, London: Butterworths.

Avery (1970) 'The Court of Chancery under the Lancastrian Kings', 86 LQR 84.

Baker (2002) *Introduction to English Legal History*, 4th edn, Oxford: Oxford University Press.

Bigwood (2002) 'Undue influence in the House of Lords: principles and proof', 65 MLR 435.

Birks (1985) *An Introduction to the Law of Restitution*, 2nd edn, Oxford: Oxford University Press.

Birks (2005) *Unjust Enrichment*, 2nd edn, Oxford: Oxford University Press.

Birks and Chin (1997) 'On the Nature of Undue Influence' in *Good Faith and Fault in Contract Law*, ed. Beatson and Freidman, Oxford: Oxford University Press.

Borkowski (1999) *Deathbed Gifts*, London: Blackstone Press.

Bright and McFarlane (2005) 'Personal liability in proprietary estoppel', Conv. 14.

Brundage (1995) *Medieval Canon Law*, London: Longmans.

Burns (2002) 'Undue Influence Inter Vivos and the Elderly', Melbourne University Law Review.

Capper (1998) 'Undue influence and unconscionability: a rationalisation', 114 LQR 479.

Chambers (1997a) *Resulting Trusts*, Oxford: Oxford University Press, p. 88.

Chambers (1997b) *Resulting Trusts*, Oxford: Oxford University Press, p. 63.

Chesterman (1979) *Charities, trusts and social welfare*, London: Weidenfeld & Nicholson.

Clarke (1992) 'The family home: intention and agreement', *Family Law*, 72.

Clarke (1994) All ER Rev 250.

Clements (2004) 'Bringing trusts law into the twenty-first century', 2 Web JCLI.

Conaglen (2003) 'Equitable compensation for breach of fiduciary dealing rules', 119 LQR 246.

Conaglen (2005) 'The nature and function of fiduciary liability', 121 LQR 452.

Critchley (1999) 'Instruments of fraud, testamentary dispositions and the doctrine of secret trusts', 115 LQR 631.

Davies (2003) 'The integrity of trusteeship', 119 LQR 1.

Devonshire (2002) 'Freezing orders and the problems of enjoining non-parties', 118 LQR 124.

Dixon (2005) 'Resulting and constructive trusts of land: the mist descends and rises', 69 Conv. 79.

Dockray and Laddie (1990) 'Piller Problems', 106 LQR 601.

Doggett (2003) 'Explaining *Re Rose*: The search goes on', 62 CLJ 263.

Draper (1999) 'Undue influence: a review', 63 Conv. 176.

Duggan (1997) 'Is equity efficient?', 113 LQR 601.
Elliott and Edelman (2003) 'Target holdings Considered in Australia', 119 LQR 545.
Emery (1982) 'The most hallowed principle', 98 LQR 551.
Finn (1977) *Fiduciary Obligations*, Sydney: Law Book Company.
Finn (1985) *Essays in Equity*, Sydney: Law Book Company.
Fletcher (1996) 'Charities for the advancement of education', 112 LQR 557.
Ford (1985) 'Dispositions for purposes', in Finn (ed.) *Essays in Equity*, Sydney: The Law Book Company.
Fox (1998) 'Constructive notice and knowing receipt: an economic analysis', 57 CLJ 391.
Gardner (1993) 'Rethinking family property', 109 LQR 263.
Gardner (1996) 'Knowing assistance and knowing receipt: taking stock', 112 LQR 56.
Gardner (2003) *Introduction to the Law of Trusts*, 2nd edn, Oxford: Oxford University Press.
Garton (2003) 'The role of the trust mechanism in the Rule in *Re Rose*', Conv. 364.
Glister (2004) 'The nature of Quistclose trusts: classification, reconciliation', CLJ 632.
Gurry (1985) 'Breach of confidence', in Finn (ed.) *Essays in Equity*, Sydney: Law Book Company.
Guy (1980) *The Public Career of Sir Thomas More*, Brighton: Harvester Press.
Halliwell (2003) 'Perfecting imperfect gifts and trusts: have we reached the end of the Chancellor's foot?', Conv. 192.
Hanbury and Martin (2005a) *Modern Equity*, 17th edn, London: Sweet & Maxwell, p. 124.
Hanbury and Martin (2005b) *Modern Equity*, 17th edn, London: Sweet & Maxwell, p. 131.
Harris (1971) 'Trust, power and duty', 87 LQR 31.
Harris (1975) *Variation of Trusts*, London: Sweet & Maxwell.
Hayton (1994) 'Uncertainty of subject matter of trusts', 110 LQR 335.
Hayton (1996) 'The Irreducible Content of Core Trusteeship' in Oakley (ed.) *Trends in Contemporary Trust Law*, Oxford: Oxford University Press.
Hayton (2001) 'Developing the obligation characteristic of the trust', 96 LQR 117.
Hayton (2005) *Commentary and Cases on the Law of Trusts and Equitable Remedies*, London: Sweet & Maxwell.
Hayton and Marshall (2005) *Commentary and Cases on the Law of Trusts and Equitable Remedies*, 12th edn, London: Sweet & Maxwell, pp. 70–104.
Histed (1998) 'Election in equity: the myth of mistake', LQR 621.
Honore (2003) 'Trusts – The Inessentials' in Getzler (ed.) *Rationalising Equity and Trusts: Essays in Honour of Edward Burn*, London: Butterworths.
Jones (1997) 'Uses, trusts and a path to privity', 56 CLJ 175.
Keay (2003) 'Transfers to defeat creditors: the problem of purpose under s. 423 of the Insolvency Act 1986', 67 Conv. 272.
Ker (1953) 117 Conv. (N.S.) 273.
Kerridge (1994) 'Taxation of trust income', 110 LQR 84.
Kodilinye (1982) 'A fresh look at the Rule in *Strong* v. *Bird*', Conv. 14.
Koh (2003) 'Once a director, always a fiduciary?', 62 CLJ 403.
Law Commission Annual Report (1996) LC 244.
Law Commission (2002) Discussion Paper 'Sharing homes'.

Law Commission Consultation Paper 146 (1999) 'Trustees' powers and duties'.
Law Commission Consultation Paper 154 (1999) 'Illegal transactions: The effect of illegality on contracts and trusts'.
Law Commission Consultation Paper 171 (2003) 'Trustee exemption clauses'.
Law Commission Consultation Paper 175 (2004) 'Capital and income in trusts: classification and apportionment'.
Law Reform Committee (1982) *Powers and duties of trustees*, twenty-third report on powers and duties of trustees. London: Reform Law Committee.
Law Society (2000) Law Reform Advisory Committee, *Matrimonial Property*.
Maitland (1936) *Essays on Equity*, 2nd edn, Cambridge: Cambridge University Press.
Martin and Hayton (1984) 'Certainty of objects: what is heresy?', Conv. 304.
Mason (1977) Foreword to Finn, *Fiduciary Obligations*, Sydney: Law Book Company.
Mason (1994) 'The place of equity and equitable remedies in the common law world', 110 LQR 238.
Matthews (1984) 'A heresy and a half in certainty of objects', Conv. 22.
Matthews (1996) 'The New Trust: Obligations without Rights?' in Oakley (ed.) *Trends in Contemporary Trust Law*, Oxford: Oxford University Press.
Maudsley (1979) *The Modern Law of Perpetuities*, London: Butterworths.
McIlroy (2003) *Christian Perspectives on Law: A Biblical View of Law and Justice*, Carlisle: Paternoster Press.
Meager (2003) 'Secret trusts: do they have a future?', Conv. 203.
Miller (1998) 'On the application of s. 433 of the Insolvency Act 1986', Conv. 362.
Millett (1985) 'The Quistclose Trust, who can enforce it?', 101 LQR 269.
Millett (1991) 'Tracing the proceeds of fraud', 107 LQR 76.
Millett (1998) 'Equity's place in the law of commerce', 114 LQR 214.
Millett (1998) 'Restitution and constructive trusts', 114 LQR 399.
Moffat (1999) *Trusts Law*, 3rd edn, London: Butterworths.
Morris (1996) 'Equity's reaction to Modern Domestic relationships' in Oakley (ed.) *Trends in Contemporary Trust Law*, Oxford: Oxford University Press.
Musson (2001) *Medieval Law in Context*, Manchester: Manchester University Press.
Oakley ed. (1996) *Trends in Contemporary Trust Law*, Oxford: Oxford University Press.
Oakley (1997) *Constructive Trusts*, 3rd edn, London: Sweet & Maxwell.
Parry and Clark (2002) *The Law of Succession*, 11th edn, London: Sweet & Maxwell.
Pascoe (2000) 'S. 15 of the Trusts of Land and Trustees Act 1996: a change in the law?', 64 Conv. 315.
Perrins (1972) 'Can you keep half a secret?', 88 LQR 225.
Pettit (2005) *Equity and the Law of Trusts*, 9th edn, London: Butterworths.
Phang, A. (1998) 'Specific performance: "Explaining the roots of settled practice"', 61 MLR 421.
Phillipson (2003) 'Transforming breach of confidence? Towards a Common Law right of privacy under the Human Rights Act', 66 MLR 726.
Plucknett (1948) *A Concise History of the Common Law*, 4th edn, London: Butterworths.
Polden (2002) 'Mingling the waters: personalities and politics in the making of the supreme court and judicature', 61 CLJ 575.
Poole (2004) *Textbook on Contract Law*, 7th edn, Oxford: Oxford University Press.
Ridge (2004) 'Equitable undue influence and wills', LQR 120.

Roper (1979) *A Life of Thomas More*, Folio Society Edition.
Rotherham (2004) 'The property rights of unmarried cohabitees: the case for reform', 68 Conv. 268.
Simpson (1986) *A History of the Land Law*, Oxford: Oxford University Press.
Strauss (1967) Note on *Vandervell* v. *IRC*, 30 MLR 461.
Swadling (1996) 'A new role for resulting trusts', LS 110.
Swadling (ed.) (2004) *The Quistclose Trust: Critical Essays*. Oxford: Hart.
Tee (1998) *Themes and Perspectives in Land Law*, Oxford: Oxford University Press.
Thompson (1996) 'Mere formalities', Conv. 366.
Thompson (2003) 'My home is not my castle', Conv. 516.
Underhill (1995) *Law of Trusts and Trustees*, 15th edn, London: Butterworths.
Virgo (2003) 'Restitution Through the Looking Glass: Restitution within Equity and Equity within Restitution' in Getzler (ed.) *Rationalising Property, Equity and Trusts: Essays in Honour of Edward Burn*, London: Butterworths.
Warburton (1997) 'Charities, members, accountability and control', 61 Conv. 372.
Wells (1999) 'A restrictive approach to proprietary estoppel in the Court of Appeal', 63. Conv. 462.
Willoughby (1999) *Misplaced Trust*, 2nd edn Saffron Walden: Gostick Hall Publications.
Wishart (1997) 'The O'Brien principle and substantine unfairness', 56 CLJ 60.
Worthington (2003) *Equity*, Oxford: Oxford University Press.
Yeo (2005) 'The great peace: a distinct disturbance?', 121 LQR 393.
Zuckerman (1993) 'Mareva injunctions and security for judgement in a framework of interlocutory remedies', LQR 432.

Index